Managing Change
A Critical Perspective

2nd edition

Mark Hughes

Chartered Institute of Personnel and Development

Published by the Chartered Institute of Personnel and Development,
151, The Broadway, London, SW19 1JQ

This edition first published 2010
First published 2006
Reprinted 2007, 2010

© Chartered Institute of Personnel and Development, 2010

Typeset by Fakenham Photosetting Ltd, Norfolk

Printed in Great Britain by The Charlesworth Group

British Library Cataloguing in Publication Data
A catalogue of this publication is available from the British Library

ISBN 978 1 84398 241 8

The views expressed in this publication are the author's own and may not necessarily reflect those of the CIPD.

The CIPD has made every effort to trace and acknowledge copyright holders. If any source has been overlooked, CIPD Enterprises would be pleased to redress this in future editions.

Chartered Institute of Personnel and Development, CIPD House,
151 The Broadway, London, SW19 1JQ

Tel: 020 8612 6200
E-mail: cipd@cipd.co.uk
Website: www.cipd.co.uk
Incorporated by Royal Charter
Registered Charity No. 1079797

Managing Change
A Critical Perspective

2nd edition

Mark Hughes

Mark Hughes is a Senior Lecturer in Organisational Behaviour in Brighton Business School, at the University of Brighton. Mark teaches managing change on MBA programmes and professional programmes, and he is a former course leader of the MA Change Management. Mark's work with colleagues in the Business School is focused upon facilitating change in large public service organisations.

The Chartered Institute of Personnel and Development is the leading publisher of books and reports for personnel and training professionals, students, and all those concerned with the effective management and development of people at work. For details of all our titles, please contact the publishing department:

tel: 020 8612 6204

e-mail: publish@cipd.co.uk

The catalogue of all CIPD titles can be viewed on the CIPD website:

www.cipd.co.uk/bookstore

This textbook is dedicated to
Derek Hughes (1936–2009)

Contents

List of figures

List of boxes

Journal research cases

Acknowledgements

I reflect back on the past 12 months with great gratitude for my close family: Mum, Clair, Stuart, Rob and Beth and all their loving kindness. I fondly remember what my Dad taught me through his words and actions and I am grateful to have this opportunity to dedicate this textbook to his memory.

Once again I have enjoyed the encouragement of the CIPD editorial team to write and keep on writing the book. They have kept me grounded and focused, which is a tall order for the academic 'butterfly' mind. My dealings on this edition have been with Ruth Anderson, Kirsty Smy and Georgie Smith, to whom I publicly record my thanks. I am aware that behind the scenes there are many others, particularly the anonymous reviewers, so thank you.

I have developed many good friendships and learnt so much from both colleagues and postgraduates at Brighton. I am very tempted to offer a roll call of all the names at this point, but I will limit myself to three, this time around. I thank Aidan Berry for his belief in me back in 1987, when my own self-belief was lacking. I thank Steve Reeve for co-facilitating many enjoyable MA Change Management and external client workshops. And I thank Lew Perren for many supportive conversations whilst writing this edition, which helped make the writing process a joy rather than a chore.

Finally, invariably I find my chapter writing accompanied by the wonderful apocalyptic compositions of Godspeed You Black Emperor – their belief in 'quiet revolutions' says it all.

Mark Hughes
Brighton

Preface to the second edition

Since the first edition of this textbook was published early in 2006 I have been aware of change within myself, within the groups and teams that I belong to, within the university that employs me and the wider society. It is tempting to describe such processes as a revolution, but largely it has been an evolution – I barely notice the few extra grey hairs that appear each day. In a similar manner this textbook has evolved over the last few years informed by my experiences and by helpful feedback.

In introducing this new edition, probably the most tangible change is in terms of the title, changing from *Change Management* to *Managing Change*. The new title is believed to better indicate the dynamic and processual nature of changing. The second edition presents an opportunity to make many other enhancements to the textbook, which include the reordering of chapters into distinct parts and the addition of six new chapters, ensuring a breadth of coverage of managing change debates.

The purpose of the book

The aims of the textbook remain the same in seeking to:

- advance understanding about managing change from a critical perspective
- encourage an appreciation of managing change at different levels
- provoke debate in terms of understanding the past, the present and the future of managing change.

Adopting a critical perspective is integral to understanding managing change. Both the theory and practice of managing change are hampered by the myths and assumptions that managing change generates. This textbook informs understanding about organisational change at different levels, ranging from the individual, through groups and teams and the whole organisation, through to change at the sectoral and societal level. Managing change initially appears to be preoccupied with uncertain futures; however, this textbook emphasises that both the present and the past have a profound influence upon organisational change and how organisational change is understood.

The approach of the book

In writing this textbook, three guiding principles have informed its development: breadth, depth and rigour. The textbook offers a breadth of coverage of managing change topics and debates. The goal has been to include important topics such as history, ethics, power, resistance and change agency, which are often neglected in traditional management textbooks. It has been necessary to balance this breadth with depth. Each chapter of this new edition explores managing change debates in greater depth than the first edition. Finally, this textbook is rigorous in the sense that assertions are evidence-based. The textbook allows the reader to take a position on managing change debates informed by an extensive literature review of managing change research and scholarship.

The organisation of the chapters

All chapters follow a generic structure with the exception of the first and last chapters, which introduce and conclude debates about managing change. Chapters 2 to 19 are organised around the following generic structures. The **learning outcomes** orientate the reader in terms of what each chapter is seeking to achieve, with the introduction defining key terms and introducing the structure of the chapter. The **managerial approaches** section reviews the orthodoxy with specific reference to practices of managing change. The **critical perspective** offers a counterpoint in terms of how thinking is changing and how the latest research is informing managing change.

The **journal research cases** sections signpost research cases that have been published in leading academic journals. These research cases often feature famous organisations and the cases benefit from being developed through undertaking original research. Through following up the references to the case studies, it is possible to access real accounts of how change is being managed. The **concluding commentary** draws together debates featured in the **managerial approaches** and **critical perspectives** sections.

The end-of-chapter **case studies** offer an opportunity to test out understanding of theories introduced in the chapter through application. The case studies have been developed specifically for this textbook to ensure the potential application of theories to realistic change scenarios. In a similar manner the **discussion questions** offer an opportunity to discuss the ambiguities that arise out of managing change debates. The chapters conclude with **key readings**, suggesting books that are very relevant to issues discussed in the chapter.

The organisation of the book

The textbook is divided into five major parts: Introduction; External and Internal Change Contexts; Managing Change; Developments in Managing Change; and Conclusions.

Part 1 Introduction

Chapter 1 introduces the debates that make managing change so fascinating, yet simultaneously so contentious. Any serious study of managing change needs to clarify the subject of study and this is achieved through Chapter 2. History plays a large and often unacknowledged role in shaping both the theory and practice of managing change; Chapter 3 develops this historical perspective. History reveals the many competing paradigms and perspectives informing understanding about managing change, and these are introduced in Chapter 4.

Part 2 External and Internal Change Contexts

The unique nature of both external and internal organisational contexts is the focus of Part 2. Chapter 5 reviews the range of contextual factors that are believed to drive change. Chapter 6 considers the many choices that inform organisational design. Chapter 7 discusses changes affecting whole organisations. Chapter 8 is concerned with how organisations change through groups and teams changing. Chapter 9 features the individual transitions that take place as part of wider change initiatives.

Part 3 Managing Change

In this part activities that have been considered integral to managing change are featured. Chapter 10 highlights how managing change in isolation may be insufficient, without considering leading change. Chapter 11 looks at how change messages are conveyed and potential barriers and blockages. Chapter 12 questions the orthodoxy that resistance is something that must always be overcome. In Chapter 13, the realism of espoused cultural change is questioned. Chapter 14 makes the connections between learning and changing.

Part 4 Developments in Managing Change

Chapter 15 draws attention to an often intangible yet significant aspect of managing change in terms of power and politics. The earliest managing change writings emphasised the ethical management of change; in Chapter 16, major ethical debates are reviewed. Chapter 17 is concerned with the different individuals, groups and teams that make change happen through change agency. Managing change potentially offers a significant role for HR professionals, which is the focus of Chapter 18. Chapter 19 acknowledges that technological change and organisational change can no longer be viewed as independent.

Part 5 Conclusions

Chapter 20 takes stock of both the outcomes of managing change and the status of studying managing change.

Appendix – The organisational Change Field Guide

The 'Organisational Change Field Guide' is modelled upon a natural history field guide. The guide offers concise guidance about 20 of the most common/enduring organisational change initiatives.

Walkthrough of textbook features

LEARNING OUTCOMES

At the beginning of each chapter a bulleted set of learning outcomes summarises what you can expect to learn from the chapter, helping you to track your progress.

INTRODUCTION

Introductions to each chapter outline the structure of that chapter and define the key terms you can expect to come across.

MANAGERIAL APPROACH

The first part of each chapter focuses on specific practices of managing change.

CRITICAL PERSPECTIVES

The second part of each chapter explores relevant developments in the managing change school of thought and looks at the impact of recent research.

JOURNAL RESEARCH CASE 2.1

Slavs (division of a UK subsidiary of a multinational)

Sector: Motor vehicle manufacturing
Research methods: Participant observation, intensive interviews, analysis of documents and company literature

of its time, remains a classic. The paper drew upon the work of Foucault to demonstrate that discipline was embedded within routine social practices. The researchers were able to study

JOURNAL RESEARCH CASES

Access real accounts of how change is being managed by following up on these cases, published in leading academic journals and often featuring high-profile organisations.

CONCLUDING COMMENTARY

At the end of each chapter, a concluding commentary draws together the debates featured in the Managerial Approach and Critical Perspectives sections.

GREENSHIRES COUNTY COUNCIL IN SHOCK RESTRUCTURING

CASE STUDY: APPLYING THEORY TO PRACTICE

The headline above appeared in the local newspaper. The following is a summary of the main themes from the newspaper article. Greenshires County Council was planning to change through the removal of one level of management located at the main council offices. It was believed that this would result in a flatter organisational hierarchy for the council. The background to this change was that senior management had become increasingly frustrated with regards to what they perceived as excessive bureaucracy within the county council. The councillors had unanimously agreed with a proposal to embark upon delayering in due to the bureaucratic practices of middle management; while managers had initially appeared very enthusiastic, they had failed to adopt the new ways of working. The announcement about delayering had been made to senior management at an away-day at a local hotel. Senior managers were subsequently required to cascade this information down the organisational hierarchy of the county council, informing those individual managers directly affected by delayering in face-to-face meetings. The chief executive had made clear that he regarded this change as very significant when compared with previous changes

CASE STUDIES:
APPLYING THEORY TO PRACTICE

End-of-chapter case studies and accompanying questions encourage you to test your understanding of the theories introduced through practical application.

DISCUSSION
QUESTIONS

1 Collins (1998) was sceptical about the 'What is change?' narrative. What do you think was the basis for his scepticism?

2 Are classifications of change likely to be more evident in academic or in organisational explanations of change? Why?

3 In terms of the ten change classification questions specified in the framework, which are going to be the most difficult to answer?

4 What drives interest in perspectives such as complexity and postmodernism?

DISCUSSION QUESTIONS

These are designed to get you thinking about the ambiguities that arise out of managing change debates – consider them alone or discuss them in groups.

KEY READINGS

Edited books of key readings provide a useful orientation when faced with the large and diverse body of managing change literature. The three following edited readers offer effective introductions to many of the debates that feature in this textbook.

BEER, M. and NOHRIA, N. (eds) (2000) *Breaking the code of change*. Boston: Harvard Business School Press.

This collection of readings was drawn from a conference held at Harvard Business School in 1998. Although the book is now inevitably dated, its impact on current debates should not be underestimated. The conference and book drew together leading writings on change and one of its strengths is the inclusion of writers who originated debates within the broader study of managing change. The book was very

a comprehensive reader. San Francisco: Jossey Bass.

This reader is an evolution of a classic book, *The Planning of Change*, with the focus now more upon planned organisation change. The book includes 75 articles and runs to 998 pages. An innovation or frustration, depending upon your perspective, is the inclusion of ten additional chapters accessible via the web.

PRICE, D. (ed.) (2009) *The principles and practice of change*. Basingstoke: Palgrave Macmillan. Published in association with the Open University.

This reader draws together a collection of both classic and contemporary writings on change with chapters organised into themed sections, such as types of change, managing change,

KEY READINGS

Delve further into areas of particular interest by accessing the books, articles and websites listed in these end-of-chapter sections.

THE ORGANISATIONAL CHANGE FIELD GUIDE (APPENDIX)

An introduction to twenty popular and enduring approaches to organisational change. For each approach, we have included: essence and origins, pros (why) and cons (why not), where to find it (where to look) and how to identify it (what to listen for), as well as one managerial and one critical reference to encourage further exploration.

ONLINE RESOURCES FOR STUDENTS

- Annotated weblinks – click through to a wealth of up-to-date information online

Visit **www.cipd.co.uk/sss**

ONLINE RESOURCES FOR TUTORS

- Lecturer's Guide – a commentary on the case studies and questions in the book
- PowerPoint slides – build and deliver your course using these ready-made lectures

Visit **www.cipd.co.uk/tss**

PART 1

Introduction

CHAPTER 1

The managing change conundrums

The theory and practice of managing change is simultaneously fascinating and frustrating, with many riddles or conundrums evident about how organisational change is managed and studied. Myths and assumptions about managing change are well documented (Binney and Williams 1995; Conner 1998; Crom and Bertels 1999; Jarrett 2003). In response to the prevalence of these myths and assumptions, academic research and scholarship into organisational change has strived to inform understanding about managing change. However, despite considerable ongoing interest in studying managing change evident within many academic disciplines, a consensus does not exist and is unlikely to ever exist. What quickly becomes apparent is the centrality of the conundrums managing change raises and their role in the development of understanding about managing change. In this chapter, 11 major managing change conundrums are identified and discussed, by way of introducing major debates featured in this textbook. These conundrums are not the only conundrums, but they are believed to be significant conundrums. The origin of each conundrum is traced back to the practice of managing change, before explaining how the conundrum relates to the study of managing change. The goal is not to solve these conundrums, although readers will have their own preferred position on each conundrum; instead the goal is to demonstrate how ongoing debates, grounded in practice, inform the study of managing change. In the summary section of this chapter the question that each conundrum seeks to address is concisely stated and the chapters in which a particular conundrum features prominently are indicated.

THE MANAGING CHANGE CONUNDRUMS

THE DEFINITION CONUNDRUM

What does managing change mean?

The topicality of terminology such as 'managing change', 'change management' and 'organisational change' ensures that most readers possess working definitions of these terms. However, this does not mean that in terms of the practice of managing change a consensus definition exists. Invariably managers in organisations will not define key terms, and ambiguous references to 'managing change' may even be beneficial; changes in organisations are believed to be never clearly defined (Dawson 1994). In studying managing change, good practice emphasises the need to define key terms. However, the conundrum relates to the lack of any universal definition of managing change. Two textbook definitions of change management help to illustrate this point:

> Definition of change management: 'the leadership and direction of the process of organisational transformation – especially with regard to human aspects and overcoming resistance to change' (Fincham and Rhodes 2005, p525).

> Definition of change management: 'the process of achieving the smooth implementation of change by planning and introducing it systematically, taking into account the likelihood of it being resisted' (Armstrong 2009, p424).

In reviewing the two definitions of change management there are similarities and differences. Both authors depict change management as seeking to overcome resistance to change: in the case of Fincham and Rhodes through leadership and direction, and in the case of Armstrong through planning and systematic implementation. However, these apparently neutral definitions of change management are informed by significant assumptions shaping the study of managing change, which are discussed in Chapter 4.

The terminology of organisational change is never neutral and even the term 'change management' may be challenged. For example, Clegg and Walsh (2004) believe that the term change management is inappropriate and misleading because of its implementation focus and managerial focus. The waters are further muddied by the many guises that change takes: 'transformation, development, metamorphosis, transmutation, evolution, regeneration, innovation, revolution and transition to list but a few' (Stickland 1998, p14). While the definition of managing change remains a conundrum, in the context of this textbook the following definition of managing change is used: attending to organisational change transition processes at organisational, group and individual levels. This definition acknowledges the potential involvement of all employees in ongoing processes of changing, rather than necessarily a single heroic manager, although the amount of involvement may vary considerably at different hierarchical levels. Also, the definition acknowledges that change may be planned or emergent, and the terminology of 'attending to' seeks to avoid prescribing a 'one best way' approach to organisational change. In summary, a conundrum exists about the meaning of managing change.

THE CONSTANT CHANGE CONUNDRUM

Is organisational change the only constant?

Peters' (1988, p2) assertion that 'excellent firms don't believe in excellence – only in constant improvement and constant change' became an often repeated mantra within organisations. This goal of constantly changing is evident in the following quotation from Kotter (1996, p144): '… without sufficient leadership, change stalls, and excelling in a rapidly changing world becomes problematic'. As Child (2005, p277) warned, 'change, paradoxically, has become an organisational norm'. While not grounded in any empirical evidence, this evangelical rhetoric to constantly change proved popular (gauged by book sales) with managers. This practical view of organisational change as a constant suggests the need for managing change and leading change.

However, academics have been far more suspicious about such exhortations. The conundrum is concerned with debates relating to both the natural appeal of constant change and academic scepticism about both the reality and desirability of constantly changing. The danger in overemphasising organisations as constantly changing is that organisational continuities and stability may be discounted. The most troubling manifestation of constant-change thinking is the notion that all change is beneficial. As Alvesson and Sveningsson (2008, p32) warn, 'there is a myth about the inherent good in changes just because they are changes'.

While constant-change rhetoric initially appealed to managers as a means of legitimising managerial activities, they became suspicious of such exhortations. A survey of management practices found that 'managers are rightly sceptical of the evangelical exhortations to change radically, and often show a much greater understanding of the complex implications than do the experts and consultants' (Ezzamel et al 1995, p8). Also, there has been a growing recognition of phenomena such as change fatigue, or what Abrahamson (2004a) has referred to as 'repetitive-change syndrome'. In summary, a conundrum exists around the claims made for organisational change as a constant.

THE HISTORY CONUNDRUM

Does history play a role in managing change?

On one level history appears to have very little relevance to the forward-looking practice of managing change. For example, Kotter (1996, p142) advocated purging history: 'cleaning up historical artifacts does create an even longer change agenda, which an exhausted organisation will not like. But the purging of unnecessary interconnections can ultimately make transformation much easier.'

The practical dilemma is how realistic it is to purge 'unnecessary interconnections'. This line of reasoning suggests practical merit in engaging with history as part of a forward-looking process of managing change. Organisational histories and traditions are an important component of organisations suggesting that it can be more fruitful to work with rather than against the past (Cummings

2002). Equally, previous experiences of change initiatives inform the subsequent reception (positive or negative) of subsequent change initiatives.

What has been written previously about managing change informs what is being written today about managing change. Cooke (1999) criticised the ahistorical and acontextual study of managing change and, more generally, Pettigrew et al (2002) stated that history is well placed to ask big questions over long time spans as a counterpoint to the largely ahistorical field of strategic management. New academic journals such as *Management and Organizational History* (launched in 2006) are encouraging far greater appreciation of history and how history is written, which is discussed further in Chapter 3. In summary, a conundrum exists about the degree of emphasis to be placed upon history as part of understanding organisational change.

THE PERCEPTION CONUNDRUM

Is it possible to reconcile the multiple perceptions of organisational change?

Perception with its emphasis upon how information from our senses is interpreted is relevant to management in general. In terms of managing change, practitioners may work from the position that there is a common understanding of a specific change or that competing understandings of a specific change exist. The perception conundrum offers an antidote to unitarist approaches to managing change and universal explanations of managing change. Perceptions tend to lack reliability, which has implications for organisations (Thompson and McHugh 2009).

While unitarists view organisations as essentially co-operative, integrated and harmonious wholes (Collins 1998), acknowledging the multiplicity of perceptions that exist begins a process of questioning this harmony. Is it really realistic to assume that within a large organisation everyone shares a common perception of an organisational change? Beginning to engage with different perceptions of organisational change encourages an appreciation of important debates relating to ethics, diversity, power and politics. In summary, this conundrum is concerned with the merits of understanding organisational change in terms of either a common perception or a diversity of perceptions.

THE 'ONE BEST WAY' CONUNDRUM

Is there one best way to manage and study change?

Managing change practitioners understandably look for the one best way to manage change. Publishers have responded with an extensive amount of literature that appears to offer the one best way to manage change. A good example of this approach was evident in the writings of Peters and Waterman (1982), which were very influential in encouraging managers to attempt to manage cultural change in the 1980s. Their key message was: '"My way or the highway" – that is, there is "one best way" to business excellence via cultural management' (Brewis 2007, p356). This approach encouraged later management gurus to offer their own one-best-way recipes for managing change. While these prescriptions are often greeted with academic scepticism, they remain influential: '… modern gurus of management tend to be looked upon as the state of the art, or the highest evolutionary stage of management's development' (Collins 1998, p21).

The study of managing in general and managing change in particular reveals the many contingent variables that potentially impact upon processes of managing. For example, managing change in a large global bank will be very different from managing change in a small social enterprise. This line of reasoning questions the one-best-way approach to managing change; inevitably the recipes for managing change are unlikely to be transferrable to the very different organisational contexts evident in a diverse world. This is further compounded by the ambiguities that characterise managing change and tensions '… between change management that puts employees' well-being first and change management that serves only business needs' (Walton and Russell 2004, p143).

A far more subtle form of the one-best-way approach is apparent within the academic managing change literature, which either implicitly or explicitly prescribes how best to study managing change. Competing perspectives have an important role to play in advancing understanding about managing change, but equally there can be merit in adopting a pluralist approach that draws upon many competing perspectives. Dunphy (1996) noted that in studying organisational change, there is no agreed theory of change and there is unlikely to be one; he argued for the existence of competing theories of change (see also Van de Ven and Poole 1995):

> What we do need instead, however, as do all truly scientific fields, is not a single theory but comprehensive competing theories of change and a healthy debate about their respective value bases and biases and empirical investigation of the extent to which their claims to achieve their preferred ideals can in fact be substantiated. (Dunphy 1996, pp545/6)

This eloquent appeal for competing theories remains highly relevant to this day.

In summary, the variability of organisational change with particular reference to different organisational contexts has implications for both how to manage change and how to study managing change.

THE MANAGEABILITY CONUNDRUM

Is organisational change manageable?

Wilson (1992, p7) described 'the leitmotiv of modern management theory is that of understanding, creating and coping with change'. The earliest approaches to managing change in the 1940s and 1950s advocated a planned approach. An early account defined planned change as originating '… in a decision to make a deliberate effort to improve the system and to obtain the help of an outside agent in making this change' (Lippitt et al 1958, p10). Planned change offers a systematic approach to managing change. This approach was to inform the development of organisational development in the late 1960s and remains influential today.

However, in recent decades an alternative approach, which acknowledges the emergent nature of change, has gained prominence. Weick (2000, p223) has written about emergent change as follows:

> The hyperbole of transformation has led people to overestimate the liabilities of inertia, the centrality of managerial planning, and the promise of fresh starts, and to underestimate the value of innovative sense making on the front line, the ability of small experiments to travel, and the extent to which change is continuous.

Burnes (1996, p16) concluded his review of planned and emergent approaches to change by writing that 'rather than seeing the argument between the planned and emergent approaches to change as a clash of two fundamentally opposing systems of ideas, they can be better viewed as approaches which seek to address different situational variables (contingencies)'. The manageability conundrum is also concerned with the popular appeal of being seen to be managing change:

> The ideology of good management, however, associates managers with the introduction of new ideas, new organizational forms, new technologies, new products, new slogans, or new moods. Consequently, some fraction of organizational resources is dedicated to running unlikely experiments in changes as unwitting altruistic contributions to the larger world. (March 1981, p573)

Wilson (1992) and Sorge and van Witteloostuijn (2004) have commented upon the organisational and societal pressures to be seen to be managing change. However, there is an irony in such change rhetoric, as Dawson (2003, p20) notes: 'it is as important to recognise when not to change as it is to identify when there is a need for change'. In summary, the manageability conundrum focuses upon arguments for and against planned change.

THE CHANGE AGENCY CONUNDRUM

Who manages change?

This conundrum is related to the manageability conundrum, in that if you believe that change is manageable, this raises questions about who manages change. Change agents and change agency are the focus of Chapter 17; at this stage one of the major debates relates to top–down change versus bottom–up change. The traditional approach regards the most senior manager or managers as the change agents. Managing change is cascaded down through the hierarchical levels of the organisation. The strength of such an approach is that change can be planned with a clear strategic direction. The weakness of such an approach is that organisational change may be misunderstood or wrongly implemented at lower levels in the hierarchy. The bottom–up approach addresses these weaknesses through dispersing change agency to lower levels in the organisation in the belief that, if employees design and develop change initiatives, they are more likely to succeed. A hybrid of top–down change and bottom–up change may prove to be the optimum arrangement. In summary, the change agency conundrum is concerned with who manages change, which is predicated upon how change agency is dispersed throughout an organisation.

THE MANAGING AND LEADING CHANGE CONUNDRUM

Managing change or leading change?

The theory and practice of managing and leading are well documented; what is less clear is the practical requirement for managing change or leading change. The best-selling book *Leading Change* (Kotter 1996) gave considerable impetus to an emphasis upon leading change rather than managing change. However, in studying managing change, distinctions between leading and managing change are less clear cut. Caldwell (2003c) found that rather than thinking in terms of either change leaders or change managers, there was a need for both. In summary this conundrum is concerned with the requirement for change management, change leadership or a combination.

THE SUCCESS/FAILURE CONUNDRUM

What is the outcome of managing change?

Beer and Nohria (2000a, p133) wrote in the influential *Harvard Business Review* that 'the brutal fact is that about 70% of all change initiatives fail'. This very blunt statistic had a huge influence upon both the practice and theory of managing change. Managing change was depicted as being susceptible to high failure rates, but it was suggested that with the help of consultants, practitioners would be able to more successfully manage change. In the case of academics, high failure rates fuelled scepticism about the manageability of change. The whole area of evaluating managing change has been plagued by a lack of empirical evidence and the vested interests of those commenting upon success and failure: 'when pessimistic opinions are suppressed, while optimistic ones are rewarded, an organization's ability to think critically is undermined' (Lovallo and Kahneman 2003, p60). These debates have implications for an organisation's capacity for organisational learning, which is discussed further in Chapter 14. The most expedient answer to the question 'does managing change succeed or fail?' is that 'it depends'. It depends upon the many variables that shape a process of changing as well as how managing change is evaluated, which is explored in Chapter 20. In summary, the success/failure conundrum focuses upon the outcomes of change initiatives and the effectiveness of these initiatives.

THE CHANGE/CHANGING CONUNDRUM

Is organisational change a 'thing' or a 'process'?

The first edition of this textbook used the title *Change Management*, whereas this edition uses the title *Managing Change*. The different titles reflect practical and theoretical perspectives on managing change. Change management depicts organisational change as a thing, something with very clear boundaries.

Managing change depicts organisational change as an ongoing process without clear boundaries. On a practical level, how change is managed will be influenced by whichever of these views is dominant. The earlier discussion about planned and emergent change may be related to this conundrum. In academic terms this conundrum goes back as far as ancient philosophers, such as Democritus and Heraclitus, with Van de Ven and Poole (2005) highlighting ongoing disagreements between scholars about whether organisations consist of things or processes. In summary, this conundrum is concerned with two very different ways of thinking about organisational change as a thing and as a process.

THE FUTUROLOGY CONUNDRUM

How feasible is it to manage into the future?

The conundrums introduced in this chapter challenge many espoused certainties about managing change in order to inform the overarching conundrum that neither practitioners nor academics can talk or write about the future with certainty. The existentialist nature of this conundrum is effectively conveyed in the following quote: 'a person's ability to deal with change is related to how comfortable they are with mystery, with the loss of control and limits of rationality that any emergence from mystery reveals' (Steiner 2001, p156).

The planned approach to managing change offers a degree of control, certainty and rationality when faced with an uncertain future. Kotter (1996, p186) concluded his book with the following 'authoritative' observation: 'As an observer of life in organizations, I think I can say with some authority that people who are making an effort to embrace the future are a happier lot than those who are clinging to the past.' While Kotter makes reference to working with companies over the past decade, his rhetoric largely aligns with his forward-looking conclusions. His concerns relate to establishing a sense of urgency, developing visions and strategies, generating short-term wins, consolidating gains and producing more change. This rhetoric may prove appealing to task-orientated managers, but it is very difficult to reconcile with any notion of advancing academic knowledge about organisational change.

Beckhard and Harris (1987, p687) explained organisational change in terms of three states: '… any major organizational change involves three distinct conditions: the future state, where the leadership wants the organization to get to; the present state, where the organization currently is; and the transition state, the set of conditions and activities that the organization must go through to move from the present to the future.' Presented in this way the organisational change process appears rational and the goal appears eminently achievable. However, March (1981, p572) warned that '… our plans are based on a future that we know, with certainty, will not be realized'. Equally, Dawson (2003, p11) warned that '… change involves a movement to some future state that comprises a context and time that remain unknown'. The academic challenge is that while managing change is concerned with imagined futures, knowledge claims are traditionally located in the verifiable past. In summary, while the practice of managing change is inevitably preoccupied with the future, theories of managing change are grounded in the empirical past.

SUMMARY

In this chapter, 11 managing change conundrums have been introduced. Inevitably there are overlaps between conundrums. While each conundrum is summarised as a question, there are no definitive answers. Instead, managing change conundrums highlight ongoing managing change debates. In Box 1.1 each conundrum is succinctly stated, with chapters of particular relevance to exploring a conundrum specified.

Box 1.1 Summary of the managing change conundrums

The definition conundrum (What does managing change mean?)
Chapters 2, 4 and 19
The constant change conundrum (Is organisational change the only constant?)
Chapters 5, 7 and 14
The history conundrum (Does history play a role in managing change?)
Chapter 3
The perception conundrum (Is it possible to reconcile the multiple perceptions of organisational change?)
Chapters 8, 9, 15 and 16
The 'one best way' conundrum (Is there one best way to manage and study change?)
Chapters 4 and 11
The manageability conundrum (Is organisational change manageable?)
Chapters 7, 12 and 13
The change agency conundrum (Who manages change?)
Chapters 10, 17 and 18
The managing and leading change conundrum (Managing change or leading change?)
Chapter 17
The success/failure conundrum (What is the outcome of managing change?)
Chapter 20
The change/changing conundrum (Is organisational change a 'thing' or a 'process'?)
Chapters 4 and 5
The futurology conundrum (How feasible is it to manage into the future?)
Chapters 3 and 20

Edited books of key readings provide a useful orientation when faced with the large and diverse body of managing change literature. The three following edited readers offer effective introductions to many of the debates that feature in this textbook.

BEER, M. and NOHRIA, N. (eds) (2000) *Breaking the code of change*. Boston: Harvard Business School Press.

This collection of readings was drawn from a conference held at Harvard Business School in 1998. Although the book is now inevitably dated, its impact on current debates should not be underestimated. The conference and book drew together leading writers on change, and one of its strengths is the inclusion of writers who originated debates within the broader study of managing change. The book was very popular with strategists in business schools and MBA students and, for a time, rather than merely relaying debates, it helped to shape debates.

BURKE, W.W., LAKE, D.G. and PAINE, J.W. (eds) (2009) *Organization change: a comprehensive reader*. San Francisco: Jossey Bass.

This reader is an evolution of a classic book, *The Planning of Change*, with the focus now more upon planned organisation change. The book includes 75 articles and runs to 998 pages. An innovation or frustration, depending upon your perspective, is the inclusion of ten additional chapters accessible via the web.

PRICE, D. (ed.) (2009) *The principles and practice of change*. Basingstoke: Palgrave Macmillan. Published in association with the Open University.

This reader draws together a collection of both classic and contemporary writings on change, with chapters organised into themed sections, such as types of change, managing change, resisting change and leading change. The final ingredient in this reader is an eclectic inventory of 15 tools and techniques, which may be used during the processes of planning, implementing and evaluating change.

CHAPTER 2

Organisational change classifications

LEARNING OUTCOMES

After reading this chapter you should be able to:

- appreciate the rationales for classifying organisational changes
- classify organisational change using the change classifications framework
- consider practical applications of the change classifications framework
- think about the change classifications framework as a point of view
- understand complexity theories as a counterpoint to change classifications
- understand postmodernist explanations as a counterpoint to change classifications.

INTRODUCTION

By way of introducing organisational change, this chapter addresses the innocent question: what is organisational change? The dilemma quickly becomes apparent that 'organisational change literature encompasses a vast and diverse body of work that encompasses micro and macro views of the firm, as well as varying foci (scale of change, type of change, interventions in change and people in change)' (Frahm 2007, p946). There is no consensus about organisational change; the word change is characterised as a container concept, and searching for the word's underlying values results in a whole range of meanings (De Caluwe and Vermaak 2003). For example, Stickland (1998, p14) identifies many guises of change, including 'transformation, development, metamorphosis, transmutation, evolution, regeneration, innovation, revolution and transition... '.

While ambiguities are acknowledged, organisational change scholars have been concerned that not enough has been done to understand change itself (Stickland 1998). The ambiguities of change are not purely academic, with changes in organisations believed to be never clearly defined (Dawson 1994). Jones (2010, p31) has defined organisational change as '... the process by which organisations move from their present state to some desired future state to increase their effectiveness'. This broad definition accommodates the range of discussions that inform a pluralistic understanding of managing change within this textbook.

In the 'Managerial Approaches' section, a ten-question literature-based framework has been developed and is introduced. The change classifications framework, through a process of questioning, offers a means of classifying organisational changes in the belief that this will deepen understanding and move debates away from generalised discussion about organisational change. In the 'Critical Perspective' section, the certainties and rationality of the change classifications framework are questioned. This questioning is used to illustrate the role of competing perspectives in explaining organisational change. In this way complexity theories and postmodernist explanations of organisational change are introduced as critical counterpoints to the change classifications framework.

MANAGERIAL APPROACHES

In this section the rationale for why the change classifications framework was developed is presented. Each of the ten change classifications framework questions is located and explained in terms of relevant literature and the potential use of the framework as an analysis tool inside organisations is discussed.

CLASSIFYING ORGANISATIONAL CHANGE

Whereas Stickland (1998) devoted a fascinating book to what is change, Collins (1998) was more sceptical, noting that the 'What is change?' narrative can be found in what he perceived as basic textbooks on change. However, the position of Collins, writing in 1998, can be contrasted with recent managing change textbooks, which increasingly engage with the meaning of organisational change in more sophisticated ways. The classifications of Andriopoulos and Dawson (2009), Burke (2008), Burnes (2009a), De Caluwe and Vermaak (2003) and Paton and McCalman (2008) illustrate this point, as depicted in Box 2.1.

In the classifications in Box 2.1 there are similarities and differences. Classifying organisational change is a prerequisite to more comprehensively understanding organisational change. The process of classifying change is informed by competing paradigms and perspectives, which are discussed in the 'Critical Perspective' section and in Chapters 3 and 4. In essence, each classification reflects a slightly different viewpoint on organisational change. The following rationales for developing the change classifications framework featured here were identified.

Firstly, the question 'What is change?' is frustrated by the breadth and occasionally the depth of the organisational change literature. Writers from very different academic disciplines and perspectives offer competing explanations of organisational change. A consequence of these ongoing debates is a large, disparate and at times contradictory body of literature relating to classifications of change and even the value of change classification, which is discussed in the 'Critical Perspective' of this chapter. Consequently, the first rationale for

Box 2.1 Organisational change classifications (literature based)

Andriopoulos and Dawson (2009) identify four dimensions: the substance of change, the scale and scope of change, the politics of change, and the timeframe of change (see also Dawson 2003).

Burke (2008, p21) offers a typology of the current language in use of scholars and practitioners:

– revolutionary versus evolutionary
– discontinuous versus continuous
– episodic versus continuing flow
– transformational versus transactional
– strategic versus operational
– total system versus local option.

Burnes (2009a) has developed a framework for change incorporating four quadrants and two axes. The diagonal axis ranges from slow transformation/slow change through to rapid transformation/rapid change. The horizontal axis ranges from turbulent environment/large-scale transformation through to small-scale change/stable environment.

De Caluwe and Vermaak (2003, p70) identify six elements of planned change: outcome, history, actors, phases, communication and steering.

Paton and McCalman (2008, p25) developed the TROPICS test '… as an early warning device to access both the impact and magnitude of the impending change'. This mnemonic stands for Time scales, Resources, Objectives, Perceptions, Interest, Control and Source.

developing this framework was to draw upon this disparate literature in order to inform a focused classification of organisational change.

The second rationale for developing the framework was to refocus discussion away from generalised organisational change towards thinking about specific aspects of organisational change. Plenty of generalisations exist about 'change being the only constant' or 'the one best way to manage change'. These generalisations misinform, rather than inform, the study of managing change. Rigorous empirical studies of specific organisational changes in specific organisations inform the study of organisational change and these studies are the best antidote for popular generalisations.

The third rationale for classifying what is known about a specific organisational change is that it potentially also highlights what is not known. The change classifications framework can be viewed as a form of audit that seeks to establish what is known, as well as what is not known, about a particular organisational change. It is anticipated that, for example, a reason for a change may not be made public. Acknowledgement of the unknown is particularly pertinent to managing change given that change involves movement to some future state that comprises a context and time that remain unknown (Dawson 2003).

The final rationale for developing this question-based framework was the belief that inquisitive questioning deepens understanding about organisational change. The emphasis upon asking good questions draws upon action learning (Revans 1982), which is discussed in the Organisational Change Field Guide (see

Appendix). Asking good questions encourages a range of answers reflecting the diversity of thinking about organisational change.

THE CHANGE CLASSIFICATIONS FRAMEWORK

In the following discussion the ten questions in the change classifications framework are explained, with specific reference to their location in the literature. When you begin to apply the change classifications framework, it can be helpful to have a real organisational change in mind (even if you do not possess detailed information about that organisational change). The other point to acknowledge is that Chapter 5 encourages understanding organisational change within context (both internal and external) and that the context will inform the classification of a specific organisational change. The ten questions that make up the change classifications framework are drawn together at the end of this section.

The first question in the framework is based upon the belief that it is more informative to engage with specific organisational change, rather than generalising about organisational changes. Dawson (2003, p18) referred to 'the essential nature and content of the change in question', and it is this content of a change that is the focus of the first question. Burke (2008) regards the content of change as usually beginning with an organisation's leaders responding to changes in an organisation's external environment. Examples of specific organisational changes include: a merger or acquisition, a programme of cultural change, total quality management and downsizing, discussed in the Organisational Change Field Guide (see Appendix). It is acknowledged that these changes are unlikely to be happening in isolation, but that there will always be merit in specifying what is being studied. Major changes invariably take place against a backdrop of everyday changes; 'organisations change all the time, each and every day' (Burke 2008, p1). The reasons for change and the scale of change feature in subsequent questions. However, the quotation warns that given the prevalence of everyday changes, specifying change requires careful consideration, aided by clarification of the scale and scope of the change. The first classification question is: What organisational change is taking place?

The second question is informed by discussions featured in Chapter 3 and relates to the history and historiography of managing change. The recent history of organisational change informs its classification; 'what causes change is embedded in the organisation's history up to the present' (De Caluwe and Vermaak 2003, p79). In a similar manner, Cummings (2002) acknowledges organisational histories and traditions and the difficulty in making people forget them; it can be more fruitful to work with rather than against the past. For example, employees' experiences of a change initiative such as total quality management in an organisation will inform the subsequent reception (positive or negative) of a subsequent change initiative, such as business process reengineering, discussed in the Organisational Change Field Guide (see Appendix). Darwin et al (2002, p11) believe that 'most, if not all, currently fashionable ideas are reinventions'. The concern is that employees become sceptical of repackaged change initiatives, with Abrahamson (2004b) identifying repetitive change syndrome as a growing malaise in an increasing number of organisations. The second classification question is: What has been the recent organisational history of change?

The third question encourages consideration about both the explicit and implicit reasons for an organisational change. Many potential causes of organisational change are discussed in Chapter 5, ranging from a change in the environment in which an organisation operates through to the appointment of a new chief executive. As Palmer et al (2009, p60) note, 'all organisations are not the same and not all managers respond to external pressures for change in the same way: Some resist them; some are slow to respond; some may not recognise them as a real threat in the same way that other managers do.' Equally, rationales for organisational change are not always made explicit, or politically expedient reasons are offered as opposed to the real reasons for change. For example, a bank may declare that it is removing back-office operations from branches in order to improve customer services, while at the same time making considerable cost savings through this change. The third classification question is: What rationale has been offered for this organisational change?

The fourth question seeks to identify the person or persons making a decision to change. Answering this question provides insights into the significance of an organisational change, as well as encouraging consideration about issues of power and politics, discussed in Chapter 15. For example, was the decision made by a dominant coalition of senior managers, or perhaps an incoming chief executive wishing to herald a change of direction? Paton and McCalman (2008) highlight the role of problem owners in the context of change; Chapter 17 includes further discussion about change agency. Frequently a top–down (Kotter 1995) approach to change is adopted. However, there is also support for bottom–up approaches to change (Beer et al 1990a). The fourth classification question is: Who made the decision to change?

The fifth question addresses the enormous variability in the scale and scope of organisational changes. One of the most influential differentiations of organisational change was offered by Dunphy and Stace (1988) in terms of: participative evolution, charismatic transformation, forced evolution and dictatorial transformation. Evolutionary change, which focuses upon incremental change, can be contrasted with revolutionary change, which focuses upon radical change. However, there is a need for caution when classifying the scale of change, because despite potential managerial rhetoric that radical revolutionary change is being undertaken, '… more than 95 per cent of organisational changes are evolutionary' (Burke 2008, p69). The rhetoric of large-scale change is echoed in the literature, as depicted in Box 2.2.

Judging the scale of change can be complicated, with Abrahamson (2000) noting oscillations between big and small changes helping to ensure dynamic stability in organisations (see also Romanelli and Tushman 1994 for a discussion of their punctuated equilibrium model of change). The challenge of classifying the scale of change becomes apparent in notions such as 'long marches', where apparently small-scale changes contribute to a larger-scale transformation.

Box 2.2 The rhetoric of large-scale change language

> **Quantum change:** changing many elements at once instead of piecemeal change (Mintzberg et al 2009, citing Miller and Friesen 1984).
>
> **Transformation:** massive programmes of comprehensive change to turn around or renew an organisation (as noted by Mintzberg et al 2009).
>
> **Turnaround:** quick dramatic revolution (as noted by Mintzberg et al 2009).
>
> **Bold strokes:** major and rapid changes imposed top–down (Kanter et al 1992).
>
> **Long marches:** small-scale short-term incremental changes leading to longer-term transformation (Kanter et al 1992).

Often the scope of a change is related to the scale of a change, with 'scope' referring to who or what will be affected by the change. For example, the scope of a large-scale redundancy programme may refer specifically to middle management. An important element of the scope of change is the identification of the level or levels to which organisational change applies. Scope in terms of individual, group and organisational levels can range from one individual or group being affected to the whole organisation. The fifth classification question is: What is the scale and scope of this organisational change?

The sixth question addresses the precision or imprecision of organisational change timescales. For example, the relocation of a head office can be undertaken within a very precise timescale, whereas the timescale for achieving cultural change will be far less precise. Senior management may specify that they want to change an organisational culture over six months, but it is likely to take years to change the attitudes, values and beliefs that inform an organisational culture (discussed further in Chapter 13). In a similar manner, the logistics of relocation can be dealt with over six months, whereas new working relationships and ways of working may take years to settle down. As Burrell (1992) acknowledges, change is very reliant upon a conception of temporality, and Van de Ven and Poole (2005, p1394) have described time as '... the "ether" of change. We judge that change has occurred against a background of time.' On a more mundane level, Burke (2008) identifies four phases of change: pre-launch, launch phase, post-launch phase and sustaining phase. While Burke acknowledges that change is unlikely to follow exactly such a linear pattern, the phases are a useful aid to thinking about organisational change in terms of time. The sixth question is: What is the timescale for this organisational change?

The seventh question addresses an integral aspect of managing change relating to change communications (discussed further in Chapter 11). Communication has been defined as an '... exchange of ideas, emotions, messages, stories and information through different means including writing, speech, signals, objects or actions' (Clegg et al 2008, p302). For some commentators, without appropriate communication to employees, organisational change initiatives fail (Barrett 2002). The question focuses upon internal organisational communications and processes of communicating. Once again, what is not communicated can be as informative as what is communicated. The variables influencing the nature of communications include: the type of change, the degree of urgency, the speed of change and the reactions to the change (Quirke 1995). The focus is not solely upon the content of change messages. Processes of communicating change and barriers to communications potentially offer insights into the exercise of power and politics with regard to a particular change. The seventh classification question is: How is this organisational change being communicated?

The eighth question is based upon the belief that who is managing change and how it is managed informs the classification of an organisational change. Choices relating to change agents and change agency are featured in Chapter 17. One of the most frequently cited typologies of change strategies was developed by Kotter and Schlesinger (1979), which suggested that change strategies range from education and communication through to explicit and implicit coercion. As with the other classifications, it is important to remember that organisations and changes are dynamic, so that although it is possible to identify how change was managed at one point in time, such an approach to managing change is unlikely to remain static. The eighth classification question is: Who is managing this organisational change, and how is it being managed?

The ninth question encourages identification of a successful outcome of a particular organisational change. The problematic nature of judging the efficacy of change programmes is acknowledged (Iles and Sutherland 2001). In Chapter 20, an evaluation of organisational change outcomes is featured, and one of the main findings of that discussion is how difficult it is to conclusively establish success and failure of organisational change initiatives. There is believed to be a tendency for change initiatives to fail (Kotter 1995; De Caluwe and Vermaak 2004; Burke 2008). In the context of the change classifications framework, the concern is if the criteria for judging success have been made explicit or are the criteria left implicit within a change initiative. Has a successful outcome been specified and openly communicated and, if so, what will be the criteria for establishing the achievement of the successful outcome? The ninth classification question is: How will the success of this organisational change be evaluated?

The tenth question is again political in seeking to identify different parties who can influence a particular organisational change. The establishment of the nature of a successful outcome of change in question nine informs the process of identifying those individuals and groups that are potentially influential in the success or failure of an organisational change. This question speaks to the politics of change in terms of whether a change is accepted as central and worthwhile or threatening and challenged (Dawson 2003). One approach to analysing such influences is the force-field analysis (discussed in Chapter 12). Resistance has been defined as 'behaviours acted out by change recipients in order to slow down or terminate organisational change' (Lines 2004, p198). The question encourages consideration about how resistance impacts upon an organisational change, either negatively or positively. Also, change agents' influence upon the success or failure of a change depends upon how effectively they undertake the task. The tenth classification question is: Who can influence the success of this organisational change?

In Box 2.3 the ten change classifications framework questions are gathered together. It is believed that answering at least some of these questions offers a more focused approach to understanding organisational change.

Box 2.3 The change classifications framework

1 What organisational change is taking place?
2 What has been the recent organisational history of change?
3 What rationale has been offered for this organisational change?
4 Who made the decision to change?
5 What is the scale and scope of this organisational change?
6 What is the timescale for this organisational change?
7 How is this organisational change being communicated?
8 Who is managing this organisational change, and how is it being managed?
9 How will the success of this organisational change be evaluated?
10 Who can influence the success of this organisational change?

This framework has the potential to inform discussion about organisational change within organisations. Greater conceptual clarity about organisational change would benefit organisations because 'it facilitates clearer communication between people involved, it characterises dominant paradigms in groups or organisations as a whole, it provides a map to deal with possible strategic issues and it offers change agents a tool for reflection' (De Caluwe and Vermaak 2004, p214). In an organisational change special issue of the journal *Human Relations*, Dunphy (1996) identified three distinct groups among the contributors: the analysts (primarily interested in analysing organisational change), the activists (primarily interested in intervening in organisations to produce change) and the futurists (primarily interested in discerning the direction of future change). The target audience for this textbook is the group that Dunphy referred to as the analysts.

However, Dunphy's identification of three groups signposts time horizons inside organisations. In organisations the focus is likely to be activists working in the present. The change classifications framework has the potential to inform their discussions about ongoing changes. The framework offers an agenda for activists that can begin a dialogue around a change. The change classifications framework can also be used inside organisations to aid the reflection of analysts. For example, important questions about learning from a previous organisational change (discussed further in Chapter 14) can be facilitated through using the framework. Finally, the futurists inside organisations could use the framework in order to encourage employees to begin engaging with a future change and, through dialogue, begin a process of changing.

CRITICAL PERSPECTIVE

In the following discussion, the change classifications framework is used to illustrate the concept of a perspective on organisational change. Complexity theories and postmodernism are introduced as critical counterpoints to assumptions informing the change classifications framework.

THE CHANGE CLASSIFICATIONS FRAMEWORK AS A POINT OF VIEW

In the next two chapters the history of managing change thought and the role of paradigms and perspectives informing managing change are introduced. These concepts can appear quite abstract, and so at this stage it is informative to highlight how the change classifications framework is both informed by and encourages a point of view about organisational change. Box 2.1 highlighted that the change classification framework is not the only classification of change, but one of many. The use of a classification framework initially appears objective and neutral. However, inevitably it reflects the subjective choices of the author. It is biased in the sense of what is included and what is excluded. In this way, the change classifications framework offers a particular perspective on organisational change with the usual advantages and disadvantages of adopting a particular perspective.

In terms of the advantages, the change classifications framework brings a very reassuring order to uncertainties relating to both the theory and practice of managing change; it draws upon relevant literature and maps a process of organisational change. The disadvantages of the framework are that it is based upon assumptions about the planned nature of change, the desirability of organisational change and that change benefits all stakeholders. Burnes (2009a), in his own introduction to complexity theory and postmodernism, raises criticisms of more traditional organisation theories, which appear applicable to discussions about the change classifications framework. Traditional theories tend to assume that workers and managers share a common frame of reference. They adopt the belief that contextual factors can be easily accommodated or that they are irrelevant. They assume that managers cannot change situational variables. They ignore growing scepticism about their reliance upon rational objective science. They fail to deal effectively with the role of organisational culture, power and politics. Finally, organisation theories tend to explicitly or implicitly reject choices. While Burnes (2009a) was not specifically critiquing the change classifications framework, exploring competing counterpoints (perspectives) is at the heart of academic study. In complexity theory and postmodernism, counterpoints to the change classifications framework are evident.

COMPLEXITY THEORIES AND ORGANISATIONAL CHANGE

The origins of complexity theories can be traced to physics, mathematical biology, meteorology, computer science and systems thinking (Caldwell 2006). Caldwell (2006, p92) captured the essence of complexity when he wrote, 'the central idea of "complexity science" is that natural systems are characterized by dynamism, non-linearity and unpredictability, rather than simply equilibrium, order and predictability'. Critical commentators have begun to look to complexity theories for explanations of organisational change regarding organisations as natural systems that do not necessarily follow the strategic plans of managers.

A complex system has been defined as consisting '… of aggregates of interacting subunits, or agents, which together produce complex and adaptive behaviour patterns (hence the term "complex adaptive systems")' (Boal and Schultz 2007, p413). Caldwell (2006) focuses upon four core concepts of complexity science: ordered unpredictability, strange attractors, small changes/large effects and self-organisation. A brief explanation of each of these complexity concepts is included in Box 2.4.

Box 2.4 Four core concepts of complexity science

Ordered unpredictability: This departure from other organisation theories acknowledges the limits about what is known about organisations and change, and that unpredictability is underplayed (Stacey 2007).

Strange attractors: The concern here is with the paths that complex adaptive systems take in operating far from equilibrium. For example, Disney was viewed as a company moving towards strange attractors because, despite his death, employees still asked, 'What would Walt do?' and would then act accordingly (Boal and Schultz 2007).

Small changes/large effects: This is the principle that small changes in interactively complex systems alter the long-term behaviour of systems, often referred to as the 'butterfly effect'. However, in terms of change theory, empirical studies have not been able to support this view to date (Caldwell 2006).

Self-organisation: Systems on the edge of chaos exhibit spontaneous processes of self-organisation (Caldwell 2006). The radical implications of self-organisation are that organisations would need to be organised on democratic principles (Burnes 2009a).

Over the past decade academics and practitioners have begun to view how organisations should be structured and changed from a complexity perspective (Burnes 2009a). A critique of the change classifications framework based upon complexity theories could take the following form. The change classifications framework implies equilibrium, order and predictability in organisational change processes, whereas complexity theorists regard organisational change as being far more dynamic, non-linear and unpredictable than the framework suggests. The framework implies that organisational change is the outcome of a planned process, whereas complexity theorists would suggest that change emerges out of complex and adaptive behaviour patterns operating within a system.

POSTMODERNISM AND ORGANISATIONAL CHANGE

Postmodernism in the context of change has been defined as a counterpoint to modernism: 'the prevailing modern view of organisational change is that sufficient scientific analysis will ultimately reveal all that is important,' whereas postmodernism suggests that knowledge '… is relative rather than absolute, determined by social reality rather than some universal truth' (Graetz et al 2006, p18). Postmodernist perspectives on organisational change can be challenging, suggesting disorientation and chaos, with their use of complex language conveying unfamiliar ideas in often cryptic ways (Darwin et al 2002).

Morgan and Sturdy (2000, p29) in their differentiation of competing social approaches to organisational change concisely capture the essence of a postmodern approach: '… emphasis is placed on the detailed processes whereby forms of knowledge are constructed and become productive, as well as constraining, of forms of subjectivity and patterns of action'. In Journal Research Case 2.1, an early example of adopting a postmodern perspective upon organisational change is highlighted.

JOURNAL RESEARCH CASE 2.1

Slavs (division of a UK subsidiary of a multinational)

Paper title: Disciplining the shop floor: a comparison of the disciplinary effects of managerial psychology and financial accounting

Sector: Motor vehicle manufacturing

Research methods: Participant observation, intensive interviews, analysis of documents and company literature.

Authors: Knights, D. and Collinson, D.

Year: 1987

Journal details: *Accounting, Organizations and Society*. Vol 12, No 5. pp457–477.

Commentary: This paper, which was ahead of its time, remains a classic. The paper drew upon the work of Foucault to demonstrate that discipline was embedded within routine social practices. The researchers were able to study the disciplinary effects of psychological- and financial-accounting-based managerial power upon an all-male group of shop floor workers. Shop floor workers at Slavs tended to dismiss the company magazine as propaganda, whereas the financial accounting information had far more influence, acting as a disciplinary force upon management–worker relations.

Another illustration of postmodernism at work is evident in Grey's (2003) polemical critique of the orthodoxy of change management. Grey (2003) acknowledged the writings of Michel Foucault, which are believed to have subsequently informed management and organisation theory. He engages with the discourse of change with what he describes as radical scepticism. Discourse can be defined as talking or writing that frames how people understand and act with regard to that aspect of the world (Watson 2006). What is informative for this textbook is the way that Grey is able to take taken-for-granted assumptions about change management and show how they are informed by a dominant discourse of change. In this way he challenges popular views that change management failures arise out of imperfect implementation, resistance to change and poor leadership. These debates are explored in subsequent chapters of this textbook, but the role they serve according to this postmodern perspective is to protect the dominant discourse of change management.

However, I am not arguing that change discourse is a 'lie' fabricated by some conspiratorial group. On the contrary, I suspect that for many who so enthusiastically articulate that discourse it is less a tool of 'exploitation' and more a way of sustaining a particular sort of identity. (Grey 2003, p16)

This position highlights how postmodernist emphasis upon discourse encourages a different world view, which can be related to the paradigms and perspectives discussed in Chapter 4. Grey (2003, p11), in this polemical critique of change management, is unequivocal '… that the whole business of change management should be given up on'. In writing polemically he caricatures the discourse of change, but in this way helps to inform understanding about his radical perspective upon organisational change.

A critique of the change classifications framework based upon postmodernism could take the following form. The change classifications framework reflects a modernist view of knowledge with literature viewed as informing universal truths about organisational change, at the expense of more relativistic and subjective knowledge. The change classifications framework can be critiqued as reflecting a dominant discourse of managing change that takes for granted that change should be managed, implying that effectively managing change is in everyone's interest; in this way competing voices and debates are silenced.

This strong critique illustrates the strength of feeling that academic study generates. There are a range of very different viewpoints informing understanding about organisational change. In this textbook many competing perspectives will be introduced with the expectation that the reader can choose which appear most applicable to their studies.

CONCLUDING COMMENTARY

In order to study organisational change it is necessary to clarify and classify organisational change. The chapter introduced ten classification questions that help understanding of organisational change in terms of what is known and not known about a particular change. This classification process is good academic practice, but also informs the practice of managing change. Specific organisational change can be classified in terms of how it was managed, or how it is being managed, or how it is going to be managed. Instead of organisational change being dismissed as ambiguous, classification informs managing change.

The 'Critical Perspective' offered a counterpoint to the reassuring concept of the change classifications framework. Complexity theorists, in depicting organisations as natural systems, have emphasised the non-linearity of change and the unpredictability of change. In a similar manner postmodernists have questioned the universal truths that exist about organisational change and the espoused advance of science. The irony of both complexity theory and postmodernism is that they have captured the imaginations of more enlightened change practitioners. Increasingly managers do not regard organisational change as linear and predictable. Also, they are less likely to favour universal truths about the one best way to manage change. In conclusion, the change classifications framework is believed to advance the theory and practice of managing change.

However, this needs to be tempered by the acknowledgement that human systems will never behave exactly as either we want or expect them to behave.

CASE STUDY: APPLYING THEORY TO PRACTICE

GREENSHIRES COUNTY COUNCIL IN SHOCK RESTRUCTURING

The headline above appeared in the local newspaper. The following is a summary of the main themes from the newspaper article. Greenshires County Council was planning to change through the removal of one level of management located at the main council offices. It was believed that this would result in a flatter organisational hierarchy for the council. The background to this change was that senior management had become increasingly frustrated with regard to what they perceived as excessive bureaucracy within the county council. The councillors had unanimously agreed with a proposal to embark upon de-layering in order to reduce bureaucracy. The decision to de-layer the organisation had been made by the incoming county council chief executive and he had taken advice from a team of external management consultants. The management consultants had agreed to act as change agents in terms of carrying out the de-layering in the county council. However, overall responsibility for the change initiative remained with the chief executive. The de-layering would be managed through a negotiated process involving full consultation with representative bodies. As an outcome of this change the chief executive very publicly stated that once the de-layering was completed, all committee paperwork was to be processed within a maximum of one week of each committee meeting and fully actioned within one month of that committee meeting.

The last major change management initiative in the county council emphasised the need for improvements in service quality. 'Quality Council through Quality Service' was believed to have floundered due to the bureaucratic practices of middle management; while managers had initially appeared very enthusiastic, they had failed to adopt the new ways of working. The announcement about de-layering had been made to senior management at an away-day at a local hotel. Senior managers were subsequently required to cascade this information down the organisational hierarchy of the county council, informing those individual managers directly affected by de-layering in face-to-face meetings. The chief executive had made clear that he regarded this change as very significant when compared with previous changes initiatives that had taken place at the county council. However, he conceded in talks with his senior management team that the focus was very much upon middle management, rather than upon the whole workforce of the county council. His target was for all redundancies in the county council to be completed within one year, with a further year envisaged for adjusting to the new arrangements. Many of the individual managers affected by the change were supportive because of the size of their redundancy payments. However, representative bodies were sceptical and critical of de-layering, perceiving it to be a crude cost-cutting exercise.

Case study questions

1 Apply the change classifications framework to this organisational change (please answer all ten questions).

2 What further classification questions could be asked to inform understanding about this particular organisational change?

DISCUSSION QUESTIONS

1   Collins (1998) was sceptical about the 'What is change?' narrative. What do you think was the basis for his scepticism?

2   Are classifications of change likely to be more evident in academic or in organisational explanations of change? Why?

3   In terms of the ten change classification questions specified in the framework, which are going to be the most difficult to answer?

4   What drives interest in perspectives such as complexity and postmodernism?

KEY READINGS

BURKE, W. W. (2008) *Organization change: theory and practice*. 2nd ed. Thousand Oaks, CA: Sage Publications.

In this textbook the author has managed to reconcile the theoretical with the practical (many books are either excessively theoretical or excessively practical). This book favours a planned approach, rather than an emergent approach to organisational change, which makes it very compatible with discussions in this chapter about the change classifications framework. Chapters about the levels of organisational change and conceptual models for understanding organisation change are particularly pertinent.

DARWIN, J., JOHNSON, P. and MCAULEY, J. (2002) *Developing strategies for change*. Harlow: FT Prentice Hall.

This deeply philosophical textbook is recommended for anyone who wants to read more about complexity theories and postmodernism as applied to organisational change. The book adopts a thought-provoking style of writing and acts as an antidote to the functionalism of many change management textbooks.

STICKLAND, F. (1998) *The dynamics of change*. London: Routledge.

This textbook has a different feel from many of the other textbooks on change. When you read this book you can imagine Stickland trying to make sense of change himself. One of the strengths of this book is its interdisciplinary nature. Particularly relevant to this chapter is Stickland's discussion entitled, 'What is this thing, change?'

CHAPTER 3

History and organisational change

INTRODUCTION

To appreciate contemporary themes and thinking about organisational change, there is a need to revisit traditional themes (Frahm 2007). Managing change in moving from what is known to what is unknown is inevitably forward looking; however, this should never be at the expense of overlooking the past. The academic dilemma is that the legacy of the past is too often unacknowledged or misrepresented. For example, Cooke (1999) criticised change management for being ahistorical and acontextual, with similar criticisms being levelled at strategic management (Pettigrew et al 2002). In engaging with contemporary organisational change, it is essential to acknowledge the past: 'too many people fall into the trap of thinking that management has no past, or at least that nothing can be learned about management today by studying the past' (Witzel 2003, pxiii).

In this chapter, the focus is upon the historical legacy that informs and misinforms understanding about organisational change. In the 'Managerial Approaches' section, the six most popular management writing idea families are introduced as a means of mapping out key management writing and its implications for organisational change. In the 'Critical Perspective', the focus shifts from history to the historiography of organisational change, in particular highlighting the dangers of traditional textbook orthodoxy, which present a very particular and selective account of organisational change.

MANAGERIAL APPROACHES

POPULAR MANAGEMENT WRITING

The challenges of organisational change go back much further than the literature featured in this textbook. Burke (2008, p27) highlighted how 'organisation change is as old as organisations themselves', citing examples of building projects such as the Egyptian Pyramids and the Great Wall of China. In looking to collections of management writing, Witzel's (2003) survey of the 50 key management figures is different from the norm in that he goes back as far as the sixth century BC to feature the ancient Chinese philosopher Lao Tzu and the sixteenth-century Italian statesmen Niccolo Machiavelli.

However, the norm has been histories favouring Anglo-American management figures. As Cummings (2002, p6) sceptically notes, '... the network of objects that we refer to as management's primary elements emerge in the US in the period around 1900'. The textbook orthodoxy is then to feature chronologically writers on management and organisation (largely Anglo-American) from 1900 to the present day (see, for example, Pugh and Hickson 2007). Even within these artificial boundaries it is still contentious who should be entered into the management thought hall of fame.

Huczynski (2006, p30) offered a way forward, which is favoured in this chapter. His survey of popular management ideas of the twentieth century included academics and practitioner writers and a content analysis of professional journals, as well as popular texts of selected readings and reprint series. His analysis led him (2006, p31) to suggest that 'more recent writers did not appear often in the voting. The length of the final list indicated that beyond a hard core of writers, there is little consensus as to who the really influential contributors are.' Huczynski (2006, p32) identified the following hard core of the most popular management writers: joint first – Henri Fayol, Douglas McGregor; joint third – Peter Drucker, Frederick Herzberg, Tom Peters; and joint sixth – Frederick Winslow Taylor, Rensis Likert and Chris Argyris.

In total Huczynski (2006) identified 129 management writers, based upon references to authors in his literature review constituting a vote for each author. In reviewing this analysis for broad patterns Huczynski (2006) found that there were only six truly popular management idea families over the past 100 years. He defined a management idea as '... applied to all abstract thought units or systems of such units... where there can be said to be sufficient similarity between these ideas or systems of ideas, then the term family of management ideas will be used' (2006, p30). The six management idea families that he identified were: bureaucracy, scientific management, administrative management, human relations, neo-human relations, and guru theory. Each of these management idea families is introduced in terms of key writers and how they inform understanding about organisational change.

Bureaucracy

Bureaucracy can be defined as '… an organisational form consisting of a hierarchy of differentiated knowledge and expertise in which rules and disciplines are arranged not only hierarchically in regard to each other but also in parallel' (Clegg et al 2008, p486). Weber (1947), through translations of his writing, gave impetus to understanding organisations as bureaucracies and structuralist approaches to organisational behaviour. Structuralism suggested that the way organisations were structured was beyond choice and was instead an outcome of modern, scientific and rational principles (Huczynski 2006). Weber (1947) was interested in economies and societies, rather than organisations; however, he was well placed to comment upon advances in formal rationality and authority. He (1947) identified three major bases of authority: rational-legal, traditional and charismatic. Rational-legal authority was concerned with following rules and general principles. Traditional authority was concerned with following previous precedents, and charismatic authority was grounded in the 'magic' of the authority figure. To differentiate bureaucracy from other administrative forms, Weber constructed an 'ideal type' of bureaucracy, which had the following defining characteristics: specialisation, hierarchy, rules, impersonality, appointment, progression, exclusivity, segregation and accurate written records.

Weber (1947) was open-minded about bureaucracy: 'for Weber on the one hand was persuaded that bureaucracy was becoming the dominant organisational form while, on the other hand, he bemoaned even despaired of this fact' (Grey 2007, p494). In terms of the first of the six management ideas families, interest was not so much focused upon the validity of Weber's work as the appeal bureaucracy has had over the years for managers (Huczynski 2006). The concept of bureaucracy is very relevant to organisational change debates. For example, debates about organisational design (Chapter 6) are informed by different perceptions of the advantages and disadvantages of bureaucracy. In a similar manner, interest in cultural change, which emphasises the informal organisation, is a reaction to perceived disadvantages of bureaucracy.

Scientific management

Scientific management as a popular management idea has focused upon the shop floor and techniques to maximise manual workers' productivity (Huczynski 2006). The origins of scientific management can be traced back to F.W. Taylor (1911) and the landmark publication of *The Principles of Scientific Management*. Taylor (1911), as the founder of scientific management (sometimes referred to as Taylorism), advocated increased managerial discretion over work through calculating and defining how work was undertaken. Witzel (2003, p293), reflecting upon his work, offers the following evaluation: 'there is no doubt, that when properly implemented, scientific management can increase efficiency, often many fold. The fault of Taylor's system was that it failed to build in mechanisms to temper efficiency with humanity,' discussed further in the 'Critical Perspective'. The appeal of scientific management as a popular management idea family has been the implications it has for how jobs are designed and organisations are designed. Although Taylor was writing at the beginning of the last century, elements of scientific management are still evident in contemporary organisational changes (see, for example, business process reengineering and Lean Six Sigma, which are featured in the Organisational Change Field Guide (see Appendix)).

Administrative management

Writers in this management idea family sought to optimise efficiency through determining types of specialisation and hierarchy, with the outcome of invariably mechanistic forms of organisational design (Hucyznski 2006). The analysis of Huczynski (2006), cited earlier, locates Fayol as the most popular management writer. Fayol's famous work *General and Industrial Management* was originally published in French in 1916 and appeared in English translation in 1949. Fayol (1949), with a background in engineering, worked in a French mining company and rose to become managing director. One of the major contributions of Fayol was his classification of activities of organisations in terms of: technical, commercial, financial, security, accounting and managerial. He identified 14 general principles of management, which are featured in Box 3.1.

Many of the terms featured in Box 3.1 have become part of the everyday lexicon of management and many are discussed in Chapter 6. However, *esprit de corps* requires clarification: the term means emphasising harmony and cohesion among organisation members. Fayol played an important role in management thought, offering a classification of the activities of managers; many of the 14 principles are still evident in organisations today. In terms of organisational change, the origins of debates about the manageability of change can be traced back to Fayol. Drawing upon his own experiences as a managing director, Fayol offered insights into processes of managing that subsequently informed attempts to understand managing change.

Box 3.1 General principles of management (based on Fayol, 1949)

1 division of work	8 centralisation
2 authority	9 scalar chain (line of authority)
3 discipline	10 order
4 unity of command	11 equity
5 unity of direction	12 stability of tenure of personnel
6 subordination of individual interest to the general interest	13 initiative
7 remuneration	14 *esprit de corps*

Human relations

Critical writers have argued that human relations represented a change of management tactics rather than any fundamental shift in the objectives of scientific management (Huczynski 2006). The pivotal role of the Hawthorne studies in organisational theory is widely acknowledged (Thompson and McHugh

2009). The Hawthorne studies drew upon a major research project, which commenced in the mid-1920s at the Hawthorne plant of American Telegraph and Telephone. Two important conclusions were drawn from undertaking these studies: first, the influence of intervention in the workplace, particularly in terms of interventions by psychologists and sociologists; and second, the interpretation of the results formed the basis of the human relations school of thought and subsequent management practice (Thompson and McHugh 2009).

A key publication of this era was *The Human Problems of an Industrial Civilization* (Mayo 1933). The book discussed the famous Hawthorne studies, which were largely undertaken by Mayo's colleagues, and in particular those human relations witnessed by researchers at the Hawthorne plant. In his own history of organisational change, Burke (2008) identified reasons why he believed the Hawthorne studies were a significant precursor to understanding organisational change: they highlighted psychological and human factors influencing productivity and morale; they signposted variables impacting upon worker satisfaction and encouraged more humanistic treatment of workers; they informed later theoretical developments, such as the writings of Herzberg et al (1959) and provided stimulus and data for studies of group dynamics.

Neo-human relations

In his analysis of popular management idea families, Hucyznski (2006) identified neo-human relations as the most popular management idea family. Neo-human relations writing can be traced back to the late 1950s, with the unifying theme being a belief in employees' desire to grow and develop on the job. Four neo-human relations writers featured in the ranking of the most popular management writers: McGregor, Herzberg, Likert and Argyris.

McGregor (1960) identified assumptions (Theory X and Theory Y) about motivation and human behaviour, which he believed were implicit in management literature, theory and practice. Theory X assumptions suggested people had an inherent dislike of work and would avoid work if they could; consequently people needed to be controlled, directed and threatened with punishment in order to achieve organisational goals. By contrast, Theory Y assumptions emphasised the potential inherent satisfaction within work and suggested less need for management controls.

The two major aspects of Herzberg's contribution were the theory itself and the technique of job enrichment (Huczynski 2006). Job enrichment involves expanding the scope of jobs and increasing decision-making by job-holders. Herzberg et al (1959) surveyed engineers and accountants in Pittsburgh. They were able to identify factors that were believed to be strong determinants of job satisfaction: achievement, recognition, the work itself, responsibility and advancement (often referred to as motivators). They also identified reasons for job dissatisfaction: company policy and administration, supervision, salary, working conditions and interpersonal relations (often referred to as the hygiene factors). Again, Huczynski (2006) highlighted how a theorist such as Herzberg has often been misrepresented: the hygiene factors and motivators together influenced worker motivation, rather than the hygiene factors being less important than motivators.

Likert's (1967) System 4 theory emphasised the importance of democracy in management and was psychologically focused, advocating integration of individuals into the organisation through groups (Huczynski 2006). Likert developed the Likert scale, allowing organisations to be classified according to their management approach: autocratic management (system 1), benevolent autocracy (system 2), consultative management (system 3) and participative management (system 4). Likert (1967) believed that the way forward was for all organisations to adopt a participative management approach (system 4). Goal congruence theory was concerned with individuals developing healthy personalities within organisations (Argyris 1973). Argyris highlighted six dimensions through which he believed individuals progressed. He was also concerned with the ingredients of administrative theory, which informed the development of the formal organisation. However, he was sceptical that formal organisations were compatible with the development of healthy personalities (Huczynski 2006).

Neo-human relations offer a rationale for managing the human aspects of organisations. In terms of organisational change, the origins of organisational development (OD) in the 1960s are closely aligned with neo-human relations theories, beliefs and values, discussed in the Organisational Change Field Guide (see Appendix). Many of the debates about the 'human side of managing change' featured in this textbook relate to neo-human relations theories.

Guru theory

Huczynski (2006) defined guru theory as seeking to help managers build strong business systems to successfully compete in their chosen market segment. He (2006) acknowledged that guru writing can appear to be a random collection of diverse contributors. Huczynski (2006) identified five beliefs underpinning guru theory, which are summarised as follows. Firstly, innovations in products and services depend upon many 'tries' by many employees. Secondly, individuals' actions leading to feelings is favoured over individuals' feelings leading to action. Thirdly, organisations can co-ordinate through culture and value systems, rather than rules and commands. Fourthly, the main source of innovation is customers. Fifthly, management attitudes and behaviour towards staff is influenced by a strong customer orientation. Huczynski (2006) distinguished three sub-schools of guru theory: the academic guru school, the consultant guru school and the hero-manager guru school.

Witzel (2003, p73) has described Drucker as '... arguably the most popular and widely read management writer of all time. A guru who fully deserves his status, he regularly tops opinion polls amongst business men as the most influential management thinker and writer of the twentieth century.' Drucker wrote extensively about management. In particular he is remembered for highlighting problems and pitfalls associated with moves towards the knowledge economy. Drucker was concerned with how knowledge workers would be controlled and disciplined, given that they were a highly skilled and mobile elite (Collins 2000). Also, Drucker is remembered for introducing management by objectives (Drucker 1954) and management by results (Drucker 1964) into the management vocabulary.

Peters is one of the more recent gurus and was prominent in the 1980s and 1990s; he was a consultant by training and drew upon his own business experiences (Witzel 2003). His work will be featured in later chapters, particularly in terms of cultural change; however, one of his most famous works was *In Search of Excellence* (Peters and Waterman 1982), which he co-authored with Robert Waterman.

Guru theory is particularly applicable to organisational change. However, it is difficult to be conclusive about the impact of guru theory upon the theory and practice of organisational change. Fincham and Evans (1999) regard management gurus as creating a climate of expectations about organisational change, preparing the ground for consultants as the live actors in firms. It is difficult to differentiate management gurus and consultants driving change from the influence of management fashions (Abrahamson and Fairchild 1999). In recent years a new literature has emerged, which, rather than being written by gurus, is written about gurus (see, for example, Argyris and Jackson 2001; Jackson 2001; and Clark and Fincham 2002).

CRITICAL PERSPECTIVE

Booth and Rowlinson (2006, p21) have referred to '… an historic turn underway in management and organisation theory requiring the reorientation of organisation theory particularly in terms of critical management studies and gender'. In the following 'Critical Perspective' the historiography of organisational change is introduced and explained, in order to encourage reflection upon the traditionally ahistorical treatment of organisational change (Cooke 1999). How history has been written and key details of this history are critically questioned, raising questions about traditional notions of the espoused linearity of the theory and practice of organisational change.

HISTORIOGRAPHY AND ORGANISATIONAL CHANGE

The popular management ideas that provided the structure of the 'Managerial Approaches' in this chapter were a pragmatic choice. Many other competing collections of management writing exist (see, for example, Witzel 2003; Pugh and Hickson 2007). Textbook orthodoxy of management thought is very reassuring in its emphasis upon research underpinning theory and implying a progressive historical and linear evolution of theory.

The study of how history is written is referred to as historiography. The following historiography of organisational change is informed by Cooke's (1999, p81) fascinating paper, which highlighted the historiography of change management. He argued that 'change management's very construction has been a political process which has written the left out, and shaped an understanding of the field as technocratic and ideologically neutral'. The concept of historiography suggests that there will be many histories of organisational change with certain accounts of history privileged over others. Cooke (1999, p83) explains how this process works: 'history, our knowing of the past, is constructed by identifying some of these events as significant, and, by implication, others as not, and by giving these events particular meaning'.

In deconstructing management's history, Cummings (2002) develops two themes. Firstly, conventional history helped to establish management and strategy as dominant fields, although this was a fabrication. Secondly, this fabrication, now perceived as fundamental, limits the study of management and strategy. In reviewing the historiography of organisational change, three related themes become apparent: the accuracy of the research evidence, the misrepresentation of theorists, and gender myopia/blindness.

Historiography questions the legitimacy of research-based theories and encourages critical review of the original research underpinning these theories. A good example of such a critical evaluation applies to Taylor's (1911) scientific management. In studying management history it is difficult to avoid F.W. Taylor, despite his contribution to management thought being regularly contested (Booth and Rowlinson 2006). The concept of scientific management was given added legitimacy through his research undertaken at the Midvale Steel Company and Bethlehem Steel Company. However, Wrege and Hodgetts (2000) analysed the original documents upon which Taylor's famous pig iron observations of 1899 were based. Troublingly, Wrege and Hodgetts (2000) found that his observations were erroneous. Taylor and his associates had made many mistakes, most importantly simplifying the results of their study and glossing over inconsistencies, as discussed in Journal Research Case 3.1.

👁 JOURNAL RESEARCH CASE 3.1

1899 Pig Iron Observations

Paper title: Frederick W. Taylor's 1899 pig iron observations: examining fact, fiction, and lessons for the new millennium
Sector: Iron Production
Research methods: Documentary sources including diaries and weather records
Authors: Wrege, C.D. and Hodgetts, R.M.
Year: 2000
Journal details: *Academy of Management Journal.* Vol 43, No 6. pp1283–1291.

Commentary: The paper, while acknowledging the impact of Taylor's findings on management, explores through analysis of original documents what really happened during the famous pig iron observations of 1899. The research evidence did not support Taylor's principles of scientific management; the book was largely supported through Taylor's anecdotes about the pig iron observations. One of the ironic revelations of the paper is that senior managers at that time in history never replicated Taylor's methods: 'Taylor told a good tale, but he could not sell it to senior-level managers who focused on facts not anecdotes' (Wrege and Hodgetts 2000, p1289).

Almost a century later the critical evaluation of Taylor's research appears pedantic, yet scientific management at the turn of the last century was the major means of change (Thompson and McHugh 2009) and scientific management today remains influential in terms of management and organisational behaviour thinking (see Cummings 2002 and Darwin et al 2002 for further discussion). There is a growing body of literature questioning the research that underpins the history of management thought (see Wren 1987 and Booth and Rowlinson 2006 for critical overviews of this literature).

A second concern is that in trying to ensure theories fit prevailing management logic, theories are misrepresented either intentionally or unintentionally. The writings of both McGregor and Herzberg have frequently been misrepresented to fit the prevailing management logic of achieving productive and efficient employees. Cummings (2002, p80) highlights a more general problem with traditional accounts of the history of modern thought: 'indeed the pioneering historians got the story "down pat" so quickly that no significantly new general history of management has been written since the early 1970s: new editions of these men's classics were considered more than adequate to relate a history that was already fully understood'.

In terms of organisational change, Cooke (1999) uses managerialist accounts of the work of Kurt Lewin, John Collier and Edgar Schein to illustrate how despite these writers drawing upon ideas of the political left, the left is airbrushed out of what now appears in management textbooks. The misrepresentation of Lewin is particularly pertinent to concerns within this textbook, given his central role in the development of theories of organisational change. Burnes (2004) has convincingly encouraged a reappraisal of the work of Lewin, although he is the exception rather than the rule among management academics. Lewin's concepts of unfreezing, changing and refreezing and force-field analysis were enthusiastically adopted by management academics as theories to help explain organisational change. 'However, in the past 20 years, Lewin's approach to change, particularly the 3-step model, has attracted major criticisms' (Burnes 2004, p977). Through his careful reading of Lewin's original work and through setting Lewin's work within its political and social context, Burnes (2004) has been able to counter these criticisms. As Burnes (2004, p979) highlighted, 'for most of his life Lewin's main preoccupation was the resolution of social conflict and, in particular, the problems of minority or disadvantaged groups'. Managerialist accounts of Lewin's work tend to neglect this fact when evaluating his work in terms of contemporary management logic.

A third concern relates to the gender blindness/myopia of traditional histories of management thought. Wilson (2001) gets to the heart of the matter in the preface to her reassessment of organisational behaviour: 'there are any number of standard OB textbooks, indistinguishable from each other, and almost all written from a male, managerialist, and often ethnocentric, viewpoint. They perform a certain function, but not one that I find satisfying, because they affirm the current order.' In writing the 'Managerial Approaches' section of this chapter, the gender imbalance was very apparent. While Taylor, Fayol and Mayo have been heavily criticised, their omission would equally have been criticised. The problem is that through this accumulation of management theories, male authors are included and female authors excluded.

Cooke (1999) explained how in the 1984 edition of the classic French and Bell organisational development textbook, the contribution of women such as Mouton, Schindler-Rainman and Seashore to the development of OD was not acknowledged, whereas in the 1996 edition of the same classic textbook their contribution was acknowledged. The events being written about had not changed between 1984 and 1996, but how this aspect of history was written about had changed. This reappraisal gives some hope, but equally it highlights the selective nature of the historiography of organisational change. While Foreman (2001) in her chapter on organisational change discusses why gender must be incorporated into analyses of organisational change and how this goal can be achieved, offering competing accounts of management history is more problematic.

A consequence of questioning the accuracy of the research evidence, the misrepresentation of theorists and gender myopia/blindness is to raise doubts about modernist notions of progress and the associated linearity of management thinking.

Implicit and often explicit in the organisational change literature is the notion that each theory of organisational change is an improvement on earlier theories, with the practice of organisational change reflecting a similar progressive linearity. However, such modernist notions of progress have been questioned:

> Organisational change is not linear; if it has any direction, it is very often cyclical. Many current forms of organisational change, although they are described as if they were the very latest in modern thinking, have been around before, often more than once and sometimes very long ago, although often under a different name. (Salaman and Asch 2003, p3)

A radical new organisational change initiative, such as business process reengineering, presented to managers as a break with the past is a revision and repackaging of the principles of scientific management (Cummings 2002; Hughes 2009). Darwin et al (2002, p11) raised similar concerns 'that most, if not all, currently fashionable ideas are reinventions: old wine in new bottles, with packaging and presentation the critical factors'. The notion of change as cyclical is informative in terms of understanding organisational change. Burrell (1992) has challenged notions of linearity and chronarchy, promoting the notion of spiral time (depicted pictorially as a coiled serpent). Cummings (2002, p180) has also challenged assumptions about the linearity of organisational change, arguing for 'a vision of time not as a straight line but as a spiral, with past, present and future intermingled'.

As well as questioning the linearity of change, historiography encourages questioning of popular rhetoric that we are living through turbulent times, exemplified in the writings of Drucker and critically questioned by Thompson and O'Connell Davidson (1995). In a similar manner, Eccles and Nohria (1992) address the question of whether the 1980s and 1990s were truly a time of organisational transformation and discontinuous change as Drucker suggested, concluding that future business historians will be better placed to make this assessment than are any contemporary writers. Cooke (1999, p98) has argued persuasively that 'all understanding of management and organisation theory are shaped by historiographical processes'. However, as he warns, this concern is as equally applicable to critical perspectives as it is to managerial perspectives.

CONCLUDING COMMENTARY

The task of managing change can be traced back to the earliest civilisations as highlighted in visible achievements such as the Pyramids and the Great Wall of China. What happened next is more contentious. A broad body of management literature is now evident, which has been informed by many writers over many centuries. The textbook orthodoxy has been to trace these writings from 1900 onwards and to favour Anglo-American accounts of managing. Even within these pragmatic parameters, there is a large body of contradictory writing about management. The idea of popular management idea families, favoured in this chapter, signposts commonalities and differentiates writers in terms of six idea families: bureaucracy, scientific management, administrative management, human relations, neo-human relations, and guru theory. Each of these idea families has implications for managing change, with neo-human relations and guru theory being particularly significant.

However, the dilemma that this chapter has highlighted is that many different histories of management thought exist. The version presented in this chapter is just one version. The concept of historiography appears to be an academic abstraction, but it has a profound impact upon both the theory and practice of managing change. Managing change in an organisation today can never completely be separated from that organisation's past. History has determined what aspects of managing change are regarded as significant and what should be studied and, by association, not studied; the tragedy is that scrutiny of famous writers such as Lewin reveals that their work is frequently misrepresented.

CASE STUDY: APPLYING THEORY TO PRACTICE

Reflecting upon the NHS Next Stage Review

Introduction

The National Health Service (NHS) Next Stage Review, led by Lord Darzi, engaged with patients, staff and the public with a view to developing a shared vision for the future of health and healthcare. The review will be seen as a milestone in the history of the NHS. In this case study two perspectives on the NHS are presented. Perspective one is the preface written by the Prime Minister, Gordon Brown, in 2008 for the final report produced as part of the review. Perspective two summarises a newspaper article from the *Sunday Times* that appeared on the Times Online website. Please read both perspectives before answering the case study questions.

Perspective One – Preface by the Prime Minister to the NHS Next Stage Review final report

The National Health Service is not just a great institution but a unique and very British expression of an ideal – that healthcare is not a privilege to be purchased but a moral right secured for all. For 60 years it has carried the support of the British people because it speaks to our values of fairness and opportunity for all and because it is always there for us when we are most vulnerable and in need. That is why it is right that we should seek to renew the NHS for the 21st century. To meet the rising aspirations of the public, the changing burdens of disease and to ensure

that the very latest, personalised healthcare is available to all of us, not just those able to pay.

Over the last 10 years we have improved the basic standards of the NHS. In 2000, the NHS Plan set out to tackle the challenges which chronic underinvestment had created. Since then we have invested in 80,000 more nurses and 38,000 more doctors, including 5,000 more GPs. Access to care has improved dramatically, and outcomes have improved as a result: 238,000 lives have been saved in the last 11 years as a result of significant improvements in cancer and heart disease survival rates in particular. This report builds on those reforms and will, I believe, have an even more profound effect on NHS services and our experience of them. If the challenge 10 years ago was capacity, the challenge today is to drive improvements in the quality of care. We need a more personalised NHS, responsive to each of us as individuals, focused on prevention, better equipped to keep us healthy and capable of giving us real control and real choices over our care and our lives.

Lord Darzi's report is a tremendous opportunity to build an NHS that provides truly world class services for all. It requires Government to be serious about reform, committed to trusting frontline staff and ready to invest in new services and new ways of delivering services. It is a bold vision for an NHS which is among the best healthcare systems in the world – a once in a generation opportunity that we owe it to ourselves and our families to take. I would like to thank Lord Darzi and the thousands of those who have been involved in the review locally and nationally for their contributions. As a Government the renewal of the NHS must be one of our very highest priorities and we will rise to the challenge you have set us.

Gordon Brown
Prime Minister

Source: Darzi, A. (2008) *High quality care for all: NHS next stage review final report.* Department of Health, Norwich: The Stationery Office.

http://www.dh.gov.uk/prod_consum_dh/ groups/dh_digitalassets/@dh/@en/ documents/digitalasset/dh_085828.pdf (accessed 08/12/09). Crown Copyright 2008.

Perspective Two – Labour hid ugly truth about National Health Service (NHS)

Summary of an article by Lois Rogers published on 7 March 2010 in the *Sunday Times*.

The main theme of the article is that the Government suppressed three reports that were critical of the state of the NHS. These reports were commissioned by Lord Darzi as part of his review of the progress of the NHS. Their existence was revealed through a freedom of information request. The article suggested that the pursuit of political and managerial targets was the root cause of hospital scandals that resulted in thousands of lost lives. The reports were prepared by the Massachusetts-based Institute for Healthcare Improvements, the US-based Joint Commission International and the US-based Rand Corporation.

Lord Darzi was cited as saying the previous week that 'the NHS is continuing a journey of improvements, moving from a service that has rightly focused on increasing the quantity of care to one that focuses on improving the quality of care,' while a Department of Health spokesperson was cited explaining that the reports were never intended for 'wider circulation'. However, the spokesperson suggested that they were discussed by the experts who advised Lord Darzi on the production of his report.

The full article is available at the following website:

http://www.timesonline.co.uk/tol/news/ uk/health/article7052606.ece (accessed 14/04/10).

Case study questions

1 What do you believe was the motivation of each author when writing their piece and how may they contribute to the history of the NHS?

2 Compare and contrast the two extracts in terms of what contemporary aspects of the NHS the two authors chose to focus upon.

3 What aspects of each extract give legitimacy to the views expressed?

DISCUSSION QUESTIONS

1 In written histories of management thought, which groups and roles are likely to have been over-represented and under-represented?

2 What are the potential consequences of adopting an ahistorical approach to understanding organisational change?

3 Is the history of organisational change fixed, or does the history itself change over time?

4 What are the dangers implicit within historiography?

KEY READINGS

In adopting a historical perspective towards organisational change, there is merit in reading original publications, rather than secondary accounts. In the absence of such primary sources, the following readings are recommended.

BURKE, W.W. (2008) *Organization change: theory and practice*. 2nd ed. Thousand Oaks, CA: Sage Publications.

In his chapter 'A brief history of organisation change', Burke outlines the historical evolution of thinking about organisation change. There are interesting sections on coercion and confrontation and management consulting. He believes that much can be learned from responses to coercive and confrontational techniques in terms of understanding organisational change. The chapter may be read as one of the better examples of textbook orthodoxy in terms of the evolution of management thinking. Alternatively, it may be read as a counterpoint to this chapter and another example of the historiography of change management.

CUMMINGS, S. (2002) *Recreating strategy*. London: Sage Publications Ltd.

The innocent title of this book belies the sophistication of the ideas within it. The book is recommended here because of its emphasis upon historiography. In particular, the author adopts a critical perspective to highlight how history has been misrepresented in developing understanding about organisational behaviour, management and strategy. The tone of the book is critical throughout, and the book has the capacity to provoke alternative thinking about taken-for-granted aspects of organisations. For anyone reading his textbook selectively, there is a very relevant chapter on regenerating change. The only cautionary note would be that the modernist/postmodernist themes may prove hard work for the uninitiated.

WILSON, E. (ed.) (2001) *Organizational behaviour reassessed: the impact of gender*. London: Sage Publications Ltd.

In the 'Critical Perspective' it was suggested that histories of organisational change had been written by men, for men and about men. In fairness the critique is far more sophisticated than this and it is difficult to do justice to the critique in the confines of a chapter covering broader themes. In this edited reader most of the major management and organisational debates are covered from a gender perspective.

CHAPTER 4

The role of paradigms and perspectives

LEARNING OUTCOMES

After reading this chapter you should be able to:

- understand how paradigms frame thinking about organisational change
- appreciate the contribution of Burrell and Morgan to understanding paradigms
- understand the concept of perspective with regard to organisational change
- appreciate Sturdy's contribution in understanding the adoption of ideas/practices
- understand what constitutes a critical perspective
- appreciate why a critical perspective has been adopted for this textbook.

INTRODUCTION

Burnes (2006, pviii) acknowledged that '… we cannot understand organisational change sufficiently, nor implement it effectively, unless we can map the range of approaches and evaluate what they seek to achieve how and where they can be applied, and, crucially, the evidence which underpins them'. In undertaking these tasks, theory plays a significant role. Theory can be defined as '… an explanation of observed regularities…' (Bryman and Bell 2007, p7); while this chapter introduces and explains paradigms and perspectives, in essence the chapter is concerned with explaining organisational change.

The task should not be underestimated: 'explaining how and why organisations change has been a central and enduring quest of scholars in management and many other disciplines' (Van de Ven and Poole 1995, p510). The chapter is informed by discussions in the previous chapter tracing the history and historiography of organisational change. The writings of the management writers who featured in the previous chapter were informed by different philosophical positions and implicit or explicit perspectives (viewpoints).

Writing with specific reference to managing change, Palmer et al (2009, p23) suggest that metaphors, frames or perspectives '… are held by us often without our being aware either of their existence or of how they affect our thinking, perceptions, and actions. They act as mental models, pointing us in certain directions in order to make sense of things going on around us.' However, in beginning to engage with these mental models it becomes apparent that organisational change cannot be regarded as a distinct academic discipline with rigid and clearly defined boundaries. The theory and practice of managing change draws upon a number of social science disciplines and traditions (Van de Ven and Poole 1995; Burnes 2009a), which explains why Willcocks and Mason (1987) found that there are as many perspectives on change as people in the organisation affected. The challenge facing students and researchers is the diversity of theoretical perspectives and prescriptive frameworks that relate to organisational change (Palmer and Dunford 2008).

In a chapter entitled 'One hundred theories of organizational change: the good, the bad and the ugly', Mohr (1999) highlighted the central dilemma that this chapter addresses – making sense of many competing accounts of organisational change. Frustratingly, Mohr does not list 100 theories, as his title tantalizingly suggests; however, he does signpost the breadth (one hundred), the wealth (the good) and the weaknesses (the bad and the ugly) of organisational change theory. This textbook does not attempt to feature all theories; instead the choice of theories must always be selective. Often a pragmatic choice will be made to focus upon theories relevant to a single perspective or a small group of perspectives while acknowledging the existence of competing perspectives. The real advantage of such pragmatic choices is that they potentially enable far deeper understanding. No academic or student of organisational change can ever master all of the many thousands of theories in this field. However, in studying organisational change, commonalities in basic assumptions (paradigms) and perspectives become apparent. In this way paradigms and perspectives frame understanding about organisational change.

The 'Managerial Approaches' section makes explicit the role of philosophies and perspectives informing the study of organisational change. In discussing paradigms, four major philosophical positions are identified: functionalism, interpretivism, radical humanism, and radical structuralism. The relevance of the concept of perspective with regard to studying organisational change is illustrated through Sturdy's (2004) classification of perspectives relating to the adoption of management ideas and practices. In the 'Critical Perspective', what constitutes a critical perspective and why it has been adopted in the context of this textbook are explained.

MANAGERIAL APPROACHES

Collins (1998, p1) suggested that 'a key problem with much of the study of change management in organisations is that the authors active in the field tend not to discuss, explicitly, the theoretical models and frameworks which guide their analysis'. The following discussion explicitly explains the role paradigms and perspectives play in underpinning the study of organisational change. This terminology appears inappropriate for a 'Managerial Approaches' section. However, 'we cannot rid ourselves of the burdens of theory since, even if we fail to realize it, we are always at some level guided by the tools and insights of some theoretical model, however imperfectly we understand its finer points' (Collins 1998, p33). In this way the managerial rhetoric such as 'the customer is always king' can be traced back to a particular paradigm and perspective.

PARADIGMS OF/FOR CHANGE

The word paradigm has a particular meaning in academic study: 'it is a term which is intended to emphasise the commonality of perspective which binds the work of a group of theorists together in such a way that they can be usefully regarded as approaching social theory within the bounds of the same problematic' (Burrell and Morgan 1979, p23). There are still likely to be debates within paradigms, but commonalities in basic assumptions are shared. In reviewing the organisational change literature, references to different paradigms become apparent, for example, Butler et al (2003) applied modernist and postmodernist paradigms in evaluating organisational change, as discussed in Journal Research Case 4.1.

JOURNAL RESEARCH CASE 4.1

Evaluating the Action Thinking Program

Paper title: Evaluating organizational change: the role of ontology and epistemology.
Sector: Manufacturing
Research methods: Longitudinal data set for 35 individuals (data collection methods not specified).
Authors: Butler, J., Scott, F. and Edwards, J.
Year: 2003
Journal details: *TAMARA Journal of Critical Postmodern Organization Science*. Vol 2, No 2. pp55–67.

Commentary: The research featured in this paper employed an action research design as the management wanted to move their organisation towards the ideal of a learning organisation. The researchers collaboratively evaluated the change programme, which was called the Action Thinking Program. The major theme of the paper was the demonstration of how adopting different ontological and epistemological paradigms leads to very different evaluations of the Action Thinking Program.

Another way of thinking of paradigms is to regard the writings of the management gurus as a paradigm (Collins 1998). This discussion suggests that competing accounts of what constitutes a paradigm exist that configure academic debates about organisational change in different ways.

In this textbook, Burrell and Morgan's (1979) four paradigms are used as means of differentiating organisational change theorists and introducing the philosophical positions that underpin their studies. Wilson (1992), Collins (1998) and Randall (2004) have effectively applied the Burrell and Morgan framework to the study of strategic change, organisational change and managing change respectively. Burrell and Morgan (1979) have received many bouquets and brickbats since their publication over 30 years ago (see Grant and Perren 2002 for an overview).

Figure 4.1 Four paradigms for the analysis of social theory

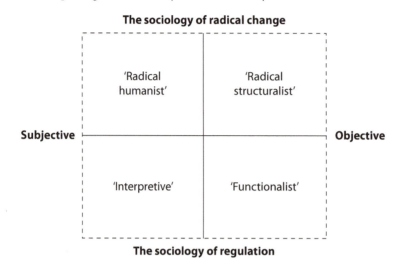

Source: Burrell, G. and Morgan, G. (1979) *Sociological paradigms and organisational analysis.* London: Heinemann, p22. Reproduced with permission from Ashgate Publishing Limited.

In Figure 4.1, Burrell and Morgan's (1979) distinction between the sociology of regulation and radical change is highlighted. The sociology of regulation referred to theorists primarily concerned with explanations of society that emphasise underlying unity and cohesiveness. In contrast, the sociology of radical change explains society in terms of deep-seated structural conflict, modes of domination and structural contradiction characterising modern society. This distinction between regulation and radical change theorists is highly applicable to the dynamic orientation of the study of organisational change.

The other axis in Figure 4.1 differentiates theorists in terms of their research interest in either individuals' subjective experiences or the hard objective realities of scientific research. Thinking in terms of paradigms begins to explain how subjective experiences inform understanding about organisational change, as well as objective research studies. The four paradigms of functionalism, interpretivism, radical humanism and radical structuralism are underpinned by philosophical assumptions, which it is necessary to clarify as this terminology will be used in later chapters.

Figure 4.2 A scheme for analysing assumptions about the nature of social science

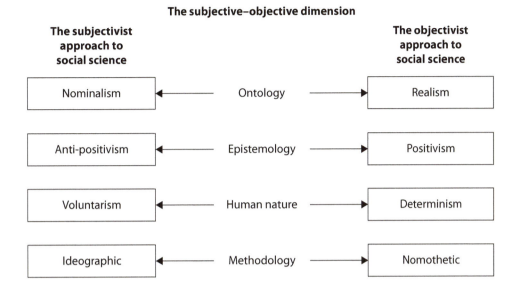

Source: Burrell, G. and Morgan, G. (1979) *Sociological paradigms and organisational analysis.* London: Heinemann, p3. Reproduced with permission from Ashgate Publishing Limited.

Burrell and Morgan (1979) explain competing philosophical assumptions in terms of four polarised debates: ontological, epistemological, human nature, and methodological, as featured in Figure 4.2.

Assumptions of an ontological nature concern the very essence of the phenomena being studied. Nominalists regard the social world external to individual cognition as made up of names, concepts and labels, whereas realists regard the social world external to individual cognition as made up of hard, tangible and immutable structures. Assumptions of an epistemological nature are concerned about the grounds of knowledge, with positivists favouring traditional natural science approaches, whereas anti-positivists are against the search for laws or regularities in the world of social affairs. The 'human nature' debate is concerned with the model of man reflected in social science theories, with determinists regarding activities as being completely determined by the situation or 'environment', whereas voluntarists view people as completely autonomous and free-willed. The ontological, epistemological and human nature debates have implications for how the subject of study is investigated – the methodological debate. Ideographic approaches favour understanding the social world by obtaining first-hand knowledge of the subject under investigation, whereas the nomothetic approach lays emphasis upon systematic protocol and technique. In the following discussion each of the four paradigms is defined and an illustration of organisational change writing informed by each paradigm is offered. The vast majority of the organisational change literature is located in the functionalist quadrant of Figure 4.1.

Functionalism = '... characterised by a concern for providing explanations of the status quo, social order, consensus, social integration, solidarity, need satisfaction and actuality.' (Burrell and Morgan 1979, p26)

Functionalism is concerned with regulation and objectivity, and while the vast majority of organisational change literature is located within this quadrant, this literature seeks to maintain the status quo in society. In Chapter 3, Huczynski (2006) identified eight of the most popular management writers. All of these writers can be located within the functionalist quadrant. While functionalism dominates the study of organisational change, the implication is that the three other paradigms have the potential to offer informative alternative ways of thinking about organisational change. The other paradigm concerned with regulation is interpretivism; however, whereas functionalism is interested in objective accounts of organisational life, interpretivism is interested in subjective accounts of organisational life.

Interpretivism = '... a concern to understand the world as it is, to understand the fundamental nature of the social world at the level of subjective experience.' (Burrell and Morgan 1979, p28)

Page's (1998) *The Diary of a Change Agent* is a good example of writing within this paradigm. Page uses a diary format to share his daily experiences of being a change agent. He does not make any claims to objectivity, but instead offers his subjective experience of being a change agent. Interpretivism can be differentiated from radical humanism in that Page is involved in maintaining the status quo (regulation), rather than seeking any radical change through his writing.

Radical humanism = '... concern to develop a sociology of radical change from a subjectivist standpoint.' (Burrell and Morgan 1979, p32)

A good example of a radical humanist perspective on organisational change is Hochschild's (2003) *The Managed Heart*. In this book, first published in 1983, she explains how women's emotional labour was commercialised in roles such as flight attendants. Her goal was not simply to report what was happening and maintain the status quo (regulation), but instead to critically question such practices (radical change) with her work informed by the experiences of her research subjects.

Radical structuralism = '... advocate a sociology of radical change from an objectivist standpoint.' (Burrell and Morgan 1979, p33)

Braverman (1974) is a good example of radical structuralist writing in his concern to highlight the exploitative nature of capitalist production. In *Labor and Monopoly Capital* he gave considerable impetus to organisational change debates specifically relating to tendencies to deskill labour and increase management control. It is ironic that his most vociferous critics were fellow radical structuralists.

The process of thinking about theorists in terms of functionalism, interpretivism, radical humanism and radical structuralism begins to clarify the very different world views and philosophical positions that inform understanding about organisational change. Locating theorists within different quadrants is not so much the issue as acknowledging that theorists adopt very different standpoints in their explanations of organisational change. This should help to reconcile the contradictions that will be encountered when reviewing the diverse organisational change literature.

A shortcoming with using Burrell and Morgan's (1979) framework is that it has never been updated to reflect more recent developments in theorising. As Grey (2000) warns in his review of Collins (1998), application of Burrell and Morgan (1979), Foucault, postmodernism and feminism are neglected from this form of analysis. While acknowledging paradigms makes explicit philosophical assumptions informing the development of theories, thinking in terms of perspectives offers a narrower focus upon differences between organisational change theories.

PERSPECTIVES ON ORGANISATIONAL CHANGE

A beautifully concise definition of a perspective is '... the foundation for theoretical inspiration' (Graetz et al 2006, p8). In practical terms a perspective can be viewed as a viewpoint, with perspectives informing organisational change being many and varied. Graetz et al (2006), for example, identified ten different perspectives that they believed were pertinent to organisational change. They do not claim that their list is a definitive list; instead perspectives highlight different values informing the study of organisational change. Dunphy (1996, p542) captured this view as follows: 'in the field of organisational change, theories are necessarily infused with ideology. Our theories are value driven, often self-serving, grounded in social movements and driven by social forces'.

Frequently, organisational change writers do not explicitly refer to a particular perspective; instead the perspective will be implicit within their writing. For example, the functionalist organisational change literature featured in the previous chapter was largely written from a managerialist perspective. Managerialism can be defined as 'a belief that modern societies, and the institutions within them, should be run by qualified managers who can organise society rationally on the basis of their expert knowledge – thus replacing the divisiveness and inefficiency of debate and democracy' (Watson 2006, p455). Writing from the perspective of a manager can prove informative for a manager, but will tend to exclude the experiences of the managed and wider social interests. Debates about power, politics, ethics and gender are far less likely to be covered in a managerialist textbook. In this way, perspectives can be understood as intentional biases within organisational change writing, seeking to include and exclude certain debates from discussion.

As it is not practical to list all perspectives informing organisational change, a pragmatic choice has been made to illustrate the concept of a perspective with specific reference to how different perspectives potentially inform understanding about a specific topic – the adoption of organisational change ideas and practices. Sturdy (2004) identified six different perspectives that help to explain the adoption of management ideas and practices: rational, psychodynamic, dramaturgical, political, cultural, and institutional. While Sturdy's focus was far broader than organisational change, his classification illustrates how different perspectives offer different explanations for the adoption of organisational change ideas and practices. In the following discussion, each of the six perspectives identified by Sturdy (2004) is defined and illustrated with an organisational change example.

A rational perspective suggests that new ideas and practices are adopted because they work or promise to work, with the goal being the adoption of tried and tested techniques. This perspective is highly applicable to organisational change. Rigby (2001) reported the Bain and Company (global business consultants) survey of management tools and techniques with the implication that a management tool that worked in company X would work equally well in company Y. In the Organisational Change Field Guide (see Appendix) all of the featured change initiatives reflect this rational perspective towards change.

A psychodynamic perspective on the adoption of new ideas and practices highlights underlying anxieties and yearnings with a corresponding need for the comfort of order and identity and/or control. An example of this perspective would be the popular management ideas families discussed by Huczynski (2006) in the previous chapter. Managers gravitated towards a relatively small number of management ideas when faced with the considerable breadth of management writing. In terms of organisational change writing, Vince's (2002b) account of psychodynamics at Hyder Plc illustrates this perspective.

A dramaturgical perspective (rhetoric) is concerned with the persuasiveness, rather than the content, of new ideas and practices. Gurus, consultants, academics, trainers and authors utilise charisma and presentation techniques in seeking to persuade their audiences. Peters and Waterman's (1982) *In Search of Excellence* recipe for managing cultural change is an effective illustration of a dramaturgical view. Their identification of the eight attributes of successful companies offered a recipe that other managers could follow and was presented in an easily digestible manner.

A political perspective highlights the use of ideas to secure power and their discursive power effects. Pettigrew (1985) highlighted the centrality of power and politics in processes of organisational change and, more recently, Buchanan and Badham (2008) highlighted interrelationships between power, politics and organisational change.

A cultural perspective draws attention to the nature of how knowledge is locally embedded, with culture acting as either a bridge or a barrier to knowledge transfer. In advocating his eight steps for leading change, Kotter (1995) drew upon locally embedded knowledge in America. The question becomes: How transferable is Kotter's recipe for leading change to countries other than America?

Finally, an institutional perspective highlights various social influences on organisational practices, with the work of DiMaggio and Powell (1991) explaining the tendency for institutions to mimic each other (discussed further in Chapter 5).

Sturdy (2004) identified three problems arising out of organising the field in terms of broad theoretical perspectives. Firstly, the boundaries of a field can be highly permeable. Secondly, the allocation of labels tends to be fairly arbitrary. Thirdly, theorists rarely in practice adopt a single or coherent perspective. However, thinking in terms of perspectives informs understanding about organisational change in general and the particular viewpoints of different authors in particular. As the above discussion demonstrates, the answer to the question, 'why do managers adopt particular organisational change ideas and practices?' is very much dependent upon the perspective of the person answering the question. Many perspectives on managing change will be introduced in this textbook, although often without the explicit label of perspective being used. The one perspective unifying diverse debates in this textbook is the critical perspective, which is the focus of the next section.

CRITICAL PERSPECTIVE

Gabriel (2001, p23) warned that 'our theories have mostly given up on the Marxist idea of changing the world and even on the more modest one of understanding and critiquing it'. While questioning and critique are integral to academic study, they potentially also inform management: '… senior management may still not understand the responsibility they hold as role models and builders of structures which encourage challenge and questioning' (Johnson 1992, p35). In the following discussion, competing definitions of a critical perspective help to inform what constitutes a critical perspective in this textbook. The second half of the discussion presents rationales for adopting a critical perspective with specific reference to studying organisational change.

WHAT CONSTITUTES A CRITICAL PERSPECTIVE?

Critical theory is an influential strand of the broader palette of critical approaches. Fay (1987, p33) captures the essence of critical theory: 'a Critical Theory wants to explain a social order in such a way that it becomes itself the catalyst which leads to the transformation of this social order'. Burrell and Morgan's (1979) earlier differentiation between the sociology of regulation and the sociology of radical change is informative here, with critical theory seeking radical change, rather than maintaining the status quo. However, critical theory is far more than simply being critical. Writers such as Alvesson and Willmott (1996) have emphasised that critical theory is guided by an emancipatory intent, which draws particularly upon the writings of Habermas (1971). This textbook makes no claims to be a critical theory textbook; such a conception is an oxymoron when linked to the practicalities of managing change (see Dawson 1994 and Collins 1998 for further discussion of textbook orthodoxy with regard to organisational change).

Critical management studies (CMS) reflects another influential strand of critical theorising, particularly pertinent to the study of management. Fournier and Grey (2000, p16) offer the following definition of CMS: '… at the most basic level, to say that there is something wrong with management as a practice and as a body of knowledge, and that it should be changed'. They do not favour such a definition because this would include most of management studies. However, their quotation highlights that most academic writing about management incorporates varying degrees of critical thinking.

Fournier and Grey (2000) do advance a much more specific definition of what CMS means to them: 'CMS is unified by an anti-performative stance, and a commitment to (some form of) denaturalization and reflexivity.' Performative knowledge refers to knowledge contributing to the production of maximum output for minimum input, with performativity believed to subordinate knowledge/truth to the production of efficiency. Spicer et al (2009) have questioned the anti-performative stance within the above definition of CMS, instead favouring what they refer to as critical performativity.

Denaturalization is concerned with deconstructing the mask of science and naturalness that pervades twentieth-century management theory (Fournier and Grey 2000). A good illustration of this is the discussion of historiography in the 'Critical Perspective' section of the previous chapter. The goal becomes '… writing in what has been written out which would seem to link many otherwise diverse critical writings on management' (Fournier and Grey 2000, p18). The final ingredient in a unified account of CMS is reflexivity, with specific reference to the epistemology and ontology of management studies. While this textbook makes reference to CMS authors, no claims are made to this textbook being a CMS textbook.

Critical theory and CMS are important strands of academic thinking, yet the potential trap would be to invoke these terms without fully committing to their emancipatory and anti-performative agendas. This is a personal choice yet an important choice relating back to earlier discussions in this chapter. Watson (2006), who has offered a rigorous critique of many aspects of organising and managing, chose to differentiate himself from CMS with particular reference to notions of transformation at both personal and social levels.

> It is felt that the choices that these transformations would entail are a matter for political and moral debate in society generally and for contestation within organisations themselves. They are not transformations which social science can or should push people towards. (Watson 2006, p13)

This is a highly contentious point, yet it is the favoured position within this textbook. The textbook radically challenges myths and assumptions that are believed to impede understanding about managing change through highlighting the lived experiences of many diverse stakeholders in processes of organisational change. In this sense the textbook encourages debates that are rarely given an airing in more mainstream textbooks.

Another way of thinking about what constitutes a critical perspective with specific reference to writing textbooks is to look for exemplars already published. One way of denaturalising management theory is to rethink the style, structure and content of popular textbooks introducing management theories.

> In leading textbooks, OB tends to be presented as largely cut-and-dried and settled, thus lacking any controversy, conflict or contest, yet such appearances are deceptive. There are fundamental differences of view – cultural, political and ethical – about how organisations are organised, how they should be organised and how they can be studied. (Knights and Willmott 2007, p13)

The work of Clegg et al (2008), Knights and Willmott (2007) and Thompson and McHugh (2009) have proved an inspiration in writing this textbook, but what constitutes a critical perspective with particular reference to their textbooks? Clegg et al (2008) is intriguing in that it effectively conveys many critical debates without ever labouring the point that it is a critical text. Instead, the creativity and innovation of the text is emphasised, which subtly encourages the reflexivity commended earlier.

Knights and Willmott's (2007, pxii) edited reader draws together authors sharing their own critical perspective on management and organisational behaviour, '... exploring what the mainstream literature says, and what it fails to say, about issues of identity, (in)security, freedom, power, inequality and knowledge – the six central concepts around which the more critical content of this book is organised'. In this way their textbook benefits from encouraging readers to engage with ongoing debates, rather than seeking out the certainties of an artificial consensus.

Thompson and McHugh (2009) clarify what a critical approach means to them in introducing their critical textbook on work organisations. They advocate reflexivity in the examination of how accounts are generated, encouraging critical reflection upon and the challenging of existing attitudes and practices. They argue that critical approaches need to be historical and contextual, locating organisational processes within their structural settings. The complexities and levels of human behaviour require multilayered and multidimensional explanations. They regard many critical theorists as utilising a dialectical perspective to explain the dynamics of organisational change. They define dialectical as denoting '... a reciprocal interaction, between structure and human agency or between conflicting groups' (Thompson and McHugh 2009, p15). Finally, they believe that critical approaches can and should still embrace the 'practical' and applied.

WHY ADOPT A CRITICAL PERSPECTIVE TOWARDS MANAGING CHANGE?

The study of managing change from a critical perspective is potentially informative and timely: '... there is much to question and challenge within the field of organisational change' (Frahm 2007, p952). In the following section, rationales for adopting a critical perspective towards the study of managing change are discussed, as they both further explanations about what a critical perspective entails and explain its emphasis within this textbook. Box 4.1 summarises reasons for adopting a critical perspective.

Box 4.1 Reasons for adopting a critical perspective towards managing change

1 This epistemological stance challenges myths and assumptions prevalent in the prescriptive managing change literature.
2 This ontological stance seeks to understand managing change in terms of the diversity of experiences that inevitably inform processes of changing.
3 The critical common sense of those managing change requires acknowledgement.
4 The study of managing change still needs to be informed by rigorous research.

The following discussion is organised around the four reasons outlined in Box 4.1.

In terms of epistemology, the state of knowledge about managing change is disappointing (Ezzamel et al 1995; Dawson 2003; Caldwell 2006) given its perceived centrality to organisational life. Adopting a critical perspective towards the study of managing change encourages questioning both about what is known about managing change and what is not known. This epistemological stance allows myths and assumptions prevalent in the prescriptive managing change literature to be surfaced and challenged. It is only through understanding beliefs and assumptions beneath popular change prescriptions that they can be critiqued.

> The critical starting point is to recognize that 'managing change' is not an unambiguous term because no one common ontological assumption underlies either the notion of 'managing' or that of 'change'. (Palmer and Dunford 2008, S27)

Functionalist and managerialist preoccupations about how best to manage change result in questions about the lived experience of the diversity of stakeholders in processes of organisational change being neglected. Weary debates about overcoming resistance to change adopt an ontological stance, which neither serves the interests of managers nor the managed. Chapter 12 argues that rather than overcoming resistance to change there is a need to engage with diverse and human 'responses' towards organisational change. A critical perspective explicitly seeks to understand managing change in terms of the diversity of experiences that inevitably inform processes of changing. The critical perspective adopted in this textbook acknowledges the scepticism managers themselves have with regard to implementing many of the fads and fashions of managing change. Ezzamel et al (1995, p8) identified in their survey of changing management practices that:

> ... managers are rightly sceptical of the evangelical exhortations to change radically, and often show a much greater understanding of the complex implications than do the experts and consultants.

Watson (2006, p11) has referred to this capacity as critical common sense 'analysis based on the basic logic, rationality, hard-headedness to be found in human beings whenever they step back from the immediate situation and critically put their minds to an issue or problem'. This concept relates to both Collins (2000) advocating a critical–practical perspective with regard to management fads and buzzwords and Dawson's (2003) belief in critical reflective awareness when understanding processes of organisational change.

In the discussion of historiography in the previous chapter, research underpinning famous management studies was critiqued; however, this does not negate the need for social science to be informed by rigorous research. Adopting a critical perspective to studying managing change encourages research that tests popular taken-for-granted assumptions about managing change.

CONCLUDING COMMENTARY

The paradigms, perspectives and theories that this chapter has featured inform both the theory and practice of managing organisational change. However, frequently neither academics nor practitioners make explicit the assumptions and viewpoints underpinning their work. In undertaking an academic study of organisational change, the real danger in not acknowledging paradigms, perspectives and theories is that the literature can appear very confused and very contradictory. Through understanding differing viewpoints and assumptions it is possible to appreciate the different writings about organisational change that are informed by competing paradigms and perspectives. In the spirit of being explicit about one's perspective, this textbook is subtitled 'a critical perspective'. This choice is informed by the belief that there is a real need to critique existing accounts of organisational change.

CASE STUDY: APPLYING THEORY TO PRACTICE

Identifying perspectives and paradigms in four journal papers

The following case study features summaries of four very different journal papers. It is not essential to understand the research methods used, but please look for assumptions and viewpoints evident within these summaries. Read the four summaries and then answer the questions at the end of the case study.

PAPER ONE: Steiner, C. (2001) A role for individuality and mystery in 'managing' change. *Journal of Organizational Change Management*. Vol 14, No 2. pp150–167.

Summary: This paper focuses upon why people have trouble understanding, coping with and managing change. The paper offers an account of human nature,

suggesting people are 'naturally' capable of coping with change, but that they have forgotten, because of their intellectual history. The paper suggests that scientific paradigms and rationalism have turned people into conformists, afraid to trust their own individual experiences and reliant on others to validate them. Change makes conformity difficult because people do not know who to rely on for validation. The paper suggests current management remedies for responding to the conformity problem, while acknowledging that some remedies may exacerbate the problem. The paper offers philosophical analysis as a tool to interpret/evaluate remedies from a new perspective.

PAPER TWO: McCabe, D. (1999) Total quality management: anti-union Trojan horse or management albatross? *Work, Employment and Society*. Vol 13, No 4. pp665–691.

Summary: This paper reviews a co-operative union–management approach towards total quality management (TQM) through a case study based in the auto components manufacturing sector. The first purpose of the paper is to suggest, in contrast to much critical thinking, under certain conditions TQM may not undermine trade unions. A more moderate trade union stance towards TQM may prove a more effective form of resistance than a militant stance. The second purpose of the paper is to provide insights into how TQM reinforces existing power relations, hierarchies, bureaucracy and inequality. TQM does not simply enhance management control in a uniform manner; it also presents management with dilemmas and contradictions. TQM is part of the continuing and complex effort by management to balance control and consent within employment.

PAPER THREE: DiGeorgio, R.M. (2002) Making mergers and acquisitions work: what we know and don't know – Part I. *Journal of Change Management*. Vol 3, No 2. pp134–148.

Summary: This paper, published in two parts, summarises what is known and not known about making mergers and acquisitions (M&A) work. The paper identified best practice and reviewed relevant literature. Areas requiring further research are identified. In conclusion a much more systematic approach is required with regard to thinking about M&A if the success rate is going to improve. This paper suggests critical elements of a systems approach that would aid M&A work. Change agents and managers are offered guidance on the key levers for them to focus upon when undertaking M&A work.

PAPER FOUR: Rafferty, A.E. and Griffin, M.A. (2006) Perceptions of organizational change: a stress and coping perspective. *Journal of Applied Psychology*. Vol 91, No 5. pp1154–1162.

Summary: Organisational change studies rarely identify aspects of change relevant to individuals and influencing well-being. In this paper, the authors identify three change characteristics: frequency, impact and planning of change. A cognitive phenomenological model of stress and coping was used. This model proposed ways that change characteristics influence individuals' appraisal of uncertainties in the change process. The three change perceptions featured were moderately to strongly intercorrelated with change perceptions, displaying differential relationships with outcomes. In the discussion section the focus is upon systematically considering individuals' subjective experience of change.

Case study questions

1 In terms of the perspectives (rational, psychodynamic, dramaturgical, political, cultural and institutional) identified by Sturdy (2004), please identify the perspective most applicable to each of the journal paper summaries, explaining your reasoning.

2 Please match each of the four journal papers to at least one of Burrell and Morgan's (1979) four paradigms (functionalist, interpretive, radical humanist and radical structuralist), explaining your reasoning.

DISCUSSION
QUESTIONS

1 Why does the functionalist paradigm dominate the study of organisational change?

2 What is the downside of adopting a critical perspective towards studying organisational change?

3 What is the downside of not acknowledging any perspective in studying organisational change?

4 Why have critical perspectives not featured more prominently in previous accounts of organisational change?

KEY READINGS

BURRELL, G. and MORGAN, G. (1979) *Sociological paradigms and organisational analysis.* London: Heinemann.

In 1979 this textbook was a challenge to the functionalist orthodoxy of organisational analysis. The book encouraged alternative thinking and writing and importantly legitimised the role of other academic disciplines in the study of organisations. The book has inevitably received many bouquets and brickbats, and it is a great pity that a second edition has never appeared, which would allow the authors to reflect upon recent academic developments. However, the book remains an informative guide to a great range of intellectual territory.

COLLINS, D. (1998) *Organizational change: sociological perspectives.* London: Routledge.

One of the central themes of this chapter has been how the study of managing change is informed by different perspectives. Collins offers an unashamedly sociological perspective on organisational change. The sociological perspective that he adopts determines what is included and excluded from the book and how he chooses to configure debates featured in the book. The book is also recommended for anyone interested in further application of the Burrell and Morgan framework specifically to organisational change.

THOMPSON, P. and MCHUGH, D. (2009) *Work organisations: a critical approach.* 4th ed. Basingstoke: Palgrave Macmillan.

Critical approaches sometimes feel/ appear abstracted from everyday experiences within work organisations as social theorists attempt to out-theorise each other. This textbook illustrates what is possible when two knowledgeable academics apply a substantial body of knowledge to critically understanding work organisations. They demonstrate that by asking a different set of questions, the concept of a management and organisational behaviour textbook can be transformed. This textbook is an inspiration.

PART 2

External and internal change contexts

CHAPTER 5

Why organisations change

INTRODUCTION

This chapter – in engaging with competing explanations of why organisations change – builds upon the change classifications and the paradigms and perspectives introduced in previous chapters. McLoughlin (1999, p69) posed a useful initial focusing question: 'is change within organisations an essentially adaptive activity determined by broader economic and technological imperatives or a consequence of organisation-specific processes of choice and politics?' How you answer this question determines the explanation you favour of why organisations change. There is no consensus upon why organisations change; the skill is acknowledging competing explanations. The identification of underlying, often hidden, logics of change or motors of change has a long history in ancient and modern philosophy (Morgan and Sturdy 2000). The differentiation between determinists and voluntarists was made in the previous chapter and this differentiation helps to clarify explanations of why organisations change.

A key element of determinism is the emphasis upon cause–effect relationships (Darwin et al 2002). For example, organisational change can be regarded as being determined by the economic environment. In simple models of organisational change it is usually assumed that action is taken in response to the environment, without the environment being affected by organisational action (March 1981). Alternatively, voluntarism emphasises managerial choices and actions influencing organisational change. For example, a senior management team could choose to close down a division of a business because it has been making a loss for the past decade. The danger with favouring a determinist, rather than a voluntarist, explanation is captured by Salaman (2007, p142): '... current analyses of change which seek to explain executive decision making on the nature and design of change tend to underplay and neglect the role of managers as active, interpretive agents and instead to define them, if implicitly, as simple relays of larger societal forces'.

The two polarised positions of determinism and voluntarism explain competing popular explanations of why organisations change. However, the reality inside organisations is likely to be far less polarised and far more of a hybrid of these two positions. In the 'Managerial Approaches' section, traditional determinist notions of change being triggered or driven by external forces are discussed and contextualist explanations of organisational change are introduced, in particular the contributions of Pettigrew and Dawson. The 'Critical Perspective' introduces Van de Ven and Poole's (1995) typology of different change theories: life-cycle, teleology, dialectical and evolutionary. New institutional theory offers an alternative explanation of organisations changing through mimicking other organisations, which is related to understanding organisational change as management fads and fashions.

MANAGERIAL APPROACHES

TRIGGERS AND DRIVERS OF ORGANISATIONAL CHANGE

The following discussion of why organisations change draws upon popular triggers and drivers terminology (related terminology includes motors and engines). This type of explanation can broadly be regarded as determinist, depicting organisational change as caused by external factors within the wider environment. The writings of Tichy (1983) are a good illustration of this line of reasoning. He believed that managers adopted a one-size-fits-all approach to managing change and argued that 'once the change process has been triggered it may be managed in various ways' (1983, p17). Tichy (1983, p147) believed that large-scale strategic change was 'triggered by a large-scale uncertainty – in the form of either a threat or an opportunity'. He discussed four types of trigger that necessitated strategic change. Firstly, the environment, such as increasing competitive pressures, can trigger strategic change. Secondly, diversification into new business lines can necessitate strategic change. Thirdly, rapid technological shifts can require strategic change, and fourthly, people, such as new types of people entering an organisation, can trigger strategic change. Tichy (1983, p152) subsequently discussed how triggering information can be interpreted in organisations, as summarised in Box 5.1.

Box 5.1 Interpreting triggering information (based upon Tichy 1983)

1 historical comparisons, for example between current and past performance
2 planning comparisons, for example current performance against future projections
3 extra-organisational comparisons, for example comparisons with firms in the same industry
4 other people's expectations, for example starting change projects envisioning positive careers outcomes

Although Tichy's emphasis upon triggers suggests a determinist approach to organisational change, this is a soft determinism, in that in Box 5.1 and throughout his book he acknowledges that strategic change can also be influenced by internal and more human factors.

The following possible triggers with specific reference to managing change have been identified: government legislation; process or product technology advances; changes in consumer requirements, expectations or taste; competitor/supply-chain activities; general economic and social pressures; unpredictable environmental catastrophes; acquisitions and mergers (Paton and McCalman 2008). Dawson (2003) identified potential triggers of change, although he warned that their relative importance was open to debate. There is no consensus listing of change triggers/drivers explaining all changes in all contexts, and there never will be. However, there is merit in differentiating drivers at different levels. Price (2009) discusses drivers for change with specific reference to change management at three levels of the environment: the far (macro) level, the near (meso) level and the internal (micro) level. A PESTLE analysis used to discuss the drivers for change present within the far environment is summarised in Box 5.2.

Box 5.2 PESTLE analysis identifying drivers for change (based upon Price 2009)

P – Political drivers include governmental ideologies, practices and systems.
E – Economic drivers include taxation, interest rates and exchange rates.
S – Socio-cultural drivers include the standards set by society at large.
T – Technological drivers include new uses of technology and new means of production.
L – Legal drivers include organisational regulatory systems.
E – Environmental drivers include ethical and environmentally friendly ways of working.

The differentiation between the far environment and the near environment is informative, with managers believed to have little control over the far environment but a more reciprocal relationship with their near environment. In terms of the near environment, Price (2009) identifies the following examples of stakeholders: suppliers, customers, competitors, collaborators, partners and potential stakeholders. These stakeholders are viewed as potential drivers of change dependent upon the nature of their relationship with the organisation.

The danger with this discussion of triggers and drivers is that it overemphasises notions of continuous change in a single linear direction, as characterised by popular 'change is the only constant' rhetoric. Leana and Barry (2000) identified forces that drive organisations' pursuit of flexibility and continuous change: adaptability, cost containment, impatient capital markets, control and competitive advantage. What is different about their account of forces that drive change is their acknowledgement of tensions between stability and change as an inevitable part of organisational life. This type of reasoning can be traced back to Lewin (1947), who regarded status quo as being the balance between forces for change and forces for stability, so that change consequently arose out of an increase in the forces for change and a reduction in the forces for stability (see Palmer et al 2009 for further reasons why organisations may not change in the face of external environmental pressures).

CONTEXTUALIST APPROACHES TO ORGANISATIONAL CHANGE

The explanations of why organisations change closely relate to the contexts in which an organisation operates. Dawson (2003) identified the context of change, the politics of change and the substance of change as determinants shaping the change process. The substance of change was discussed in Chapter 2 and the politics of change will be discussed in Chapter 15. In Journal Research Case 5.1 an illustration of a contextualised approach to understanding organisational change is featured.

👁 JOURNAL RESEARCH CASE 5.1

GlaxoWellcome

Paper title: Devising context-sensitive approaches to change: the example of Glaxo-Wellcome.
Sector: Pharmaceuticals
Research methods: Longitudinal research utilising qualitative and quantitative data.
Authors: Hope Hailey, V. and Balogun, J.
Year: 2002
Journal details: *Long Range Planning.* Vol 35, Issue 2. pp153–78.

Commentary: The authors presented an extended case study of organisational change in the large pharmaceuticals company Glaxo-Wellcome. One of the strengths of this case study was that changes in the organisation were analysed with particular reference to the context of the organisation. The authors use their change kaleidoscope in order to facilitate a contextual understanding of the case for readers.

In focusing upon the context of organisational change, the following discussion draws upon the contributions of Pettigrew and Dawson. The writings of Pettigrew offer a good example of this type of approach to organisational change. Morgan and Sturdy (2000) explain how political approaches, rather than completely rejecting managerialist approaches, offer more sophisticated cultural engineering. While factors trigger change, the emphasis upon these factors changes through the actions and interpretations of different interest groups.

Major contributions of Pettigrew to understanding strategic change include highlighting the significance of power in shaping strategy (Pettigrew 1973, 1977), highlighting the language of culture (Pettigrew 1979), a large-scale study of change processes in ICI (Pettigrew 1985) and combining the content, process and context of strategic change with longitudinal data (Pettigrew and Fenton 2000). Pettigrew encouraged the study of both the processes of change and the contexts of change. Instead of regarding change as a single event, change is understood as a process happening over time, with major strategic change typically taking place over many years. In studying change longitudinally and processually, there is also a need to study the context in which changes take place. When Pettigrew was developing these ideas, processual/contextualised accounts of change were not the norm: few studies of change allowed the change process to be revealed in a temporal or contextual manner (processual approaches to organisational change are discussed in the next chapter).

Pettigrew (1990, p269) defined a contextualist analysis as drawing 'on phenomena at vertical and horizontal levels of analysis and the interconnections between those levels through time'. He (1990) emphasised four key points when analysing change in a contextualist mode. Firstly, embeddedness, specifically in terms of the interconnected levels of analysis, was important. Secondly, temporal interconnections in terms of the past, the present and the future were important. Thirdly, exploring context and action and how context is a product of actions was important, and fourthly, he acknowledged that the causation of change was neither linear nor singular and that a grand theory of change was unlikely to be fruitful. These key points are pertinent to earlier discussions about drivers/triggers of change.

A contextualist analysis of organisational change is unlikely to explain change in terms of a single dominant 'trigger' or 'driver'. Instead, why an organisation changes is likely to be explained in terms of different levels of analysis (embeddedness), the past, present and future (temporal), how actions shape the context, and avoiding linear or singular explanations of change. In terms of why organisations change, Pettigrew et al (1992) suggest that the why of change is derived from analysing the inner and outer context of an organisation.

Similarly, Dawson (2003, p47) suggested that we need to think about both internal contexts and external contexts temporally: 'the contextual dimension refers to both the past and the present external and internal operating environments, as well as to the influence of future projections and expectations on current operating practice'. What does Dawson mean by the external and internal context of change? What one writer refers to as a trigger or driver of change, another writer refers to as the context of change. The difference tends to be one of emphasis, with a determinist placing more emphasis upon factors triggering or driving change, whereas a voluntarist emphasises the context in which senior managers make change decisions. Examples of external contextual factors include: 'changes in competitors' strategies, level of international competition, government legislation, changing social expectations, technological innovations and changes in the level of business activity' (Dawson 2003, p47). Internal contextual factors relate to what Price (2009) referred to earlier as the internal (micro) environment, which is predominantly controlled by the management of the organisation. In terms of the internal context, Dawson (2003, p47) cites Leavitt's (1964) internal contextual factors: 'human resources, administrative structures, technology and product or service, as well as an additional category labeled the history and culture of an organisation'. The above reasoning signposts the need to address at least six elements when contextualising a specific organisational change, which are summarised in Box 5.3.

Box 5.3 Understanding internal and external organisational environments (based upon Dawson 2003)

1 past internal (inner) organisational environment
2 past external (outer) organisational environment
3 present internal (inner) organisational environment
4 present external (outer) organisational environment
5 future internal (inner) organisational environment
6 future external (outer) organisational environment

The contextualist approach highlighted in Box 5.3 encourages a much more subtle answer to the question 'why do organisations change?' Instead of regarding change as triggered or driven exclusively by the external environment, a range of internal and external factors shaping change are acknowledged. The rhetoric of organisational change emphasises notions of rapidly changing environments; Pettigrew (2003) explained this partially in terms of Americans' infectious enthusiasm about the future and the belief that it will be better than the past, although Sorge and van Witteloostuijn (2004) offer a critique of such rhetoric. Box 5.3 highlights the role of both the internal and external environment in the past shaping organisational change. For example, in discussing the change classifications framework, the influence of the recent organisational history of change was emphasised and, more broadly, in Chapter 3 the role of history was acknowledged. The present environmental conditions are relevant, but Box 5.3 highlights how the internal environment as well as the external environment shapes organisational change.

March (1981, p572) warned that '… our plans are based on a future that we know, with certainty, will not be realised'. In Box 5.3 the acknowledgment of future environments is based upon the view that organisational change involves movement from a known state to an unknown state (Dawson 2003). While strategic analysis tools (such as PESTLE analysis, Porter's model, scenario-writing and SWOT analysis) aid the analysis of the environment, such analysis can never predict the future with complete certainty. However, consideration of the future internal and external environment of an organisation will be another factor shaping change. Dawson (2003, p179), who himself advocated including the future as an element of contextualising change, is quite philosophical about the outcome of such an endeavour: 'the essential unforeseeable character of change means that the process cannot be predicted and that outcomes are often only understood in retrospect. But this does not negate the need for some form of consideration of the future context – however speculative.'

A major implication of this discussion is that the internal and external context for each organisation will be unique, resulting in very different answers to the question 'why do organisations change?' Organisational change researchers and scholars will tend to specialise in different contexts, such as multinationals or charities or small and medium-sized enterprises or trade unions. A good example of this has been differentiating organisational change in the different contexts of public, third and private sector organisations. Iles and Sutherland (2001) reviewed managing change literature with specific reference to NHS organisational changes. They cited Golembiewski et al (1982) and Robertson and Seneviratne (1995), suggesting that knowledge, theories and models developed in the private sector can be transferred to the public sector. However, more recently the appropriateness of private sector organisational change models explaining public sector organisational change has been challenged (Joyce 1998; McAdam and Mitchell 1998; Sminia and Van Nistelrooij 2006). The 'it depends' maxim is pertinent here in that treating public sector organisations as a homogenous category is problematic, given their different types of activity, scales of activity and histories. This suggests that for each organisation their internal and external contexts will be unique, even if sectoral commonalities can be identified.

CRITICAL PERSPECTIVE

The 'Managerial Approaches' section reflected the orthodoxy with regard to why organisations change, with contextualist approaches highlighting more subtle organisational processes of changing. The differentiation between determinism and voluntarism helped to introduce debates about why organisations change. However, the notion of organisational change being independently triggered by factors beyond the control of senior management has been questioned (Collins 2000). The environment does not force change upon actors, but rather actors work within a context and act to shape this context. In the 'Critical Perspective' Van de Ven and Poole's (1995) typology offers a more sophisticated explanation of why organisations change. New institutional theory and management fads and fashions are introduced and discussed as further explanations for why organisations change.

LIFE-CYCLES, TELEOLOGY, DIALECTICS AND EVOLUTION

Van de Ven and Poole (1995, p511), through an extensive interdisciplinary literature review of theories explaining processes of change in the social, biological, and physical sciences, identified '... fundamentally different event sequences and generative mechanisms – we will call them motors – to explain how and why changes unfold'. This analysis offered change scholars an influential typology of different explanations of why organisations change. Van de Ven and Poole (1995, p511) do not regard the theories as being hierarchically superior, but instead the '... different perspectives are viewed as providing alternative pictures of the same organisational processes without nullifying each other'. The four basic types of process theories that they identified were: life-cycle, teleological, dialectical and evolutionary. In the following discussion each type is introduced and explained. More recently they have explored epistemological and ontological disagreements with regard to the study of organisational change (Van de Ven and Poole 2005).

Van de Ven and Poole (1995) defined life-cycle theories as regarding change as being imminent, with an underlying form, logic, programme or code regulating the process of change and moving the entity towards a subsequent end that is prefigured in the present state. While such a theory initially appears abstracted from organisational change, it informs understanding of approaches such as Lewin's (1947) three-step process and Rogers' (1962) stages of innovation and is very evident within the organisational change literature. This type of approach grounds explanations of why organisations change in natural processes of changing, drawing upon the metaphor of organic growth. Managers manage this process through steps or stages, with resistance to change presented as irrational and unnatural. The downside of this type of approach is that it suffers from the shortcomings of determinism, discussed earlier.

Teleological explanations for why organisations change are particularly evident in goal-setting, planning, functionalist, social constructionist and symbolic interactionist theories; they reflect the doctrine that a purpose or goal guides the movement of an entity (Van de Ven and Poole 1995). Van de Ven and Poole (1995, p516) differentiate teleology from life-cycle theory in that '... teleology does not prescribe a necessary sequence of events or specify which trajectory development of the organisational entity will follow'. This type of explanation emphasises the purposeful involvement of managers in processes of changing reflected in the large body of prescriptive, 'how to manage change' literature. The downside of this type of explanation is the limitations of prescriptive 'one best way' accounts of managing change.

Van de Ven and Poole (1995) suggest that, according to dialectical theory, change occurs when opposing values, forces or events gain enough power to challenge the status quo. In the business world, Burke (2008, p139) acknowledged that '... acquisitions and hostile takeovers often represent resolutions that are not necessarily creative'. Dialectical explanations tend to be more applicable to critical/radical explanations of why organisations change than managerial explanations. For example, Braverman's (1974) explanation of organisational change in terms of deskilling and increasing management control illustrates a dialectical explanation.

Finally, evolutionary explanations of change emphasise the recurrent and cumulative, progression of variation and selection of organisational entities (Van de Ven and Poole 1995). The theory suggests that those organisations best able to adapt are the most likely to survive (see for example Hannan and Freeman 1977). Van de Ven and Poole (1995) acknowledge that which entities will survive or fail cannot be predicted; overall population persists and evolves according to specific population dynamics. This can again be regarded as a determinist approach to explaining why organisations change.

Figure 5.1 Process theories of organisational development and change

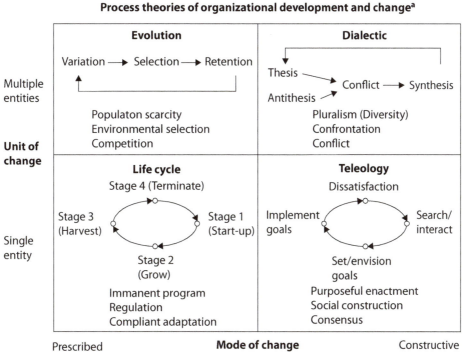

Source: Van de Ven, A.H. and Poole, M.S. (1995) Explaining development and change in organizations. *Academy of Management Review*. Vol 20, No 3. p520. Reproduced with permission from www.copyright.com.

In drawing upon a range of philosophies, literatures and disciplines, Van de Ven and Poole's typology can initially appear obtuse. However, in Figure 5.1 they illustrate the four ideal-type theories and four distinguishing characteristics of theories. Firstly, processes are viewed as different cycles of change events. Secondly, change events are governed by different motors or generating mechanisms (the focus of this chapter). Thirdly, motors operate upon different units of analysis, and fourthly, they represent different modes of change.

NEW INSTITUTIONAL THEORY

The origins of institutional theory can be traced back to the 1950s and 1960s, with the earliest contributions emphasising conflict and negotiated order between different interest groups (Clegg et al 2008). In their analysis of organisational change, Morgan and Sturdy (2000, p8) refer to social approaches that examine 'how management practices and knowledges are constructed and reproduced in particular institutional and social settings'. Institutional theory is a form of social approach pertinent to concerns in this chapter, offering an alternative yet persuasive explanation for why organisations change.

While not writing specifically about institutional theory, March (1981, p572) highlighted the problem as '... one of introducing new ideas into organisations at a rate sufficient to sustain the larger system of organisations, when such action is not intelligent for any one organisation'. In these instances, there tends to be an understandable tendency to look to what managers in other organisations are doing. Organisational decision-makers under conditions of uncertainty are forced into action resembling the lead taken by others in the field (Grint 2005a).

DiMaggio and Powell (1983) were influential players in the development of new institutional theory (see DiMaggio and Powell 1991 for acknowledgement of other influential contributors). The essence of their position on organisational change was that '... rational actors make their organisations increasingly similar as they try to change them' (DiMaggio and Powell 1983, p147). The title of their paper, 'The iron cage revisited', acknowledged Weber's imagery of the iron cage of bureaucracy, as discussed in Chapter 3. However, they argued that the causes of bureaucratisation and rationalisation had changed: 'instead, we will contend, bureaucratization and other forms of organisational change occur as a result of processes that make organisations more similar without necessarily making them more efficient' (DiMaggio and Powell 1983, p147). They referred to these processes of homogenisation as isomorphism. DiMaggio and Powell (1983, p150) identified three mechanisms through which institutional isomorphic change occurred, which are summarised in Box 5.4.

Box 5.4 Institutional isomorphic change mechanisms (based upon DiMaggio and Powell 1983)

1 coercive isomorphism – stems from political influence and the problem of legitimacy
2 mimetic isomorphism – results from standard responses to uncertainty
3 normative isomorphism – associated with professionalisation

An explanation of why organisations change in terms of coercive isomorphism is that organisations are complying with legislation. For example, managers could encourage bids to provide services in a public service organisation in order to comply with particular legislation, or car manufacturers could fit seat belts in all new cars because legislation requires them to do so. Explaining organisational change in terms of mimetic isomorphism suggests that senior management wish to emulate the success of exemplar organisations in their sector. For example, in the UK in recent years Tesco has been regarded as a successful retailer and other retailers may look to the successful loyalty card or online shopping operation of Tesco and decide to mimic these activities. An explanation of why organisations change in terms of normative isomorphism relates to the norms that develop among groups of professionals. In Chapter 17, project management approaches to managing change are introduced. Among certain groups of professionals using project management, specific types of project management methodology to manage change could become the norm. In these instances it can become difficult for a manager to ignore such norms (the persuasiveness of norms is discussed further in Chapter 8). In terms of further reading, the *Academy of Management Journal* (2002, Vol 45, No 1) devoted a special issue to new institutionalism and explanations of change.

MANAGEMENT FADS AND FASHIONS

In Chapter 3, guru theory was introduced and discussed as a potential driver of organisational change. In the context of this chapter, it is worthwhile critically reflecting upon the influence of management fads and fashions upon organisational change. Tichy (1983, p291) cited a beautifully mischievous quotation from Kaplan (1964): 'I have found that if you give a little boy a hammer, he will find that everything needs pounding.' A cynic might argue that a major outcome of the gurus' and consultants' prescriptions to change is that they are in the business of manufacturing the hammers, regardless of the organisational need for hammers (or, coincidentally, Hammer).

More recently, Sorge and Van Witteloostuijn (2004) warned of organisational change becoming the *raison d'être* of the consultancy and management professions, with their involvement self-sustaining once it has set in. Although they do not offer empirical evidence to support this view, the implications are troubling that organisational change is driven not so much by any interplay of internal and external factors, as discussed in this chapter, but in order to serve the financial interests of the global management consultancies.

As Collins (2000, p4) warned, 'management's fads and buzzwords do not fall like rain. They do not occur naturally. They are created and disseminated by groups of people working within an apparatus, which has grown to become an industry in itself.' Salaman and Asch (2003, p22) neatly articulate the dilemma that managers must face when attempting to choose between the practical prescriptions of consultants and the more evidence-based criticisms of management fads and fashions offered by academics:

> Consultants try to sell them packages, beautifully presented, forcefully marketed, clearly stated in persuasive language, which promise radical dramatic organisational transformation… On the other hand, academic commentators – Cassandra-like – warn against too easy acceptance, noting numerous problems with the advice and recommendations on offer, pointing out inconsistencies, contradictions and simplifications.

The temptation to criticise the contribution of gurus and consultants is very strong, and the criticisms have been very strong. For example, Jackson (2001, p16) highlighted some of the labels given to gurus' work: 'intellectual wallpaper', 'business pornography', 'shameless narcissism', 'behavioural fast food' and 'commonsensical in the extreme'.

CONCLUDING COMMENTARY

Despite many practitioner books asserting that there is one best way to manage change, there is not one best way to manage change. In a similar manner there is no single consensus explanation for why organisations change. The paradigms and perspectives introduced in the previous chapter help to explain the existence of contradictory explanations for why organisations change. The determinist view emphasises change being driven or triggered, whereas the voluntarist view places greater emphasis upon managerial choices. Pettigrew and Dawson highlight the importance of context in shaping changes. Many competing explanations for why organisations change still remain, and in the 'Critical Perspective' more theoretical explanations were featured, which have been particularly influential among change scholars. The concepts of life-cycle, teleological, dialectical and evolutionary theories offer a typology that can embrace most explanations of why organisations change. New institutional theory offers an explanation for why organisations mimic the changes of other organisations. An outcome of such processes can be the depiction of organisational change as managers following fads and fashions.

CASE STUDY: APPLYING
THEORY TO PRACTICE

Changing times at Factory Bank

A brief history of Factory Bank: The origins of Factory Bank can be traced back as far as the late eighteenth century. The bank began in Yorkshire serving two functions – financing developments in the new industrial towns and acting as a savings bank mainly for the factory workers. In the nineteenth century the bank grew from being a regional bank into being a large national bank. This process was facilitated through a series of mergers with smaller banks. Despite the mergers and acquisitions, Factory Bank still had a disproportionate number of branches in the north. The bank was regarded as being a steady if uninspiring institution. The following discussion of Factory Bank is structured around three time horizons reflecting the recent past, the present and the future of Factory Bank.

Factory Bank – the 1990s: The 1990s were a challenging decade for Factory Bank: employee numbers were reduced from 100,000 to 60,000. The bank had always had a different culture from other clearing banks due to its unique historical origins and the fact that it was the only

bank to have worker representatives on the board. In the early 1990s when other clearing banks began implementing cost-cutting strategies, Factory Bank had bucked this trend with its provocative 'Caring for Customers not Conning Customers' campaign. This had initially won them customers but had alienated them in relations with the other clearing banks. Despite the appearance of fierce competition among the clearing banks, they still co-operated closely and the campaign proved costly in terms of strategic alliances. However, one of the major catalysts for change was the increasing prominence in the marketplace of the building societies. The major building societies targeted the same demographic groups as Factory Bank, and by the mid-1990s there was talk of crisis. The costs of the building societies were a fraction of Factory Bank's, and throughout the bank there was a realisation that the bank would struggle to survive in its current form.

In summary, the bank abandoned its regional structure that had served it so well in previous decades. The goal of survival was used as the rationale for removing the worker representatives from the board, who were replaced by representatives of the institutions who had become major investors in Factory Bank. Despite this investment, or because of this investment, Factory Bank embarked upon a radical cost-cutting programme involving branch closures and compulsory redundancies. There was industrial action and strikes closed the branches for a week – the first time in the history of Factory Bank. Many employees became bitter and disillusioned and voluntarily left the bank. However, the financial press expressed delight with progress, and when Factory Bank declared record profits, the headlines announced that 'Factory Bank Comes of Age'.

Factory Bank – today: The current chief executive of Factory Bank is the charismatic Tommy Wilson. He used to be a television company executive and was deliberately brought into Factory Bank to introduce greater financial realism into the operation. It was he who personally oversaw the refurbishment of branches and the rebranding of Factory Bank products with his 'New Order' campaign. Competition for financial services was fierce, with the recent entry into the market of retail stores. He had engineered a very lucrative partnership arrangement with Merryweather superstores, whereby Factory Bank provided them with financial services products that were promoted using the Merryweather superstores brand. Also, Factory Bank had purchased a regional building society in the south-east, which helped rectify a discrepancy in its branch network. The industrial action in the 1990s left a legacy of poor industrial relations, although the banking union had benefited from increased membership. Tommy Wilson was reputed to have said at a banker's dinner: 'I do not care about the commitment of the workforce as long as they work hard for their salaries.' This had become an urban myth, but what was real was the staff share ownership scheme that he had aggressively promoted. This had resulted in 20% of shares in Factory Bank being owned by employees – a sizeable proportion for any bank.

Factory Bank – the next decade: Nobody can predict the future with certainty, but the following offers a flavour of the forecasts about the next decade that the bank has been working on. The diversification of delivery channels is expected to continue to gather momentum. Whereas in the 1990s the majority of financial services were delivered via the branch networks, increasingly telephone banking and Internet banking are becoming the norm. The branches are being repositioned as sales outlets rather than service outlets. However, it is privately envisaged that the branch network will have to be considerably reduced. What was once an asset has become a huge liability in terms of costs to the bank.

The competition from the retail sector will continue to grow, but more troublingly is the increasing threat of global competition. The Internet has made it possible for traditionally loyal customers to invest their savings with overseas financial service providers at far better rates of interest. The joint arrangements with Merryweather superstores will have worked very well, leading to a series of joint ventures with other, smaller retailers. There is even speculation that Factory Bank might rename itself Retail Bank to draw a line under its industrial past and signpost the retail future.

Case study questions

1 Drawing upon the recent past, present and future external context of Factory Bank, what potential drivers of change may be identified?

2 How might the recent past, present and future internal context of Factory Bank help or hinder managing change within Factory Bank?

DISCUSSION QUESTIONS

1 Why is there no consensus about why organisations change?

2 What would trigger an organisation to stop changing?

3 What factors encourage organisations to mimic each other?

4 Why has management guru-generated literature proved so popular?

KEY READINGS

COLLINS, D. (2000) *Management fads and buzzwords: critical–practical perspectives.* London: Routledge.

In his fascinating account of management fads and buzzwords, Collins advances what he refers to as a critical–practical perspective, drawing upon critical social science while acknowledging the practicalities of managing change. The introductory chapters offer a provocative overview of management gurus and the fads and fashions that they promote. Subsequent chapters feature critical reviews of what Collins perceives as fads and buzzwords, including: total quality management, empowerment and globalisation.

DIMAGGIO, P. and POWELL, W.W. (eds) (1991) *The new institutionalism in organisational analysis.* Chicago: University of Chicago Press.

This edited reader brought together key writings on institutional approaches, in particular writings from American sociological journals over the previous 15 years.

The book sought to differentiate neo-institutional approaches from earlier classical institutional approaches, highlighting how new/ neo-institutionalism arose out of the writings of a group of writers.

DAWSON, P. (2003) *Understanding organizational change: the contemporary experience of people at work.* London: Sage Publications Ltd.

In explaining the contexts of change, this chapter has encouraged the use of frameworks developed by Dawson. The approach to change that Dawson advocates can be seen as a development over time of his writings. The book is recommended here for anyone who wishes to read further about processual/contextualised approaches to organisational change. In particular, the book benefits from a series of research-based case studies that illustrate different experiences of organisational change within their own unique contexts.

CHAPTER 6

Organisational design and change

LEARNING OUTCOMES

After reading this chapter you should be able to:

- identify major challenges that organisational design seeks to address
- discuss the development of major organisational design theories
- identify different organisational forms
- acknowledge recent developments in terms of changing organisational forms, processes and boundaries
- understand the contribution of the INNFORM survey
- understand dualities with regard to organising.

INTRODUCTION

An organisation may be compared to a human body in terms of its organisational structure (anatomy), its organisational processes (physiology) and its organisational culture (psychology) (Bartlett and Ghoshal 1995; De Wit and Meyer 2004). This analogy with the human body is a helpful starting point in discussing debates relating to organisational structures and processes, with culture the focus of Chapter 13. Many organisational structures have been proposed with claims that they offer the one best way in terms of organisational design (see Eccles and Nohria 1992 for further discussion). However, as the previous chapter highlighted, contextual variables (both internal and external) make such aspirations unrealistic. While organisational design is influenced by environmental factors, it is also likely to be influenced by managerial choices and power relations.

Organisational design has been defined as 'the process by which managers select and manage aspects of structure and culture so that an organisation can control the activities necessary to achieve its goals' (Jones 2010, p31). This definition highlights the interrelationships between structure and culture. Organisational structure has been defined as 'the formal system of task and authority relationships that control how people coordinate their actions and use resources to achieve organisational goals' (Jones 2010, p29).

The 'Managerial Approaches' section introduces major organisational design choices in terms of the challenges they seek to address and influential theories that have shaped thinking about organisational design. However, there has been a reaction against traditional conceptions of organisational design, in favour of a more emergent and processual emphasis upon new forms of organising. This new emphasis acknowledges changing processes and changing boundaries as part of change processes. The 'Critical Perspective' questions the belief in the ascendancy of new forms of organising, instead favouring a duality of change and continuity, valuing both old and new forms of organising.

MANAGERIAL APPROACHES

THE CHALLENGES OF ORGANISATIONAL DESIGN

In the large organisations that impact upon everyone's life everyday, structures, cultures and processes are invariably already established. In this sense it is easy to neglect organisational design decisions shaping the development of an organisation. However, while all organisations are unique, it is possible to identify generic organisational design challenges that managers face. In Box 6.1 the organisational design challenges that Jones (2010) identified are summarised.

Box 6.1 Organisational design challenges (based upon Jones 2010)

Design challenge one – how to address lack of clarity in terms of responsibilities and reporting (who to speak to and co-ordinating people's activities)
Design challenge two – how to address the inability to get people to communicate and co-ordinate (specification of tasks and roles builds barriers between people and functions)
Design challenge three – how to address employees' lack of responsibility or risk-taking (avoiding the tendency to look to the boss for direction)
Design challenge four – how to address a culture of too much attention being paid to rules by employees (consequent unwillingness to break rules)

In Box 6.1, generic challenges that managers encounter in terms of organisational design are outlined. The following discussion is organised around these four design challenges. Jones (2010) regards differentiation as the principal design challenge (design challenge one). Differentiation involves allocating people and resources to tasks. A consequence of differentiation is that it establishes and controls the division of labour in the organisation. Vertical differentiation refers to the hierarchy and creation of reporting relationships, and horizontal differentiation refers to the grouping of tasks into roles and subunits.

In Figure 6.1 a simple organisational hierarchy is depicted with both vertical differentiation (that is, Team A, Supervisor X and Manager) and horizontal differentiation (that is, Supervisor X and Supervisor Y). Many writers appear to have an aversion to hierarchy, although '… hierarchy continues to provide the backbone of almost every company in every part of the world' (Child 2005, p9).

Figure 6.1 A simple organisational hierarchy

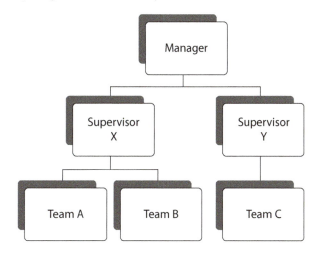

In terms of change, this challenge can be related to debates about the suitability of tall (Figure 6.2) and flat hierarchies (Figure 6.3).

In Figures 6.2 and 6.3, two caricatures of hierarchy are depicted in order to highlight potential organisational design choices. In Figure 6.2 the organisation has nine levels, between the most junior position in the organisation and the most senior position, whereas in Figure 6.3 a flatter hierarchy is depicted.

The second design challenge is concerned with integration, which Child (2005) also regards as another key organisational choice. Jones (2010, p121) defines integration as 'the process of coordinating various tasks, functions, and divisions so that they work together and not at cross purposes'. Potential integrating

Figure 6.2 Tall hierarchy

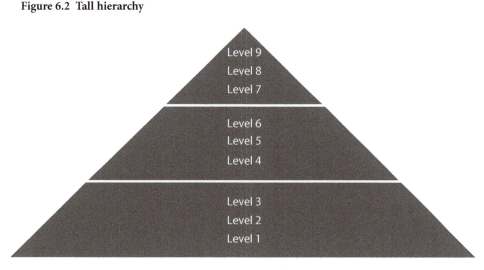

Figure 6.3 Flat hierarchy

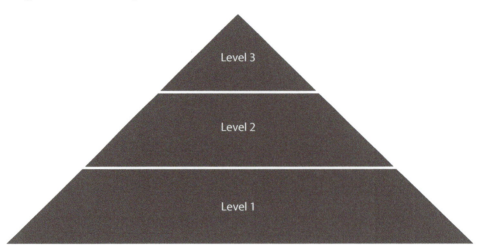

mechanisms include: hierarchy of authority, direct contact, liaison roles and task forces.

The third design challenge relates to centralisation or decentralisation of authority with arguments for and against each option. Jones (2010) favours a balance of centralisation and decentralisation. In terms of change, these choices have implications with regard to how power is dispersed within an organisation. This challenge speaks to debates about the suitability of top–down or bottom–up approaches to managing change.

Figure 6.4 is again a caricature. Brian favours a top–down approach, generating ideas for change himself and then relaying them to the teams via his supervisors. Bill favours a bottom–up approach in which ideas for change are generated by the teams and relayed to Bill via the supervisors. The reality inside organisations is likely to be a hybrid of top–down and bottom–up approaches; these debates will be revisited in subsequent chapters.

Figure 6.4 Top–down and bottom–up approaches to managing

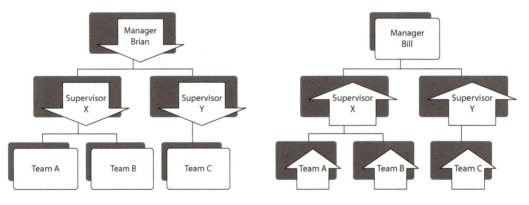

Design challenge four is concerned with norms about appropriate ways of behaving that develop in organisations and processes of socialisation shaping these norms (norms are discussed further in Chapter 8). There are design choices in terms of how mandatory or discretionary rules and schedules should be (Child 2005). This design challenge also acknowledges the importance of the informal organisation. While organisational charts depict formal organisations, the informal organisation can play a significant role in organisational effectiveness. In terms of change, this challenge speaks to the degree of emphasis placed upon formal and informal aspects of organising.

The above organisational design choices have implications for the effectiveness of organisations; these implications include: dealing with contingencies, gaining competitive advantage, managing diversity, increasing efficiency and managing innovation (Jones 2010). The discussions around design choices traditionally lead to classic organisational structural types: functional (see Figure 6.5), multidivisional (see Figure 6.6), matrix (see Figure 6.7).

The functional structural type is depicted in Figure 6.5. In this instance the organisation is designed around the functions, in this case HR, sales, marketing and finance and operations. This simple organisational structure can be very effective for small to medium-sized enterprises because it simplifies communications and controls. One of the downsides of this structure can be co-ordination between functional areas.

The multidivisional structural type is featured in Figure 6.6. In this instance the functions will be duplicated in each division. This classic structure is much more appropriate for larger organisations, particularly those working in different geographical regions. A potential benefit is that each division can focus upon a specific strategy. A downside is that there can be duplication of work.

The matrix structural type is featured in Figure 6.7. In the example, Group A would comprise employees working in the UK on retail sales. Matrix structures are regarded as being far more flexible than traditional structures. The principles

Figure 6.5 Functional structural type

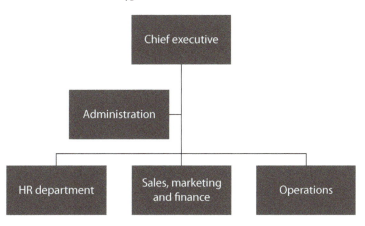

Figure 6.6 Multidivisional structural type

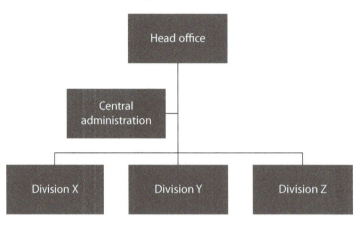

Figure 6.7 Matrix structural type

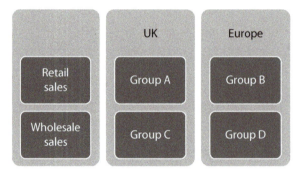

can be applied right across an organisation or within part of an organisation. Potential dangers with matrix structures can arise through multiple reporting lines.

Many other structural types have been proposed; however, they should be regarded as templates because they are unlikely ever to correspond exactly with what happens in organisations and inevitably are intermediate structures. Eccles and Nohria (1992) have warned that analysing the structure of even a modest-sized organisation is likely to be messy and complicated because they are always in flux and organisation charts reflect only one person's perception of the organisational design at one moment in time.

THEORISING ORGANISATIONAL DESIGN

In the following discussion key milestones in theorising organisational design are discussed. The writings of both Taylor (1911) and Fayol (1949) (first published in French in 1916) attempted to explain and classify management, which began an ongoing process of searching for the most effective organisational structures. The engineering background of Taylor (1911) shaped his thinking with regard to engineering the design of jobs, and Fayol (1949), who also came from an engineering background, sought to focus upon positions rather than people (Clegg et al 2008). However, the problematic nature of deficient organisational structure as illogical, cruel, wasteful and inefficient was recognised at an early stage (Urwick 1947). The application of the writings of Weber (1947) (discussed in Chapter 3) encouraged further discussion about organisational structure and consideration about authority and rationality within organisations. In the 1960s, rather than the structuralist approach, contingency theorists presented organisational structures as being contingent upon a range of different variables.

The contingency approach advocated by Burns and Stalker (1961) was informed by research with Scottish manufacturing firms; their findings highlighted two types of organisation structure, which appeared to be responses to the environment in which the firms operated – these were mechanistic structures and organic structures. Mechanistic structures displayed a clear definition of jobs, standardised policies and procedures governing organisational decision-making and rewards determined by adhering to supervisory instructions. Organic structures displayed a decreased emphasis upon formal job descriptions and a view of the formal organisation that was fluid and changeable. Burns and Stalker were able to argue from their research that the adoption of a mechanistic structure or an organic structure suited specific markets. In this classification the origins of debates about the merits of 'flat' versus 'tall' organisations were apparent (as depicted in Figures 6.2 and 6.3). The mechanistic structure favoured a tall structure, whereas the organic structure favoured a flat structure. Organisational moves to flatter structures reflected moves towards organic organisations. Woodward (1965) was another influential contingency theorist whose research findings suggested that organisational structure could be related to the technology in use, either unit, batch or mass, discussed further in Chapter 19.

Mintzberg et al (2009) traced the origins of strategic management back to Chandler's (1962) path-breaking book *Strategy and Structure*. Chandler, a historian of business and management, in looking at responses to the challenges of growth and diversification, showed how managers responded to strategic imperatives through developing new forms of organisation (Witzel 2003). Chandler's book was built around four detailed case studies of successful companies: Du Pont, General Motors, Standard Oil and Sears Roebuck. 'Chandler argues that this success was in part based upon early adoption of a new form of business organisation, the multi-divisional form or M-form, which allowed these corporations to grow and diversify' (Witzel 2003, p58). This important work was to inform the belief that structure follows strategy.

In moving from structuralist to more contingent accounts of organising, managerial choices became increasingly apparent. Both the work of Mintzberg (1983) and Miles and Snow (1984) offered more strategic perspectives in terms of the perceived fit between organisational structures and the environment in which they operate. Mintzberg (1983) identified five organisational forms: simple structure, machine bureaucracy, professional bureaucracy, divisional form and adhocracy. The simple structure consisted of the operating core and the strategic apex (individuals directing the organisation). In the machine structure, decisions were still made at the strategic apex. However, the involvement of administrative staff and the technostructure (technical support staff) was acknowledged. The professional structure possessed few levels between the strategic apex and professional employees in the large operating core (transforming inputs into products and services). In the divisional structure, emphasis was placed upon the autonomous work of divisions. Finally, the adhocracy, as its title suggests, was the most flexible and organic form, which Mintzberg believed was suited to smaller organisations.

Miles and Snow (1984, p10) wrote about what they perceived as a simple yet core concept '... of fit among an organisation's strategy, structure, and management processes'. In a manner similar to Chandler, they traced the evolution of organisational structures from the 1800s through to contemporary times, identifying patterns of strategy–structure linkage: defender strategies, prospector strategies, analyser strategies and reactor strategies, which are summarised in Box 6.2.

Box 6.2 Defender, prospector, analyser and reactor strategies (based upon Miles and Snow 1984)

Defender strategies = trying to maintain a traditional approach in the face of changes in the environment
Prospector strategies = exploiting new options through product and market innovations
Analyser strategies = not being the first mover in product-market innovations, but being an early adopter of successful competitors' innovations
Reactor strategies = hanging on to an approach regardless of poor performance

In Box 6.2 the essence of each of the strategies is summarised. A major outcome of Miles and Snow's (1984) research was identifying the evolution of historical forms of organising, which they were able to trace back to 1800. The earliest form was agency: '... small firms had relied on an informal structure in which the owner-manager's immediate subordinates acted as all-purpose agents of the chief executive, solving whatever problems arose' (Miles and Snow 1984, p25). The second form they identified was functional, which allowed companies to specialise in a limited set of products and markets and to become very large (see Figure 6.5). The third form was divisional, facilitating more organisational growth and diversification in both products and markets (see Figure 6.6). They regarded the matrix organisational form as the breakthrough, combining elements of functional and divisional forms in a single system (see Figure 6.7). The final form that they believed was emerging at the time of writing was what they referred to as the dynamic network organisation. This form placed far greater emphasis upon networks of relationships and subcontracting. Theorising about organisational design in recent years has increasingly focused upon the search for new forms of organisation. New organisational forms can be defined as:

Organisational designs for structure seeking to be non-bureaucratic –
indeed are often anti-bureaucratic stressing flat structures rather than tall
hierarchies, multiskilled capabilities rather than a rigid division of labor,
informality rather than a high degree of formality. (Clegg et al 2008,
p556)

New challenges are believed to encourage managers to move to new forms
of organising; these challenges include: globalisation, new technologies, the
knowledge-based society, hyper competition and social expectations (Child
2005).

CHANGING FORMS, PROCESSES AND BOUNDARIES

Managers appear to have become more creative in their forms of organising,
with a movement away from traditional emphasis upon organisational structures
and greater emphasis placed upon informal relationships and processes. Morgan
(1989) identified six different models: the rigid bureaucracy, bureaucracy with
a senior management team, bureaucracy with project teams and task forces, the
matrix organisation, the project organisation and the loosely coupled organic
network.

The bureaucracy reflected a traditional rigid bureaucracy; it was depicted as a
pyramid with the chief executive at the top. It reflected the choices that have
been made about organisational design challenges, particularly in terms of
integration and differentiation. The bureaucracy with a senior management
team reflected an evolution of the rigid bureaucracy in order to reflect a
more flexible form and the dispersal of power to a senior management team.
The bureaucracy with project teams and task forces acknowledged that when
senior managers could not handle all issues there was a need for project teams.
The matrix organisation followed the logic of project teams and moved to a
matrix form of organising. More or less equal priority was given to functional
departments such as finance, marketing and sales. In the project organisation
most core activities were tackled through project teams, with traditional
functional departments now playing a supporting role. Finally, an organisation
operating in a subcontracting mode was described as a loosely coupled
network.

An ongoing academic dilemma has been establishing which of these forms or
which new form is the most appropriate explanation for a particular situation.
Although, as Ackroyd (2002, p169) cautioned, 'there is a great deal of variation
in organisational forms, it is not helpful to think of the main task of organisation
studies as being to identify the one new and distinctive organisational type
that fits most observable examples'. As well as new forms of organising, the
terminology of organisational design is changing: 'the term has fallen out
of favour because it implies the conscious, rational pre-planning of formal
organisational arrangements, whereas contemporary thinking places greater
emphasis on a more adaptive, emergent process of organising to suit ever
changing circumstances' (Child 2005, p6).

Child encourages shifting the debate away from organisation design towards changing organisational forms, highlighting three integral components of organisation. The structural component is concerned with basic structural issues and procedures. The processual component is concerned with integration/co-ordination, control and reward. The boundary-crossing component is concerned with outsourcing, virtual organisation, alliances, organising across borders (outsourcing and strategic alliances are featured in the Organisational Change Field Guide (see Appendix)). Organisational design challenges are still present, but also more contemporary challenges of organising are evident, such as outsourcing and business process reengineering. Boundary-crossing/spanning has implications for both organisational forms and the management of change. The research featured in Journal Research Case 6.1 begins an important research agenda relating to new forms of change agency that new forms of organising raise.

JOURNAL RESEARCH CASE 6.1

Pharma, Consult and Engco

Paper title: Managing change across boundaries: boundary shaking practices
Sector: Pharmaceuticals, Consultancy and Automotive
Research methods: Interviews and focus groups
Authors: Balogun, J., Gleadle, P., Hope Hailey, V. and Willmott, H.
Year: 2005
Journal details: *British Journal of Management.* Vol 16, Issue 4. pp261–278.

Commentary: This intriguing paper acknowledges boundary-spanning as a potential new form of organising, with the authors focusing upon the boundary-shaking activities of individuals. This is an interesting new research agenda. The researchers locate their work within the field of change agency – notoriously difficult to research because of issues of organisational access. The researchers were able to gain access to their case studies through a consortium of companies involved in an ongoing research agenda. The findings from the research suggest that their research subjects were active movers and shakers working within existing networks and creating new networks.

Child (2005) suggests that there has been a move away from 'organisation' to 'organising' as a process. The work of Pettigrew and Dawson was discussed in the previous chapter in terms of acknowledging contextual perspectives on organisational change. The following discussion of Pettigrew and Dawson illustrates how processual perspectives increasingly inform understanding about organisational change.

Pettigrew wrote extensively about strategy with reference to power, politics, processes and change (see Pettigrew 2003 for an overview of this work). The INNFORM research project is particularly pertinent to debates in this chapter. The INNFORM programme of research involved a network of researchers undertaking a large-scale standardised survey of new organisation practices in Europe, Japan and the United States. The leadership and co-ordination of the network was undertaken by Pettigrew, based at Warwick Business School. One of the strengths of the research was the opportunity to compare through their survey innovative forms of organising in the different countries in 1992 and 1996.

Pettigrew et al (2000, p260) explain the three main programme aims: 'to map the extent of development of new forms of organising in Europe, Japan and the USA; to test for the performance benefits of such changes; and to examine the management processes as organisations move from more traditional to novel forms of organising'. The nine areas of change measured in the INNFORM survey may be summarised as follows. In terms of structures, the areas were: decentralising, de-layering and project forms of organising. In terms of processes, the areas were: communicating horizontally and vertically, investing in IT and practising new human resources. In terms of boundaries, the areas were: downscoping, outsourcing and developing strategic alliances.

Pettigrew et al (2000) suggest that a range of factors were driving the emergence of innovative forms of organising: economic, technological, informational and political. Pettigrew et al (2000, p259), reporting on the European and Japanese findings, identified a '... tendency for firms in both regions to seek new forms of organising by simultaneously altering their structures, processes and boundaries'. They believe these changes were widespread, although not revolutionary. The researchers conclude their paper with the following caveat: 'managing such a complementary change agenda is likely to take very considerable top management awareness, confidence, commitment and skill, qualities that our survey findings and case studies suggest may still be rare'.

Dawson (2003), in a manner similar to Pettigrew, sought to rectify the downplaying of the processual and ongoing nature of organisational change. He identified three general timeframes, comprising initial conception, process and operation of new work practices, which provide a framework from which to examine the process of organisational change (Dawson 2003). Three groups of determinants were believed to shape the process: the politics of change, the context of change and the substance of change, which Dawson explains as follows. Politics referred to activities such as consultation, negotiation, conflict and resistance. Context referred to both the internal and external context in the past, present and future (as discussed in Chapter 5). The substance of change encompassed: the scale and scope, the defining characteristics, timeframe and perceived centrality of the change. This processual approach underpins the case studies presented in his book and, as he acknowledges, this frame or lens shapes the outcomes of the analysis: 'under a processual perspective, our main concern is with how people variously experience the change process and how this dynamic non-linear process is shaped over time' (Dawson 2003, p48). Processual accounts of organisational change encourage engagement with the lived experience of organisational change and the dynamic, rather than static nature of organisational change.

Organisational designs are informed by managerial choices and contingencies, resulting in a wide range of organisational forms and structures with consequences for employment relations of these new organisational forms (see Rubery et al 2002 and Storey 2005). It is difficult to comment conclusively on these dynamic processes of changing; with the passage of time it will be possible to be more conclusive in a manner similar to the retrospective analyses undertaken by both Chandler, and Miles and Snow. As Pettigrew et al (2000, p260) noted when reporting their research findings, 'theoretical developments are also problematic when the appropriate analytical language is still emerging to capture empirical developments which themselves are also still in the process of evolution'. In the following 'Critical Perspective' the duality of change and continuity that potentially informs organisational design is acknowledged as a counterpoint to popular notions of new forms of organising replacing old organisational designs.

DUALITIES IN FORMS OF ORGANISING

In the 'Managerial Approaches' section, the implication was that traditional organisational structures were being replaced with new forms of organising in order to respond more effectively to changing circumstances. The notion of the static organisation was being replaced with the notion of the dynamic organisation and a greater appreciation of the permeability of traditional organisational boundaries, because 'it is widely believed that conventional forms of organisation can no longer adequately meet the challenge' (Child 2005, p29).

However, Graetz and Smith (2008, p265) highlighted the paradox in discussions about new forms of organising '... that, if organisations discard the key planning, co-ordinating and direction-setting mechanisms of traditional forms of organising, they also remove the stabilising dimensions of organisational form that are essential in periods of uncertainty and change'. Graetz and Smith (2008) undertook an extensive literature review of dualities with reference to organisational forms, which informs the following discussion. They acknowledge a central tension within organisations between continuity and change and the need to reconcile this tension through managing this duality in terms of different organisational forms. In reviewing and synthesising the dualities literature, they identified five duality characteristics: simultaneity, relational, minimal thresholds, dynamism and improvisation.

Simultaneity is the most basic characteristic and refers '... to the presence of traditional and new forms of organising within a single structural reference frame' (Graetz and Smith 2008, p271). While this duality has historically been recognised in organisations (see for example Lawrence and Lorsch 1967), its acknowledgement is a counterpoint to the idea that new forms are replacing old structures. Dualities are also relational and interdependent in nature. Graetz and Smith cite Palmer and Dunford (2002), arguing against the popular belief that new organisational practices are designed for flexibility, whereas traditional practices were designed for stability. Instead they suggest that new organisational practices have evolved in order to strengthen traditional practices. A third dualities characteristic is the need for a minimal threshold – only minimal enabling forces are required in order to enable, for example, self-organising forms.

Dynamism is a consequence of working with the dualities of continuity and change, and the final duality characteristic identified by Graetz and Smith (2008, p273) is improvisation, which '… reinforces the importance of two organising forces working dynamically and mutualistically to shape decision-making through bidirectional feedback between the two duality poles'. They cite Weick (1998), who has been influential in encouraging acknowledgement about improvisation in organisations through fusing intended actions and emergent actions.

Thinking in terms of dualities provides a useful counterpoint against some of the rhetorical depictions of new forms of organising that suggest the replacement of traditional organisational designs. Van de Ven and Poole (2005) highlighted an ongoing debate in studying organisational change about whether organisations consist of 'things' or whether they consist of 'processes'. The organisational design debates featured in this chapter initially depicted organisations as very solid 'things', such as the M-form. However, as this chapter has demonstrated, there has been an increasing acknowledgement of the significance of organisational 'processes'. The organisational dualities of change and continuity highlighted by Graetz and Smith (2008) suggest the merits of a pluralistic approach, a position favoured by Van de Ven and Poole (2005).

CONCLUDING COMMENTARY

This chapter has mirrored traditional histories of management thinking – beginning with early classifications of organisational design and then acknowledging human aspects of organisational design, followed by an acknowledgement of contingency variables shaping organisational designs. As organisations have had to respond to new contingencies, the search has continued for new forms of organising. It is difficult to be conclusive about these new forms of organising at present. However, the danger is in believing that new forms are necessary for a new age. The four basic organisational design choices still appear relevant today. Particularly in terms of large organisations, it appears sensible to explain change in terms of dualities with new forms of organising addressing change and traditional forms of organising maintaining continuities.

CASE STUDY: APPLYING
THEORY TO PRACTICE

New organisational forms at the University of Midchester

The University of Midchester successfully delivers a mix of research, teaching and scholarship, benefiting students, clients and the wider community. The vice-chancellor for the past five years has been the charismatic and strident Professor Hope Sandoval. Professor Sandoval, whose background was as a senior academic at Harvard Business School, has enjoyed the challenge of running a large academic institution and has been supported by a very capable senior management team. Once a week this senior management team have met with Professor Sandoval to discuss strategic and operational matters. At these meetings there has been a standing item entitled 'twenty-first-century university', which entails an ongoing discussion about correctly positioning the university for the challenges of the twenty-first century. For these discussions, the need to bring together the work of the separate faculties of IT and business has been identified as a priority.

The university has ten faculties, each faculty comprising a number of academic departments. Each faculty is led by a dean, beneath whom heads of department head up individual departments. The focus has been upon the Faculty of IT and the Faculty of Business. Each faculty has approximately 400 staff (a mix of academics and administrators) and each faculty has approximately 4,000 students, who include part-time and full-time students – undergraduates and postgraduates. Bringing these two areas together was believed to be beneficial and would be appropriate to an increasingly competitive higher education environment. A closer relationship would allow the university to offer more business courses with IT and more IT courses with business. Also, there were potential commercial benefits to bringing together IT and business in terms of the research services the university offered. The financial environment was very influential in terms of senior management

thinking. Although the University of Midchester was financially successful, the senior management team was aware that many universities were in debt and wanted to avoid such a situation by being proactive. As a consequence of discussions at the previous week's meeting, Professor Sandoval had been tasked with sketching out ways forward for bringing the two faculties together. She presented her ideas to the senior management team as Designs A, B and C. She believed each design had merit and was keen for an informed evaluation of each design.

Design A

The obvious choice was to merge the two faculties into a single faculty under the provisional title of the Faculty of Business and Information Technology. There would be cost savings in terms of one fewer dean's salary and one fewer faculty administration team. It was envisaged that the small number of staff affected would be offered alternative positions or generous redundancy packages. For staff and students in the two faculties, the impact of the merger would be minimal. Current staff and students would continue as normal. However, in the future opportunities were envisaged in terms of new courses and new research. One potential obstruction to merging the two faculties was that they were based on two different parts of the campus.

Design B

This involved the two faculties maintaining their existing structures but radically changing their processes, as would be enabled through IT. Committees overseeing, for example, academic quality and research strategy would become joint faculty committees with an equal representation of members from each faculty. In a similar manner, heads of department from both faculties would meet together on a regular basis. Communications and report structures would become more collaborative, involving joint reports on key strategic partnerships. The cost savings of a single faculty office would not be achieved, but estimates suggested that the joint working proposed would be less costly than Design A. Students and staff would experience no disruption under the new arrangements, although again potential developments in terms of new courses and research were envisaged. One potential hurdle was the increased levels of bureaucracy. Staff already moaned about the amount of paperwork and there was a danger of increasing the number of committees under the joint arrangements.

Design C

The most radical proposal was the closure of the Faculty of IT, and for the subcontracting of specialised IT expertise to a neighbouring university with which the university already had many collaborative arrangements. In the designs it was acknowledged that the consequences for staff would have to be managed and that some staff would join an expanded Faculty of Business whereas others might be offered opportunities to join the neighbouring university. The thinking behind this was that Midchester was unable to attract IT students like the neighbouring university, and that collaboration was believed to be a better long-term arrangement than competition. The neighbouring university did not have a business faculty – which was another argument in favour of Design C. Although student places on courses would be safeguarded, this was the most disruptive option for staff and students. The biggest hurdle to Design C would be the anticipated industrial action that would arise.

Case study questions

1 What factors are likely to inform the organisational design choices?

2 Evaluate each of the three designs in terms of their strengths and weaknesses.

DISCUSSION QUESTIONS

1 What information is likely to inform organisational design choices?

2 Why do managers place less emphasis upon designing effective organisational structures these days?

3 Will a universal optimum organisational design ever be discovered?

4 What are the organisational advantages of reconciling change and stability?

KEY READINGS

CHILD, J. (2005) *Organization: contemporary principles and practices*. Oxford: Blackwell Publishing.

Child is a respected theorist who has influenced thinking about management and organisational behaviour over many decades. This textbook is recommended because of its coverage of organisational design debates. The book is divided into four major sections: the broad picture, new internal forms, new network forms and evolving effective organisations. The strength of this book is that Child is well versed in earlier theorising, allowing him to comment upon contemporary organisational developments in an informed manner. The other strength of the book is its readability; he has a gift to make the complex accessible.

JONES, G. (2010) *Organizational theory, design and change*. 6th ed. Global edition. Boston: Pearson.

As the title suggests, this textbook is very pertinent to many of the debates that have been introduced in this chapter. The textbook, now in its sixth edition, straddles the gap between organisational theory books with little coverage of organisational change and organisational change books with little coverage of organisational design. The textbook is organised into three main parts: the organisation and its environment, organisational design and organisational change.

PETTIGREW, A.M. and FENTON, E.M. (eds) (2000) *Innovating new forms of organizing*. London: Sage Publications Ltd.

This edited reader is one of the major outputs of the INNFORM project discussed earlier in the chapter. The strength of this grouping was that an international research network was established in order to study innovative forms of organising. The book allows the commonalities in findings from very different international contexts to be made explicit.

CHAPTER 7

Strategic-level change

LEARNING OUTCOMES

After reading this chapter you should be able to:

- differentiate approaches to strategy and strategic change
- understand planned approaches to change
- recognise managing change challenges of mergers and acquisitions
- understand emergent approaches to change
- question popular strategic change assumptions
- critically review the effectiveness of mergers and acquisitions.

INTRODUCTION

This chapter focuses upon relationships between two large and sometimes contradictory bodies of literature – strategy and change. There is neither consensus about how to effectively manage/explain change, nor consensus about how to manage/explain strategy. The lack of agreement about strategy has been acknowledged (Whittington 2001). As a consequence this chapter selectively acknowledges different schools of strategic management informed particularly by Mintzberg et al's (2009) *Strategy Safari*, which offers a 'roadmap' through this disparate body of literature.

In this textbook, discussions about topics such as communications, leadership and culture invariably refer to strategic-level changes. In this way the subject of managing change is often depicted as strategic. Placing the adjective 'strategic' in front of programmes such as strategic change and strategic human resources has proved politically useful (Frahm 2007). In the context of a textbook it is necessary to go beyond using strategic as a politically expedient label and consider more deeply the origins and theories of strategic change. This chapter, with its strategic-level focus, draws far less upon psychology and sociology and far more upon economics. Strategic management has been promiscuous in drawing upon other disciplines and sub-fields of management, however strategic management has consistently drawn upon economics (Pettigrew et al 2002).

In this chapter, the 'Managerial Approaches' section introduces and differentiates major approaches to strategy, informing understanding about strategic change. The planned approach to change is introduced and illustrated in terms of mergers and acquisitions as an example of the planned approach to change. In the 'Critical Perspective', managerial emphasis upon planned change is contrasted with more emergent approaches to change, strategic change is questioned and the effectiveness of mergers and acquisitions is critically reviewed.

MANAGERIAL APPROACHES

STRATEGY AND STRATEGIC CHANGE

In focusing upon strategic-level change, an understanding of strategy is necessary. The concerns of strategists typically include '... the purposes, direction, choices, changes, governance, organisation and performance of organisations in their industry, market and social, economic and political contexts' (Pettigrew et al 2002, p3). While there are commonalities in strategic concerns, there is no consensus about the meaning of strategy. In mapping out the strategic terrain, five possible definitions of 'strategy' have been suggested – as a plan, a ploy, a pattern, a position and a perspective (Mintzberg 1987). There is an ongoing critical questioning of strategy and through this questioning four generic approaches have been identified: classical, evolutionary, processual and systemic (Whittington 2001).

The classical approach most closely reflects traditional views of strategy and may be regarded as the textbook orthodoxy. This approach can be closely related to functionalism, discussed in Chapter 4. This approach emphasises rational planning and senior management preparing strategic plans and specifying objectives. The evolutionary approach is more organic in its emphasis upon senior managers responding to markets, with less emphasis upon processes of planning. The theoretical foundations of this approach are rooted in population ecology, which espouses that only the fittest organisations survive. The processual approach challenges both the rationality of strategic planning and the supposed efficacy of markets. Instead, a far more emergent approach is favoured that acknowledges political compromise and the influence of cultures and subcultures. Finally, the systemic approach suggests that social systems shape strategic goals and processes so that strategies reflect both organisational and societal interests.

There is no one best way to undertake strategic change. Proponents of the classical approach will favour a planned approach to strategic change as part of wider strategic planning. Proponents of the evolutionary approach will argue that strategic change needs to be informed by developments in the environment. Proponents of the processual approach will emphasise strategic change as an ongoing process that is inherently political. And proponents of the systemic approach will emphasise the role of social systems shaping strategic change. There is merit in each approach, and throughout this textbook theorists from different approaches are featured. The downside of this multiplicity of approaches is that there is little synthesis between different approaches, yet synthesis may be fruitful given the interdisciplinary nature of both strategy and change.

In their definition of strategic change, De Wit and Meyer (2004) made reference to business systems and organisational systems: the business system refers to how businesses make money and the organisational system refers to how people work together in carrying out business. They identified three components of the organisational system: organisational structure, organisational processes and organisational culture. Organisational structure is concerned with the clustering of tasks and people, reflecting debates introduced in Chapter 6. Organisational processes are concerned with arrangements, procedures and routines controlling and co-ordinating people, again reflecting debates in Chapter 6. Organisational culture is concerned with the world view and behaviour patterns of members of an organisation (culture is the focus of Chapter 13). While acknowledging the pervasive nature of change, it is apparent that not all organisational change is strategic; organisations undertake operational change on a regular basis and this is likely to be the norm in most organisations.

Strategic change has been defined as impacting upon the way an organisation does business (its business system) and on the way an organisation has been configured (its organisational system) (De Wit and Meyer 2004). The specification of these systems differentiates operational change from strategic change, with strategic change referring to fundamental alterations to the business system or organisational system. In emphasising 'renewal', they suggest examples of strategic change, which include: reorganisation, diversification, shift in core technology, business process redesign and product portfolio reshuffle (De Wit and Meyer 2004).

In a similar manner to De Wit and Meyer, Johnson et al (2008, p434) couch their discussion of strategic change in terms of configuration, defining an organisation's configuration as consisting of '... the structures, processes and relationships through which the organisation operates'. The strength of acknowledging configuration is that otherwise disparate strategic concepts are unified. In *Strategy Safari* the configuration school reconciles and integrates messages from other schools of strategic management. Transformation is regarded as an '... inevitable consequence of configuration. There is a time for coherence and a time for change' (Mintzberg et al 2009, p318). The warning in this quotation is that strategic change is an oxymoron, because as well as strategic change addressing transformation, strategy is concerned with continuities. While practitioner rhetoric about transformation is echoed in the prescriptive literature, organisational change is far more subtle than this. Often debates are couched in terms of evolutionary and revolutionary change.

Evolution has been defined in terms of '... prolonged periods of growth where no major upheaval occurs in organisation practices', whereas revolution refers to '... those periods of substantial turmoil in organisation life' (Greiner 1972, p38). Evolutionary phases create the need for revolutionary phases in the form of an organisational life-cycle. Greiner argued that an organisation's future may be determined less by outside forces (as suggested by traditional evolutionary approaches) and more by an organisation's history. Greiner identified five essential dimensions of organisational development: the age of the organisation, size of the organisation, stages of evolution, stages of revolution and growth rate of the industry. This led him to suggest that there were five stages of growth as follows. Evolutionary phases are characterised by the dominant management style that achieves growth; revolutionary phases are characterised by the dominant management problem that requires solving for growth.

Phase one was concerned with the birth of the organisation and creating a product and market. The first revolution results from a crisis of leadership, with the founders reluctant to step aside. Phase two for those companies that survive was about a directive leadership embarking upon sustained growth. The second revolution resulted from a crisis of autonomy when lower-level management demanded greater autonomy. Phase three involved growth through successful application of a decentralised organisation structure. The third revolution resulted from a control crisis, with top management seeking to regain control. Phase four involved the use of formal systems for greater co-ordination and top executives taking responsibility for the initiation and administration of new systems. The fourth revolution – referred to as the red-tape crisis – resulted from a lack of confidence between line and staff and between headquarters and the field. Phase five involved strong interpersonal collaboration and greater spontaneity in action through teams. At the time of writing, Greiner did not have the historical data to specify the revolution resulting out of phase five. In reviewing the strategic change literature, debates about planned approaches to change (top–down) and emergent approaches to change (bottom–up) are very prevalent. A good way to think about evolutionary and revolutionary change is in terms of the paradox a manager encounters when attempting strategic change:

> On the one hand, they usually realise that to fundamentally transform the organisation a break with the past is needed… On the other hand, they also recognise the value of continuity, building on past experiences, investments and loyalties. (De Wit and Meyer 2004, p170)

This quotation highlights a danger in regarding revolutionary change as strategic and evolutionary change as operational (De Wit and Meyer 2004). Strategists are just as likely to be involved in evolutionary change despite the existence of revolutionary organisational change rhetoric. Burke (2008, p69) suggests that 'more than 95 per cent of organisational changes are evolutionary', while Johnson et al (2008, p179) acknowledged that 'strategies of organisations change gradually'.

PLANNED APPROACHES TO CHANGE

The debates about whether strategic changes are planned or emergent mirror larger debates about the planned or emergent nature of strategy (emergent change is discussed in the 'Critical Perspective' section). Schein (1980) acknowledged Lewin as the intellectual father of planned change. Lewin's vision of the planned approach to change was as a well-integrated system, with field theory, group dynamics, action research and the three-step model making a unified whole. These elements supported and reinforced each other at the individual level, group level, organisation level and societal level (Burnes 2004). In his reappraisal of Lewin's planned approach to change, Burnes acknowledged that Lewin promoted an ethical and humanist approach to change. These themes are discussed in Chapter 16; however, they highlight a potential strength of planned change in its transparency when compared with more emergent conceptions of change.

Planned approaches to change were given impetus by the popularity of strategic planning. The 1970s witnessed a huge growth in strategic planning and related literature, both within academic circles and the popular business press. However, the origins of strategic planning may be traced back to Ansoff (1965), who was also influential in the early shaping of the field of strategic management. Mintzberg et al (2009) suggest that planning became not just an approach to strategy formation, but a religion to be promoted with missionary fervour. Strategic planning involved gathering information and applying appropriate techniques in the belief that the outside world and the organisation itself could be made predictable and shaped in accordance with the careful plans of top management (Whittington 2001). Strategic planning assumptions allowed organisations to predict the course of their environment, to control their environments, or simply to assume that the environment was stable (Mintzberg et al 2009, p72).

The origins of step/stage models so prominent in the managing change literature are evident in the rationality of planned approaches to change. Many of the models that prescribe an approach to managing change are deeply rooted in this planned change tradition. Wilson (1992, p27) captures the potential of such approaches in the following caricature: 'In the extreme, planned change strategies would be those processes in which there was a smooth transition from some previously articulated strategic vision towards a future desired state (such as an envisaged portfolio of potentially successful products and services).'

After Lewin's death organisational elements of his work were given prominence through the creation of organisational development (OD) (Burnes 2004). The dominant model that was to arise from OD was one of incrementalism, incorporating planned change and orderly transitioning (Dunphy and Stace 1988). OD developed in the late 1960s and 1970s, suiting the prosperity and stability of those eras. The case for incremental change arose when environments were characterised by unidirectional growth and relative environmental stability and organisations operated primarily within the bounds of national economies (Dunphy and Stace 1988). Cummings and Worley (2008, p29) proposed a general model of planned change that was closely aligned with organisational development; the model involves four major change activities: entering and contracting, diagnosing, planning and implementing change, and evaluating and institutionalising change. They further differentiate planned change in terms of the magnitude of organisational change, the degree to which the client system is organised, and whether the setting is domestic or international.

Dunphy and Stace (1988) suggested that the type of strategic change depended upon the strategic analysis of the situation. They identified four types of strategic change: participative evolution, charismatic transformation, forced evolution and dictatorial transformation. Participative evolution was when organisations made minor adjustments with key groups favouring change. Charismatic transformation was when there was support for radical change, yet little time for extensive participation. Forced evolution was when there was a need for minor adjustments, but key interest groups opposed change. Dictatorial transformation was when there was no time for participation and there was no support for radical change, yet radical change was believed to be vital. In this contingent view Dunphy and Stace feared that change agents might have a preferred change strategy, which might not be compatible with a particular change situation. In Journal Research Case 7.1, the Dunphy/Stace matrix is applied to four Australian service industry organisations.

⊙ JOURNAL RESEARCH CASE 7.1

Macquarie Bank, Westpac Bank, Advance Bank and MLC Life

Paper title: The strategic management of corporate change
Sector: Banking, insurance, aviation and international telecommunications
Research methods: Structured interviews and Delphi Group interviews
Authors: Dunphy, D. and Stace, D.
Year: 1993
Journal details: *Human Relations*. Vol 46, No 8. pp905–920.

Commentary: This classic paper describes field research undertaken to test the applicability and usefulness of the Dunphy/

Stace (1988) change matrix. The research was conducted with 13 Australian service industry organisations during 1988–89. The final third of the paper contains four case studies, which are drawn from the larger research project. The case studies are believed to demonstrate how each of the four major change strategies can be used in specific circumstances to maintain high performance. The four change strategies were: participative evolution, charismatic transformation, forced evolution and dictatorial transformation.

MANAGING MERGERS AND ACQUISITIONS

Mergers and acquisitions (M&As) present very real examples of strategic-level change, often favouring a planned approach to change. M&As are regarded as catalysts for change in that they are unique opportunities to shake and shape organisations because of people expecting change (Hubbard 2001). The incidence of mergers and acquisitions tends to be highly cyclical (Rees and Edwards 2003, p5). Gaughan (2002) mapped out five waves of M&A activity, with the first wave being traced back to between 1897 and 1904.

In recent years senior managers have favoured M&As as a means of gaining scale and global scope, which has been reflected in the cross-border nature of many M&As. M&As potentially offer opportunities for firms to substantially enhance their value to stakeholders, shareholders in particular; they respond to and anticipate external changes in the environment and proactively influence their immediate context (Angwin 2007). Corporate takeovers are typically differentiated into four types: mergers, acquisitions (friendly or hostile), proxy contests and leveraged buyouts. Mergers involve similar-size organisations, whereas acquisitions will have clear winners and losers (Hubbard 2001).

As well as acknowledging the problematic nature of mergers and acquisitions, DiGeorgio (2002, 2003) cites Cisco Systems and GE Capital as case examples of companies that were successful in their M&A activity. DiGeorgio (2003) advocated a very systematic approach, both in terms of selection and integration. Palmer et al (2009) identify managing change challenges that M&As raise; these include: overvaluing cost savings, merging different cultures, balancing change and continuity, retaining employees, lack of contingency planning and communication difficulties. Three key areas in terms of HR's contribution to international mergers and acquisitions are: pay and benefits, management selection and development, and harmonisation and integration (Rees and Edwards 2003).

CRITICAL PERSPECTIVE

In this 'Critical Perspective' emergent approaches to change are discussed as a counterpoint to planned approaches to change, the concept of strategic change is questioned and claims made for mergers and acquisitions are critically reviewed.

EMERGENT APPROACHES TO CHANGE

Caldwell (2006) suggests that there was a need to reappraise planned change, due to far-reaching workplace transformations over the previous two decades. Planned change was challenged in the early 1980s due to the increasingly competitive international climate. Companies were competing across national boundaries with far less stability in markets. Burke (2008, p14), an advocate of planned approaches to change, was realistic about the unanticipated consequences of plans: 'we must plan change yet understand that things never turn out quite as we planned. It's a paradox.' In a similar manner it has been acknowledged that models and practices of planned change are still at a formative stage of development and that there is considerable room for improvement (Cummings and Worley 2008).

However, proponents of emergent change, rather than seeking to improve the planned approach to change, developed an important counterpoint. This was driven by the perceived need for more appropriate models to both guide and explain the major changes that were taking place. In order to understand emergent change, it is necessary to acknowledge schools of strategic management that address emergence, in particular the learning school (discussed further in Chapter 14). Emergence is far more prevalent in organisations than strategic planning implies; strategy 'emerges constantly in a firm as different people respond to and reinterpret their sense of the organisation's identity and purpose' (Eccles and Nohria 1992, p87). Mintzberg et al (2009), in introducing the learning school, make the connection between learning and strategies emerging as people acting individually, but more often collectively, learn about a situation and their organisation's capability of dealing with it. Mintzberg et al (2009) acknowledged the contribution of Lindbolm (1959) in initiating this school in his article *'The Science of Muddling Through'*. This school of thought raised awkward questions about: how do strategies actually form in organisations? There was an acknowledgement that strategies could be informed by individuals at any level in the organisation.

In tracing the origins of the learning school, Mintzberg et al (2009) differentiated the 'disjointed incrementalism' of Lindbolm's muddling through from the 'logical incrementalism' of Quinn (1980). The concept of logical incrementalism acknowledged emergence, but with an underlying logic that allowed strategists to promote their strategic visions while simultaneously acknowledging that these strategic visions were changing and improving. This line of reasoning was to have implications for managing change. The evolutionary theory of Nelson and Winter (1982) challenged rational and planned approaches to change, instead explaining change as emerging from changes in routines. Routines were perceived as being very prevalent in organisations and a major source of organisational stability: 'the interaction between established routines and novel situations is an important source of learning. As routines are changed to deal with new situations, larger changes come about' (Mintzberg et al 2009, p194).

Weick (2000) gave considerable impetus to emergent change debates. In explaining this approach to organisational change he offered the example of Allan Leighton and Archie Norman and their work in changing the UK-based ASDA supermarket chain. While they established the strategic direction for the supermarket chain, the actual changes were a mix of local initiatives, experiments and formalising informal routines. The trend that Weick detected and highlighted in his writings was organisational change as ongoing, continuous and cumulative. This was not a particularly grand proposal, but it did provide an important counterbalance to planned change orthodoxy. Weick began to shift interest away from traditional static preoccupations with finding the right organisational form, featured in Chapter 6, towards more dynamic processes of organising. More recently Leybourne (2006) has argued for greater acknowledgement of improvisation alongside planned changes in managing change projects.

Child (2005), in his discussion of planned and emergent change, contrasts business process reengineering (BPR) with Kaizen (discussed in the Organisational Change Field Guide (see Appendix)). BPR can be understood as a planned approach to change seeking to radically change the whole organisation. Child regards BPR as failing to live up to its claims (see Hughes 2009 for further evaluation) and in this way may be regarded as an example of failed planned change. Child contrasts this with Japanese practices of continuous improvement (Kaizen) and innovating through project teams, which he regarded as an emergent approach towards change and a more successful approach than planned change.

The danger in discussing emergent change as a counterpoint to planned change is that a polarised either/or divide is encouraged. This partisan approach may have been encouraged by the torrent of criticisms of planned change in the early 1980s onwards (Burnes 2009a). However, careful reading of the writings of Weick (2000) and Burnes (2009a) favours a more balanced approach. Weick (2000, p237) concludes that 'if leaders take notice of emergent change and its effects, however, they can be more selective in their use of planned change'. Instead of the either/or dichotomy, planned and emergent change may be complementary. Burnes (2009a) concludes that both planned change and emergent change have much to recommend them, but equally they have significant shortcomings. His line of reasoning suggests that different approaches may suit different situations, but that some situations may require a completely different approach.

QUESTIONING STRATEGIC CHANGE

Strategic change – in drawing upon a variety of mutually exclusive conceptual approaches – surfaces different issues about understanding and managing strategic change (Wilson 1992). In essence the weakness of one approach to strategic change is the strength and rationale for an alternative approach to strategic change. As with managing change, the goal of the one best way either to strategically change or explain strategic change is illusory. Understanding about strategic change is shaped by a series of ongoing critical debates about the meanings, explanations and prescriptions of strategy. There have been periodic cries for a unifying paradigm in strategic management: 'one has not appeared, it is unlikely to do so, and it would be creatively destructive if it did arrive' (Pettigrew et al 2002, p11). The theory and practice of strategy has strengths and weaknesses similar to other fields of study. In reviewing the strategy literature there is an apparent lack of reflexivity (Whipp 1996; Pettigrew et al 2002). An explanation for this lack of reflexivity centres upon the divide between theory and practice – specifically the need to meet the expectations of the various stakeholders interested in the subject (Pettigrew et al 2002). A tension consequently exists between the critical development of appropriate theories and practical requirements made of strategy by managers.

The influence of economics on strategic management was acknowledged earlier in the chapter, and this emphasis is informative in suggesting preferences and biases built into strategic management. Processes of individual-level change, discussed in Chapter 9, may be neglected in strategic accounts of change due to the economic orientation of strategy. Even differentiation between organisations may be challenging in terms of economic analyses: 'economic theory is unable to distinguish effectively between firms, except through glib generalities about comparative efficiency of the firm's production function' (Pavitt and Steinmueller 2002, p345). The danger is that '… economic theory and management theory are unable to transcend their own paradigmatic boundaries' (Wilson 1992, p26). It is unlikely that economic theories or, by association, strategy can address the diversity of individuals that comprise contemporary organisations.

Organisations have no unity, yet the notion of 'strategy' implies multitudinous individuals who make up an organisation uniting around the effective pursuit of a coherent goal (Whittington 2001). Strategic change, particularly planned approaches to change, appears to rest heavily upon unitarist conceptions of organisations that may not reflect their diversity of stakeholders. Sorge and Van Witteloostuijn (2004, p1213), in a polemical attack on what they regard as the nonsense of organisational change, criticise popular notions of strategic change. They challenge the preoccupation of strategists with radical change: 'strategies and structures need credibility, consistency, and legitimacy in order to mobilise people'. The central contradiction of strategic change is that strategy itself is not about change at all, but about continuity in terms of either a deliberate plan to establish patterns of behaviour or as an emergent pattern (Mintzberg et al 2009). However, Sorge and Van Witteloostuijn's (2004, p1213) main target is the perceived preoccupation of strategists with an increasing rate of environmental change: 'empirically, we have not seen any demonstration that the rate of environmental change has uniformly increased across the board over a longer time span… It is an unsubstantiated myth so far shamefully tolerated or cultivated by scholars.'

A pragmatic concern about focusing upon strategic change is that it may detract from focusing upon other aspects of managing change. Earlier the political usefulness of using the 'strategic' adjective was noted (Frahm 2007). This may equally be applied to the discourse of business academics using the 'strategic' prefix in order to enhance their subjects. As far back as the 1980s management researchers were highlighted shifting attention away from the management of changes towards strategic change, although limiting attention to strategic change may be unrealistic and misleading (Buchanan and Boddy 1992).

Cummings (2002), in his critical strategy text, highlights modernist preconceptions about managing change, which may selectively be summarised as follows. There is an emphasis upon change following a linear, input–process–output approach, with organisations moving through a series of steps. Equally time and history are regarded as moving in a step-by-step linear manner, changing tangible things in the present for the future. Finally constancy is seen as second best, with organisational change regarded as the primary imperative. Many of these themes are explored within this textbook; however, at this point these preconceptions resonate with discussions about strategic change. Strategic change appears to promise a progressive linearity leading towards increasingly more effective strategically managed organisations. However, Greenwood and Hinings (1988) offered a sobering view of strategic change in their theoretically complex paper about the dynamics of strategic change. Their use of terminology can be rather obtuse, meriting clarification.

In writing about design archetypes they draw upon underlying organisational interpretive schemes and their associated structural arrangements (this concept may be related back to the organisational design choices featured in the previous chapter). They regard an organisation's track in terms of the temporal relationship between an organisation and one or more design archetypes.

> The language of tracks has to provide for the study of organisations over time, allowing for the possibilities not only of radical transformations but of abortive shifts between design archetypes and of the absence of change. We must allow for a complex array of tracks. (Greenwood and Hinings 1988, p303)

Greenwood and Hinings (1988) envisaged four possible tracks, which are summarised in Box 7.1.

Box 7.1 Summary of organisational tracks (based upon Greenwood and Hinings 1988)

Track A: inertia – the design archetype most organisations gravitate towards (although very little literature exists about inertia)
Track B: aborted excursions – for whatever reason, movement away from the starting archetype
Track C: reorientations (transformations) – movement from one archetype to another, including linear progression, oscillations and delays
Track D: unresolved excursions – focus moves away from successful change to encompassing aborted or unresolved excursions.

While Track C allows for and acknowledges the linear progress in terms of transformations, Box 7.1 highlights how even with the best intentions strategic change may not lead to linear progress, but aborted and unresolved excursions. Also, Box 7.1 suggests that inertia, rather than change, may be more the norm. It is difficult to offer empirical evidence to confirm or disconfirm the prevalence of organisational tracks, and Greenwood and Hinings (1988) concluded that there was a need for further research.

CRITICALLY REVIEWING MERGERS AND ACQUISITIONS

In the 'Managerial Approaches' section the popularity and rationales for M&As were discussed, raising the question: 'Do M&As deliver what senior managers expect?' The resounding answer appears to be no. Hubbard (2001, p11), acknowledging the different measures of success and failure, concludes that 'regardless of the measurement, the results are remarkably similar – over half of acquisitions fail to meet the objectives of the parties involved' (see also Sorge and Van Witteloostuijn 2004). Copeland et al (1993) found that '61 per cent of their sample of acquiring firms in the 1980s have not even been successful in recovering the capital cost of their acquisitions'. DiGeorgio (2002, 2003) reviewed relevant literature as well as drew upon his own experience as a consultant working on mergers and acquisitions; he highlighted the overview of previous studies undertaken by LaJoux (1998):

> LaJoux cites 15 major studies of the success or failure of acquisitions. For the studies reporting failure rates, the rate ranged from 40 per cent to 80 per cent, with the exception of one study done in 1965, which reported a 16 per cent failure rate. (DiGeorgio 2002, p135)

The large volume of literature highlighting the high incidence of M&A failure begs the question: why do M&As tend to fail? The reasons M&As do not work include inadequate due diligence, lack of a compelling strategic rationale, and unrealistic expectations. The reasons for acquisition failure may be divided into two categories – fit and process issues. Fit issues are concerned with the juxtaposition of the acquirer and target and include: size issues, diversification, previous acquisition experience, organisational fit, strategic fit, cultural fit and other demographic factors (Hubbard 2001). Process issues relate to the transaction and implementation process, which the acquirer has more influence over, and include: negotiation issues, inadequate pre-acquisition planning, insufficient information-gathering, price paid and method of payment for the target, people problems, implementation issues and communication. Johnson et al (2008, p359) also suggest that: 'As many as 70 per cent of acquisitions end up with lower returns to shareholders of both organisations.' They suggest that the most common mistake is paying too much for a company and being over-optimistic about the benefits of the acquisition.

CONCLUDING COMMENTARY

The study of strategic change raises similar challenges to the study of managing change; despite considerable interest and a large body of literature, there is very little consensus and there is never likely to be. An ongoing process of critical questioning helps to advance knowledge, with schools of strategic management increasingly being delineated. The planned approach to change can be traced back to the pioneering work of Lewin. Even though in recent decades the emergent approach to change has become fashionable, the best way forward is to regard these approaches to change as complementary rather than contradictory. Mergers and acquisitions offer a strategic-level example of a planned approach to change, depicting organisational change as planned, linear and rational. The high failure rate of mergers and acquisitions is well known among practitioners and academics. However, by addressing the emergent as well as planned nature of mergers and acquisitions, greater understanding is possible, which may inform the practice of managing mergers and acquisitions.

Strategic change at Higson's Plastic Parts

CASE STUDY: APPLYING THEORY TO PRACTICE

Higson's Plastic Parts (HPP) is a family firm established over 60 years ago and has one factory that employs 320 people in roles ranging from production to administration. The company moulds specialised plastic parts for a range of large organisations that manufacture cars, buses, lorries and trains. The business was successfully run by Walter Higson, who passed away ten years ago, and has since been jointly run by the Higson brothers Charlie and Bobby, who succeeded their father. Over the past decade the brothers have repeatedly clashed over the strategic direction of the business, which may account for why a once prosperous business is now in financial difficulties. At the suggestion of a friend they have engaged a business consultant, who has agreed among other things to act as a mediator between the two brothers.

She spent her first day with the brothers touring the site and meeting many of the long-serving staff. She had also had a chance to 'eyeball' the accounts and talk with the sales and marketing team. Also, towards the end of the day she had an opportunity to talk with each of the brothers independently of each other and together as a pair. After what had been a long yet productive day she sat down to write up her notes.

In order to orientate herself she started by sketching out a simple SWOT analysis. HPP had been very successful and appeared to be a respected supplier of plastic parts. The workforce was very skilled, loyal and committed to HPP. However, in terms of weaknesses, HPP was no longer operating as a profitable business and was reliant upon cash reserves that had been accumulated in more profitable times. Sales and marketing staff saw opportunities to diversify into new lines of business that had not existed in the past. Also, it was believed that the workforce was very flexible and would be prepared to work differently to secure the long-term future of the business. The threats were the most troubling part of the analysis. HPP was reliant upon five major contracts, which were renewed annually. The plant, which had been an asset in the past, was becoming obsolete and would need replacing with the latest advanced manufacturing technology in the near future. However, the biggest threat was now from Asia, where the competition was increasingly able to produce plastic parts at far lower costs.

The consultant's discussions with Charlie and Bobby was hard work because they appeared to favour very different positions, particularly in terms of ways forward. At times they contradicted each other and at times they even contradicted themselves. She doodled: 'Strategic change at Higson's over the next five years?'

Charlie was the more assertive of the two brothers and the keener to remember his father's ways of working. His father had schooled him in the use of the 'Plan'. The Plan involved the manipulation of a series of fairly simple sales and costs ratios, which had helped to determine the rate at which the business had grown in the past. Inside HPP the Plan had been the secret ingredient that had given the business its competitive advantage. Every six months the Plan was recalculated and heads of the functional areas of the business would wait with anticipation for their budget forecasts. Information would then be cascaded down throughout the organisation, to such an extent that shop-floor employees looked to the Plan as a barometer of how the

business was doing. At one point Charlie had asserted that 'the Plan has served us well in the past, it serves us well in the present, and it will serve us well in the future.' Despite this he was now in search of a Plan B, which would not replace the Plan but would complement it. In particular, he was interested in the development of more sophisticated financial models that would help with more effective business planning. When challenged about the threat of competition from Asia, he retorted that their absence at the Plastic Mouldings Traders Association conference had been rather conspicuous. In terms of the next five years the Plan suggested that the time was not right in terms of sales and costs to invest in expensive technology. However, when the time was right his preference would be to bring in a consultant to carefully manage the change he envisaged. He favoured a five-stage approach to change, which had worked effectively 15 years ago when the new production line was introduced. In the short term, though, it was important to consolidate the strengths of the business.

Bobby was initially reticent to talk, appearing to live in his brother's shadow. However, with encouragement he began to talk very freely about his hopes and even dreams for HPP. He was disparaging about the Plan, questioning its relevance and its predictive capabilities. He mumbled that what his father had taught him was not the importance of numbers but the importance of people. 'People make our products, people sell our products, and people buy our products – that's my plan.' He explained that every day he would tour the site talking to employees. His brother thought he was time-wasting, but he would always respond that he was listening to the business talking. He was popular with employees and was beginning to hear concerns from employees about the likelihood of future generations working at HPP. He had deliberately located his office alongside the sales and marketing office. The recurrent message from that office was that there were many requests for small plastic mouldings, but that reluctantly they had to turn away this business because the company was concentrating upon large production runs. His fact-finding trip to Taiwan had left him anxious. He had seen the new highly automated factories and knew that HPP would be unable to compete and – more troublingly – could no longer afford the investment in advanced manufacturing technology in order to compete. He explained that for some months he had been in a deep depression but that the solution had emerged out of an informal discussion with staff in the canteen the previous month.

They had been asking for advice on how they could set up their own businesses in order to serve the lucrative and expanding small-production-run market. At this point he began to see a very different future for HPP. Parts of the manufacturing site could be sold to employees who would operate independently of HPP but still gain the benefits of being on a single site, possibly subcontracting personnel and sales functions back to HPP. These businesses would be less susceptible to overseas competition and the existing technology would be an asset rather than a liability, in terms of small-scale production runs. He believed there was an urgency, but was also interested in getting into a serious dialogue with their five main clients, believing other options might arise out of such discussions.

Case study questions

1 Evaluate the visions of Charlie and Bobby in terms of their strengths and weaknesses.

2 Which of the brothers is more likely to favour planned change and which is more likely to favour emergent change?

3 If you were the consultant, what advice would you give to the brothers about strategic change in Higsons?

DISCUSSION QUESTIONS

1 Why is there a lack of any consensus in academic writing about strategic management?

2 Why do senior managers employ the rhetoric of revolutionary change when evolutionary change appears to be the organisational norm?

3 As an employee, would you prefer to work in an organisation which favoured a planned approach to change or which preferred an emergent approach to change?

4 Why have mergers and acquisitions remained popular if the empirical evidence suggests that they invariably fail?

KEY READINGS

BURNES, B. (2009) *Managing change: a strategic approach to organisational dynamics.* 5th ed. Harlow: FT Prentice Hall.

Burnes has resolutely avoided the fashion for critiquing Lewin and planned approaches to change. The ongoing debate about planned change and emergent change appears to have become more balanced in recent years. In particular, Burnes devotes a chapter to evaluating emergent change. The chapter compares and contrasts planned change and emergent change in an informed manner.

MINTZBERG, H., AHLSTRAND, B. and LAMPEL, J. (2009) *Strategy safari: the complete guide through the wilds of strategic management.* 2nd ed. London: FT Prentice Hall.

The pluralism of this book is highly compatible with the pluralism of this managing change textbook. The authors are very clear that there is no one best way either to study or undertake strategic management. Consequently the book is organised around ten major schools of strategic management. The style is highly readable and engaging and at times provocative.

PETTIGREW, A., THOMAS, H. and WHITTINGTON, R. (eds) (2002) *Handbook of strategy and management.* London: Sage Publications Ltd.

The volume of strategy literature and the volume of many strategy textbooks can be daunting for anyone outside this specialism. However, this handbook, edited by respected academics in the strategy and management field, offers an informative collection of readings, giving a flavour of the many debates that shape thinking about strategy and management.

CHAPTER 8

Group- and team-level change

INTRODUCTION

This chapter focuses upon groups and teams within processes of organisational change. The downside of discussions about strategic change in the previous chapter was that the involvement of groups and teams was downplayed. Groups have been referred to as the 'building blocks' of organisations (Thompson and McHugh 2009), and the primary work group has been described as the most important subsystem within an organisation (Burke 2008). Equally, emphasis upon individuals (the focus of the next chapter) can downplay the involvement of groups and teams, with Andriopoulos and Dawson (2009) warning about the overemphasis upon individuals in Western cultures. Coghlan (1994) suggested that understanding organisational change involves an understanding of how individuals react to change, as well as how groups and teams function and deal with change. This suggests that this chapter and the next chapter need to be regarded as closely connected. In this chapter and the next chapter the focus is primarily upon hierarchical levels, which may be differentiated from the subsystems that make up an organisation as a living system: individuals, working teams, interdepartmental groups and organisations (Coghlan and Rashford 2006).

In the 'Managerial Approaches' section, four influential theories explaining groups and teams in organisations are introduced, before discussion of the involvement of groups and teams in processes of organisational change.

Socio-technical systems are introduced as an approach that places emphasis upon teamworking. In the 'Critical Perspective', theories of groups and teams are critiqued and the tyranny of teamworking ideology is highlighted.

MANAGERIAL APPROACHES

GROUPS AND TEAMS IN ORGANISATIONS

There is a tendency to treat groups and teams as indistinguishable; however, in terms of academic study, differentiating these terms – as depicted in Box 8.1 – is informative.

Box 8.1 Defining groups and teams (Clegg et al 2008, p92)

Definition of a group
… two or more people working towards a common goal, but there is no psychological contract between them; the outcomes are less dependent on all the members working together, and there is usually no shared responsibility and accountability for outcomes.

Definition of a team
… two or more people psychologically contracted together to achieve a common organisational goal in which all individuals involved share at least some level of responsibility and accountability for the outcome.

The definitions in Box 8.1 highlight similarities and differences between groups and teams. Although all teams are by definition groups, not all groups are teams. Often emphasis is placed upon the applied work-based nature of teams, with teams focusing upon specific outputs and held accountable for the completion of their output (Weiss 2001). Social psychologists tend to be interested in groups and group work, whereas managers are primarily interested in teams and effective teamworking (Brooks 2008). As the early pioneering work of Lewin made reference to 'groups' and more recent managing change literature refers to 'teams', the label 'group and team' will be used in this chapter except for those instances where a commentator is referring specifically to a group or a team.

As well as differentiating between groups and teams, it is common to differentiate groups. Classifications include: primary groups versus secondary groups, formal groups versus informal groups, and permanent groups versus temporary groups. Individuals will belong to many different groups inside organisations and in the wider society. For example, an individual may be a member of a large factory trade union. This group may be classified as secondary in terms of limited social interaction among members, formal in terms of being a formalised group, and permanent in the sense that it seeks to tackle ongoing issues. By contrast, the same individual may be a member of the group campaigning for a vending machine in the staff room. This group is a primary group in that the six employees lobbying for the vending machine regularly interact with each other. It is informal in that the group simply came together out of their collective annoyance at the lack of a vending machine. And it is temporary because the group will cease to exist once the vending machine has been installed or if it has no success in the campaign. The important point here is not so much to note the variety of classifications as to acknowledge that groups and teams differ considerably contingent upon a range of variables, such as type of task, type of organisation, level in the hierarchy and sectoral background. Every group and team is unique in a manner similar to the unique nature of organisations and individuals.

The writings of Asch (1952), Tuckman (1965), Janis (1972) and Belbin (1981) are major milestones informing understanding about groups and teams in organisations. These writers largely favour a human or neo-human relations approach in terms of Huczynski's (2006) popular management ideas families, featured in Chapter 3. In the following discussion the contribution of each writer is summarised and the implications of their work for managing change signposted.

Asch (1952) conducted one of the most frequently cited studies in this field, asking individuals in a group to judge the lengths of three different lines. Seven of the eight individuals gave the wrong answer, about which two lines were the same length, in collusion with the researcher. The answers of the seven tended to influence the answer of the eighth individual (unaware of the research), who often gave a wrong answer in order to conform to the group norm. Norms represent '… the tacit and unspoken assumptions and informal rules, the meaning of which people negotiate in their everyday interactions' (Clegg et al 2008, p218). Coghlan (1994) has referred to them as the 'unwritten rules' and 'atmosphere' of the group. Norms are only guides or expectations about behaviour, offering potential indications as to how others will behave; however, researchers found that group norms exert a considerable influence over individuals. Group norms have been identified as being very influential in organisational change processes, and they are discussed further in the next sub-section with reference to the work of Lewin.

Another important contribution to understanding groups was the identification of the concept of groupthink by Janis (1972). Groupthink occurs when group members' motivation for unanimity and agreement overrides their evaluation of the risks and benefits of alternative choices. Janis demonstrated real-life policy-making groups making poor choices. He cited the highly visible example of US foreign policy fiascos, such as that of the Bay of Pigs in the 1960s. The symptoms of groupthink that he identified were: the illusion of invulnerability, assumptions of morality, rationalisations, stereotyping, self-censorship, and illusions of unanimity, mind-guarding and direct pressure. The concept still appears relevant today when analysing irrational senior management decisions in teams that are composed of apparently able and rational individual senior managers. Journal Research Case 8.1 is intriguing in terms of the level of access gained to a senior management team.

JOURNAL RESEARCH CASE 8.1

Beta Co.

Paper title: Confronting strategic inertia in a top management team: learning from failure
Sector: Publishing
Research methods: Multiple methods including interviews and workshop activities.
Authors: Hodgkinson, G.P. and Wright, G.
Year: 2002
Journal details: *Organization Studies*. Vol 23, No 6. pp949–977.

Commentary: The case study of Beta Co. is referred to here because the authors gained access to the workings of a senior management team. Many of the issues raised in this case study are, however, equally relevant to the discussion about organisational learning in Chapter 14. Beta Co. represents a pseudonym for a global publishing business, which was described as having a reasonably secure short-term future but a highly uncertain longer-term future. The authors focused their qualitative research upon the senior management team, including the chief executive officer. They were working with the senior management team and facilitating the use of scenario-planning techniques and related procedures. The authors admit that their attempts were largely unsuccessful. But they offer extensive discussions of their interactions with the senior management team and use theories to explain the defensive avoidance strategies at work. They argue that the reality of a team faced with an uncertain future proved too stressful for the team members, giving rise to a variety of coping strategies.

Tuckman (1965) made an important contribution to understanding group development, proposing that permanent groups go through four stages of development, which he labelled as forming, storming, norming and performing. In the case of temporary groups there was believed to be a fifth stage: adjournment (Tuckman and Jensen 1977). Coghlan (1994) has suggested that when using groups as a medium and target of change, there is a need for attention to forming and maintaining groups in order to enable them to function effectively; in this way the process of group formation is dynamic in a manner similar to processes of organisational change.

Belbin (1981) proposed a typology of personality-based team roles through his observations of managers' participation in training course activities at the Henley Centre. Belbin (1981) was interested in what team roles needed to be covered in order to make an effective team. He identified nine roles in an effective team: co-ordinator, shaper, 'plant', monitor/evaluator, implementer, teamworker, resource investigator, completer/finisher and technical specialist. The typology acknowledged that one team member may cover the weakness of another team member and vice versa. In terms of organisational change, the typology highlights the roles required in terms of selecting an effective change team.

GROUP AND TEAM INVOLVEMENT IN ORGANISATIONAL CHANGE

In organisations undergoing change it is unrealistic to work with every single one of the individuals who comprise the organisation, consequently there is a heavy reliance upon the use of work groups (Burke 2008). The following discussion focuses upon four themes: the contribution of Lewin, groups and teams within organisational development, self-managed teams and the emergence of change teams.

The pioneering work of Kurt Lewin became a catalyst for the group dynamics school. This school emphasised the role of groups in organisational change and highlighted how groups exert pressure on members to conform to group norms. Lewin was influential in encouraging an appreciation of the role of groups in achieving organisational change. Lewin's main concern was the resolution of social conflict, particularly among minority or disadvantaged groups. He maintained 'that it is fruitless to concentrate on changing the behaviour of individuals because the individual in isolation is constrained by group pressures to conform' (Burnes 2004, p983). Group dynamics was one element of his integrated planned approach to change, which also included field theory, action research and the three-step model (Burnes 2004). Group dynamics sought to bring about organisational change through teams and groups in the belief that achieving organisational change through changing the behaviour of individuals was futile; instead the focus should be at group level, in terms of changing the group's norms (Burnes 2009a). In the context of groups, norms exert a considerable unacknowledged influence upon individuals, particularly in terms of how people respond to organisational change. Burnes (2004, p480), in reappraising Lewin's work, highlights the centrality of groups in organisational change processes:

> [Lewin] demonstrated that the most effective method of convincing people to change their behaviour was by providing groups with information for them to evaluate and discuss, and letting the group come to its own decision. Once the decision had been made by the group, it exerted a strong pressure on all the individuals concerned to adhere to the group's decision.

Burnes (2004, p986) clarified why Lewin advocated the often derided 'refreezing' element of his three-step model: 'Lewin saw successful change as a group activity, because unless group norms and routines are also transformed, changes to individual behaviour will not be sustained.' The frequently misunderstood concept of 'refreezing' needs to be viewed in terms of establishing the new norms and routines. It is unfortunate that general interest in field theory waned with Lewin's death (Burnes 2004) because an appreciation of field theory contributes considerably to the integrated system that Lewin was proposing, with changes in behaviour believed to stem from changes small or large in the forces within the field (Lewin 1947) (force-field analysis is discussed in Chapter 12).

Lewin's pioneering work was taken up and extended by the organisation development (OD) movement. Lewin's work is believed to have had a more pervasive influence upon OD, both directly and indirectly, than any other person (Burke 2008). Cummings and Worley (2008) explain how interpersonal and group process approaches form an integral part of the practice of OD, viewing process consultation, third-party interventions and team-building as among the most enduring OD interventions. These activities may be summarised as follows. Process consultation aids groups in identifying and solving interpersonal problems, which are regarded as often blocking the solution of work-related problems. Third-party intervention is only used in special situations where both parties are willing to engage in a process of direct confrontation, in which case they focus directly upon dysfunctional interpersonal conflict. Finally, team-building is used to improve team performance and help individuals to meet their work needs.

Teamworking has been described as a powerful strategy for managing organisational changes (West et al 2004). Teamworking options for managing change include: self-managed teams and change agency through change teams. Self-managed teams have been defined as: '... teams are responsible, and collectively accountable, for performance and monitoring of one or more tasks (often an entire product or service) and managing interpersonal processes within the team' (Iles and Sutherland 2001, p55). Iles and Sutherland (2001, p55) evaluated the evidence relating to self-managed teams. They cite the research of Cummings and Molloy (1977) and Pearce and Ravlin (1987), highlighting improvements arising out of the introduction of self-managed teams. Beekun (1989) and Macy et al (1994) were conversely more circumspect in their evaluations of self-managed teams. Elmuti (1997), in his paper reviewing the case for and against self-managed teams, is able to draw some relevant conclusions. Overall, Elmuti believed that they can make a positive contribution to organisations.

A change team may be formed specifically to facilitate a change process, with major generic change initiatives such as the learning organisation, TQM and BPR emphasising teamworking. Caldwell (2003a) identified change teams in his fourfold classification of change agents, highlighting their recent emergence and tracing their origins back to Lewin (1947). He identifies a number of explanations for why there has been a shift from individual change agents to change agency as a team process, which may be summarised as follows. The emergence of change teams reflects the growing emphasis upon self-managed teams. Change teams potentially help with co-ordination across an organisation. The complexity and high risk of large-scale change suggests the need for a team-based approach. The emergence of change teams may be explained as a reaction to disillusionment with charismatic or heroic leadership. The formation of change teams allows the combination of internal and external expertise. Finally, dispersing change agency to teams helps to institutionalise behavioural change. Caldwell (2003a, p139) regards the learning organisation, discussed in the Organisational Change Field Guide (see Appendix), as the most influential model of a change agency team-based approach.

SOCIO-TECHNICAL SYSTEMS APPROACHES

A socio-technical system is 'an approach to work design in which the technical and the social/psychological aspects of the overall workplace are given equal weight and are designed at the same time to take each other into account' (Watson 2006, p336). Socio-technical systems are pertinent to this chapter because of their emphasis upon teamworking. Trist and Bamforth (1951) were the earliest proponents of this approach. Trist, a social psychologist, and Bamforth, an ex-miner, studied the advent of mechanisation in the mining industry. They developed the concept of the working group, which they regarded as an interdependent socio-technical system. The long-wall method of coal mining that they studied was being facilitated through mechanisation, such as pneumatic drills and conveyor belts. Under this system miners were far more closely supervised than in the past, when they had used picks to extract the coal and they were able to organise themselves. Despite mechanisation the anticipated benefits had not been realised. Analysis of these mining studies suggested that '... change initiatives which focus on either the purely technical or social aspects of work are likely to have limited "success" as they create a situation where the whole is sub-optimized for developments in one dimension' (Andriopoulos and Dawson 2009, p50).

In terms of managing change, this approach suggested a need to equally weight the social and technical aspects of work and many subsequent studies developed from this starting point. For example, high-performance work systems can be traced back to the early UK research. The characteristics of high-performance work systems include: a way of thinking about an organisation, principles for designing an organisation, a process for applying the design principles and a variety of organisational design principles (Nadler and Gerstein 1992). Socio-technical design relied upon teams in managing interdependent work, in particular empowering teams to manage work processes and flows. More recently, lean manufacturing and the Toyota Production System may be viewed as developments of socio-technical systems.

CRITICAL PERSPECTIVE

The following critical perspective offers a critique of groups and teams research and highlights the tyranny of teamworking ideology.

CRITIQUE OF GROUPS AND TEAMS RESEARCH

Lewin made a convincing case, cited earlier, for changing individuals through groups, highlighting how groups shape the norms of individuals about organisational change. This approach was viewed within a broader context of studying groups and teams within organisations. The historical origins of group-level analysis in psychology are informative. The experiences of the world wars shaped psychological research and theorising about groups, with individuals increasingly viewed from the perspective of the larger entity of the group (Rose 1989). War provided both the impetus to research group processes and the means by which real groups could be researched. Behaviour during combat was found to relate to bonds between soldiers, rather than to the unreal and distant principles and causes of war (Rose 1989). These insights help to place in historical context the body of management and organisational behavioural work that developed in relation to groups and teams.

> The concept of the group was to become the organising principle of psychological and psychiatric thought concerning the conduct of the individual... The invention of the 'group', the conception of 'social' or 'human' relations as key determinants of individual conduct, were the most consistent lessons of the psychological and psychiatric experience of war. (Rose 1989, p48)

The historical perspective developed by Rose suggests that management and organisational behaviour was at a crossroads at the time of the world wars and that the unit of analysis became the group, rather than the individual. History also helps to explain how groups and teams research tended to be preoccupied with performance: 'the problems of economic reconstruction would insert these issues of the group into the heart of economic debate, managerial practice and psychological innovation' (Rose 1989, p52).

Since the Second World War, individuals have increasingly been understood in relation to the groups to which they belong. This may be regarded as a more sophisticated and contextualised approach than understanding individuals in isolation. However, the concern is that we begin to lose sight of individuals when the unit of analysis becomes the group. Also, the reification of the group as a manageable thing suffers from deficiencies similar to the reification of organisations as manageable things.

While group and team theories featured in the 'Managerial Approaches' section have proved influential, they have also attracted criticisms. The research of Asch (1952) remains an important milestone in the study of conformity within groups. However, since the early 1950s levels of conformity have declined, with levels of conformity varying dependent upon the collectivist or individualistic nature of national cultures (Robbins and Judge 2009). Again groupthink, identified by Janis (1972), usefully highlights how groups may marginalise a lone dissenter. However, groupthink is not applicable to all groups; it tends to occur in situations where group members have a positive image of their group that they wish to protect from external threat (Robbins and Judge 2009).

The Tuckman (1965) model of group development appears eminently plausible, which may explain its longevity. However, Tuckman never viewed the model as being universally applicable. Reynolds (1994) and Gersick (1988) highlighted an alternative 'punctuated equilibrium' model of group development. Belbin's (1981) typology remains very popular with practitioners, whereas most academics are sceptical about its academic validity, due to the data being gathered in the artificial setting of training games, rather than in real-life groups. Thompson and McHugh (2009, p373) suggest that it '... is difficult to use outside training sessions and is mainly useful as a heuristic device for scripting managerial behaviour'.

While groups and teams can make a positive contribution to organisations, the concept of 'social loafing' has been cited as an example of the potentially negative side of group work, particularly pertinent to the practical challenges of managing change. Social loafing has been defined as 'the tendency for individuals to expend less effort when working collectively than when working individually' (Robbins and Judge 2009, p333). Social loafing is more colloquially known as 'shirking', 'bludging', 'free riding', or 'laziness' (Clegg et al 2008). Ringelmann, a German psychologist, identified social loafing in the late 1920s, at a time when organisational change was less prevalent. He was able to measure individual and group performance through a rope-pulling task, and subsequent replications of his study broadly supported the conclusion that 'group performance increases with group size, but the addition of new members to the group has diminishing returns on productivity' (Robbins and Judge 2009, p334).

THE TYRANNY OF TEAMWORKING IDEOLOGY

Managerial approaches are informed by positive assumptions about groups and teams. There is an almost evangelical feel to the groups and teams literature, implying that anyone who is not part of a group is in some way deviant. In a polemical yet practical critique of teamwork, Robbins and Finley (1998, p21) suggest that 'despite human beings' attraction to belonging to a team, we are not willing to uproot our individual lives and priorities for the sake of some lousy workgroup'. They explain why they believe teams do not work. Among the problems identified are mismatched needs, unresolved roles, personality conflicts and bad leadership.

The title of this section is based upon a polemical paper by Sinclair (1992) questioning the ubiquitous nature of teamworking in organisations. Her concerns are that despite research and theory-building about teamwork in many disciplines, teamworking ideology prevails among management consultants, experts, trainers and educators. This ideology in terms of teams results in what is labelled as constructive and disruptive being determined by the dominant power-holders. Marshak (2006), in his discussion of covert processes at work with regard to organisational change, highlights covert issues in work groups. He regards overt issues as being task related and rational and defined through group norms as being legitimate. Whereas covert issues, such as relationship-related and emotionally based issues, are defined through group norms as illegitimate and inappropriate. Marshak believes that it is important to address these covert dynamics of organisational change, although this is not necessarily the norm.

Sinclair regards the benefits of teams as occupying a central and unquestioned place in changing organisations, with team ideology espoused consistently. The team is invariably presented as the solution to the problems of organisational life. The prevalence of teamworking ideology is relevant to the theory as well as the practice of teamworking. Knights and McCabe (2003) acknowledge that despite the popularity of practical applications of teamworking, the development of theoretical analysis has been fairly leisurely. They acknowledge that contingency thinking has been the norm, with analyses invariably concluding that teamworking is always contingent upon its context.

In reviewing a discursive and often contradictory literature, the authors deliberately restrict themselves to manufacturing, by way of focusing and also in order to inform their own study of teamworking in the automobile industry. They use the concepts of power, knowledge and subjectivity to offer new theoretical insights into teamworking with regard to human relations perspectives, socio-technical systems approaches and lean production.

The human relations perspective was introduced in Chapter 3. The analysis of Knights and McCabe suggests that knowledge was derived from the bank wiring experiments with regard to how informal norms exercise considerable power over group members through conformity to peer pressure. Through managers joining the groups they could reconstitute groups into teams and influence how team members saw themselves and their work (subjectivity).

The influential socio-technical systems approach was featured in the 'Managerial Approaches' section. However, Knights and McCabe (2003) question the historiography of this landmark in the study of organisational change. They highlight that the autonomous, self-regulated teamworking of the miners could be viewed as their exercise of power drawing upon their knowledge of the work. Teamworking helped to make the work safer and more socially collaborative. While this analysis highlights the influence of power, knowledge and subjectivity, the traditional conception of socio-technical systems emphasised systems concepts – equilibrium and integration.

Knights and McCabe (2003) highlight the Japanese approach to teamworking, known as 'lean production' (see Organisational Change Field Guide in the Appendix for further discussion) and promoted as the one best way for car manufacturing (Womack et al 1990). They regard Womack et al's production of teamworking knowledge as assisting managers to exercise power over employees. The implication is that employee subjectivity is realigned with managerial objectives, both in terms of how individuals perform tasks and make sense of their work.

In summary, while teamworking is presented neutrally as a practical solution for workplace problems, it may also be regarded as dominant ideology shaping beliefs about managing and organising. The critical analysis of Knights and McCabe (2003) illustrates how the existence of a dominant teamworking ideology may obscure explanations of teamworking in terms of power, knowledge and subjectivity.

CONCLUDING COMMENTARY

Groups and teams play an important role in managing change, with research since the world wars helping to explain group dynamics in general and group dynamics in particular with reference to organisational change. Lewin was a great advocate of organisational change through groups and it was his legacy that was to inform the organisational development movement. Groups and teams offer an opportunity for employees to be involved in organisational change, which is very evident in undertaking change agency through change teams. In pragmatic terms, groups and teams are likely to remain the building blocks of organisations, and in this sense they remain an integral element of any thorough understanding of managing change. The caveats are that the diversity of individuals who comprise groups and teams may be overshadowed when the unit of analysis is the group or team. This was particularly prevalent in the notion of the tyranny of the team. The apparently neutral concept of the team may mask more subtle processes of power, knowledge and subjectivity.

CASE STUDY: APPLYING THEORY TO PRACTICE

All change in the technical support team

A total of 250 people work at the head office of the Mighty Lemon Drop Company (MLDC). The head office covers all the functional areas of the business, such as personnel, marketing and finance, and has been located on the same site for the last 30 years. It has something of a hierarchical feel to it, with the more senior staff located at higher levels in the multi-storey building. The technical support team are located in the basement of the building. In their large, artificially lit rooms there are many metal shelves on which computers and parts are stacked neatly. The rooms have also been personalised with old chairs and equipment salvaged from the building over the years, and unlike the rest of the building there are many inappropriate posters.

The technical support team provide day-to-day technical support for the whole head office. The workload of the team has increased over the years, reflecting the increasing workplace emphasis upon IT, although more strategic large-scale IT projects have been subcontracted to external providers. The members of the team used to be Alf, Bill, Jane and Ted. Bill was the team leader and was referred to as Head Technician. Jane's specialism was software problems, whereas Ted's specialism was hardware problems. Alf was part of the team, although he had no real interest in IT and so would deal with more DIY-oriented technical matters - it was privately acknowledged that he was working his time until retirement in two years. They were known as the TT team,

although nobody could remember why. As a team the four of them had been together for five years and had become quite close over that time.

Apart from software and hardware upgrades that they instigated, they tended to be fairly reactive in how they operated. A wide range of head office staff would contact them through a range of communication channels and in a variety of emotional states. A member of the TT team would then go and sort out the problem as best he or she could.

Bill tended to have good days and bad days. Unfortunately, most days were bad days. He was responsible for checking that requests for assistance were dealt with promptly, but he did not take this responsibility very seriously. He was very capable and would help a small number of staff in the head office who he had got to know well over the years. The rest of the time he could be found slumped in his armchair smoking - which was strictly against MLDC policy - and staring into space. Other team members over time had begun to follow this example. The team were even once disciplined for drinking at work, which was also against company policy. Despite these problems effective technical support was provided, although in a very reluctant and reactive manner.

It was the early retirement of Alf on health grounds that presented senior management with an opportunity for change. They were due to introduce an intranet for company communications, and although the development work would be subcontracted, they wanted the intranet to be run and maintained in-house. Also, they wanted to shake up the technical support function but were aware that lax ways of working had become deeply ingrained.

They used the spare staff establishment post to appoint Felicity. She was not to report to Bill but to report directly to the head of the personnel department. She took over one of the other rooms in the basement. These new arrangements were communicated to the TT team who, although they were initially annoyed, claimed not to care.

There were elements of Felicity's role that were not disclosed to the TT team. Primarily, she represented the new model of IT support – she had an extensive budget and postgraduate qualifications in IT. Her office was refurbished to a high standard, sharing the same corporate livery as the other offices in the building. On the door there was a bold metallic sign proclaiming IT Solutions, with the slogan underneath 'Here to help'. She was careful to define her role in terms of the newly introduced intranet site. However, more subversively, she began placing practical guides to IT problems onto the intranet. She also established message boards that encouraged people

to anonymously post discussions about their IT problems. It was not long before the whole company was reading posts about 'the dreary people who live in the dungeon'. In her role as moderator she would then ask TT team members if they wanted these offensive messages removed.

Over time things began to change in the basement. Jane spent more and more time with Felicity in the IT solutions office and asked if there was any way she could be seconded into the office. Bill left MLDC to study philosophy as a full-time student. When Ted and Jane requested that their office be refurbished, it was suggested that this might be the opportunity to rededicate the whole of the basement to the challenges of IT solutions.

Case study questions

1　Is the TT team a team or a group?

2　How could the concept of group norms be used to describe the behaviours of the TT team before the arrival of Felicity?

3　How could the concept of group norms be used to describe the behaviours of the TT team after the arrival of Felicity?

4　In what alternative ways could the introduction of the intranet have been managed?

DISCUSSION QUESTIONS

1　Why do writers attempt to differentiate between groups and teams, and does such differentiation help or hinder the study of managing change?

2　Why is teamworking such a popular managerial approach?

3　Do you believe groups and teams will play a greater or a lesser role in managing change in the future?

4　Why is an ideology of teamworking regarded as problematic?

KEY READINGS

ANDRIOPOULOS, C. and DAWSON, P. (2009) *Managing change, creativity and innovation*. London: Sage Publications Ltd.

The authors devote a substantial chapter to coverage of groups and teamworking, highlighting the centrality of teams in change, creativity and innovation. The book benefits from balancing the many relevant theories with practical application.

COGHLAN, D. and RASHFORD, N.S. (2006) *Organizational change and strategy: an interlevel dynamics approach*. London: Routledge.

This is an intriguing book that brings together many contemporary debates in a highly innovative manner. The authors have consistently written about groups and organisational change and this book draws upon their earlier work. The book also draws upon their action research interventions in order to present the reader with an integrated inter-level model of organisational change.

KNIGHTS, D. and MCCABE, D. (2003) *Organization and innovation: guru schemes and American dreams*. Maidenhead: Open University Press.

Knights and McCabe offer a coherent and consistent critique of many of the managing change initiatives featured in this textbook. Their chapter on teamworking and resistance is particularly relevant to debates featured in this chapter.

CHAPTER 9

Individual-level change

LEARNING OUTCOMES

After reading this chapter you should be able to:

- appreciate the concept of individual differences
- understand how individual perceptions inform change processes
- differentiate explanations of individual change processes
- review approaches to managing individuals through organisational change
- identify covert dimensions of organisational change
- question the role of pain in organisational change.

INTRODUCTION

The central theme of this chapter is the involvement of individuals in processes of organisational change. This micro-level focus may be contrasted with the macro-level focus upon strategic-level change featured in Chapter 7. The downside of systemic/strategic accounts of change is that individuals are marginalised through terminology, such as the 'people problem' (see for example Clegg and Walsh 2004) or the 'soft stuff' (see for example Jorgensen et al 2009).

Organisations only change and act through their members, and even collective activities that take place in organisations are the result of an amalgamation of the activities of individuals (George and Jones 2001). In this chapter, individuals are valued and placed at the centre of the analysis. This level of analysis was evident in the earliest managing change writings (see Lewin 1947) and has been identified as the major theme in popular management writing (Huczynski 2006). Until recently there has been a deficit of writing about individual-level change with regard to managing change. This has been explained by French and Delahaye (1996) as a consequence of managing change developing at a group or systems level. However, even differentiation between organisational change at group or systems levels is absent from much of the managing change literature, with writers conflating the process of change at different levels into one seamless series of events (Randall 2004).

In the 'Managerial Approaches' section, unique differences that differentiate individuals are acknowledged with particular emphasis placed upon different perceptions of organisational change. This is a precursor to explaining processes of individual change, and these differences and processes suggest the need to manage individuals through organisational change initiatives. The 'Critical Perspective' highlights often-overlooked covert dimensions of organisational change and questions the espoused role of pain in processes of organisational change.

MANAGERIAL APPROACHES

UNDERSTANDING INDIVIDUALS

As Clegg et al (2008, p5) suggest, 'being an individual means that each body – and all that it contains – is as unique as the fingertips we leave or the DNA that constructed us'. As well as acknowledging the diversity of individuals within organisations, there is a need to acknowledge that broader social factors help to shape individuals (Thompson and McHugh 2009). Individual differences often feature prominently in the study of organisational behaviour (OB). Typically OB textbooks devote chapters to different individual variables, such as motivation, attitudes, perception, learning, values and personality. While these themes will feature as part of broader discussions in this textbook, it is not feasible to cover them all in detail. However, by way of illustration, perception explains how individuals in the same organisation may interpret the same organisational change in very different ways.

Perception has been defined as '… the process of receiving, attending to, processing, storing, and using stimuli to understand and make sense of our world. The stimuli can be experiences through any and all of the senses such as sight, sound, smell, taste, and touch' (Clegg et al 2008, p664). Perception is often misunderstood as merely our senses – that is, how (and what) we hear or see. However, as the definition suggests, it is concerned more with the interpretation of various sense inputs. Everyday processes of perception are susceptible to distortions (often unacknowledged); these distortions include: stereotyping, the halo effect, the self-fulfilling prophecy, selective perception and projection. In Box 9.1 these distortions in perception are illustrated using hypothetical managing change examples.

Box 9.1 Perceptual distortions (hypothetical managing change examples)

'All change management consultants are only interested in making as much money as possible.' This is an example of a stereotype in terms of using a standardised impression of a group.
'The manager had a university education, so I knew he could manage the complexities of change.' This is an example of the halo effect, which magnifies one characteristic (university education), thus overshadowing other characteristics.
'We repeatedly reassured employees that we anticipated Project Hercules would be successful – and it was successful.' This is an example of expectancy – in particular, the self-fulfilling prophecy.

Employees help to fulfil the prophecy that Project Hercules will be successful because they believe it will be successful.

'While the new office is ergonomically designed and employs state-of-the-art technology with plenty more space for employees, I believe the magenta paint on the door of the toilets will lead to colleagues rejecting these new offices.' This is a caricatured example of selective perception by which an employee pays more attention to the colour of the toilet door than to the office as a whole.

'If only Project Daisy had commanded top management support, it would have succeeded.' This is an example of projection, which often involves blaming others rather than taking responsibility for a situation such as the demise of Project Daisy.

In considering the examples cited in Box 9.1, the issue is not about the accuracy of the statements as much as the ways in which individuals often unconsciously distort their perception of an individual or a situation. The implication is that each individual maintains their personal interpretation of change and what it means to them (Doyle 2001). Coghlan and Rashford (2006) highlighted the centrality of perception in processes of mandated change, linking the perception of the change, assessment of impact and the individual's response. They regard the perception of an organisational change as comprising the meaning the change has for those mandated to change, the degree of control individuals have over the change and the degree of trust individuals have in those mandating the change. They viewed perception as informing the assessment of the impact of the change, which leads to responses that can range from embracing the change to open opposition. In Journal Research Case 9.1, perceptions of organisational change within American hospitals are featured.

◉ JOURNAL RESEARCH CASE 9.1

American hospitals

Paper title: Perceptions and misperceptions of major organizational changes in hospitals: do change efforts fail because of inconsistent organizational perceptions of restructuring and reengineering?

Sector: Healthcare

Research methods: 208 individuals interviewed at 11 hospitals, documentary sources reviewed.

Authors: Walston, S.L. and Chadwick, C.

Year: 2003

Journal details: *International Journal of Public Administration*. Vol 26, No 14. pp1581–1605.

Commentary: The authors demonstrated that employees' perceptions of organisational change differed from the objective outcomes of change and that these misunderstandings had negative implications for the performance and sustainability of change efforts. They (2003, pp1582/1583) identified four important factors that they believed '… may influence these perceptions: (1) the degree to which change effort goals are seen as balanced; (2) the perceived consistency of change effort intensity; (3) persons' level in the organisational hierarchy; and (4) the passage of time'. These factors are informative in considering perceptions of organisational change in different contexts and at different levels. They concluded that the research suggested that employees are often unaware of positive effects of restructuring efforts and, contrary to reality, may believe that cost and quality have deteriorated when it has improved.

The research findings reported in Journal Research Case 9.1 have implications for many of the managing change debates featured in this textbook, such as leading change and communicating change. However effectively a change is led or communicated, perception has an important role to play in how it is interpreted.

EXPLAINING PROCESSES OF INDIVIDUAL CHANGE

The diversity of individuals is mirrored in their diverse experiences of change, and in this way change can be a threat or an opportunity, a cause of mourning or celebration, surprising or predictable, controlled or uncontrolled (Antonacopoulou and Gabriel 2001). Individual changes are an inevitable process for everybody, with changes ranging from major-life adjustments to more trivial everyday changes. The Social Readjustment Rating Scale (Holmes and Rahe 1967) famously attributed values, in terms of their severity, to adjustments required after individuals experience different life events, such as the death of a partner or being sacked from work. This helps both to differentiate everyday changes that occur on a regular basis from those that occur far less regularly and to begin to differentiate the impact upon individuals of such changes.

Elrod and Tippett (2002), in their review of human responses to change and transition, identified different models of the change process. Two of their main conclusions were that most models followed Lewin's (1947) three-step model of change and that the models described a degradation of capabilities in the intermediate stages of change processes. This meant that things often got worse before they got better. The three-step model of change is a useful starting point in explaining processes of individual change. In the three-step model Lewin renamed methods that had been used by Wesley 200 years earlier and described by Aristotle earlier still (Huczynski 2006). Lewin intended the three-step model to be integrated with field theory, group dynamics and action research as elements comprising the planned approach to change (Burnes 2009a). More recently the three-step model has been applied at group and organisational levels of analysis (see Hendry 1996 and Cummings 2002 for overviews). The three-step model involves the three steps of unfreezing, moving and refreezing. The first two steps created conditions for change, with the third step stabilising change that had occurred. Lewin recommended the three-step model when one was seeking to change strongly held attitudes (Huczynski 2006). The first step was concerned with addressing the preference for stability in individuals, which has been applied to inertia at an organisational level. The second step was concerned with individuals changing their attitudes and beliefs and has been applied to planned change at an organisational level. The third step was concerned with refreezing, which involved individuals integrating new behaviours into their overall behaviour and personality that has been applied to cultural change at an organisational level.

Elrod and Tippett's (2002) second conclusion was that there was a degradation of capabilities in the intermediate stages. In attempting to make sense of processes of individual change, the work of Kubler-Ross (1969) has proved to be very influential. In *On Death and Dying* she identified five stages that individuals go through when facing up to death. The first stage was denial and isolation, during which the dying patient questioned the truth of their diagnosis. The second stage was anger, with the dying patient experiencing feelings such as anger, rage, envy and resentment. The third stage was bargaining, with the dying patient attempting to reach an agreement that would postpone the inevitable. The fourth stage was depression, with the dying patient's anger replaced with numbness and growing stoicism. The fifth stage was acceptance, when the dying patient reached a certain degree of quiet acceptance.

It feels disrespectful to compare organisational change to the experiences of a dying person. However, there has been a realisation that, for example, somebody losing their job, which had defined them for the past 20 years, appears to go through similar stages of transition before reaching acceptance. The five stages are not intended to suggest either a rational or uniform process. Individuals will not necessarily go through all five stages, but they are believed to experience at least two of them. Individuals may become stuck at one stage, such as anger, or alternatively move through each stage fairly smoothly. Importantly, rather than thinking about individual change as a single event, individual change is regarded as a process with different individual experiences at different stages of the process of changing. Burke (2008, p91) suggests that 'some organisational members fight the change "to the death", constantly denying that the change is necessary. Others embrace the change readily and move with it. Most people are somewhere in between and move through all stages.' This quotation, with its strange mix of metaphors, is not supported by empirical material, but does highlight differences with regard to how individuals respond to organisational change.

In *Loss and Change*, Marris (1974) discussed individual change with reference to balancing continuity, growth and loss. He identified three types of change: incremental/substitutional changes, growth changes and loss changes (either actual or prospective). Incremental or substitutional changes were concerned with alternative means of meeting familiar needs, such as obtaining a new bicycle or buying a different coat. These changes were routine and continuity was likely to be unbroken. The second type of change, growth changes, can be illustrated in terms of personal growth or security, with ageing fitting this category. Although these changes may be profound for the individual, continuity was still unbroken.

Marris referred to the third type of change as representing loss, such as a death or discrediting of familiar assumptions: 'the thread of continuity in the interpretation of life becomes attenuated or altogether lost ... But if life is to go on, the continuity must somehow be restored' (Marris 1974, p21). These three types of change as identified by Marris offer a categorisation of individual change that explains why change is taking place and deals with both continuities and discontinuities. His central concern was 'how loss disrupts our ability to find meaning in experience, and how grief represents the struggle to retrieve this sense of meaning when circumstances have bewildered or betrayed it' (Marris 1974, p147). The writings of Marris suggest that individuals will be able to cope with many organisational changes, but will struggle where there is a loss of continuity. The loss of continuity may explain the disproportionate reaction/unease when, for example, employees are asked to exchange offices with colleagues. Rashford and Coghlan (1989), in developing their four-stage change process, highlighted denying, dodging, doing and sustaining, which is depicted in Box 9.2.

Box 9.2 Four stages of the change process (based upon Rashford and Coghlan 1989)

Denying stage – paraphrased as 'this does not affect us'
Dodging stage – paraphrased as 'don't get involved'
Doing stage – paraphrased as 'this is very important, we have got to do it now'
Sustaining stage – paraphrased as 'we have a new way of proceeding'

In Box 9.2 a process of changing is evident, moving from initial reticence through to subsequent acceptance in a manner similar to the Kubler-Ross stages of grief. Rashford and Coghlan suggest that these four stages of behavioural reactions to change may be linked to different organisational levels: individual, face-to-face team, group/divisional and organisational strategy/policy. Elrod and Tippett's (2002) conclusion about the degradation of capabilities in the intermediate stages of organisational change may be vividly depicted in the classic change curve, as proposed by Schneider and Goldwasser (1998) (see Figure 9.1).

Figure 9.1 The classic change curve

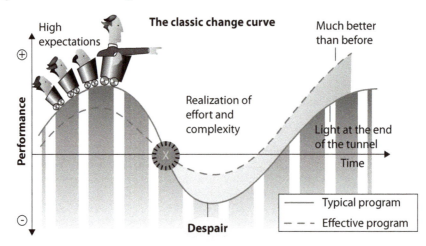

Source: Schneider, D.M. and Goldwasser, G. (1998) Be a model leader of change. *Management Review*. Vol 87, No 3. p41. Reproduced with permission from www. copyright.com.

Schneider and Goldwasser (1998) drew upon their own experiences as consultants working on change projects in their depiction of the change curve (see Figure 9.1). What they effectively convey is the despair that is invariably part of processes of changing that may be related back to the writings of Kubler-Ross (see similar 'valley of despair' discussions in Albrecht 1983 and Loh 1997).

This discussion is an important precursor to any attempt to manage individuals through organisational change, as individuals' experiences of organisational change vary, and vary over time.

MANAGING INDIVIDUALS THROUGH ORGANISATIONAL CHANGE

Woodward and Hendry's (2004, p164) survey found that managing the people aspects of change '… is still ignored by a sizeable minority, with a third of senior managers acknowledging that people aspects were ignored in their change programmes'. However, the desire to help individuals through processes of organisational change is not a new phenomenon and may be traced back to the 1950s and the origins of planned approaches to change. Lippitt et al (1958, p3), in the introduction to their guide to the dynamics of planned change, made reference to a modern world characterised by rapid change.

> The increased need to modify or invent our patterns of behavior and organisation has led naturally to a demand for professional help. This help is now available to assist us in our attempts to meet the problems of personal and social change.

They offer one of the earliest references to change agents, depicting the role of change agents as facilitators of change at different organisational levels. Change agents and agency are the focus of Chapter 17, with many of the discussions in that chapter pertinent to concerns raised in this chapter. In the following discussion, the writings of Bridges, Conner, and Balogun and Hope Hailey inform understanding about managing individuals through change.

Bridges (1986) prophesied that transition management was one of the key executive skills needed in the years ahead. He defined transition as '… a three-part psychological process that extends over a long period of time and cannot be planned or managed by the same rational formula that work with change' (1986, p25). In terms of managing people through such transitions Bridges advocated a three-phase model, with echoes of Lewin's three-step model cited earlier. Firstly, people in transition have to let go of the old situation. Secondly, they have to go through a neutral zone between the old reality and the new reality. Thirdly, they have to commence the new beginning. Individual change involved some form of contemplation as a precursor to changing that ensured the readiness of individuals for organisational change. Bridges' (1995, p32) concern was that 'planners and implementers usually forget that people have to let go of the present first'.

Conner (1998) regarded himself as a perpetual student of human transitions, working initially as counsellor of troubled individuals and families and later as a consultant on organisational transitions. He drew upon the work of Kubler-Ross, cited earlier, in order to identify eight phases people pass through when they feel trapped in change: stability, immobilisation, denial, anger, bargaining, depression, testing and acceptance. However, he contrasted this with five phases of a positive response to change: uninformed optimism, informed pessimism, hopeful realism, informed optimism and completion. Negative or positive responses to change may be explained in terms of individual differences, but equally they will be a consequence of the type of organisational change. A pragmatic view was taken about the willingness of individuals to change: 'change doesn't happen because a chief executive or other top management figure says it should; change happens because the majority of people involved willingly or unwillingly agree to change their behaviour' (Conner 1998, pviii).

Balogun and Hope Hailey (2008, p42) highlighted three design choices with regard to individual involvement in change processes: 'some change processes concentrate on attempting to change the values of employees, others emphasise behavioural change, whilst others may only seek to change the performance objectives or outputs of employees'. There are opportunities for a hybrid of these designs, however each merits clarification. Firstly, individual change through changing attitudes/values is best understood in terms of cultural change (discussed in Chapter 13). This choice encourages individuals to adopt new attitudes and values, such as valuing the customer. The downside with such an approach is that it may be superficial, as achieving real change in the attitudes and values of individuals can be challenging. Secondly, individual change can be achieved through changing behaviours and enforcing new behaviours. The case for this design choice is that individuals only change if the organisational system in which the individual operates is changed (Balogun and Hope Hailey 2008). This view was promoted in the influential writings of Beer et al (1990a).

> The common belief is that the place to begin is with the knowledge and attitudes of individuals. Changes in attitudes, the theory goes, leads to changes in individual behaviour... The theory gets the change process exactly backward. In fact, individual behaviour is powerfully shaped by the organisational roles that people play. (Beer et al 1990a, p159)

This design choice is based upon the belief that through changing roles, relationships and responsibilities attitudes will subsequently change. Whereas the attitude/values-led view of change in focusing upon individuals is based upon the view that behavioural change will follow on from changes in individuals' attitudes. Thirdly, individual change may be achieved through focusing upon performance objectives or outputs. This design choice may result in changing behaviours: 'the target is the outcome of what people do in terms of managerially determined outputs or objectives...' (Balogun and Hope Hailey 2008, p42).

This chapter has focused upon individual change as a component of larger organisational change in the belief that this level of analysis is often overlooked in traditional accounts of managing change. The caveat is that many of the other debates (resistance, power and politics, and ethics) featured in this textbook inform individuals' experience of organisational change. Individuals will always be influenced by broader group, organisational, sectoral and societal forces.

In the following discussion the covert dimensions of organisational change are featured and the espoused role of pain in organisational change is questioned.

COVERT DIMENSIONS OF ORGANISATIONAL CHANGE

In studying managing change by definition the tangible aspects of organisational change attract more attention than the intangible aspects. However, human responses to change will be influenced by a series of conscious and unconscious elements (Antonacopoulou and Gabriel 2001). Six dimensions of organisational change that have been identified are: reasons, politics, inspirations, emotions, mindsets and psychodynamics (Marshak 2006). Reason is viewed as overt whereas the other dimensions are viewed as covert. Invariably a case will be made for organisational change (reasons), as was discussed in Chapter 5. Politics is another covert dimension of organisational change, although its role is increasingly acknowledged (Buchanan and Badham 2008) in accounts of organisational change; this is discussed further in Chapter 15.

Emotions are human responses to a range of events relating to how we feel and how we express and make sense of those feelings (Hancock and Tyler 2009). Emotions are particularly pertinent to organisational change because they offer coping mechanisms enabling individuals to adapt to changing circumstances (Antonacopoulou and Gabriel 2001). The catalyst for academic interest in emotion in general and emotional labour in particular was Hochschild's book *The Managed Heart*. She defined emotional labour as requiring '... one to induce or suppress feeling in order to sustain the outward countenance that produces the proper state of mind in others – in this case, the sense of being cared for in a convivial and safe place' (Hochschild 2003, p6). The book features accounts of flight attendants' experiences of long-haul flights, in which female flight attendants had to hide their emotions when attending to sexist businessmen.

The covert dimension of inspiration can be illustrated in terms of vision statements that '... capture the essence of the desired future state: we will be the best (biggest, smartest, fastest, friendliest, most flexible, most knowledgeable) company in the world' (Marshak 2006, p8). Marshak regards inspiration as not appealing to reason or logic, but instead appealing to people's desire to do good or be part of something bigger than themselves; in this sense inspiration is closely related to culture and cultural change initiatives (see also discussion of visionary leadership in Chapter 10).

Marshak (2006, p11) referred to unexamined or untested assumptions as mindsets: 'because people generally don't think about the underlying frameworks that guide the way they reason and interpret the world, mindsets have a profound (though often covert) impact on the ways we react to change possibilities'. A good example of a mindset would be the notion that managing change is not contingent upon gender. However, organisational scholarship has been criticised as being primarily a literature written by men for men and about men (Calas and Smircich 1996). In terms of managing change, the warning is that 'contemporary literature on the management of organisational change rarely discusses the issue of gender' (Foreman 2001, p215).

A critical gendered perspective is more than an acknowledgement of the under-representation of women change management theorists. Empirical evidence exists to view gender as a central organising principle in organisations (Alvesson and Billing 1997). Paton and Dempster (2002), in their study of the Department of Social Security, raised policy implications for organisations including the existence of a female preference for a more open and collegiate approach to managing change, and the fact that ignoring gender differences disadvantages a significant proportion of the workforce. As well as implications for management practice, their study warns academics against tools for change that 'tend to offer mechanistic, systems-oriented and results-driven solution methodologies and techniques' (2002, p546). Through an analysis of gender, understanding of organisational change and managing change can be enriched (Foreman 2001, p233).

Psychodynamics is the final and most covert dimension of organisational change identified by Marshak. Psychodynamics are concerned with the unconscious dynamics of workplace settings. A psychodynamic framework informs the study of managing change in terms of the interaction of emotion and politics (Vince 2002b). Vince (2002b, p1205), through undertaking his case study research of Hyder plc, suggested a different agenda for the management of change: '... one that focuses less on what to do in order to make change happen, and more on what has already been created that mitigates against change'. In terms of covert dimensions of organisational change, work is ongoing; however, thinking in terms of intangible aspects of organisational change offers a richer understanding of processes of organisational change.

QUESTIONING THE ROLE OF PAIN IN ORGANISATIONAL CHANGE

The prescriptive managing change literature implies that everyone benefits from organisational change initiatives – according to such accounts there appear to be no losers when managing change. However, many of the debates featured in this textbook around power, politics and ethics highlight that there are invariably multiple stakeholders in processes of organisational change and that these stakeholders are inevitably unequal in terms of power and access to resources. It has been suggested that for every change proposed or achieved, someone loses something (Harvey 1990). The following discussion explores this shadow side of managing change. People in the throes of change speak in terms of being diminished, using words such as '... anger, betrayal, shock – in short, they describe dramatic emotions that rarely encompass the positive' (Jick 1990, p404).

This sense of individuals being diminished is likely to be exasperated by popular managerial preferences for initiating constant organisational change. Child (2005, p278) cites the Roman Gaius Petronius Arbiter, as long ago as AD 66, summarising the problem: 'I was to learn later in life that we tend to meet any new situation by reorganising, and a wonderful method it can be for creating the illusion of progress while producing confusion, inefficiency, and demoralisation.' The concern with notions of constant change is that heavy workloads and organisational demands can make individuals less, rather than more, responsive to demands to change (George and Jones 2001) and, in these situations, employee burnout may turn to cynicism. Abrahamson (2004a) identified three symptoms of what he refers to as repetitive change syndrome: initiative overload, change-related chaos and employee burnout. More-knowing practitioner accounts of organisational change do acknowledge despair as part of a process of changing (see Schneider and Goldwasser 1998 cited in the 'Managerial Approaches' section).

The acknowledgement of pain is a recurrent theme within both the practical literature (see for example Kotter 1996; Page 1998) and critical managing change literature (see for example Alvesson and Sveningsson 2008). Conner (1998, p98), who was featured in the 'Managerial Approaches' section, believes that 'orchestrating pain messages throughout an institution is the first step in developing organisational commitment to change'. Grint and Case (1998), in their critical study of BPR, highlighted an espoused view that '… participants have to suffer pain because it is an essential ingredient in improving the character of the individual and the organisation'. Abrahamson (2004b) attributes the origins of the espoused relationship between managing change and pain to Lewin (1947), who argued that without pain there would be no change. While agreeing with Lewin, Abrahamson adds three caveats. Firstly, it is important not to overgeneralise. Secondly, 'no pain, no change' should not become the standard for managing change; and thirdly, 'no pain, no change' cannot remain the standard for managing change.

It is a sad indictment of the state of managing change that Abrahamson, a highly respected scholar, has to question the current pain fetish. The danger in the prescriptive managing change literature is that pain becomes legitimised within managing change processes; see for example the promotion of creative destruction within the innovation literature. Abrahamson (2004a, p93) warns that 'advice on how to change varies quite a bit, but it has three features in common: "Creative destruction" is its motto. "Change or perish" is its justification. And "No pain, no change" is its rationale for overcoming a purportedly innate human resistance to change.'

In *Change without Pain*, Abrahamson (2004b) signposted a very different approach to organisational change, directly contradicting the brutalism of change initiatives of the previous decade, such as lean, six sigma and business reengineering (which are discussed in the Organisational Change Field Guide (see Appendix)). As Abrahamson (2004, ppxii–xiii) wrote, 'if anything, a growing body of careful empirical research, which I refer to throughout this book, supports our gut feeling that in many situations, such highly destructive, destabilising and painful changes can hurt more than they help'. These aspirations are shared in this textbook; it is only through critically questioning popular myths and assumptions that the theory and practice of managing change will develop along the humanistic lines originally intended.

CONCLUDING COMMENTARY

Ongoing processes of change are relevant to everyone. These experiences are influenced by our individual differences in general and our perceptions in particular. The scale of change can vary from everyday changes to life-changing events. Dealing with dying offers insights into how individuals deal with major change, and the study of individual responses to organisational change has been informed by such learning. The emphasis in these accounts is very processual, both in terms of organisational change processes and processes of individual change. What this suggests is that it is very difficult to generalise in terms of individuals' very different experiences of organisational change. However, one of the strengths of acknowledging the diversity of individuals, and their experiences of organisational change is that managers may be able to manage processes of change in a more informed and sensitive manner. Helping individuals through organisational change is not a new development and there certainly is not one best way.

Bridges emphasised letting go of the past, and for Conner the emphasis was upon individuals' different capacities for change. Another potentially fruitful approach highlighted by Balogun and Hope-Hailey was choices around change through values/attitudes, or change through behaviours or change through performance objectives. Engaging with individual-level change requires engagement with the intangible aspects of managing change and recognition of that element of work that has been defined as emotional labour. A mindset exists that pain is a prerequisite of effectively managing change; Abrahamson has done much to challenge this sadly persuasive mindset.

CASE STUDY: APPLYING THEORY TO PRACTICE

Experiencing change in Greenshires County Council

Among other things, the social services department of Greenshires County Council processes documentation relating to elderly people going into care – in particular, the department is responsible for the generation of a contract between the individual, the residential home and the council. The process inevitably generates large amounts of paperwork from a wide range of interested parties. Traditionally, one administrator has been tasked with processing all this paperwork from the initial enquiry through to the time the person takes up residence in his or her new home, and to processing the payments. The process has included gathering reports from social workers, estimates from residential homes and invoices from the council's finance department. The process

is invariably time-consuming and has to be dealt with professionally and sensitively. After many years of working in this way the manager of the department has decided to change the way contracts are processed. His story is told in his own words, together with the stories of two administrators who worked in the department.

Departmental manager's story: I have enjoyed running this department, but it is not the job it used to be. I pride myself that all contracts are processed as quickly and efficiently as possible, and I believe that the low labour turnover reflects a relatively content workforce. My problem in recent months has been that the Head of Finance required me to achieve major cost savings in order to address a significant council budget deficit. I explained that due to demographic changes the contract work was expanding and that administrators were working to full capacity. He was not satisfied with my answer and demanded a 20% cut in labour costs while simultaneously acknowledging that the work of the department will continue to increase. If that was not enough, the council's quality guru has insisted that the department must dramatically improve customer service ratings or face processing work being outsourced to a private contractor who is keen to take over from us. I seriously considered resigning when faced with these challenges, but because of my loyalty to my team, I have decided to go for one last roll of the dice. I decided not to tell my team anything about the organisational politics or potential job losses, but to present the changes as positive improvements to service delivery.

The changes that came into force three months ago are quite radical by our standards. My thinking has been influenced by writings about scientific management I read years ago and more recently in an article by Hamper and somebody who advocated radical change around reengineering processes. The contract generation process has been divided into five stages and a separate team now works on each stage, rather than individuals working on individual cases as they used to in the past. It has been a revelation to me in that I have been able to identify bottlenecks in the process that I never knew existed. Also, there is a progress wall chart in the open-plan office, which allows us all to gauge the progress that we are making. I am currently working on some interesting enhancements to the processes. However, I hear mixed reports from staff, so I have decided to talk to two of the longer-serving administrators.

Administrator's story (Justin Hinds): Yes, it's okay. It took a while for me to get used to it, but I like it. As I think you know, I enjoy my work, but generally I am quite laid back about life. I used to find working on individual cases interesting but it could be very intense. I didn't like the phone calls from the relatives enquiring about the contracts. I'd tell them to chill out, but they just got more uptight. I now work in a small team with Tina, Eric and Paula. We call ourselves the A Team, although officially I think we are the Finance Communications Team. It took a few weeks for us to 'sus' each other out and at first I thought Eric was odd, but it is just his way of working with people. We go for a beer every Friday after work and whinge a bit, but generally the team is upbeat. I don't mind the new open-plan office – although now that I am away from the window, my special plant does not seem to grow so vigorously, and that annoys me. If you'd told me six months ago we would be working in this new way, I would have laughed. That said, I take each day as it comes and life is too short to worry. Somebody told me that the new business processes had been designed by those reengineering blokes, which I thought was probably a good thing. You get an impression of everyone pulling together in the council these days, which must be good. I do think things will get better if we all work together and chill a little.

Administrator's story (Virginia Astley): When you asked to see me, I was going to decline the invitation because I am still very annoyed. I prided myself on my attention to detail and the attentive customer service that I always provided. It was a bombshell when you announced that we had to change because we had failed to deliver effective customer service. On the Friday you made your damning announcement, and on the Monday I came in to work to find all the offices had been refurbished as one open-plan office. My desk used to overlook a lovely little garden. Now I find myself sitting opposite a fire exit. At first I could not comprehend what was happening, and then an intense anger erupted inside me. I apologise most sincerely for kicking the cabinet door – that was probably the lowest point in my 20 years of working here. After my sick leave I have felt a bit more positive, and Justin has helped. All the same, my impression of the new arrangements is that it is a weary rehash of scientific management that my university lecturers were so critical about. I'm in a pleasant enough workgroup with Tracy, Sally and Jane, but they talk a lot about shoes and make-up and to me they are 'bimbos'. When I try and jolly them along, they say that as long as we deal with our bits of 20 contracts a week we are sorted. I have started to go with the flow, or lack of flow [nervous laughter]. What keeps me sane is the knowledge that in six months' time I will be out of here and studying for my PhD. If I had wanted to work in a factory I would have worked at Higson's Plastic Parts (who, incidentally, pay more money).

Case study questions

1 Explain the departmental manager's views in terms of perception.

2 Explain Virginia's transition in terms of Bridges' (1986) model of individual transitions.

3 If you had been the departmental manager, what might you have done differently to have managed this process of change?

DISCUSSION QUESTIONS

1 What happens to an organisation if individuals do not change as part of an organisational change? (Think in terms of specific changes)

2 How can individual perceptions act as an impediment to managing change?

3 Why are the covert dimensions of organisational change frequently neglected?

4 Why is there a strong association between pain and organisational change?

KEY READINGS

ABRAHAMSON, E. (2004) *Change without pain: how managers overcome initiative overload, organizational chaos, and employee burnout.* Boston: Harvard Business School Press.

Abrahamson is a highly respected academic who has papers regularly published in leading management journals. In this accessible book, he argues persuasively against the brutalism of managing change in the 1990s, favouring a far more reasoned and humanistic approach. As the title suggests, organisational change does not need to involve pain – what a refreshing and uplifting message.

HOCHSCHILD, A.R. (2003) *The managed heart: commercialization of human feeling.* 20th Anniversary ed. Berkeley: University of California Press.

This book, which was first published in 1983, encouraged sociologists to engage with workplace emotions. The book coined the phrase emotional labour, which is vividly illustrated through her discussion of the lived experiences of Delta flight attendants.

WILSON, F.M. (2010) *Organizational behaviour and work: a critical introduction*. 3rd ed. Oxford: Oxford University Press.

As the title suggests, this textbook offers a provocative and thought-provoking critical introduction to organisational behaviour. Many of the themes introduced in this chapter, such as perception, gender and emotions, are discussed in detail within this textbook.

PART 3

Managing change

The leadership of change

INTRODUCTION

Increasingly shareholders, politicians and academics have looked to leaders and leadership for solutions to organisational problems. Private sector companies look to new chief executives to lead them out of crisis, while 'super-heads' are appointed to failing schools and hospitals in order to turn them around. It has been suggested that we appear to be witnessing a new form of social theatre in which the heroic leader is a central actor (Ahn et al 2004). Leading appears to have become the new managing, although the study of leadership is not a new phenomenon. Elrod and Tippett (2002 p287) have described '... the art of leadership is the art of guiding others through change'. In this chapter, the focus is upon what we know about leaders and leadership, with specific reference to organisational change.

The 'Managerial Approaches' section begins with a clarification of the meaning of leader and leadership. There is a long history of studying these concepts and major theories are traced chronologically. Recent developments in terms of transformational and visionary leadership are featured. In the discussion of leading change, emphasis is placed upon Kotter's (1996) influential book, which shaped contemporary leading change debates. The 'Critical Perspective' presents a counterpoint to leading change rhetoric, critically questioning Kotter's contribution and the aspirational nature of transformational/visionary leadership.

The shadow side of leadership in terms of potential dangerous, dysfunctional and devious behaviours of leaders is highlighted.

MANAGERIAL APPROACHES

LEADERS, LEADERSHIP AND MANAGEMENT

The terms leader, leadership and management are common parlance both within organisations and among those studying organisations. However, there is merit in defining what is meant by these terms in order to engage with the underlying concepts.

The terms leader and leadership may be differentiated as follows. Clegg et al (2008) define leaders in terms of what they do: leading people as a ruler, inspiring people as a motivator and facilitating or guiding them as a coach or mentor. The emphasis here is upon the role of the person who leads. Whereas leadership may be defined as 'the process of directing, controlling, motivating, and inspiring staff towards the realisation of stated organisational goals' (Clegg et al 2008, p662). Leadership places greater emphasis upon processes and may be undertaken by one person or a group of people.

Northouse (2010) acknowledges similarities between leadership and management in terms of working with people and goal accomplishment. However, he also acknowledges differences between leadership and management. He traces the origins of studying leadership back to the Greek philosopher Aristotle, whereas he cites Fayol as one of the earliest studies of management. He differentiates leadership from management in terms of management emphasis upon planning, organising, staffing and controlling. Kotter (1996) has depicted management as processes keeping a system of people and technology running smoothly, whereas leadership defines the view of the future, aligning people with that vision and inspiring them to make it happen. There is merit in differentiating leadership from management, although equally there will be overlaps (Knights and Willmott 2007; Northouse 2010).

STUDYING LEADERS AND LEADERSHIP

Major generic theories of leadership, which underpin subsequent discussions about leading change, have developed over time in order to explain leadership in organisations. Explanations in this area since the 1900s have tended to focus upon personality traits, styles of leadership and more recently on situation-contingent styles and relations between leaders and group members (Thompson and McHugh 2009). The following discussion offers a chronological overview of different approaches to studying leaders and leadership, relating these theories to the chapter focus of leading change. Trait theories emerged at the beginning of the last century, although they now appear prejudiced and stereotyped. They need to be judged against the historical context of the time in which they were being proposed. Industrial modes of production required leadership and management, fuelling early interest in the development of embryonic leadership theories.

The early traits approaches to leadership were speculative, for example, suggesting that tall men make the best leaders. There was no substantive body of research to support such assertions and their relevance declined over time. Contemporary interest in personality tests and psychometric tests may be regarded as adding a degree of scientific legitimacy to traits approaches, identifying far more subtle traits such as enthusiasm and extroversion. In terms of leading change it is probable that individuals in organisations maintain their own trait-based preferences about leaders, although it may not be expedient to make these preferences explicit. Gladwell (2006), in his discussion of unconscious prejudice, cites a research project he undertook. He polled about half of the companies on the Fortune 500 list. This is a list of the largest corporations in America. He asked each company a series of questions about its chief executive officer (CEO). The survey revealed that CEOs were overwhelmingly white men and that they were virtually all tall. The CEOs were on average just a shade less than six feet, whereas the height of the average male was 5 feet 9 inches.

Behavioural theories known as the styles approach, in the middle of the last century, began to be proposed that offered an alternative to the traits approach, shifting the focus away from the traits of leaders to the behaviour of leaders. Clegg et al (2008, p132) identify two underlying behavioural structures characterising leadership, an orientation towards the following: 'interacting and relating to other human beings' and 'the task at hand, or the technical side of the work'. Unlike much of the early traits-based theorising, these theories were informed by research studies, with two of the most famous studies being the Ohio State studies and the University of Michigan studies. The Ohio State studies were a rejection of attempts to identify leadership traits; instead researchers focused upon leadership behaviours that subordinates identified in their leaders. The Michigan researchers identified employee orientation and production orientation as two significant types of leadership behaviour.

The styles approach has strengths and weaknesses, but overall may be regarded as advancing theorising about leadership. Again this line of thinking informed thinking about leading change; for example Galpin (1996), writing about leadership and the human aspects of change, identified behavioural change as a requirement for change leaders. The dilemma with this type of approach is the tendency to remain silent about contingencies influencing leadership. As Nadler and Tushman (1990, p564) warned, 'different kinds of organisational changes will require very different kinds of leadership behaviour in initiating, energising and implementing the change'.

In the 1960s, researchers began to place much greater emphasis upon understanding leadership in specific situations and with reference to specific contingencies. Fiedler (1964) encouraged an appreciation of contingencies in understanding leadership, developing contingency theory through studying the styles of different leaders in different contexts, with a specific interest in military leaders. The work of Hershey and Blanchard (1969) was influential in encouraging this appreciation that different situations required different kinds of leadership.

More recently path-goal theory made connections with the motivation literature in order to propose leadership theories that enhance employee performance and employee satisfaction. Increasingly environmental contingencies in leading change were being acknowledged. Woodward and Hendry (2004) highlighted the difficulties of defining and resolving all eventualities in organisations undergoing change. Commentators emphasise interaction with different environments as an integral element of leading change:

> The task of discerning external change and translating that discernment into strategies for internal corporate change – in terms of evolving organisational structures, group culture, and styles of personal interaction – stand as one of the most enduring challenges of leadership. (Ahn et al 2004, p121)

There is no consensus in terms of the most effective theory of leadership. However, as with many theories of management and organisational behaviour, theories have evolved historically. Although the theory and practice of leadership may be regarded as a contemporary fashion, there is a need for caution, specifically with regard to the state of academic knowledge about leadership. Grint (2005b, p1), a respected authority on leadership, while acknowledging the increase in leadership research, wrote that: 'We have yet to establish what it is, never mind whether we can teach it or predict its importance.' He (2005b, p1) identified four quite different ways of understanding what leadership is (see Box 10.1).

Box 10.1 Understanding leadership (Grint 2005b)

Person: Is it WHO 'leaders' are that makes them leaders?
Result: Is it WHAT 'leaders' achieve that makes them leaders?
Position: Is it WHERE 'leaders' operate that makes them leaders?
Process: Is it HOW 'leaders' get things done that makes them leaders?

Although the different approaches depicted in Box 10.1 are not as succinct as earlier approaches to leadership, this fourfold typology offers a way forward in beginning to understand the subtleties of leadership in very different situations. There is still a real need for further rigorous research into leadership, rather than being seduced by leadership sound bites, which appear so prevalent at present.

TRANSFORMATIONAL AND VISIONARY LEADERSHIP

In recent decades two approaches to leadership as a means of changing organisations have gained prominence: transformational leadership and visionary leadership. Major interest in transformational leadership can be traced back to the early 1980s, a time when businesses in the West were looking for new solutions to regain competitive advantage. Transformational leadership placed more emphasis upon affective and charismatic elements of leadership than earlier theories. Transformational leadership fitted the needs of work groups, who wanted to be inspired and empowered to succeed in uncertain times (Northouse 2010). In many ways transformational leadership was a variant of the traits approach discussed earlier (Knights and Willmott 2007). Downton (1973) first coined the phrase transformational leadership. However, it was Burns' (1978) study of leadership and followership that gave impetus to transformational leadership.

In particular Burns distinguished between two types of leadership: transactional and transformational. Transactional leadership was depicted as the norm, with its focus upon exchanges between leaders and their followers, whereas transformational leadership was believed to be a process of engaging with others and creating a connection, raising the level of motivation and morality of both the leader and the follower (Northouse 2010). Influential work into transformational leadership was subsequently undertaken by Bass and colleagues (see Bass and Avolio 1994).

Nadler and Tushman (1990) described the 'charismatic leader' as referring to a special quality that enables the leader to mobilise and sustain activity within an organisation through specific personal actions combined with perceived personal characteristics. Three major types of behaviour characterise these leaders: envisioning, energising and enabling (Nadler and Tushman 1990). While interest in transformational leadership was broader than leading change, inevitably 'transformational leaders are the ideal people to have during major organisational change because they have the visionary component ... ' (Clegg et al 2008, p140).

The visionary component of leadership in times of change appears to have captured the imagination of managers, as Palmer et al (2009, p249) acknowledge: 'you need to get the vision right if you want to have any chance of achieving successful organisational change'. Mintzberg et al (2009) trace the origins of visionary leadership to the entrepreneurial school of strategy management. As organisations grow, the role of leader as entrepreneur was believed to change, with the emphasis shifting to articulating and developing the vision for the organisation. Hardy (1996) referred to this approach to strategy-making as the 'great man approach', which she believed reflected an infatuation of the Western world with leadership. She cites Lee Iaccoca, John Harvey-Jones and Jack Welch as examples of charismatic figures brought in to save organisations at times of crisis.

Cummings and Worley (2008, p169) define a vision in the context of change as follows: 'generally, a vision describes the core values and purpose that guide the organisation as well as an envisioned future toward which change is directed'. The visionary leader seeks to galvanise followers around a shared vision. Creating the vision is regarded as more of a craft than a precise science and there is potential for the vision to fail. Palmer et al (2009) highlight reasons why visions may fail: the objective may be too specific, too vague, too unrealistic or inadequate. Equally visions can fail when they are blurred, are rearview mirrors, and are too complex or irrelevant.

LEADING CHANGE

The following section in focusing upon leading change draws upon earlier sections and reflects the enormous interest in the role and significance of change leaders over the last two decades (Caldwell 2003c). The impetus for interest in change leadership, since the early 1980s, again can be attributed to the severe challenges in managing innovation and culture change faced by the large American corporations (Caldwell 2003c). There was a belief that special kinds of leadership were critical during times of strategic organisational change (Nadler and Tushman 1990). Strategic change and change leadership are closely associated, although in leading change there is a need to influence groups and individuals (Morrison 1994; Woodward and Hendry 2004).

Kotter (1996, p26), a great advocate of leadership, asserted that 'successful transformation is 70 to 90 per cent leadership and only 10 to 30 per cent management'. He warned that focusing upon managing change neglected leading change; there is support for such a view in terms of the disproportionate amount of managing change research and scholarship in comparison with change leadership research and scholarship.

In 1995, 'Leading change: why transformation efforts fail', appeared in *Harvard Business Review*. The paper drew upon Kotter's experience of working with over 100 companies seeking to make fundamental changes and built upon his earlier work (Kotter 1990; Kotter and Heskett 1992). As he conceded (1995, p59), 'a few of these corporate change efforts have been very successful. A few have been utter failures. Most fall somewhere in between, with a distinct tilt toward the lower end of the scale.' As well as fuelling interest in the theory and practice of leading change, the paper encouraged interest among practitioners and academics in evaluating the effectiveness of change initiatives, which is discussed further in Chapter 20. Kotter himself acknowledged that in the space of a short paper everything may sound a bit too simplistic, and in 1996 he addressed this concern by using the eight steps as the structure for his book *Leading Change*, featured in Box 10.2.

Box 10.2 Eight-stage process of creating major change (Kotter 1996)

1 establishing a sense of urgency
2 creating the guiding coalition
3 developing a vision and strategy
4 communicating the change vision
5 empowering broad-based action
6 generating short-term wins
7 consolidating gains and producing more change
8 anchoring new approaches in the culture

The book, which received many testimonials from senior managers, had the strap-line: 'an action plan from the world's foremost expert on business leadership'. Kotter (1996) challenged the view that companies were unable to change, which was being fuelled by high failure rates, instead choosing to identify the patterns evident in the successful companies that he had studied. He argued that change was associated with a multistep process, which could never be effective without high-quality leadership. The book, as well as giving impetus to ongoing debates about leading change, fuelled interest in step approaches to managing change.

While Kotter's writings were informed by his experiences as a consultant, Caldwell (2003c) undertook original research in order to establish whether change leaders' and change managers' roles were different. His research, which was based upon a Delphi-style panel of ten change agent experts, enabled Caldwell to draw the following conclusions. As might be expected, change leaders were perceived as executives or senior managers who envision, initiate or sponsor strategic change, whereas change managers were perceived as middle-level managers and functional specialists who carry forward and build support for change. Change leadership was about creating a vision of change, whereas change management was about translating the vision into agendas and actions. The two challenges were different, yet complementary. Although Caldwell offers many relevant caveats about his research, the notion of complementarities of change leaders and change managers is intriguing in that it challenges Kotter's view about an overemphasis upon change management at the expense of change leadership. In his conclusions Caldwell suggests that we need both change leadership and change management in order to effectively deliver change.

In his writings about differences between change management and change leadership, Gill (2003) cites the findings of an American Management Association (1994) survey. In the survey of 259 senior executives in Fortune 500 companies, the following keys to successful change were identified as important: leadership (92%), corporate values (84%), communication (75%), team-building (69%) and education and training (64%). It is unsurprising that a survey of senior executives found that leadership was viewed as the most important key to successful change. However, the survey does highlight the perceived centrality of leadership in terms of successful change.

Woodward and Hendry (2004) undertook two descriptive surveys in order to examine leading and coping with change. They were able to suggest three ways in which change management skills may be enhanced. Firstly, those leading change must become more aware of their part in the change management process. Secondly, people like to appear capable and competent in the workplace at all levels. Thirdly, change leaders in adapting and coping with change may need support.

In focusing upon leading change, there is a need to acknowledge the longitudinal, processual and contextual nature of organisational change. Pettigrew has been influential in encouraging such an approach. Pettigrew and Whipp (1993) advocated an approach to leading change, which Caldwell (2006) has effectively summarised in terms of four components. Firstly, leading change is highly context dependent: all leaders and contexts are different. Secondly, leading change is complex, incremental and long term, invariably involving fragmented activities over time. Thirdly, leading change is deeply political. Fourthly, notions of a change leader or transformational leader are regarded as inappropriate with distributed leadership favoured instead.

⟨👁⟩ JOURNAL RESEARCH CASE 10.1

Pilkington (Australasia)

Paper title: Strategic change leadership
Sector: Manufacturing
Research methods: Qualitative case based upon interviewing and documentary research.
Authors: Graetz, F.
Year: 2000
Journal details: *Management Decision*. Vol 38, No 8. pp550–562.

Commentary: The author undertook qualitative research into change leadership in three organisations – Pilkington Australasia,

Ford Plastics and Ericsson Australia. Pilkington was operating in an increasingly hostile environment. A team approach to the task of leading change was adopted, although the managing director was not directly involved in selling the need for change. At the time of writing the case study, it remained to be seen whether the lack of involvement of the managing director would be detrimental to transforming Pilkington.

In Journal Research Case 10.1, the subtleties of leading change over time and at a strategic level are discussed. The leadership of change is very contingent upon the phase that an organisational change has reached. Burke (2008) highlighted how the leader's role and function in organisational change varies in terms of four primary phases: pre-launch phase, launch phase, post-launch phase and sustaining the change. At the pre-launch phase, issues that arise include the leadership establishing the need for change and providing clarity with regard to the vision. At the launch phase, the leadership communicates the need for change and deals with resistance to change. At the post-launch phase, the type of issues leadership deal with relate to maintaining consistency and repeating the message. At the sustaining change phase, leadership deals with the unanticipated consequences and launching new initiatives.

CRITICAL PERSPECTIVE

As Thompson and McHugh (2009, p343) warned, '... there is more rubbish written on leadership than on any topic other than creationism...' This very real concern among academics is magnified within the shortcomings of the leading change literature. Caldwell (2003c, p134), in considering the role of change leaders, warns that such approaches reproduce many of the weaknesses of traditional leadership theories:

> conflating leadership with change, overemphasising the leader's ability to transform an organisation, conceiving the qualities of the leader as

extraordinary, failing to clarify differences between leaders and managers, and displaying naïve overemphasis on the effectiveness of power tools and power techniques.

Against this critical backdrop the following discussion challenges Kotter's (1996) approach to leading change and more generally transformational/visionary leadership prescriptions, before discussing the potentially dangerous, devious and dysfunctional side of leadership.

CRITIQUE OF KOTTER AND TRANSFORMATIONAL LEADERSHIP

Acknowledging the influence of Kotter's model in change implementation practice, Caldwell (2006) suggests the strength of the model has been that it is pro-practice, rather than being analytically rigorous. Kotter (1996) was highly influential in shaping organisational practice in terms of leading change, but popularity alone is insufficient reason to adopt his effectively packaged prescription for leading change. The following discussion critically reviews his contribution as outlined in the 'Managerial Approaches' section.

The major academic challenge to Kotter's vision of leading change is: where is the evidence? Tantalising anecdotes are frequently offered to support the many assertions made in the book. These anecdotes helped the book to its bestseller status, superficially offering the legitimacy of a book based upon case studies, but there is so little detail provided that it is difficult to draw conclusions from any of the cases cited. For example:

> When one of the most visionary, charismatic executives I've known was appointed president of a $1.7 billion division of a large U.S. company, the level of excitement at that business rose dramatically. (Kotter 1996, p117)

Kotter elaborates upon this anecdote to support one of his steps. However, the sectoral context of the 'large U.S. company' is not disclosed, making it impossible for anyone to undertake a thorough longitudinal analysis of the subsequent success or failure of this U.S. company. Did the 'visionary, charismatic executive' lead the company to a lengthy period of success or subsequently into rapid decline? The book does not contain a list of supporting references at the end of the book and in the body of the book there are only cursory references to Kotter's earlier publications. The essence of the whole book, specifically the eight steps, is supported exclusively with a reference to Kotter's (1995) own paper. However, reading this paper in search of empirical case study evidence reveals very little. The omission of references to theory could be explained in terms of its practitioner focus. However, Kotter's work has influenced academic writing (see for example the number of critical change commentators who cite Kotter's 1995 anecdotal reference to change failure rates).

As well as the lack of explicit evidence to support the development of his eight-step model, there is no explicit evidence of successful organisational change arising out of following the eight steps. The first few pages carry endorsements from senior managers, which again imply success without their confirmation that buying into the eight steps delivers long-term successful change. There is a real danger here that Kotter and the high-profile endorsements encourage the types of isomorphism identified by DiMaggio and Powell (1991), as discussed in Chapter 5.

In offering an unashamedly prescriptive account of leading change, the book does not acknowledge the importance of context in processes of organisational change, as discussed in Chapter 5. While the complete omission of organisational context in discussions about leading change may be a good marketing ploy, it is a dangerous recipe for leading change. The anecdotes in the book appear to be largely informed by consultancy experiences gained from working within U.S. companies. This experience base may explain the macho language, but do militaristic analogies transfer to other companies in other countries with very different political, economic and social contexts? Equally there is a danger that public service organisations (or politicians) may decide to adopt this acontextual prescription in the belief that one size fits all.

Integral aspects of managing change such as culture, power, communications and employee relations are dealt with in the book in a very simplistic manner. While the defence that the book is a prescriptive guide for practitioners is reasonable, the fact that it is published by Harvard Business School Press sends out a very mixed message. Management students in business schools are taught about the ambiguities of culture, about power and politics, the subtleties of pluralistic employee relations and the complexities and barriers involved in effective change communications. Kotter sidesteps these debates, which does his practitioner readership a considerable disservice.

Collins (1998) has used the label n-step guide to refer to undersocialised models of organisational change. He highlights three features of such n-step guides. They present a rational analysis of organisational change, a sequential approach to planning and managing change and a generally upbeat and prescriptive tone. Each of these features is apparent in Kotter's eight-step guide on how to lead change. Firstly, in the eight steps to leading change a rational and achievable process amenable to the application of formal logic is presented. Secondly, the eight steps suggest a change journey with a beginning and an end. In Kotter's configuration of leading change the influence of history, as discussed in Chapter 3, is not significant; more significant is following the steps in their sequential order. Thirdly, the eight steps are unashamedly upbeat and prescriptive. Collins (1998, p86), writing about n-steps guides in general, suggests:

> These authors tend to claim that through experience or superior insight they have been able to pierce the problems and difficulties of change management, and so, are able to offer a neat and readily applicable framework which captures the essence of the processes of change and all its attendant problems.

The writings of Kotter are symptomatic of a large populist and prescriptive body of change literature. It is always going to be far more appealing than an academic textbook for managers to read, but even exclusively at the level of practice the book brings a highly spurious rationality to processes of organisational changing. Buchanan and Badham (2008) are sceptical about the applicability to practice of

Kotter's recipe for change for the following reasons. Firstly, the eight steps offer an ideal agenda, which managers may have neither the time nor the resources to adopt. Secondly, the eight steps are generic, rather than reflecting contextual differences. Thirdly, the interrelationships between the steps are not explored; and fourthly, the view that conflict is an outcome of communication failure is questionable.

Many of the criticisms of Kotter's leading change prescription are equally applicable to notions of transformational and visionary leadership. Caldwell (2006, p80) regards leadership theory '... as simply too leader-centric and voluntaristic to explain change'. In reviewing Pettigrew's (1992, 2002) work, he highlights how Pettigrew recommends the opposite of transformational leadership, suggesting that his message for leaders, change agents and strategic actors appears to 'concentrate on iterative processes of incremental change, because the emergent context of change is so complex that it will only allow for possibilities of action and choice that are the gradual continuations of the past' (Caldwell 2006, p81). Knights and Willmott (2007, p289) believe that 'the very term "transformational" when applied to leadership (or management) is an oxymoron as its intent is to renew or streamline established practices, not to transform them'.

Northouse (2010) has drawn together criticisms of transformational leadership: transformational leadership lacks conceptual clarity in the breadth of its coverage, the measurement of this vague concept is always going to be very difficult and being trait based is open to the criticisms of trait-based approaches to leadership. Tourish and Pinnington (2002, p166), writing with specific reference to transformational leadership and cults, warn of '... the potential to encourage authoritarian forms of organisation'. Transformational leadership may be elitist and anti-democratic, particularly in terms of its heroic leadership bias, and may be used for the wrong ends. Tourish and Pinnington (2002, p157) state that 'if the leader succeeds in altering the psyches of the organisation's members, one person's vision (or delusion) becomes that of many'. Tourish and Pinnington (2002, p148), in their critique of transformational leadership, argue that 'theories of TL draw sustenance from arguments stressing the central importance of culture to organisational success'. They (2002, p149) also highlight what Ciulla (1995) has referred to as the Hitler problem:

> ... can Hitler be viewed as a transformational leader? Is he in the same category as Gandhi, or other more moral leaders? If so, who sets the standards for what constitutes morality, using what criteria, and validated by whom?

This line of reasoning raises concerns about the dangerous, dysfunctional and devious side of leadership in general and change leadership in particular.

LEADERSHIP AS DANGEROUS, DYSFUNCTIONAL AND DEVIOUS

Conger (1990, p250) wrote about what he refers to as the dark side of leadership, which sometimes eclipses the bright side 'to the detriment of both the leader and the organisation'. In reviewing the literature on leadership there are frequent warnings about the problematical nature of leadership, suggesting an apparently fine line between heroic accounts of leaders and more troubling accounts of leaders as villains. Burke (R.J. Burke 2006), in reviewing the literature on why leaders fail, cites Kellerman's (2004) typology of bad leadership.

Seven types of leader were identified; the first three types of bad leader are regarded as incompetent. Incompetent leaders (1) lack will or skill to create effective action or positive change. They can be rigid (2), unable to yield or adapt to the new and intemperate (3) in that they lack self-control. Incompetent leaders are the least problematic (damaging). The last four types are regarded as being unethical. Unethical leaders are viewed as callous (4) in that they can be uncaring and unkind. They can be corrupt (5), placing self-interest first. Bad leaders may be insular (6) in ignoring the needs and welfare of those outside the group and evil (7), doing psychological or physical harm to others. Unethical leaders are regarded as the most problematic (damaging) in their inability to distinguish right and wrong.

This analysis initially offers a depressing impression of leadership, which tends to contradict the popular mythology of leadership being concerned with heroic figures with special powers. However, although impossible to quantify, good leaders may have become captivated by their own vision and subsequently turned bad (Bowditch et al 2008). Nadler and Tushman (1990) identify the following potential problems with charismatic leaders: the creation of unrealistic expectations, the encouragement of either dependency or counter-dependency, an expectation that the magic associated with charisma will continue unabated, and the disenfranchisement of the next level of management. Kets de Vries (1989) highlighted dispositions of neurotic leaders – aggressive, paranoid, histrionic, detached, controlling, passive-aggressive, narcissistic, dependent and masochistic. In his more recent (2006) work, *The Leader on the Couch*, he adopts a clinical approach to understanding leadership, suggesting that early childhood experiences may shape the inner personality of the leader. The ethical dilemmas featured here are discussed further in Chapter 16.

CONCLUDING COMMENTARY

There is currently considerable interest in leadership, both within organisations and among academics. There has been an acknowledgement of differences between leading and managing and in the context of organisational change; there is a belief that greater emphasis upon leading change may be the solution to historic managing change failures. The study of leaders and leadership is not a new phenomenon and various schools of thought offer explanations for the effectiveness of behaviours of leaders and processes of leadership. In recent years there has been an emphasis upon identifying and developing transformational and visionary leaders, with rhetoric suggesting that such leaders will deliver new organisations and ways of working. Kotter gave considerable impetus to such debates through the success of his book *Leading Change*. The book offers practitioners an eight-step process for creating major change. The impact of this book should not be underestimated, although the supporting evidence for what is being prescribed is limited, anecdotal and acontextual. The discussion of the problematic nature of leading change raises concerns about the shadow side of leadership, which appears particularly pertinent in terms of recent major corporate collapses.

Leading change in Crusty Bakeries

Crusty Bakeries Limited (CB Ltd) is one of the largest producers of bread and bread-based products in Britain. Despite fierce competition in the sector, CB Ltd products remain popular with customers and the company is also popular with institutional investors. The main operation is based in the Midlands, with satellite distribution centres radiating out from this operational hub. The Midlands site is huge and as well as producing bakery products is the location for the head office.

Jayne County, as head of human resources, is responsible for running the senior manager development programme. One element of her role has been to develop operational managers with a view to their subsequently joining the senior management team that runs CB Ltd. She has drawn up a shortlist of three potential candidates for the next place on the highly coveted senior manager development programme. Her private summary notes about each manager read as follows.

Pete Wylie (Transport Manager)

Pete has progressed from driving delivery vans to a highly influential position in CB Ltd. As transport manager he is responsible for ensuring that products are delivered daily over a wide geographical area. If anything goes wrong, it is very evident very quickly. He runs the operation like clockwork – which is not always how it was before he took over. There was an element of risk in his initial appointment in that he was one of very few managers not to have a university qualification. However, at the appointment interviews five years

ago the other graduate candidates were perceived as being rather 'green'. The role required a manager who could deal effectively with confrontation. Pete appears to thrive on confrontation – in his regular dealings with the wagon drivers much of his communications have been non-verbal. He has a huge physical frame and when he becomes annoyed he tends to clench his fists. Occasionally, when he feels a wagon driver has been shirking, he asks the driver for his keys and drives the wagon himself, even if this means driving many hundreds of miles. These stories of Pete's trips have become folklore in the depot – yet the most frequently told story relates to Project Shake.

Pete has always used his 'thick wagon driver' reputation to good effect. Those who know him well – and that is a relatively small grouping – know he is extremely intelligent and has a natural ability for logistics. He rapidly transformed the transport department and this was recognised. However, everything almost came unstuck with the bitter winter of 2003 in which record-breaking snow storms made it impossible to transport petrol along frozen roads. In a short space of time television news stories started featuring pictures of empty supermarket shelves. However, throughout this winter CB Ltd products were distributed as normal. It was a long time before it finally emerged that Pete had been warned about the imminent winter snowstorms by a friend who was an amateur meteorologist, which had enabled him to stockpile fuel at a local aircraft base. Project Shake would have caused the transport department to go into deficit if his judgement had been wrong, but as it turned out it allowed CB Ltd to gain competitive advantage over major competitors.

Kevin Coyne (Research and Development Manager)

Kevin is usually seen wearing his lab coat and spectacles. Kevin gained his PhD in America and appears to enjoy leading a team of scientists. They work on a surprisingly wide range of products with customers' health and safety of paramount importance. Kevin facilitates the weekly 'coffee club' meetings at which he updates colleagues on developments and encourages them to air any grievances. The grievances are few and far between. Most of the scientists joined because of Kevin's reputation for innovation among the scientific community. Kevin hates administration and bureaucracy and has delegated all this work to a very capable assistant. He is not popular with senior management because of his failure to attend the monthly management meetings. However, he rarely leaves the labs and has been known to work 24-hour days, driven solely by his fascination with science. A few months ago he took eight of the top scientists out to a local pub and treated them all to a ploughman's lunch. At this lunch he made the 'Dog and Duck challenge', to the effect that in 12 months' time they would return to the pub again, but that then there would be half the salt there currently was in the bread rolls. This dramatic challenge caught the imagination of the fairly staid scientists and great advances have already been made towards meeting this goal.

Mark Smith (Senior Management Accountant)

Mr Smith is the longest-serving member of staff of the three shortlisted candidates. He is a professionally qualified management accountant who provides financial and other information for management within CB Ltd, which may be used for planning, control and decision-making purposes.

He runs the management accounting department very efficiently, requiring all staff to adhere to strict (some might say overly formal) dress codes. He also insists that all staff sign in and sign out each day. These idiosyncratic requirements have caused conflict with the HR department, but Mr Smith has remained steadfast in demanding adherence to his standards.

He claims to champion the development of younger people, but there is a suspicion that he prefers less qualified staff because this maintains the gap between his and their levels of expertise. His expertise is considerable and his financial knowledge is trusted and appreciated in CB Ltd. However, his own department suffers from a high turnover of staff and he is referred to behind his back as 'Dr Death'. He has a public persona of being charming yet a tendency to be cruel to people. This is most tangible when he gathers budgetary information. He often uses this exercise to humiliate other managers, particularly in his references to how they are perceived by the senior management team.

In recent months he has again come into conflict with the HR department. In analysing his spreadsheets he identified labour costs as being a significant outgoing in many departments. He has proposed to senior management that more agency staff are appointed on different terms and conditions as a means of lowering labour costs. He has additionally tabled a paper suggesting a reduction in pension benefits for new staff.

Case study questions

1   In respect of the three candidates, is it possible to differentiate between their work in terms of their roles as managers and leaders?

2   Explain the leadership of each manager in terms of the person, result, position and process, as described by Grint.

3   What leadership behaviours in this case study do you regard as inappropriate and why?

DISCUSSION QUESTIONS

1   What are the differences between leading change and managing change and do they matter?

2   What is the potential appeal of transformational leadership for senior managers?

3   Overall do you believe *Leading Change* (Kotter, 1996) has been beneficial or detrimental for organisations?

4   Why might a 'good' leader go 'bad'?

KEY READINGS

GRINT, K. (2005) *Leadership: limits and possibilities*. Basingstoke: Palgrave Macmillan.

This book is recommended for anyone familiar with general textbook discussions of leadership who wants to read more deeply on the subject. Through drawing upon social theory, Grint encourages new ways of understanding leadership. This book questions many of the myths and assumptions that confuse the theory and practice of leadership.

KOTTER, J.P. (1996) *Leading change*. Boston: Harvard Business School Press.

This book has consistently remained a bestseller among practitioners, bringing together many of the individual elements of change management into a simple eight-stage model. The style of writing is highly accessible and the whole book could be read on a long train journey. The academic concerns the book raises relate to ambiguities about the research methods and methodology underpinning the book. While the eight-stage model is plausible, the implied generalisability is highly questionable.

NORTHOUSE, P.G. (2010) *Leadership: theory and practice*. 5th ed. Thousand Oaks, CA: Sage Publications Inc.

This book offers full coverage of the major theories and debates relating to leadership in organisations. It is an ideal book for anyone who wants to read more deeply about leadership theories in general and how they evolved. Later chapters, which consider leadership in terms of women, culture and ethics, are particularly pertinent to contemporary debates.

CHAPTER 11

Change communications

After reading this chapter you should be able to:

- understand the concept of corporate communications
- appreciate the why, where, what, when and how of communicating change
- appreciate the different options available in communicating change
- understand potential barriers and blockages in communicating change
- understand the concept of change communications as rhetoric
- understand the concept of change communications as discourse.

INTRODUCTION

Organisations are first and foremost communicating entities (Clegg et al 2008). Communication is a central process in the planning and implementation of change (Jones et al 2004) and employee communications are regarded as an important and integrative part of change efforts and strategies (Elving 2005). In the context of a managing change textbook, engagement with change communications is essential. However, the frustrating lack of research into communicating change (Lewis and Seibold 1998; Goodman and Truss 2004; Jones et al 2004; Lewis et al 2006) may explain why most textbooks do not cover change communications.

Communication has been defined as the '... exchange of ideas, emotions, messages, stories, and information through different means including writing, speech, signals, objects, or actions' (Clegg et al 2008, p302). This definition highlights the many communication choices which are available to managers resulting in a range of different communications strategies. Clampitt et al (2000) offered the following examples of typical organisation communication strategies, summarised in Box 11.1.

Box 11.1 Typical organisational communication strategies (based upon Clampitt et al 2000)

1 **Spray and pray** – showering employees with all kinds of information.
2 **Tell and sell** – more limited set of messages selling the wisdom of the approach.
3 **Underscore and explore** – development of a few core messages and clarifying understanding.
4 **Identify and reply** – focuses upon employee concerns and responds to them.
5 **Withhold and uphold** – information is withheld until necessary.

Corporate communications encompasses three main clusters of task-related communications within organisations: management communications, marketing communications and organisational communications (Riel and Fombrun 2007). Corporate communications has been defined as '... a coherent approach to the development of communications in organisations, one that communication specialists can adopt to streamline their own communication activities by working from a centrally coordinated strategic framework' (Riel and Fombrun 2007, p22). The scope of communications is very wide and in focusing upon change communications with reference to managing change, this chapter is mainly concerned with internal organisational communications.

It is acknowledged that managers are involved in communicating changes with many other groups – for example, customers or clients, shareholders and government agencies (see Ihator 2004 for further discussion). In the 'Managerial Approaches' section communication choices are discussed specifically in terms of the why, where, what, when and how of communicating change and potential barriers and blockages that can impede communicating change. The 'Critical Perspective' shifts the focus away from the functional challenges of communicating change and considers change communications as rhetoric and as discourse.

MANAGERIAL APPROACHES

COMMUNICATING CHANGE

The lack of research into communicating change, which was highlighted earlier, explains why there 'are great many choices to make and, as yet, there are few hard and fast rules on the subject' (De Caluwe and Vermaak 2003, p92). The following discussion is themed around choices, specifically the why, where, what, when and how of communicating change.

In terms of why communicate change, rationales for communicating were highlighted in the introduction. There is a view that without effective communication, change is impossible and will fail (Barrett 2002). This textbook has featured many activities that contribute to managing change, and Barrett's quotation places communications at the centre of processes of changing. Communication seeks to gain people's involvement in processes of change and in this way it is an essential element of change activities (Burnes 2009a). The danger of poor communication of change is captured in the following quotation:

> Employees report that they want to perform well at work, but are often prevented from doing so by limited understanding of what is required. This is compounded by communication with unclear meaning and which does not specify what, if any, action is required, and by information which is poorly presented and difficult to use. (Quirke 2008, p15)

Communicating change may be regarded as a subset of wider corporate communications, with change communications seeking to obtain individual buy-in, obtain commitment to change, minimise resistance and reduce personal anxiety (Goodman and Truss 2004). Historically, effective communications have been acknowledged as an important ingredient in successfully managing change (Beer 1980; Kotter and Schlesinger 1979; Kotter 1990; Beckhard and Pritchard 1992; De Caluwe and Vermaak 2003; Goodman and Truss 2004). The CIPD (2004) *Organising for Success* research programme offered empirical insights into the centrality of communication skills in the context of reorganisation. The skills of a reorganising team, which were seen as major enablers of success, were ranked as follows (the figures represent the percentages of reorganisations): skills in people management (71%); communication skills (68%); and skills in managing organisational culture (55%). These findings suggest that communication skills are perceived as important with regard to reorganisations.

The choices relating to where to communicate change are concerned with using different communication channels. The traditional choices were either word of mouth or paper-based communications. Word-of-mouth communications include meetings, focus groups and conferences. Paper-based communications include letters, memos, reports and newsletters. Technology increasingly offers many new communication channels, such as email, video, websites, intranets and videoconferencing. The dilemma is which communication channel to use. In reviewing media selection, research has identified six categories that inform the choice of media selection: source factors, organisational factors, media factors, task/message factors, receiver factors and strategic factors (Timmerman 2003).

There are many variables informing what to communicate. Four of the major variables impacting upon a change communications strategy are: the type of change, the degree of urgency, the speed of change and reactions to the change (Quirke 1995). Each organisational change is unique, being influenced by the contextual factors introduced in Chapter 5. The communication content is concerned with '… what information is conveyed to employees before, during and after the change initiative, as well as what information is sought from employees' (Goodman and Truss 2004, p219). Armenakis et al (1999) identified five key change message components: discrepancy, efficacy, appropriateness, principal support and personal valence. Discrepancy is concerned with the need for change and efficacy is concerned with confidence in the change succeeding. Appropriateness is concerned with if the change is perceived to be the correct change and principal support speaks to the level of institutional resources and commitment. Personal valence is concerned with 'what is in it for me?'

Conner (1998, pxiv) offered an interesting example of Charles Allen, the chief executive of Granada. In his change communications he stated that: 'I always brand the change programmes. Then people associate the negatives of the restructuring with the brand, and once you've made the reorganization, you shut the brand down.' Practical generic guidance on the content of change communications is very evident. For example, the change communications plan should be guided by messages being linked to the strategic purpose of the change initiative, communications being realistic and honest, communications being proactive rather than reactive and messages being consistently repeated through different communication channels (Galpin 1996). Paton and McCalman (2008) offered guidelines to follow when communicating change, which included: customising the message, setting the appropriate tone, building in feedback, setting the example and ensuring penetration. Importantly, they acknowledged the need to customise the message, as understanding change communications in terms of generic principles will never reflect the complexity and diversity of organisational life. Communication content remains very dependent upon the nature of the messages being communicated, the sender and receiver of the messages, and the wider context of the communications.

There are choices about when to communicate change. Hubbard (2001, p21), writing with reference to acquisitions, acknowledged that 'while all changes may not be palatable, the shock of change is even greater if it remains misunderstood'. This view highlights the importance of timing change communications. Balogun and Hope Hailey (2008) offered guidelines on the timing of change communications with employees, which are summarised in Box 11.2.

Box 11.2 Change communications with employees (based upon Balogun and Hope Hailey 2008)

Employees prefer hearing about change from management, rather than as rumour.
Early communications allows employees time to understand and adjust.
Employees prefer honest and even incomplete announcements to information being covered up.
Employees inevitably learn about change initiatives despite policies of silence.

There are many choices about how to communicate change, with Quirke (2008, p158) using the metaphor of a communication escalator to explain communicating change, as depicted in Figure 11.1.

The degree of change and the degree of involvement determine which of the following steps is most appropriate: awareness, understanding, support, involvement or commitment. These steps may be matched to different employees – for example, agents and suppliers may require awareness of a change whereas the sales force and customer service staff may require involvement in a change. Similarly, different communication channels may be utilised – for example, a newsletter may generate awareness about a change whereas a team meeting may create involvement in a change.

Hubbard (2001, p36) highlighted a practical dilemma arising out of processes of change and communications with regard to acquisitions:

Generally during acquisition, no target employee wants to be the bearer

Figure 11.1 The communication escalator

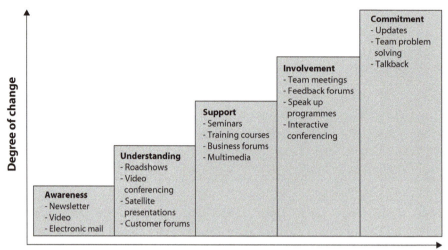

Source: Quirke, B. (2008) *Making the connections: using internal communication to turn strategy into action*. 2nd ed. Aldershot: Gower Publishing Limited, p158. Reproduced with permission from Ashgate Publishing Limited.

of good news during times of adversity; it is much more popular amongst one's peer group to tell negative stories rather than pleasant ones, thereby feeding on the already existing levels of distrust. This can mean the distortion of facts in order to make the story fit the bill.

The notion of background conversations alluded to in this quotation is intriguing. Ford et al (2002) have been influential in explaining the role of such background conversations during times of change. They argue persuasively that resistance to change is a product of the background conversations being spoken at times of change, creating the context for the change initiative and responses to it.

COMMUNICATING CHANGE BARRIERS AND BLOCKAGES

The danger with the concept of communicating change is the assumption that the act of communicating change equates to effectively communicated change. The following discussion explores why this assumption may be erroneous in terms of potential barriers and blockages to communicating change. Balogun and Hope Hailey (2008, p194) highlight that in change situations, people want to understand 'what this all means for me'. This concern is likely to be the norm and may relate to a human desire for self-preservation in the face of adversity; it can be related back to what Armenakis et al (1999) referred to as personal valence. The question signposts the need to consider not just sending messages, but also receiving messages. Against the potential backdrop of greater job insecurity, the end of jobs for life and a proliferation of change initiatives, this question is increasingly relevant.

The contemporary challenge for corporate communications is one of motivating employees with priorities vastly different from those of their organisation (Goodman 2001, p122). This has been expressed more profoundly by Finstad (1998, p717), who encourages members of an organisation to examine the existential questions: 'who are we, what do we want, and where are we going?' In this way the subtleties of change communications begin to become apparent, which are discussed further in the 'Critical Perspective'. In analysing organisational communications, a range of potential barriers and blockages to communication exist. Weiss (2001) identified: judging, criticising, sending solutions and avoiding another's concerns; while Beck et al (2002) highlighted: mechanical, psychological, semantic and organisational barriers. The barriers and blockages are many and varied, with their influence dependent upon variables discussed earlier in this chapter.

The concern with such barriers and blockages is that they reflect not only a failure to communicate, but a failure to change. Consequently, Balogun and Hope Hailey (2008) advocate message repetition as part of change communications, and Nadler and Tushman (1997) even advocated overcommunicating. Their suggestion is that at times of extreme anxiety, such as a major reorganisation, people do not effectively receive messages the first time, requiring messages to be repeated through various media. Or this may be rephrased as: 'I know you think you understand what you thought I said. But I am not sure that what you heard is what I meant' (Robbins and Finley 1998, p52).

Lewis (2000, p151) found that failures in communication contributed to stalled and/or failed programmes of change. His case-study-based conclusions, featured in Journal Research Case 11.1, suggest that communications failures may lead to change failures.

⊙ JOURNAL RESEARCH CASE 11.1

University services + 3

Paper title: Communicating change: four cases of quality programs
Sector: Various
Research methods: Observations, document analysis, interviews and questionnaires.
Authors: Lewis, L.K.
Year: 2000
Journal details: *The Journal of Business Communication*. Vol 37, No 2. pp128–155.

Commentary: The paper presents four case studies of implementing quality programmes.

All four case studies are based in the United States – university services, outreach education, veterans' hospital and messaging technology. The case studies offer empirically evidenced illustrations of communication problems as part of change initiatives. The key themes that emerge from these case studies are creating and communicating vision, sense-making and feedback, establishing legitimacy, and communicating goal achievements.

As well as barriers and blockages impeding change communication, in the context of communicating change there has been interest in processes whereby employees receive change messages, but fail to act upon them. There appears to be merit in considering almost the opposite of communication – silence. This dilemma is captured in the following quotation about senior managers' frustration with the slowness with which employees respond to change: 'Their people nod in all the right places, make all the right noises, then go off and do something quite different' (Quirke 1995, p75). This apparent paradox in organisations has been explained as 'most employees know the truth about certain issues and problems within the organisations yet dare not speak that truth' (Morrison and Milliken 2000, p706).

Morrison and Milliken (2000, p707) introduced the concept of organisational silence as follows: 'the possibility that the dominant choice within many organisations is for employees to withhold their opinions and concerns about organisational problems – a collective phenomenon that we have termed organisational silence – is one that we believe deserves serious research attention'. Organisational silence is perceived as a dangerous impediment to organisational change and development. In a similar manner, Daly et al (2003, p161) cite a manager warning that: 'Change initiatives will disappear into the cracks if management are not careful...' This notion of change initiatives disappearing, rather than being explicitly resisted, speaks to many of the debates in this textbook. However, it may prove to be easier to diagnose organisational silence than to rectify it. It is likely in the short term that managers will choose to manage the more tangible resistance, rather than the intangible silence. The effective creation of systems that encourage voice requires an understanding of complex dynamics within organisations that maintain and reinforce silence (Morrison and Milliken 2000).

On a more pragmatic level it may be possible to pre-empt communication barriers and blockages. The communication of a major change requires an 'MOT' of organisational communication processes: 'Companies cannot afford not to improve the current communication practices if they find them lacking' (Barrett 2002, p222). Although not empirically tested or supported, this is an interesting proposition. A failure to effectively communicate change may reflect a failure of broader organisational communication processes. Barrett (2002, p224) advocated an assessment of current communication practices as a necessary precursor to communicating major changes.

CRITICAL PERSPECTIVE

In this 'Critical Perspective' the focus shifts from the functional aspects of communicating change towards understanding change communications as language. Manning (1992, p4) believed that 'communication – ambiguous, paradoxical, and equivocal – should be seen as a defining feature of human beings, and an appreciation of its vagaries a valuable step toward a sensitivity to the diversity and sensibilities of people'. In this section, two very closely related approaches to understanding change communications are discussed: change communications as rhetoric and change communications as discourse.

CHANGE COMMUNICATIONS AS RHETORIC

Change communications have been depicted as powerful tools shaping images of organisational change and mindsets accompanying change, stretching the imagination and motivating people to rethink organisational possibilities (Bowditch et al 2008). In the following discussion the concept of organisational rhetoric with specific reference to organisational change is introduced: 'Communication, and language more specifically, is central not just to conveying or transmitting required changes; it is the medium through which change itself occurs' (Palmer and Dunford 2008, S26).

The study of rhetoric has a long history and may be defined as: '... the art or the discipline that deals with the use of discourse, either spoken or written, to perform or persuade or motivate an audience, whether that audience is made up of one person or a group of persons' (Corbett 1990, p3). Rhetoric is often regarded as something of a red flag, and erroneously dismissed as 'mere rhetoric' (see Eccles and Nohria 1992 and Watson 1995 for further discussion) or used to differentiate rhetoric from reality (see, for example, Poole and Mansfield 1992). However, Eccles and Nohria (1992) believed that in order to gain a fresh perspective on management it was necessary to take language, and hence rhetoric, seriously.

The accounts of change communications in the 'Managerial Approaches' section depicted communications as something largely neutral and apolitical. However, change communications inevitably employ persuasive rhetoric. Choices about what, when and how to communicate and the release of disconfirming information are invariably political issues (Dawson 2003). A good illustration of this was evident in employees' questioning total quality management: 'If the rhetoric of change does not align with the substance of change, then employees who find themselves having to do more with less resources are likely to become cynical about management change initiatives and to view TQM as a totally questionable method' (Dawson 2003, p166). The rhetorical use of change language offers a means of galvanising change, whereby people collectively create new realities through language (De Caluwe and Vermaak 2003). The symbolic significance of language in relation to change has been explained in terms of: 'Either consciously or unconsciously, change agents may employ language and metaphor to galvanise change' (Johnson et al 2008, p537). These quotations emphasise the functions change language can perform.

Rhetorical-based studies offer fresh perspectives on organisational change in many different ways. Thompson and O'Connell Davidson (1995) identified the rhetoric of discontinuity in managerial writing, highlighting how the writings of Peter Drucker over many decades regularly announced that we were entering an era of unprecedented change. Finstad (1998) identified four forms of rhetoric with specific reference to organisational change in municipal services in Norway – monocratic, opportunistic, anarchical and professional. Critical commentators, in highlighting the rhetorical construction of language, regard the lexicon of management as based upon fads and buzzwords: '… a grammar based upon commands and imperatives has been developed which will not, and cannot, countenance dissent' (Collins 2000, p386). Grint and Case (1998, p559), writing with specific reference to business process reengineering, warned that '… rhetoric associated with the workplace seems to have taken a violent turn'.

Knights and Collinson (1987) identified shop-floor workers ridiculing the new human relations strategy as presented to them in the glossy in-house magazine, regarding these communications as management propaganda (a form of rhetoric). However, shop-floor workers appeared to accept the discipline of financial accounting information. While there are overlaps between studying change communications as rhetoric and as discourse, discourse offers another informative perspective on understanding change communications.

CHANGE COMMUNICATIONS AS DISCOURSE

Caldwell (2006), in the context of his discussion of agency and change, acknowledged that there were at least four meanings of discourse: as rule-bound systems, as discursive practices, as 'power/knowledge' and discourse as Discourse (a grand meta-narrative). In the context of this textbook the following definition of discourse is used: 'a set of connected concepts, expressions and statements that constitutes a way of talking or writing about an aspect of the world, thus framing and influencing the way people understand and act with regard to that aspect of the world' (Watson 2006, p102). In this quotation the relevance of discourse to organisational change is apparent, in particular the power inherent within language. Tsoukas (2005) made a very good case for adopting a discourse analytic approach when studying the language of change, which he contrasted with behaviourist and cognitivist approaches. In the following discussion, each approach is explained using public sector change communications as an illustration.

A behaviourist explanation suggests that public service organisations in their strategic change communications seek to secure funding. They consequently follow the national policy and performance guidance of strategic stakeholders with this compliance subsequently rewarded through funding. This is succinctly captured in the concept of 'strategies as funding pitches' (Llewellyn and Tappin 2003). A cognitivist explanation suggests that public service organisations in their strategic change communications reflect more subtle shifts in thinking than behaviourists would acknowledge. A good example of a cognitivist explanation is evident in the work of Hartley and Bennington (2006, p104) on knowledge-sharing through inter-organisational networks when they pose the question: copy and paste, drag and drop – or graft and transplant? Instead of public service organisations adopting a 'copy and paste' response, there is an acknowledgement of how culture and context are likely to influence strategic change communications. This was reflected in a preference for the 'graft and transplant' approach and its implication for organisations developing, rather than merely mimicking, national policy guidelines.

A discursivist explanation is the most radical, suggesting that public service organisations in their strategic change communications seek to construct new meanings and interpretations of their activities. As Tsoukas (2005, p98) succinctly states, '... a new language is used to re-constitute the organisation'. The implication here is far greater than change as a language game: 'change must not be thought of as a property of organisation. Rather, organisation must be understood as an emergent property of change' (Tsoukas and Chia 2002, p570). The discursivist explanation suggests that through processes of strategic change communication public service organisations are reconstituted.

> While for behaviorists and cognitivists the world is projected more or less objectively on our mental screens, for discursivists the world appears, or is constructed through the way people talk and use sign systems more generally. (Tsoukas 2005, p102)

It is important to acknowledge that behaviorist and cognitivist explanations remain the orthodoxy in terms of the theory and practice of change communications, but the potential of discourse-based approaches is considerable. Oswick et al (2005, p387) believe that 'the general trend in terms of the theory and practice of organisational change management is towards an accumulating interest in intangible phenomena and, defacto, discourse'. Similarly, Woodman (2008) identified organisational diagnosis and the evaluation of OD programmes/organisational change as fruitful areas of future discourse studies.

CONCLUDING COMMENTARY

The prevalence of organisational communications is one explanation for the paucity of research into communicating change, in that communications are taken for granted. Communications have been identified as an integral aspect of managing change and for some commentators the most important aspect. However, the label organisational change covers many different activities, as was discussed in Chapter 2. As a consequence there are many choices relating to the why, where, what, when and how of communicating change. The danger is in imagining that having addressed such communication choices, effective change communication is assured. Barriers and blockages are an inevitable consequence of communicating; however, pre-empting them may help to minimise them. The second half of the chapter considered the persuasive nature of change communications and how the concepts of rhetoric and discourse are reconstituting organisations through language.

Communications about a new job evaluation scheme

Organisational context: The Office of Qualitative Social Science – affectionately abbreviated to OOqSS – provides qualitative economic, social and political data for government departments in the civil service. Invariably, it has been overshadowed by its sister office, which gathers quantitative social science data, although its staff quite enjoy the anonymity of being the office nobody has heard about. The staff are highly qualified social scientists who in most instances have chosen to work in public service rather than the private sector. One such member of staff is Robert Wyatt, who, after completing his university studies in social theory, joined OOqSS over 20 years ago. Staff in OOqSS have done their best to avoid radical change, but in a manner similar to the rest of the civil service have recently had to respond to a series of government-driven changes. One of these changes was the implementation of a job evaluation scheme, which may be explained in terms of four communication events.

Event 1: trade union meeting: Robert has been a trade unionist all his working life and attended union branch meetings out of both a sense of duty and a sense of loyalty. However, he is prone to daydreaming, and when the branch official announced the piloting of a job evaluation scheme in OOqSS, his mind was on the previous night's TV documentary about shipbuilding. He slowly began to tune back into what was being said as the official impressed upon members that this job evaluation scheme had implications for all civil service employees. In particular, there was a strong belief in the joint trade union co-ordinating group that job evaluation might lead to better pay for low-paid workers in the civil service. This was why the union was participating in the pilot, and this rationale appealed to Robert's socialist beliefs. However, the branch official warned that there was a tendency with job evaluation schemes for employees to 'talk up' what

they did, which had implications for other employees. The official emphasised that it was imperative that in the pilot interviews members did not 'talk up' their work. The meeting concluded, and although Robert was not a statistician he felt the odds were good that he would not be invited to the pilot interviews. He returned to the Poverty in Schools Project feeling that he had done his duty, but that he was not that much wiser about job evaluation.

Event 2: meeting with personnel representatives: Robert was disappointed when he learned that he was to be one of the pilot interviewees for the job evaluation scheme. He was invited to attend a briefing event organised by the personnel department, although there would also be presentations from the relevant trade unions. He enjoyed the free buffet lunch that was provided before sitting down to a very professional PowerPoint presentation on CSJE. CSJE was the unimaginative label given to the civil service job evaluation scheme. On one slide there was a definition of job evaluation:

Job evaluation offers a means to measure and evaluate jobs relative to one another. It involves a thorough analysis of the role based on information about the job. This information is then presented in a consistent format to ensure that all jobs are compared and evaluated logically and fairly.

So that is what they mean, he thought, and wondered if it would be perceived as cheeky if he went and helped himself to some more sandwiches. The personnel department spokesperson was explaining that CSJE was being introduced into the civil service in order to introduce real-world accountability into civil service work. CSJE was an integral element of the Conservative minister's modernisation crusade. Robert decided to opt for another sandwich.

Event 3: job evaluation interview: It had been agreed that a trade union representative would sit alongside each interviewee at the job evaluation interviews in order to ensure that the process was fair. It had even been jokingly suggested that the union representative would kick the interviewee under the table if he or she 'talked up' the job. Robert met the union representative in the canteen in order to ensure that he would say the right things. They then jointly went over to the personnel department. CSJE required Robert to do some preparatory work answering a series of generic questions, such as the following:

Do you have to plan, prioritise and organise work or resources to achieve agreed goals?

What knowledge and experience, however gained, do you need to carry out your basic day-to-day responsibilities?

Are you required to lift, carry or handle large or heavy objects routinely?

The questions went on and on and although Robert understood that the questions had to be sufficiently generic to apply to all civil service employees, he was quickly losing faith in the methodology. The interview required him to answer the questions in person and give specific illustrations with reference to the work that he did. He had feared that the process would somehow reveal that he was an incompetent social scientist, but it seemed that the methodology never enabled anything more than a superficial analysis. Also, as a good trade unionist he made sure that he did not oversell himself in any way. The interviewer explained at the end of the interview that the interview would be typed up and he would have a chance to check what had been said and the transcript would be verified by the head of OOqSS.

Event 4: conversation with head of OOqSS: About a month later, one evening Robert's boss drifted into his office. Robert was typing up the final report for the Poverty in Schools Project. His boss sat on a desk and they chatted both as colleagues and as friends. His boss commented that he had to sign off the CSJE transcript but it was difficult to recognise that it was meant to be an account of the work that Robert did for OOqSS. Robert believed he had a good rapport with his boss and explained that as a trade unionist he had been instructed not to 'talk up' his work. His boss cautioned that the transcript should be honest and suggested three enhancements based upon his knowledge of the work Robert did, which Robert agreed to. They then spent two hours talking about the pros and cons of research interviewing on different projects they had worked on, before the caretakers threw them out of the building.

Reflections: This case may be atypical in terms of organisational life in that everyone appears to have been a winner. Robert stayed fairly true to his trade union beliefs. The trade union protected the interests of members. The personnel department effectively carried out the CSJE interview. The head of OOqSS effectively verified the transcript – and in time the government minister had large amounts of qualitative and quantitative job evaluation information to peruse.

Case study questions

1 Explain these communications in terms of Quirke's (2008) communication escalator.

2 What communication barriers did Robert appear to experience for each of the communication events?

3 How does the concept of rhetoric help to explain this case study?

4 Is this case study a rare case of everybody winning?

1 What criteria should be used to determine what should and should not be communicated with regard to a particular change?

2 Is it possible for an organisation to remove all communications blockages and barriers?

3 Are there any occasions when a dishonest change message is acceptable?

4 Is there a need to take the rhetoric of change seriously and, if so, why?

COLLINS, D. (2000) *Management fads and buzzwords: critical–practical perspectives.* London: Routledge.

This book remains a personal favourite. The title suggests an author completely dismissive of management, but the subtitle more effectively conveys Collins' position. He is keen that critical debates and studies play a far greater role in informing the practice of management. In the context of this chapter, the whole book offers a critique of the role language plays in a host of different change initiatives.

CORNELISSEN, J. (2008) *Corporate communication: a guide to theory and practice.* 2nd ed. London: Sage Publications Ltd.

This textbook offers a good blend of coverage of major theoretical debates and practical application.

There is coverage of change communication, although fairly brief. This reading is recommended primarily as an introduction to corporate communications.

PALMER, I., DUNFORD, R. and AKIN, G. (2009) *Managing organizational change: a multiple perspectives approach.* 2nd ed. Boston: McGraw-Hill International Editions.

The treatment of change communications in managing change textbooks tends to be fairly superficial. This textbook is an exception in that two focused chapters are devoted to change communications. The authors have been influential in contributing to debates about the language of change in academic journals and this shows in their depth of understanding of relevant theories.

CHAPTER 12

Resistance to change

LEARNING OUTCOMES

After reading this chapter you should be able to:

- identify the causes of resistance to change
- identify manifestations of resistance to change
- establish options for managing resistance to change
- reflect upon the role of stability in organisational change
- appreciate the influence of change-agent-centric thinking
- think differently about resistance and resistance to change terminology.

INTRODUCTION

Understanding resistance to change is integral to both the theory and practice of change management, yet ironically most traditional change management textbooks avoid these fascinating debates. In managerial discussions there is a tendency to depict resistance to change as something that must be overcome: 'resistance to change can be difficult to overcome even when it is not detrimental to those concerned. But the attempt must be made' (Armstrong 2009, p431). This chapter explains how resistance to change initially appeared irrational and problematic; however, in recent years there has been an appreciation that resistance involves far more subtle and natural processes.

In the 'Managerial Approaches' section resistance is defined and reasons for resistance occurring are identified, manifestations of resistance are discussed and approaches to managing resistance are introduced. In the 'Critical Perspective', stability is acknowledged as being more prevalent than first envisaged, debates around resistance to change are believed to have been obscured by change-agent-centric thinking and the need to rethink resistance and resistance terminology is highlighted.

MANAGERIAL APPROACHES

THE WHAT, WHY AND HOW OF RESISTING CHANGE

The observation that resistance is in the eye of the beholder (King and Anderson 2002) highlights that even within the same organisation there will be multiple perceptions of resistance, ranging from resistance as disloyal behaviour to resistance as heroic and morally justified. The existence of different perceptions makes defining resistance to change problematic. In this section the following definition is favoured: 'resistance towards change encompasses behaviours that are acted out by change recipients in order to slow down or terminate an intended organisational change' (Lines 2004, p198). In this quotation managerial concerns about resistance to change are emphasised and the quotation raises questions about why resistance occurs and what the manifestations are of such negative resistance.

In studying why resistance to change occurs in organisations, diagnosis at the individual, group and organisational level is necessary (King and Anderson 2002). Individuals have to negotiate and manage change on a daily basis: 'we may like change and regard it as an essential feature of living: it does not mean that we always welcome it' (Fransella 1975, p135). An individual's personality can encourage resistance, with Watson (1967) identifying the following major forces. Homeostasis refers to our built-in self-regulatory mechanisms; for example, exercise raises the heartbeat until the rising heartbeat is resisted. Habit dictates that we behave in an accustomed way and may resist any deviations, for example the habit of sleeping on Sunday afternoons and subsequently resisting an opportunity to watch a film instead. Primacy refers to how we first coped with a situation, which sets a pattern, for example overeating when faced with rejection and subsequent advice to eat in moderation being resisted. Selective perception involves making sense of a situation in a particular way, for example perceiving a line manager as a bully and then resisting their instructions on the grounds that they are perceived as a bully.

Palmer et al (2009) identified further reasons why individuals resist change, including: dislike of change, discomfort with uncertainty, perceived breach of psychological contract and excessive change. An explanation of why individuals are selective in the changes they resist has been offered by Burke (2008, p93), who cites Brehm (1966): 'what comes closer to a universal truth about human behaviour is that people resist the imposition of change'. It is important to acknowledge that groups and teams may both help to facilitate change as well as resist change, as discussed in Chapter 8. Group cohesiveness, social norms and participation in decision-making have been identified as potential group factors causing resistance (King and Anderson 2002).

In terms of organisational causes of resistance to change, ironically success can result in organisational-level resistance to change. *The Icarus Paradox* drew upon Greek mythology in order to highlight how chief executives, in beginning to believe that their businesses were infallible, made their businesses more fallible (Miller 1990). Equally, Paton and McCalman (2008, p54) warn against 'change for change's sake, change for short-term commercial advantage or indeed change which may adversely affect the "common good" should be resisted...' The quotation warns against reactive change, which may occur in a climate of managerial fads and fashions. More generally many chapters in this textbook speak to potential organisational sources of resistance to change: structures, strategies, cultures and communications.

Manifestations of resistance to change will be many and varied, including: absenteeism, industrial action, procrastination, withdrawal and disruptive behaviour. It is important to appreciate that resistance to change is part of broader debates about workplace industrial relations and may be traced back over many centuries. Overt resistance of recalcitrant workers and a tendency to work limitation have been discovered again and again (Ackroyd and Thompson 1999).

MANAGING RESISTANCE TO CHANGE

In seeking to manage resistance to change it is important to acknowledge the individual differences and differences within groups and teams that have been highlighted in this textbook; there is neither one source of resistance to change nor one best way to manage resistance. People respond to change using a diverse range of defence mechanisms, suggesting that implementation of change may be more crucial than conceptualisation (Sorge and Van Witteloostuijn 2004). The influential mindset depicting resistance to change as something that must be overcome endures and consequently it is necessary to establish the historical origins of such a mindset. In particular the writings of Coch and French (1948), Lewin (1997) and Kotter and Schlesinger (1979) informed such thinking and their contributions are featured here, before considering more contemporary approaches.

Coch and French (1948) undertook their pioneering research at the Harwood Manufacturing Corporation in Virginia, USA. The plant produced pyjamas and mainly employed women. Changes in production methods were being met with resistance and the plant management wanted research to answer two questions:

1 Why do people resist change so strongly? and

2 What can be done to overcome this resistance? (Coch and French 1948, p512)

Preliminary work led the researchers to the view that individual frustrations were influenced by strong group-induced forces. Consequently they undertook an experiment varying group methods. The first variation involved group participation through representatives in the design of changes to be made in the jobs. The second variation involved groups in total participation by all members in designing changes and a third control group was used. The following conclusions were drawn from the research:

> It is possible for management to modify greatly or to remove completely group resistance to changes in methods of work and the ensuing piece rates. This change can be accomplished by the use of group meetings in which management effectively communicates the need for change and stimulates group participation in planning the changes. (Coch and French 1948, p531)

This pioneering action research informed the management of the plant and suggested potential new forms of industrial relations and industrial democracy. It is unfortunate that the major legacy of this research was to coin the phrase 'overcoming resistance to change'.

The field theory of Lewin (1997) (originally published in 1951) influenced thinking about managing resistance to change, although in ways that may never have been intended by Lewin himself. Lewin has been misrepresented and criticised; however, Cooke (1999) and Burnes (2004) encouraged a reappraisal of his work. Lewin regarded individual behaviour as a function of the group environment, or what he termed the 'field' (Burnes 2004). Lewin (1997, p351) identified two types of forces, which he referred to as driving and restraining forces: 'the forces toward a positive, or away from a negative, valence can be called driving forces. They lead to locomotion. These locomotions might be hindered by physical or social obstacles.'

In revisiting Lewin's original texts it is impossible to locate tools such as the force field analysis; however, they did originate out of his field theory and in particular his concepts of driving forces and restraining forces. Cummings and Worley (2008, p749) define a force field analysis as follows: 'a qualitative tool that analyzes the forces for and the forces resisting change. It implies two change strategies, increasing the forces for change or decreasing resistance to change.' This is a helpful definition, although it is ironic that Lewin with his preference for science and quantitative methods should be attributed with developing a famous qualitative analysis tool. The following example (Figure 12.1) highlights the driving forces and restraining forces with regard to introducing a new assembly line into a factory.

Figure 12.1 Example of a force field analysis

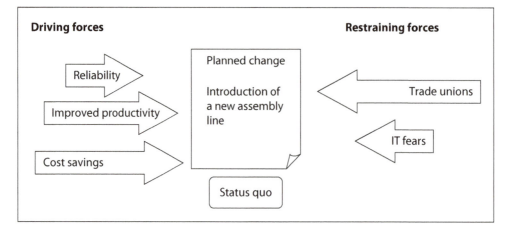

In the example in Figure 12.1 the arrows are different sizes to reflect the respective strengths of the different driving forces and restraining forces impacting upon the planned introduction of the new assembly line into the factory.

Kotter and Schlesinger (1979) argued that managers needed to be able to diagnose resistance to change and choose methods to overcome it. Their paper was very prescient in pre-empting preoccupations in American and Western companies with gaining competitive advantage over Japanese and Eastern companies. Change was increasingly being depicted as something that needed to be managed and resistance had to be overcome at all costs. Kotter and Schlesinger (1979) were able to both define the problem as resistance to change and offer their solution in the form of a repertoire of strategies for managing change. In their paper they identified what they believe to be the four most common reasons why people resist change: people's desire not to lose something of value, misunderstanding the change and its implications, believing the change does not make sense for the organisation, and their low tolerance for change. The diagnosis of reasons for resisting change subsequently informs the methods for dealing with resistance to change. Six potential approaches were prescribed: education and communication, participation and involvement, facilitation and support, negotiation and agreement, manipulation and co-optation, and explicit and implicit coercion.

They identified two common mistakes in the utilisation of these approaches, based upon their experience of working with companies: firstly, using only one approach or a limited number of approaches regardless of the situation; and secondly, approaching change in what they describe as a disjointed and incremental way, rather than as part of a considered strategy. While acknowledging subtleties and complexities of resistance, Dawson (2003) identifies change agents utilising such approaches to overcome resistance, ranging from participation and communication through to manipulation and coercion. He relates organisational development approaches to participative approaches and he relates contingency approaches more to coercive strategies.

There has been a growing acknowledgement that different perspectives in helping to identify broad causes of resistance to change inform the management of resistance to change. Burke (2008) cites the work of Hambrick and Cannella (1989), distinguishing between blind, political and ideological resistance. Individuals in the 'blind resistance' category were believed to be afraid or intolerant of any change. Individuals in the 'political resistance' category believed they may lose something of value if change was implemented. And individuals in the 'ideological resistance' category believed that change was ill-fated or against their deeply held values. Blind resistance would suggest the need for education and communication, whereas political resistance would suggest the need for negotiation, and ideological resistance would suggest the need for coercion.

A more subtle framework, identifying four predominant perspectives, has been suggested by Graetz et al (2006): the psychological model, the systems model, the institutional approach, and the organisational cultures approach.

The psychological model specifies causes of resistance to change in terms of individual behaviours. The systems model suggests that it is not change as such that people resist, but that instead people resist losing something. According to the institutionalised approach, resistance becomes embedded in organisational structures, decision-making processes and resource allocation. The organisational cultures approach explains resistance in terms of the existence of cultures and the challenges of cultural change discussed in Chapter 13. King and Anderson (2002) concluded that offering generalised models and advice on overcoming resistance to change was fraught with danger.

CRITICAL PERSPECTIVE

Managing change debates are configured in the best interests of managers, rather than in the broader interests of employees and society, which is exemplified in the misrepresentation of resistance to change as something to be overcome. Dawson (2003, p20) observed with irony that '… given the number of failed change initiatives, those who question the need for change are often cast as the villains of the piece, as unable to adapt to the dynamic changing conditions of the modern world'. In this 'Critical Perspective', the role of stability is considered as well as the role of change-agent-centric thinking. There is consequently a need to rethink resistance and resistance to change terminology.

CHANGE AND STABILITY

Instead of the caricature of senior management imposing change that employees then resist, there is an opportunity for employees to become involved in ongoing processes of changing. King and Anderson (2002, p220) offer the following colourful medical metaphor: 'we must move away from seeing organizational members who resist change only as bad patients who refuse to take their medicine; resistance may equally well be seen as a defence mechanism against the pathogens of change'. There is a need to be resourceful when dealing with resistance, rather than relying upon generalised remedies to overcome resistance to change.

It is informative to consider that notions of individual and institutional resistance to change may be rational. People tend to be selective in the changes they welcome, as discussed in Chapter 9. We may vote with our feet when a supermarket constantly changes its layout or vote through the ballot box when a government fails to support, for example, the most vulnerable in our society. When your partner 'contests "another" late night at the office, or when your child balks at a new baby-sitter, they are resisting change' (Conner 1998, p125). The urge towards stability that managerialist commentators depict as irrational resistance to change may prove to be a rational human response. One characteristic that may influence choices to resist certain changes and embrace other changes has been referred to as the conservative impulse:

> Thus the impulses of conservatism – to ignore or avoid events which do not match our understanding, to control deviation from expected behaviour, to

isolate innovation and sustain the segregation of different aspects of life –
are all means to defend our ability to make sense of life. (Marris 1974,
p11)

This is an eloquent explanation of why certain individuals may resist certain
changes; in essence, resistance to change acts as a coping mechanism to deal
with the complexities of life. In this context seeking out stability at the very
least appears understandable. The following quotation is particularly notable,
both because Schon (1963, p82) was writing in the early 1960s and because
as a mainstream writer he may be differentiated from the more radical writers
cited in this chapter: 'resistance to change is not only normal but in some
ways even desirable. An organisation totally devoid of resistance to change
would fly apart at the seams.' Burke (2008, p93), an academic with extensive
consultancy experience, regards resistance as '... a natural human response
and, like one's defence mechanisms, should be respected'. In organisational
settings, managers and employees are judged on their ability to cope with and
manage change (Sorge and Van Witteloostuijn 2004; Paton and McCalman
2008), defining any form of resistance as irrational. Job descriptions often
include references to managing change, with references to managing stability
far less evident.

The management of stability may be regarded as the antithesis of much of the
popular rhetoric of change, particularly the espousal of constant change (see for
example Matheny 1998). But what if commentators such as Abrahamson (2000)
were correct in suggesting that in changing successfully, companies should stop
changing all the time? This type of view is certainly not the orthodoxy. Eccles and
Nohria (1992) claimed that arguments for maintaining the status quo were hard
to find and even harder to defend. Both managing change successes and failures
breed new demands for change, with only the absence of change regarded as
deficiency (Sorge and Van Witteloostuijn 2004).

The critical change literature is more circumspect about the espoused case for
constant change, suggesting that we need more messages about old-fashioned
stability (Mintzberg et al 2009). These messages initially appear nostalgic, but
the implication is that we can learn from past change in terms of learning what
was bad, but equally what was good. Reed (2001, p24) argued that the belief
in constantly reengineering existing processes gives rise to anxiety and ignores
much of the good in what has gone before. Abrahamson (2000, p76) suggested
a new phrase, 'dynamic stability', defined as 'a process of continual but relatively
small change efforts that involve the reconfiguration of existing practices and
business models rather than the creation of new ones'.

Cummings (2002, p279) highlighted the paradox that managing change requires
continuity and was sceptical about greenfield site notions of change that
advocated fresh starts, believing that it is difficult for people to forget histories
and traditions. Similarly, Sturdy and Grey (2003, p652) caution against change
and continuity as alternative states: 'they are typically coexistent and coterminous;
and they are not objective because what constitutes change or continuity is
perspective dependent'. Although stability may appear to be the antithesis of

change, according to such perspectives stability may be a natural state. Managers, in seeking to overcome resistance to change, may be misunderstanding organisational change. While managers may dream of a completely compliant workforce, the concern is that such a workforce would be unlikely to effectively deliver products or services. Resistance can act as a counterbalance to ill-conceived and poorly enacted change, which is detrimental to the productive efficiency of the organisation (King and Anderson 2002). In Journal Research Case 12.1, Perren and Megginson (1996) offer case studies of managers who believed that they had made a positive difference through resisting change.

JOURNAL RESEARCH CASE 12.1

Middle managers

Paper title: Resistance to change as a positive force: its dynamics and issues for management development
Sector: Various
Research methods: Narratives told at an open space conference and on an MSc/MBA course
Authors: Perren, L. and Megginson, D.
Year: 1996
Journal details: *Career Development International*. Vol 1, No 4. pp24–28.

Commentary: Middle managers are a potentially powerful group in terms of resisting change. However, given the contentious nature of resistance it can be difficult to research resistance inside organisations. The authors gathered case illustrations of resistance to change at an open space conference themed around management development and from participants on an MSc/MBA course in technology management. The ten short, real-life cases presented in the paper illustrate how change was perceived to have been successfully resisted by middle managers. Based upon these case studies of resistance by middle managers, the authors illustrate tactics used for resistance, including: feigning agreement to change and obtaining control of the change process; say no, and link reasons to core values of the organisation; delay by continuously requesting further information and set managers involved with change against each other. They identified a potential organisational benefit of resistance as preventing folly.

CHANGE-AGENT-CENTRIC THINKING

In order to critically challenge misconceptions about resistance to change, it is informative to consider how change-agent-centric thinking has dominated the debate (change agents and agency are the focus of Chapter 17). Ford et al (2008, p362) define the change-agent-centric view as presuming '… that resistance is an accurate report by unbiased observers (change agents) of an objective reality (resistance by change recipients)'. They draw upon Weick's (1979) analogy of an umpire calling balls and strikes fairly as they observe them. Umpires and change agents inevitably offer their own observations of what is happening. Ford et al (2008) believe that it is necessary to expand the resistance story in three ways.

Firstly, by acknowledging that the resistance label may potentially be self-fulfilling and self-serving, the label may both define change recipients as resistors and simultaneously create a rationale for the presence of change agents. Secondly, change agents through their actions and inactions may contribute to the reactions of change recipients. Thirdly, acknowledging the positive contribution that so-called resistance may make to processes of changing. In a manner similar to Piderit (2000), they advocate rethinking resistance to change, advocating an approach that acknowledges the dynamic between three elements: recipient action, agent sense-making and the agent–recipient relationships. This approach is not just about offering more sophisticated forms of analysis, but also suggests new forms of change agency that place far greater emphasis upon collaboration and dialogue, rather than expending energy overcoming supposed resistors to change.

RETHINKING RESISTANCE AND RESISTANCE TERMINOLOGY

This chapter has challenged the orthodoxy that resistance should be regarded as an unfortunate aberration that change managers need to overcome, whether through education or coercion. Instead, there is a need for a re-evaluation of resistance to change, particularly in terms of the lack of sophistication of the analyses and the semantics of resistance to change. The first concern is with the lack of sophistication of analyses. Resistance is a rich and complex concept and deserves much greater attention than it often gets during managing change exercises (Stickland 1998). In this textbook the role of individuals in processes of changing has been emphasised. However, Ford et al (2002, p106) challenge individual-based explanations of resistance to organisational change: 'resistance, therefore, is not to be found "in the individual" but in the constructed reality in which individuals operate'.

Their complex although potentially enlightening argument is that resistance results out of 'background conversations' that create a reality for individuals, which is very different from notions that resistance exists within individuals. They identify three background realities: complacency, resignation and cynicism. Anyone who has experienced organisational change should be able to identify with these common background conversations. This form of analysis offers greater sophistication than the crude functionalism of earlier analyses. Also, there is a need to take into account the varied responses individuals and groups make to change: 'conceptualising employees' responses to proposed organisational changes as multidimensional attitudes permits a richer view of the ways in which employees may respond to change' (Piderit 2000, p789). This conceptualisation encourages an appreciation of the prevalence of ambivalence in individuals' responses to change.

In starting to rethink resistance to change, the problematic nature of resistance terminology is apparent. When thinking about national political systems, the semantics of government and opposition is employed, rather than government and resistance (Collins 1998). The terminology of resistance intentionally suggests something dysfunctional, whereas opposition to change (rarely used terminology) would be a more honest and constructive approach. Opposition is turned into resistance and then resistance is regarded as futile: 'the term seems to imply that those who resist are setting themselves to struggle against the inevitable...' (Collins 1998, p91). Kirton (2003, p293) takes arguments about terminology further, noting that 'the term is resistance to change – not to this change or my change. This is not to be dismissed as a subtle difference. There are no organisms that are resistant to all change – all are selective as to what change to accept and what not.'

So why is the terminology 'resistance to change' so frequently used in the context of managing change? Resistance terminology throws the entire blame for rejection (or even delay in acceptance) of a proposal for change onto those to whom it is proposed (Kirton 2003). This chapter has argued that individuals do not so much resist change as resist the uncertainty arising out of change, '... the ambiguity that results when the familiar ceases' (Conner 1998, p126). The favoured change terminology of 'resistance to change' may be misleading for those seeking to understand this concept, and may paradoxically be equally unhelpful in terms of managing change. As Piderit (2000, p792) concludes, the metaphor of resistance to change may have taken us as far as we can go. Instead, she favours retiring the phrase (see also Dent and Goldberg 2000; Merron 1993) in favour of research into employees' responses to change – in particular, their multidimensional attitudes. One of the concerns with the label 'resistance' is that it 'can be used to dismiss potentially valid employee concerns about proposed changes' (Piderit 2000, p784). It is now time to retire 'resistance to change' terminology ... although there would probably be considerable resistance from managers and mainstream management writers.

CONCLUDING COMMENTARY

Overcoming resistance to change terminology can be traced back to 1948. This terminology depicts individuals and groups as irrationally blocking supposedly rational organisational change. The goal becomes to overcome resistance and this chapter has highlighted theoretical contributions to achieving this goal. However, increasingly there has been an acknowledgement that rather than thinking in terms of resistance it is more appropriate to think in terms of responses to change. This change of emphasis is believed to better accommodate the presence of stability both within individuals and organisations and to move away from change-agent-centric thinking.

Resistance to change in Happy Homes call centre

Happy Homes call centre customer advisers design high-quality customer-focused solutions to meet all their customers' home insurance needs. This is marketing terminology for the call centre operation. The reality has been slightly different. The call centre function of Happy Homes is subcontracted to Express Efficient Calls Ltd (EEC) based in Unit B on an industrial estate. The terms of the contract between Happy Homes and EEC are very specific, involving measurable standards of service delivery and the conversion of calls into sales. The contract is regularly reviewed by Happy Homes. The manager of the call centre is Sarah Cracknell. She knows she is in fierce competition, not just with call centres in this country but also call centres globally.

Ms Cracknell is proud of EEC, which she has built up from nothing after spotting a niche for call centres 15 years ago. At any one time there might be up to 100 staff working in the call centre, working on the dawn, daylight or twilight shifts. The majority of employees work part-time. The call centre has the look of a hybrid between an open-plan office and a factory. There are rows and rows of desks, with computer monitors on each desk. Ms Cracknell has a raised glass office in one corner of the building. The walls of the building are very bare, only interrupted by neon signs flashing up details of targets and calls answered on time. Employees are divided into four colour-coded teams of approximately 25 employees. A supervisor is allocated to each team and can be seen moving from desk to desk because they wear suits reflecting the colour of their particular team.

Ms Cracknell runs a very efficient operation and everything has been going smoothly. Happy Homes have been pleased with the service delivery and sales, although enough has never quite been enough for Happy Homes. Through focus group work they have identified an innocent question for customer advisers to ask midway through each call: 'Do you enjoy living in your current home?' Their research has revealed that this question encourages customers to access good feelings about their home, and also introduces an element of informality into the conversation, yet because it is a closed question it will not lead to a discussion. Ms Cracknell has been instructed to ensure that all customer advisers ask this question during every call. She has also been warned that Happy Homes will be sampling monitored calls to ensure that this requirement is being met. Being proactive, she has decided to undertake her own monitoring in anticipation of future Happy Homes monitoring of calls.

She monitors the calls of customer advisers for one week on the busy daylight shift. Out of 100 of her employees, 80 are asking the question, and 20 employees are not asking the question. She interviews all those 20 employees to establish why they are failing to ask the question as instructed. At this stage three employees resign, stating that the job is not worth the hassle. The other interviewees are more forthcoming and explain their reasoning as best they can. Her initial hunch was that the 20 might have all come from one team, but they are from across all four teams. When she analyses the interviews, it is possible to group individuals in terms of three main reasons for resistance.

The first grouping of reasons is couched in terms of an expressed preference to stick with the status quo. Customer advisers claim that they do not want to change the way that they have always worked.

'It worked well before, so why change it?'

'Why do we have to ask this silly question?'

'I am happy continuing as I always have done.'

The second grouping of reasons relate to terms and conditions of employment and industrial relations. Only 10% of employees are in a trade union and EEC does not recognise this union as negotiating on behalf of employees. Individuals claim (erroneously, as it emerges) that any changes to their work have to go through a process of negotiation.

'I don't mind asking any question, but I must be properly reimbursed for asking the question.'

'The regional union official is due to call me back on this one.'

'Most employees feel the same as me – they are just reluctant to take industrial action.'

The third grouping of reasons is the most illuminating. Individuals acknowledge that they should be asking the question – and that initially they were asking the question – but they are gaining negative customer responses to the question, and believe this will be bad for their individual customer service ratings and the overall customer service ratings for EEC.

'Their [the customer's] tone changes negatively after you have asked the question.'

'One customer asked if I was having a laugh.'

'A customer asked if I was a robot programmed to ask the same question that I had asked them yesterday.'

Ms Cracknell now realises that an innocent question that is so important to Happy Homes has the potential to derail a lucrative contract upon which EEC is utterly dependent.

Case study questions

1 Explain the three groupings of responses with specific reference to theories of resistance introduced in this chapter.

2 If you were Sarah Cracknell, how would you deal with each of these three forms of resistance?

3 How would thinking in terms of responses to change rather than resistance to change alter your understanding of this case study?

DISCUSSION QUESTIONS

1 Is it possible to live a fulfilling life without resisting everyday changes?

2 Why is resistance to change problematic for those managing change?

3 Why is organisational change more fashionable than organisational stability?

4 What alternative terminology to 'resistance to change' could be used?

KEY READINGS

ACKROYD, S. and THOMPSON, P. (1999) *Organizational misbehaviour*. London: Sage Publications Ltd.

As the title suggests, this book reverses the concept of organisational behaviour to organisational misbehaviour. This allows the authors to feature debates and theories which are traditionally left out of OB textbooks. The book is an enjoyable and thought-provoking read.

COLLINS, D. (1998) *Organizational change: sociological perspectives*. London: Routledge.

This book, as the title suggests, covers organisational change debates from a sociological perspective. This perspective questions much of the managerialism and functionalism within management writing. The book is consequently strong in questioning many assumptions about organisational change and illustrating different ways in which debates can be configured.

KING, N. and ANDERSON, N. (2002) *Managing innovation and change: a critical guide for organizations*. London: Thomson Learning.

The chapter on 'Resistance to change' in this accessible textbook is recommended reading. In particular, the chapter reviews six pieces of literature that have been influential in advising managers on how to overcome resistance to change in their organisations. As the authors acknowledge, it would be a 'gargantuan task' to review all the resistance to change literature, and they have identified some of the more influential literature. The chapter is thought provoking and benefits from the academic background of the authors in psychology.

Cultural change

INTRODUCTION

This chapter focuses upon organisational culture, sometimes referred to as corporate culture, and in particular the practicalities and plausibility of changing such cultures. All programmes of organisational change will have a cultural change element (Salaman and Asch 2003). Cultural change attempts to change how employees think and feel about work, its purposes and priorities. Organisational cultures unfold over years without conscious design, a result of many policies and decisions that have accumulated over time (Conner 1998). The dilemma is that although cultures may have changed in the past without conscious design, the goal became to manage cultural change through conscious design. The perceived benefits of cultural change include competitive advantage, conflict reduction, co-ordination and control (Brown 1998). However, academics were sceptical that culture change could deliver what it promised.

The 'Managerial Approaches' section begins with an acknowledgement of the influence of national cultures before discussing the cocktail of factors giving impetus to managerial interest in organisational culture. The meanings and theories of culture are introduced, as well as practical prescriptions about how to manage cultural change. Critical commentators have made major contributions to understanding cultural change, although their work has not been as well publicised as the more prescriptive literature. The 'Critical Perspective' questions the manageability of cultural change and culture is considered as a potential impediment to organisational change.

MANAGERIAL APPROACHES

NATIONAL CULTURAL CONTEXTS

Large companies are increasingly organised with a view to competing internationally, with multinational, global, international and transnational structures being identified (Bartlett and Ghoshal 1989). The dilemma that emerges is that '... the Anglo-Saxon model of change has dominated the world of change management' (Trompenaars and Woolliams 2003, p362). This model is very task-oriented, seeking to forget traditions as quickly as possible, rather than celebrate cultural differences. Theories and research into managing change will increasingly have to respond to national cultural diversity. The precursor to these developments in recent decades has been research seeking to understand national cultural differences.

Hofstede (1984, 1991) became synonymous with measuring national cultures through his extensive survey work of employees working for IBM and its subsidiaries in different countries. His research and analysis identified dimensions of difference between national cultures. The five dimensions identified were power-distance, uncertainty avoidance, individualism-collectivism, masculinity-femininity and long-term short-term orientation. Power-distance referred to the distribution of power in different countries. Uncertainty avoidance referred to dealing with ambiguities at an individual and institutional level. Individualism-collectivism referred to preferences to work for oneself and family or the common good. Masculinity-femininity referred to whether masculine or feminine values were dominant in a country. Long-term short-term orientation referred to countries pursuing either long-term or short-term goals.

The writings of Hofstede have certainly given impetus to engaging with national cultural contexts. However, there remains a need for caution when imposing an explanatory mindset developed in the West upon whole countries, such as China:

> To accept Hofstede's analysis is to assume the cultural homogeneity of nations – that lines on a map inscribe a unitary, patterned, and consistent common culture. In the vast majority of cases in the contemporary world, this is hardly feasible. (Clegg et al 2008, p246)

In the context of this chapter and this textbook, Clegg et al's concerns are shared. In studying organisational cultural change, national cultures and importantly subcultures evident within countries are influential. However, this should never be at the expense of stereotyping people as belonging to a single universal national culture.

MANAGERIAL INTEREST IN ORGANISATIONAL CULTURE

In the 1980s and 1990s, there was a managerial perception of organisational culture as the most important ingredient in achieving organisational success, although this perception has subsequently been revised (Alvesson and Sveningsson 2008). What were the origins of this managerial interest in organisational cultures? Mintzberg et al (2009) identified the Scandinavian Institutes for Administrative Research, formed in 1965, undertaking the earliest pioneering academic work into culture. However, culture was not a dominant issue in management literature outside Scandinavia prior to 1980 (Willmott 1993; Mintzberg et al 2009; Watson 2006).

The timing for a new form of change initiative was right, with earlier organisational change initiatives concentrating upon changing strategies and organisational structures. The resurgence of economic neo-liberalism and the reassertion of managerial prerogative in governing employee values (Willmott 1993) offered ideological support for new forms of change initiative. More pragmatically interest in culture was fuelled by global economics. American and British companies observed the Japanese 'economic miracle', which appeared to be underpinned by specific forms of culture in organisations (Dawson 1996). Brewis (2007, pp344/5) offers a helpful summary of the challenges managers faced at this time (see Box 13.1).

Box 13.1 Late 1970s managerial challenges (based on Brewis 2007)

1 a general decline in religious belief
2 the expansion of highly technical work and the growth of service industries
3 the limitations of a mechanical, 'Theory X' approach to managing people
4 innovative production methods
5 the 'Japanese miracle'

In Box 13.1 and the above discussion it is apparent that managerial interest in changing cultures was fuelled by a range of factors and that the concept of changing cultures may be regarded as a solution to perceived organisational problems. Interest in changing cultures resulted in attempts to develop more sophisticated classifications of existing organisational cultures.

DEFINING AND CLASSIFYING ORGANISATIONAL CULTURES

Alvesson and Sveningsson (2008), in reviewing 30 years of organisation culture studies, noted that commonalities in definitions were in terms of shared meanings, interpretations, values and norms. However, the absence of any consensus definition of culture has been acknowledged (Wilson 1992; Brown 1998; Jones et al 2005) and this lack of any consensus has inevitably impaired the study of culture. The lack of consensus may be explained by the different sources informing understanding of culture, which have included: climate research, national cultures and human resource management (Brown 1998). Schein (1990) suggested that definitional problems derive from the fact that organisation itself is ambiguous. Schein's (1990, p111) definition of culture is used for this chapter. Culture can be defined as:

> a pattern of basic assumptions, invented, discovered or developed by a given group, as it learns to cope with its problems of external adaptation and internal integration, that has worked well enough to be considered valid and, therefore, is to be taught to new members as the correct way to perceive, think, and feel in relation to those problems.

The study of culture has also been hampered by ambiguous classifications. Attempts have been made to differentiate culture and climate, as well as strong and weak cultures, and to acknowledge the existence of subcultures. Organisational climate as another strand of thinking informing the study of organisational culture has been defined as '… the beliefs and attitudes held by individuals about their organisation' (Brown 1998, p2). Although, he acknowledged that in recent years interest in climate had declined.

The notion of strong cultures enabling organisations to achieve excellent performance was originally associated with writers such as Deal and Kennedy (1982). Brown (1998, p226) has suggested that 'strong' is usually used as a synonym for consistency, suggesting that strong cultures are understood as being consistent cultures, although he remains sceptical about assertions relating to the benefits of strong cultures that have been made. In studying organisational culture, it is important to acknowledge the existence of subcultures. Organisations regardless of size contain subcultures, the beliefs, values and assumptions of which often compete with the dominant culture (Brown 1998). In any large organisation, it will be possible to identify a range of subcultures, which may relate to functions, professions or the nature of work undertaken.

In the following discussion three influential theories (Handy 1978; Peters and Waterman 1982; and Deal and Kennedy 1982) that began a process of classifying and differentiating organisational cultures are introduced. These theories have also been used prescriptively to suggest how cultures could be changed. Harrison (1972), writing in the early 1970s, identified four main types of organisational culture. Handy (1978) reworked and promoted Harrison's ideas, describing the four cultures using simple symbols and references to Greek mythology. The four cultures are summarised in Box 13.2.

Box 13.2 Four organisational cultures (based on Handy 1978)

Power culture (spider's web) – emphasis upon a single power source
Role culture (Greek temple) – emphasis upon rules, procedures and job descriptions
Task culture (lattice) – emphasis upon expertise rather than position or charisma
Person culture (cluster) – emphasis upon the individual as part of a collective

In Box 13.2 the four cultures are listed in terms of what they place emphasis upon. As the title suggests, the power culture places emphasis upon a central power source, which may be an individual or a senior management team. An example of a power culture would be Rupert Murdoch's News International Group. Such cultures can have a clear sense of direction, although senior management succession can be problematic. Bureaucracies are inevitably role cultures, with emphasis placed upon rules and procedures. The classic example of a role culture is the UK civil service (although this may be a stereotype of the diverse organisations that make up the civil service). Advantages of such cultures include their predictability and stability, although the counterpoint is their inability to change, particularly in unpredictable environments.

Task cultures often focus upon specific projects and jobs, emphasising the need to bring together functional specialisms, typically through matrix structures. Management consultancies often adopt task cultures. Flexibility and task focus are regarded as advantages of these cultures, whereas achieving economies of scale can be problematic. Person cultures are the loosest form of culture in that they are often little more than collections of people undertaking similar work. The classic examples are groupings of professionals such as architects and lawyers, either working within their own practice or employed within a large organisation. An advantage can be their ability to work autonomously, although a disadvantage can be the manageability of professionals in such cultures. Handy's classifications were believed to have been influential in shaping the way culture scholars, students and practitioners understood how organisations work (Brown 1998). Even to this day upon entering a new organisation it is possible to detect signs of a power, role, task and person culture.

The success (in terms of book sales) of *In Search of Excellence* (Peters and Waterman 1982) was fuelled by and lent impetus to managerial interest in cultural change. The potential benefits of successfully managing cultural change appeared to be considerable. Peters and Waterman (1982) highlighted relationships between organisational culture and performance, based upon their studies of (at the time) successful companies, which included IBM, Boeing, Walt Disney and McDonald's. The book drew upon 'lessons from America's best run companies' in order to identify eight attributes of excellent companies. The eight attributes were: a bias for action, close to the customer, autonomy and entrepreneurship, productivity through people, hands-on, value driven, stick to the knitting, simple form, lean staff and simultaneous loose–tight properties. These attributes of excellent companies highlighted the populist language and tone of the book.

The plausibility of what Peters and Waterman were proposing captured the imagination of many at that time. *In Search of Excellence* (Peters and Waterman 1982), with hindsight, can be viewed as a timely response to many managerial concerns introduced at the beginning of this chapter; it appeared to offer an off-the-shelf solution to a managerial problem. Deal and Kennedy (1982), through examining hundreds of companies, were able to identify four general corporate culture types based upon the degree of risk and speed of feedback characteristic of a given industry. In Box 13.3 the culture types are summarised with illustrative examples.

Box 13.3 Culture types (based on Deal and Kennedy 1982)

The tough-guy, macho culture: management consultants
The work-hard/play-hard culture: computer companies
Bet-your-company culture: oil companies
The process culture: insurance companies

In the tough-guy, macho cultures risks were regarded as high, but equally feedback was rapid. A good example of this culture was among hospital surgeons. The culture emphasised getting the job done as quickly and effectively as possible, but this may be at the expense of co-operative forms of activity. The work-hard/play-hard culture was best understood in terms of high-street retail organisations, where feedback was immediate and risks were relatively low. This culture encouraged achievement in the present, although the downside was lack of understanding about future developments. Bet-your-company cultures involved high risks without the benefit of immediate feedback. The start-up of Amazon is cited as a contemporary example of such a culture. The culture encourages scientific breakthroughs, but inevitably risks were high. Process cultures were exemplified by the work that was undertaken with limited risk and slow feedback; insurance companies were depicted as process cultures. Process cultures facilitate large amounts of routine work, but they did not facilitate change in rapidly changing environments.

Deal and Kennedy (1982) encouraged managers to regard culture, rather than structure, strategy or politics, as shaping organisations. In the 'Critical Perspective', criticism of the classifications of Handy, Peters and Waterman, and Deal and Kennedy are featured.

MANAGING CULTURAL CHANGE

Attempts to differentiate organisational cultures, particularly in terms of performance, may be regarded as precursors to more full-blown attempts to manage cultural change. Implicit and sometimes explicit within the writings of Handy, Peters and Waterman, and Deal and Kennedy was the promise that by changing an organisation's culture higher performance could be achieved. Morgan and Sturdy (2000), although not advocates for such approaches, mapped out the ingredients of a cultural change programme that included identifying current shared values and norms, stating what the culture should be, identifying the gap between the two and developing a plan to close the gap.

An example of such an approach would be Sathe (1985), identifying five points at which managers seeking to create cultural change must intervene: behaviour, justifying behaviour changes, using cultural communications, hiring, and socialisation and removal of deviants. The approach offered a recipe for changing cultures. Socialisation was often regarded as an opportunity to change cultures, with socialisation most evident upon joining a new organisation, although it was an ongoing process. Socialisation varies from organisation to organisation and can be either explicit or implicit or a combination. Explicit socialisation might take the form of a formalised induction programme, whereas implicit socialisation may arise through gossip in the canteen.

Cultural change seeks to change the way existing employees think and feel about their work. Cultural change prescriptions are often couched in terms of guidelines, and the guidelines offered by Weiss (2001) are typical of the guidelines offered; they include beginning with a clear vision, senior management being actively committed to the new values and cultural change being supported in all organisation systems. In the following discussion two major contributions to understanding cultural change through the work of Schein and Johnson are featured.

Schein's work has been highly influential in explaining how organisational cultures develop and how different organisational cultures may be deciphered. Schein (1990) identified different ways a culture may be created, which included norm formation around critical incidents, leader figures modelling values and assumptions, socialisation of new members entering the group, groups changing in response to changes in their environment and the bringing together of two cultures as part of mergers and acquisitions. Another way of understanding culture formation is through an analysis of the start-up of an organisation.

Schein (2004) highlighted the steps a typical business goes through in terms of forming a culture. Firstly, the founder(s) has the idea for a new enterprise. The core group forms sharing a common goal and vision, and this group begins acting in concert and common. As more people are brought into the organisation a common history is built. Subsequently leaders are able to embed their beliefs, values and assumptions through primary embedding mechanisms and secondary articulation and reinforcement mechanisms. Examples of the primary embedding mechanisms include what the leader pays attention to and measures. Examples of secondary articulation and reinforcement mechanisms include organisational design and structure and stories about events and people.

Schein (2004) believed that cultural change was dependent upon the stage that an organisation had reached. He identified three major organisational stages: founding and early growth, midlife, and maturity and decline. Different cultural change mechanisms were relevant at each of these different stages. These mechanisms were regarded by Schein (2004) as cumulative, in that earlier mechanisms still operate while additional mechanisms become relevant.

Schein was also influential in offering a framework to analyse culture. Schein (1990, p111) suggested that 'in analysing the culture of a particular group or organisation it is desirable to distinguish three fundamental levels at which culture manifests itself: (a) observable artefacts, (b) values, and (c) basic underlying assumptions'. Artefacts in an organisation are the most observable aspects of a culture, including physical layout, dress codes, annual reports, procedure manuals and emails. They are the most tangible yet difficult to decipher accurately. Values may be studied through interviews, questionnaires or survey instruments. There is an opportunity to ask why phenomena happen the way they do. It is only through more intense observation that the taken-for-granted and often unconscious assumptions can be determined.

This framework is useful in differentiating between deep and shallow cultural change. What is interesting is that changing artefacts is more visible and may receive more attention than changing basic underlying assumptions. However, changing artefacts may have limited impact upon an organisation. Schein (2006) was well placed to offer guidance upon deciphering a company's culture, suggesting a seven-step process. The seven steps he identified were: define the business problem, review the concept of culture, identify artefacts, identify your organisation's values, compare values with artefacts, repeat the process with other groups and assess the shared assumptions.

Another influential approach for deciphering a company's culture was proposed by Johnson (1992). Johnson, through his development and dissemination of the cultural web, encouraged interest in symbolism with regard to strategic change. He (1992, p36) summarises his interest as follows: '... the social, political, cultural and cognitive dimensions of managerial activities which both give rise to the sort of incremental strategic change typical in organisations: but which can also be employed to galvanize more fundamental strategic change'. The terminology of the cultural web evoked the idea of a spider's web. At the centre of the web, Johnson (1992, pp29/30) placed the paradigm, which he defined as '... a cognitive structure or mechanism: however, this set of taken for granted assumptions and beliefs, which is more or less collectively owned, is likely to be hedged about and protected by a web of cultural artefacts'.

The cultural artefacts that Johnson identified were symbols, power structures, organisational structures, control systems, rituals and routines, and stories and myths. The cultural artefacts may be clarified as follows. The symbols included such artefacts as logos and offices. Power structures were invariably linked to the paradigm. Organisational structures reflected the organisational designs and forms discussed in Chapter 6. The control systems were believed to delineate important areas of an organisation. The rituals and routines guided people's behaviour in organisations, and stories and myths captured the influence of different narratives within organisations. In the paper, Johnson offered illustrations of cultural webs drawn up for a menswear clothing retailer, a consultancy partnership and a regional newspaper. By way of illustration the paradigm and examples of artefacts that can be identified at Arsenal Football Club are featured in Box 13.4.

Johnson explained how the cultural web may be used for undertaking cultural audits with companies. This approach was believed to allow managers to: identify the culture of their companies and how culture impacts on strategy, and understand the difficulties of changing culture. While being clear that the paper is not primarily about mechanisms of strategic change, he is able to highlight how cultural artefacts may be used to create a climate for change, how outsiders may help identify the paradigm and the significance to organisational life of symbols and routines.

Box 13.4 Cultural web (Johnson 1992) – Arsenal Football Club, an appreciative supporter perspective

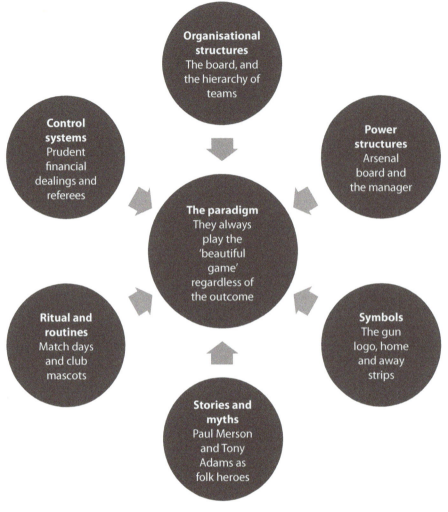

As a counterpoint to the 'Managerial Approaches' it is revealing that the wave of populist cultural change literature in the 1980s and early 1990s has not subsequently been sustained. However, while practitioners may have become disillusioned with prescriptive recipes for cultural change, unfortunately many mainstream management writers either ignore or have been unaware of critiques made of cultural management (Collins 2000). The following discussion draws upon critiques of cultural change and is organised around two themes: the manageability of cultural change and concerns about organisational cultures potentially impeding organisational change.

THE MANAGEABILITY OF CULTURAL CHANGE?

Alvesson (2002) highlighted how accounts of culture often depict existing ideas, beliefs and values as problematic, with change initiatives offering a solution within an environment in which the overall pace of change and need for change is exaggerated. This is similar to Wilson's (1992) concerns a decade earlier about the elixir-like qualities of cultural change. In questioning the populist turn in writing about cultural change, Alvesson (2002) uses the acronym MUUC (managerially-led unitary and unique culture) in order to parody how cultural change is often depicted.

Criticisms of the pioneering work of Handy, Peters and Waterman, and Deal and Kennedy are pertinent in terms of reviewing the manageability of cultural change. Wilson (2001) suggests that Handy (1978) ignores covert agendas within organisations and he ignores the perpetuation of gendered roles and gendered inequalities. Similarly, the language of Deal and Kennedy now appears dated, inappropriate and rather simplistic. Wilson (2001) has critically commented upon the gendered implications of such language.

Deal and Kennedy in 1999 had an opportunity to reappraise corporate cultural change with the benefit of almost two decades' hindsight: 'there must be a million consultants promising to help "change the cultures" of companies. Many of these consultants are even making a reasonable living from the practice. What a lot of bollocks' (Deal and Kennedy 1999, p35).

The huge commercial success of *In Search of Excellence* was relatively short-lived, with academics highlighting many flaws in the excellence recipe approach to managing change. The most striking flaw was the subsequent demise of the companies forming the basis of the research study underpinning *In Search of Excellence*. As academics began a very careful examination of the methodological and conceptual foundations of the excellence recipe for managing change, troubling shortcomings became increasingly apparent (see for example Guest 1992 and Collins 2000).

The critical literature has invariably brought realism to the exaggerated claims made about managing cultural change. Alvesson (2002, p185) warned that 'planned organisational cultural change is generally recognised as a difficult project'. Ogbonna and Wilkinson (2003), while acknowledging widespread controversy among academics about cultural change, identified three broad positions. Functionalists view culture as an organisational variable, subject to the control of management like any other organisational variables. This initially influential perspective was evident in the writings of Peters and Waterman and Deal and Kennedy on culture and was the focus of the earlier 'Managerial Approaches' section in this chapter. A second perspective may be regarded as a halfway house, suggesting some scope for cultural manipulation. The third perspective, which many critical commentators favour, is 'that the assumption that organisations can achieve planned cultural change is both intellectually flawed and practically impossible' (Ogbonna and Wilkinson 2003, p1154). It is this third perspective that critically questions the feasibility of managing cultural change.

Salaman and Asch (2003) raise doubts about the grounds of the gurus' claims and their efficacy with regard to cultural change. Firstly, organisational culture may prove to be more useful as an explanation of organisational behaviour than as a prescription on how to change an organisation. The excessive marketing of cultural change prescriptions appears to have increased this problem. Secondly, the concepts of culture and cultural change – despite excessive populist writing – remain confused and poorly defined, conceptually fuzzy and unlikely to deliver success in these terms (Dawson 1996). Despite a considerable body of literature about culture, Mintzberg et al (2009) criticised the conceptual vagueness of the cultural school.

Thirdly, it is difficult to reconcile the long-term time horizons of cultural change with the short-term time horizons of organisations. Organisational cultures do change over time, but this process takes place over years and decades, rather than days and months.

Fourthly, doubts have been expressed about the ability of senior managers to change cultures as the managerial rhetoric often implies. Many of these criticisms focus upon the difficulties of changing attitudes, values and beliefs. However, individuals' values are not open to short-term manipulation (Dawson 1996). Fifthly, cultural change initiatives are more likely to influence official as opposed to unofficial versions of an organisation. Watson (2006) defines official aspects of the organisation as all the rules, activities and values formally sanctioned by management, and the unofficial aspects are defined as rules, activities and values that develop at all levels in the organisation without formal managerial sanction.

In Journal Research Case 13.1, research-based insights into the difficulties of managing cultural change within a grocery retailer are presented.

JOURNAL RESEARCH CASE 13.1

STAR grocery retailer

Paper title: The false promise of organizational culture change: a case study of middle managers in grocery retailing
Research methods: Interviews, documents and analysis of trends.
Sector: Retail
Authors: Ogbonna, E. and Wilkinson, B.
Year: 2003
Journal details: *Journal of Management Studies*. Vol 40, No 5. pp1151–1178.

Commentary: The authors in this extended case study of grocery retailing explore the impact of culture change on one group of employees – middle managers. The case study organisation, referred to as STAR, employed over 100,000 employees at the beginning of the research in 1996. As this chapter has warned, culture can

be an area of study in which serious ambiguity can hamper effective organisational research. However, the strengths of this case study published in a leading management journal are the effective development of the context for the case and level of access to managers working in STAR. The authors are able to offer verbatim quotations from managers, highlighting perceptions of the cultural change taking place. The authors believed that middle managers might potentially have more readily identified with the espoused values of a cultural change programme. However, they found that changes in managerial behaviour related more to surveillance, direct control and the threat of sanctions rather than to any transformation of managerial values.

In seeking to manage cultural change the requirement to alter the attitudes, values and beliefs of individual employees raises ethical concerns, discussed in Chapter 16. It is worthwhile highlighting concerns at this point. In terms of considering the feasibility of changing a culture, senior management may have a perception of the culture of an organisation that differs from the perception of employees. Willmott (1993, p528) warned that 'advocates of corporate culture would like to persuade and assure us that their prescriptions are morally benign'. This is unlikely to be the case.

Bate (1994) highlighted aggressive, conciliative, corrosive and indoctrinative cultural change options. Aggressive cultural change was often initiated in response to an organisational crisis; it could be forceful and insensitive. Conciliative cultural change was based upon accommodation and egalitarianism; the emphasis was upon gradual and consensus-based change. Corrosive cultural change relied upon power and politics to change culture through manipulations of existing power relations. Indoctrinative cultural change operated through learning, development and training programmes in order to indoctrinate particular beliefs and values.

Salaman (1997, p252) argued that the dream of corporate culture books and consultants was the promise 'to be able to manage staff without their knowing or resenting this control; to get workers to accept managerial goals, authority and decisions so that they don't need managing or controlling...' Although the above discussion of the manageability of cultural change encourages a view of cultural change as another flawed fad, Salaman (1997) warned against such a view. He argued that although corporate culture programmes have not delivered the compliant and conformist individuals suggested by more prescriptive literature, they have reengineered the psychological contract between employee and employer. Individuals' sense-making and the construction of meaning are likely to have been impacted upon by corporate culture programmes.

CULTURE AS AN IMPEDIMENT TO ORGANISATIONAL CHANGE

Quirke (1995, p105), in his functionalist account of communicating change, offers a beautifully acidic aside about culture: 'the force of the culture is for the status quo; culture is the means by which we bring stability to the threat of change'. Similarly, Alvesson (2002) warned that cultural maintenance means counteracting gradual change. This cultural maintenance is achieved through everyday activities and talk and, paradoxically, may be regarded as the antithesis of managing organisational change. Managing cultures and managing change both gained prominence in the 1980s onwards, suggesting a mutual compatibility. However, commentators have questioned the potentially contradictory nature of culture and change.

According to Mintzberg et al (2009) culture can discourage necessary change in favouring the management of consistency. In emphasising tradition and consensus, a kind of stagnation is encouraged, which may explain the spectacular collapses of businesses such as Marks & Spencer and IBM. Strong cultures can reinforce beliefs that businesses are unchallengeable. Flynn and Chatman (2001) identified the apparent paradox by which cultural strength purportedly limits individual creativity. There is a real danger that a strong culture may be a barrier to diversity in that managers do not seek out and hire individuals from different backgrounds and it is difficult to reconcile strong unifying cultures with the achievement of diverse workplaces.

Wilson (2001) warned that writing on organisational culture tends to be written as if it was gender neutral, whereas it is gender blind in a manner similar to most organisational studies writing. Wilson (2001) cites Cockburn (1991) and Itzin and Newman (1995), highlighting organisational cultures as significant barriers to change when attempting to change gender relations through the development of equal opportunities policies and initiatives. In terms of mergers and acquisitions, Schein (1990) warned that the compatibility of cultures is only considered after a deal has been completed and this can be problematic. At the beginning of this chapter it was suggested that the management of culture offered a solution to perceived problems. However, as this discussion has suggested, organisational culture may be part of the problem, rather than the solution.

CONCLUDING COMMENTARY

Interest in the 1980s in managing change was closely aligned with cultural change. Organisational cultures informed by larger national cultures were perceived as malleable and requiring change. Cultural change programmes were packaged as a solution to problems of competitive advantage in the West when faced with competition from the East. In order to change a culture it was necessary to understand and classify organisational cultures. The writings of Handy, Peters and Waterman, and Deal and Kennedy offered classifications that appeared to simplify the subtleties of organisational cultures. In the 1980s there was considerable interest in changing cultures – everything was believed to be possible. However, this level of expectation was not sustainable as it became apparent that cultures were less malleable than consultants had suggested. The benefit of such scepticism was that a deeper understanding of organisational cultures was achieved, which highlighted that in certain situations a strong culture could even prove to be an impediment to organisational change.

Midlands Building Society

The origins of Midlands Building Society (MBS) can be traced back to the beginning of the last century. MBS developed through a series of mergers into being a respected if not high-profile regional building society. The society employs 1,000 staff, of which 500 staff work part-time. Staff work either at one of the 80 branches or at head office. The society is able to provide customers with a range of financial services, from deposit accounts through to loans and mortgages. It is proud to have remained a mutual building society despite overtures from a number of large financial services institutions. Although the building society has experienced mergers and has recently changed the fascias of all the branches, in other ways little has changed in MBS. Their motto, 'Community Banking: Banking on the Community', has remained the same for as long as anyone can remember.

Against this backdrop of quiet inertia Patrick Fitzgerald has joined MBS as the new chief executive. Mr Fitzgerald was deliberately headhunted by the board of MBS from a senior management position in one of the high street banks. The board had impressed upon Mr Fitzgerald that mutual status was not negotiable, but that MBS was ready for 'some radical change'. The board never expanded upon what they had in mind by this last phrase, but it was apparent that part of Mr Fitzgerald's role would be to act as a change agent. Upon his arrival, in a short message to staff he announced he would spend the first 100 days visiting every branch and meeting as many staff as possible. He was true to his word, and at the end of a gruelling schedule he felt well prepared to report to the board.

As they had anticipated, he confirmed their suspicions. Everything he had seen and heard suggested that MBS was flourishing. There was a low turnover of staff and high levels of staff commitment were apparent. Staff really did believe that they were providing a service to the community, which had been repeatedly demonstrated by the actions of staff, particularly in the branches. He had been unable to access any marketing information because there was no marketing department as such. However, the impression gained was of a loyal elderly customer base who felt assured when they deposited their savings with MBS. There had been a few rumblings from customers about the new branch fascias. In having a content workforce and a content customer base, Mr Fitzgerald as chief executive could have been regarded as being in an enviable position. However, Mr Fitzgerald was very troubled by what he had learned.

The finance function at the head office was antiquated yet very competent. They showed him forecast information, which suggested that MBS would be experiencing large and growing deficits within two more years. When he explored the reasons for the deficits, it was very apparent that costs were escalating but revenues were static. In particular, staff costs were proving to be a large drain upon resources and the rents on the high street premises were making many of the branches uneconomic to run. On the revenues side the building society gained from its large deposit base, but in potentially profitable areas – such as the provision of credit facilities – business was weak. This troubling report did not surprise the board. Mr Fitzgerald's recommendations did, however, surprise the board.

He warned that there needed to be a dramatic cultural change if MBS was to survive, and he advised that even if there was cultural change he could not guarantee the survival of MBS. In order to 'wake up' the building society he recommended the immediate announcement of plans to close eight branches (10% of the branch network). The rationale for these closures would be presented to staff as vital cost-cutting and part of a wider project, referred to internally as Project Phoenix.

Project Phoenix aimed to encourage a sales culture while maintaining the high-quality customer service that typified MBS. All branch managers would be required to attend the 'Sales through Service' management development workshops. These workshops would be deliberately challenging, and at the end of the workshop each branch manager would be required to sign a promise to deliver sales at a specified amount. Any branch manager who failed to sign the promise would be offered career counselling. A less intense version of 'Sales through Service' would be cascaded through MBS to the effect that all employees would be required to make a verbal pledge to deliver sales, on every day of every week of every year. Again, if the pledge was not made, staff would be encouraged to rethink their future with MBS. The Phoenix facilitators would visit branches at six-monthly intervals to check that the new attitudes, values and beliefs had been adopted through a series of questionnaires and interviews. The facilitators would also ensure that sales targets had been exceeded. All the data would be gathered to establish the six-monthly branch grading that might be 'Sales Competent', 'Sales Confusion' or 'Sales Incompetent'. An urban myth was deliberately spread throughout the branches that any branch graded as 'Sales

Incompetent' would be top of the list in the next anticipated wave of closures.

The board was shell-shocked at the end of the presentation. Three board members walked out of the room mumbling that this was the death of the society as they knew it. The remaining members were more philosophical, arguing for an evolution rather than a revolution. They argued quite persuasively that the change would be too radical for both staff and customers. Certain board members felt uneasy with a sales culture that they saw as contradicting the long-established service culture MBS had developed. However, Mr Fitzgerald was adamant that either the board adopted Project Phoenix or he would resign because he was otherwise unable to envisage a future for MBS.

Case study questions

1 Explain what is being proposed, with reference to theories of cultural change.

2 How are employees being socialised into new ways of thinking and behaving?

3 What would be the impediments to achieving this cultural change?

4 How could this cultural change be managed differently?

DISCUSSION QUESTIONS

1 Are the ambiguities of culture an analytical strength or weakness?

2 In what ways may all change management be considered a form of cultural change?

3 How may culture impede or enhance attempts to change an organisation?

4 What do you believe the future holds for understanding culture and our attempts to manage cultural change?

KEY READINGS

ALVESSON, M. and SVENINGSSON, S. (2008) *Changing organizational culture: cultural change work in progress.* **London: Routledge.**

It is easy to dismiss cultural change as a fad of the 1980s and 1990s that subsequently proved illusory. Critical accounts of cultural change often challenge the concept of managing cultural change without informing understanding about the lived experience of cultural change. This book fills that gap in that the authors offer an extended and up-to-date case study of cultural change within Technocom. In adopting this approach the reader gains rich insights into the longitudinal/processual nature of organisational change and can read first-hand accounts of employees experiencing organisational change.

SCHEIN, E.H. (2004) *Organizational culture and leadership.* **San Francisco, CA: Jossey Bass.**

This book, now in its third edition, was first published in 1985 at the height of interest in organisational culture. Schein is one of those writers who effectively straddle the theory and practice divide of change management. In this sense the book informs both theorising and understanding about organisational culture within organisations, as well as informs practice in organisations. The book is particularly strong on classifications of organisational culture and cultural change and is very readable.

PETERS, T. and WATERMAN, R. (1982) *In search of excellence.* **New York: Harper and Row.**

This book with hindsight proved to be a publishing phenomenon, selling millions of copies to managers and aspirant managers seeking the recipe for organisational success. It gave huge impetus specifically to the cultural change debate featured in this chapter and more generally offered a prescription about how to manage change. However, the book has not stood the test of time; the eight ingredients in its recipe for success appear simplistic and, more troublingly, subsequent studies of claims made in the book have highlighted its many methodological and conceptual weaknesses.

CHAPTER 14

Organisational learning

LEARNING OUTCOMES

After reading this chapter you should be able to:

- appreciate the different approaches to understanding learning
- understand the concept of organisational learning
- understand the concept of the learning organisation
- appreciate criticisms of organisational learning
- appreciate criticisms of learning organisations
- understand the concept of organisational forgetting.

INTRODUCTION

The concepts of learning and changing are closely related, which reflects the difficulties that organisations encounter in defining and resolving all eventualities arising out of organisational change (Woodward and Hendry 2004). The collective nature of learning is believed to be especially important in complex and turbulent environments, as in such circumstances senior managers may not be the best-placed individuals to identify opportunities and threats. Hendry (1996, p638) believed that '… learning theories can contribute to the understanding and management of different facets and stages of organisational change'. Drivers of organisational learning that have been identified include the inexorability of change, the unpredictability of the future and the importance of imagination (Starkey et al 2002).

The aim of this chapter is to evaluate the contribution of organisational learning and learning organisations to managing change. In the 'Managerial Approaches' section, broad schools of thought about learning are presented by way of an introduction to organisational learning. Organisational learning and learning organisations are differentiated and discussed in terms of their implications for managing change. In the 'Critical Perspective', the critiques of organisational learning and learning organisations are offered. The concept of organisational memory and forgetting is presented as a counterpoint to the popular rhetoric of organisational learning.

APPROACHES TO LEARNING

Learning has been described as 'a dynamic transformational process, continuously extended and redefined in response to the context in which it takes place' (Antonacopoulou and Gabriel 2001, p439). This quotation highlights both the appeal of learning and the subtleties required to understand learning. A precursor to understanding organisational learning is to understand broad schools of thought relating to learning in general. Reynolds et al (2002), while acknowledging that learning is subject to fashion, highlighted four 'clusters' of what is common in human learning, identifying learning as: behaviour, understanding, knowledge construction and social practice. Each of these clusters usefully introduces broad themes within this chapter. Theories that associate learning with behaviour are most commonly associated with Skinner (1974). Behavioural explanations of learning underpin all other explanations of learning, with reinforcement identified as the key feature:

> ... a reinforcer is anything that strengthens the desired response. It could be verbal praise, a good test result or a feeling of increased accomplishment or satisfaction. Reinforcers may be positive or negative. (Reynolds et al 2002, p16)

Burke regards Skinner's theories as contributing to the understanding of controlling behaviour within organisational change in general and organisational development in particular. Burke (2006) recommended Skinner's (1948) novel *Walden Two* as a depiction of a utopian community adopting Skinnerian principles. Learning as behaviour is believed to raise dilemmas, which include if behavioural reinforcement results in learning directly or is a stimulus to other learning processes, the transferability of skills acquired and unequal roles and power relations (Reynolds et al 2002).

Learning as understanding is also referred to as cognitive learning. This approach regards '... the learner as a powerful information-processing machine whose task is to internalise knowledge about the world' (Reynolds et al 2002, p19). Sauquet (2004) regards this approach as broadening the more limited perspective that behaviourism offers, with a focus upon cognitive processes and the limitations of human beings. Key dilemmas of this learning approach relate to employees knowing facts, but being unable to translate them into appropriate actions and the effective assessment of internalised learning (Reynolds et al 2002).

Learning as knowledge construction '... holds that people are active agents of their own learning, such that learning is not separated from personal action' (Reynolds et al 2002, p22). Dialogue is regarded as providing a primary vehicle for knowledge construction through discussion, debate and collective analysis; in this way learning is highly context-specific. The resulting dilemmas are about the consistency of thought and the manageability of such processes (Reynolds et al 2002).

Learning as social practice locates learning '... in the process of co-operation ... learning requires a social setting to occur, and to be applied' (Reynolds et al 2002, p25). The potential of this approach exceeds the other three approaches; however, key dilemmas include organisational culture determining the degree to which social learning is possible, the extent to which shared understanding can be reached and learning is dependent upon personal disposition and social skills (Reynolds et al 2002).

The implication of this discussion is that there is no one best way to understand learning, with competing schools of thought offering competing explanations of processes of learning (see also Probst and Buchel 1997). Mintzberg et al (2009, p186), in their guide to the major schools of strategic management, highlighted how an appreciation of learning informs understanding about strategic management. An inspiring aspect of the learning school is how informed individuals in an organisation can contribute to strategy (Mintzberg et al 2009). According to the learning school, strategies emerge out of people acting individually or collectively learning about a situation and their organisation's capability of dealing with it.

The learning school, in a manner similar to the paradigms and perspectives discussed in Chapter 4, offers another means of understanding organisational change. In the context of managing change there are many benefits, with an approach that values the contribution of individuals as well as groups and teams in processes of changing. Mintzberg et al (2009) acknowledged how the learning school focuses attention on internal processes, particularly those dealing with innovation and change. Focusing on learning draws attention to how an organisation's past affects its present and how learning raises important issues about the future (Starkey et al 2002). Other factors believed to have fuelled interest in organisational learning relate to a perceived increase in the pace of change and competitive threats arising from globalisation (Burnes et al 2003).

ORGANISATIONAL LEARNING

The first explicit theorising about organisational learning can be traced back to Cangelosi and Dill (1965). However, it is Argyris who has become synonymous with the concept of organisational learning. Argyris, one of the leading protagonists in debates about organisational learning, has written about organisational learning for over 40 years. He distinguishes organisational learning from learning organisations as follows:

> We divide the literature that pays serious attention to organisational learning into two main categories: the practice-oriented, prescriptive literature of the 'learning organisation', promulgated mainly by consultants and practitioners, and the predominantly sceptical scholarly literature of 'organisational learning', produced by academics. (Argyris 1999, p1)

In reality the distinction is not this precise, as Argyris subsequently acknowledges. However, this distinction offers a way forward in understanding these related concepts. In this section the focus is upon organisational learning and in the next section the focus shifts to the learning organisation.

Fulmer and Keys (2002), in conversation with Argyris, cite Argyris explaining the early reactions of book publishers to the proposed concept of organisational learning: 'we know you and we know Don (Schon) and respect both of you, but do you think this topic will ever be of interest to the business community?' Despite the initial apprehension of the publishers, organisational learning did capture the imagination of both practitioners and academics, resulting in a large and at times contradictory body of literature. Theories of organisational learning have been identified in the disciplines of social psychology, management theory, sociology, information theory, anthropology and political theory (Argyris and Schon 1978). However, a generally agreed model or definition of organisational learning does not exist (Child 2005).

In their review paper, Burnes et al (2003) defined organisational learning in terms of four common propositions that underpin the concept, which may be summarised as follows. Firstly, organisations now need to learn at least as fast as the environment they operate in changes. Secondly, movement away from traditional forms of learning to organisational learning depends upon the amount of instability in the environment. Thirdly, maintaining alignment with an organisation's environment is no longer solely the responsibility of senior management. Fourthly, the whole workforce must be involved in the identification of the need for change and implementing change and learning. In these four propositions the rhetorical thrust of organisational learning is apparent. Organisational learning is a philosophy that values the contribution of groups and individuals in learning about changes in the environment and responding to them. The following discussion selectively considers those organisational learning debates, which have particular relevance to managing change: first-, second- and third-order change, double- and single-loop learning, organisational defensive routines, reflection and communities of practice.

In their discussion of learning and change, Coghlan and Rashford (2006) highlight the contribution of Bartunek and Moch (1987) in identifying first-order, second-order and third-order change. First-order change refers to a specific change that is implemented in line with existing ways of thinking, for example, communicating forthcoming change using a different communication channel. Second-order change refers to change informed by lateral thinking and questioning core assumptions. For example, many of the cultural change initiatives featured in Chapter 13 can be regarded as second-order change. Third-order change refers to employees learning to constantly question their own assumptions and develop new ones. For example, the discussion of complex adaptive systems featured in Chapter 2 illustrates third-order change. In differentiating levels of change in this way the implication is that different forms of learning are required.

The concepts of single-loop learning and double-loop learning are closely related to debates about first-, second- and third-order change and reflect the learning as understanding approach introduced in the previous section.

> Single-loop learning occurs when matches are created, or when mismatches are corrected by changing actions. Double-loop learning occurs when mismatches are corrected by first examining and altering the governing variables and then the actions. (Argyris 1999, p68)

The easiest way to understand these two obtuse forms of learning is in terms of their origins, which can be related back to the electrical engineering of a central heating system. A thermostat (single-loop learner) may be programmed to detect states of 'too cold' or 'too hot' and correct this by turning the heat on or off. If the thermostat asked itself why it was set at 68 degrees Fahrenheit, or why it was programmed as it was, then it would be a double-loop learner (Argyris 1999). Argyris believed that single-loop and double-loop learning were required by all organisations. However, in terms of organisational change, he regarded single-loop learning as the norm.

'Unfreezing', introducing new values and behaviour and 'refreezing'-type change models (Lewin 1951) are useful for single-loop learning, but gaps exist when attempting to produce double-loop learning using such models. The importance of this distinction as part of understanding organisational learning is that it signposts the potential need for individuals in organisations to move from single-loop to double-loop learning and in this way learn about change in ways that inform how individuals deal with change.

Another significant contribution Argyris (1999) made to organisational learning debates was highlighting the existence of organisational defensive routines. These routines were believed to be activated when participants deal with business or human problems that are embarrassing or threatening; the routines were regarded as being overprotective and anti-learning.

> Organisational defensive routines are any action, policy, or practice that prevents organisational participants from experiencing embarrassment or threat and, at the same time, prevents them from discovering the causes of the embarrassment or threat. (Argyris 1999, p58)

Argyris argued that for learning to persist, managers and employees needed to look inwards and reflect critically upon their own behaviours to identify how they inadvertently contribute to organisational problems. He used the example of professionals to demonstrate defensive routines at work. He found that professionals criticised others in order to protect themselves from embarrassment (defensive routine). Professionals did not perceive their own behaviours as resistance. Indeed, 'they were to be respected, if not congratulated, for working as well as they did under such difficult conditions' (Argyris 1999, p130).

While Argyris was not exclusively concerned with organisational change, his findings are very significant for managing change in that they make explicit the potential intangible resistance to change of managers and professionals, which traditionally goes unacknowledged. It is human nature to undertake face-saving behaviour when confronted with embarrassment. However, in his concept of organisational defensive routines, Argyris was interested in the institutionalised nature of such defences. Argyris (1985) differentiated organisational defensive routines from individual defensive routines in four ways, summarised in Box 14.1.

Box 14.1 Differentiating organisational from individual defensive routines (based on Argyris 1985)

1 The routines persist despite individuals leaving and joining the organisation.
2 Very different individuals use the routines in similar ways.
3 Routines are learned through socialisation.
4 Routines are triggered by concern/being realistic, rather than personal anxiety.

In recent years there has been growing interest in reflection as a catalyst for change. Reflection is regarded as both a catalyst for learning and a response to learning (Ghaye 2005). Ghaye believed that the potential exists both to learn from failure and reflect upon success. Kolb (1984) proposed a cycle that explained how learning was captured from experience. The Kolb (1984) learning cycle incorporated a concrete experiences stage, an observational and reflective stage, an abstract conceptualisation stage, and an active experimentation stage. Overall, the Kolb learning cycle encouraged reflection, which, according to Ash et al (2001, p5), 'appeared to be of a paramount importance for learning and growth. As change is about learning and growth, the two seemed to go hand in hand.'

Vince (2002a) focused upon the practice of reflection, specifically with regard to organisational learning and change. He undertook action research in Fairness plc (pseudonym for a large UK private company). He identified four reflective practices that represented a way of organising for learning and change: peer consultancy groups, role analysis and role analysis groups, communities of practice, and group relations conferences. The communities of practice identified by Vince merit further discussion, as they are particularly pertinent to debates featured in this chapter.

Communities of practice (Lave and Wenger 1991) are part of the learning as social practice approach introduced in the previous section. Rather than thinking of organisational learning as something facilitated or arranged by management, learning is regarded as a social norm.

> Learning is therefore distributed among co-participants in a community of practice, and knowledge is embedded within it. Newcomers acquire, through participation, a sense of how people act in relation to tasks and towards each other; in doing so they become members of the community themselves. (Reynolds et al 2002, p26)

In terms of managing change, thinking in terms of communities of practice is fruitful. The discussions about groups and teams in Chapter 8 emphasised the influence of norms and, through communities of practice, a better understanding of how they develop is apparent. Acknowledging communities of practice is also informative in understanding the role of professionals in organisational change and may be related back to earlier discussion about organisational defence routines.

THE LEARNING ORGANISATION

Mintzberg et al (2009) regard interest in the 'learning organisation' as burgeoning after publication of Peter Senge's (1990) book *The Fifth Discipline*. Although Senge has become closely associated with the learning organisation, Pedler et al (1997) identify writers who contributed to shaping the idea of the learning organisation (these include Argyris and Schon 1978; Peters and Waterman 1982; Deming 1986; Harrison 1995; Dixon 1994). Jackson (2001), in his review of Senge and the learning organisation, highlights variants, which have included 'the learning company' (Pedler et al 1991), 'the knowledge-creating company' (Nonaka 1991) and 'the living company' (De Geus 1997). The appeal of the learning organisation concept is that the vision and search for strategy promote individual self-development in a continuously self-transforming organisation (Starkey et al 2002).

Managing change is often perceived as being dominated by management fads and buzzwords (Collins 2000). However, one of the strengths of Senge's conceptualisation of the learning organisation has been its longevity, with the first edition appearing in 1990 and a revised and updated version appearing in 2006. In *The Fifth Discipline*, Senge (1990, p4) employed a simple yet persuasive rhetoric to promote the learning organisation: 'learning organisations are possible because, deep down, we are all learners... Learning organisations are possible because not only is it our nature to learn but we love to learn.' Senge identified five component technologies or disciplines of a learning organisation, summarised in Box 14.2.

Box 14.2 The five disciplines of the learning organisation (based on Senge 1990, 2006)

Systems thinking – thinking in terms of systems
Personal mastery – defined as high levels of proficiency
Mental models – understanding the mental models at work
Building a shared vision – developed by people working together
Team learning – team intelligence exceeds that of the individuals

The five disciplines that comprise the learning organisation are featured in Box 14.2; each discipline merits further explanation. Senge gave impetus to interest in systemic thinking, acknowledging that businesses and other human endeavours need to be understood as systems. He defined systems thinking as '... a conceptual framework, a body of knowledge and tools that has been developed over the past fifty years, to make the full patterns clearer, and to help us to see how to change them effectively' (Senge 2006, p7). In terms of personal mastery he was concerned with gaining high proficiency, rather than gaining dominance. Through lifelong learning it was possible to achieve the highest results: 'personal mastery is the discipline of continually clarifying and deepening our personal vision, of focusing our energies, of developing patience, and of seeing reality objectively' (Senge 2006, p7).

Mental models were concerned with assumptions that inform how we see the world and how we act; these mental models may be used unconsciously. Senge (2006) believed that working with mental models started with turning the mirror inward to unearth our internal pictures of the world and bring them to the surface and hold them rigorously to scrutiny. Building shared vision was concerned with shared pictures of the future. These pictures can inspire in an organisation the fostering of genuine commitment and enrolment rather than compliance (Senge 2006). Team learning involved the intelligence of the team exceeding the intelligence of individuals in the team. The discipline of learning in teams starts with dialogue and the capacity of members of a team to suspend assumptions and genuinely think together (Senge 2006).

CRITICAL PERSPECTIVE

In this 'Critical Perspective' organisational learning in general and the learning organisation in particular are critically reviewed. Organisational memory and forgetting are considered as a counterbalance to popular assumptions that organisations learn.

CRITICALLY REVIEWING ORGANISATIONAL LEARNING AND LEARNING ORGANISATIONS

In its purest form organisational learning may be regarded as empowering and egalitarian, hinting at a very different approach to organising and managing change.

Consequently, Mintzberg et al (2009) acknowledged the merits of organisational learning and the challenge of critiquing something they support because it challenges the 'rational' deliberateness, dominating the literature and practice of strategic management. Argyris (1999) identified challenges to organisational learning arising from sceptical organisational learning scholars. These were that organisational learning is contradictory, that organisational learning is a meaningful notion but not always beneficent, and do real-world organisations learn productively? Each of these challenges may be explained as follows.

The potentially contradictory nature of organisational learning relates to the belief that individuals, rather than organisations, learn. Most theories of learning in general – and organisational learning in particular – begin from a starting point of individual learning. However, individual learning is rarely encouraged in organisations except within very narrow parameters (Denton 1998). Conceptual concerns may be raised about whether we are concerned with an object called organisation learning or with learning on the part of individual members of an organisation. Van der Bent et al (1999) raised the question of whether organisations as entities can do anything in their own right. Although organisational learning is regarded as a neutral term, organisational learning may not always be used for good purposes. Argyris cites the emotive example of Nazi learning about carrying out evil. Also, the ability of organisations to remember past events, analyse alternatives, conduct experiments and evaluate the results of action has been questioned.

Burnes et al (2003), in their review, highlighted three reservations that have been raised about organisational learning: firstly, the lack of any consensus definition of the abstract concept of organisational learning; secondly, the scarcity of rigorous research in the area; and thirdly, problems of generalising theories across different contexts, particularly in terms of generalising from studies of organisational learning undertaken in different countries. There is a danger that in focusing upon organisational learning, other aspects of managing change are neglected. Wilson (1992) argued that change cannot be restricted solely to behavioural aspects of learning; there needs to be a blend of the behavioural with the economic and historical with future-oriented decision-making. Mintzberg et al (2009, p237) express similar pragmatism, writing: 'the learning organisation is all the rage right now, and mostly for good reason. But it is no panacea for anything. People have to learn, but they also have to get on with doing the regular work efficiently (Horses wear blinders for good reason).'

Argyris (1999), with his sustained interest in organisational learning, is well placed to evaluate the learning organisation and, as might be imagined, he offers both bouquets and brickbats. He believes that prescriptions that the likes of Senge offer are useful guides with regard to organisational structures, processes and conditions, enabling productive organisational learning. However, his concerns include ignoring analytical difficulties posed by organisational learning, no serious attention paid to processes that threaten the validity and utility of organisational learning, and the short shrift given to implementation difficulties.

A critical review of the learning organisation concept is impeded by the absence of any consensus definition of a learning organisation. Ortenblad (2007), through careful analysis of *The Fifth Discipline*, highlighted 12 different interpretations using Senge's own terminology of what he meant by the term learning organisation. This criticism is particularly significant, as Ortenblad (2007) warns that the problem with vague management ideas is the difficulty of knowing what to criticise. In a similar manner, Jackson (2001) criticised the organisational and rhetorical strategies used by Senge to maintain interest in his vision, and Friedman et al (2005) have questioned the mystification of the theory and practice of organisational learning. The rhetoric of the learning organisation places it within a unitarist framework of relationships in the pursuit of shared goals, achieved through collaborative high trust and rational resolution of differences (Coopey 2002). However, the concern is that there is a lack of empirical evidence to support such a utopian vision, noting '... that the learning company can be perceived as scientific hypothesis without empirical evidence' (Coopey 2002, p537).

Jackson (2001) drew together major criticisms of the learning organisation, which included: the learning organisation is ambiguous, amorphous and ill-defined, Senge's books are based on the author's consulting experience rather than on systematic or rigorous research, and questions remain about the ethical and moral basis behind the rhetoric of the learning organisation. The criticisms of the learning organisation tend to be at a conceptual level; however, given that the learning organisation is believed to have been driven by practitioners, it is worthwhile considering an example of its application, as featured in Journal Research Case 14.1.

JOURNAL RESEARCH CASE 14.1

Banks A, B, C, D and E

Paper title: The learning organisation – myth and reality? Examples from the UK retail banking industry
Sector: UK retail banking
Research methods: Interviews
Authors: Harris, L.
Year: 2002
Journal details: *The Learning Organisation*. Vol 9, No 2. pp78–88.

Commentary: The cases featured in this paper address learning on new technology projects in five anonymous banks referred to as Banks

A to E. The cases were based upon interviews with 42 bank managers and industry consultants over 18 months. The author was also able to draw upon ten years' experience in the industry. The projects in Banks A, B and C were categorised by the participants as failures. The projects in Banks D and E, by contrast, were regarded as successful. The author believes that the case studies provide evidence that learning from past mistakes or past successes continues to be the exception rather than the rule.

ORGANISATIONAL FORGETTING

The assumption running through this chapter has been that in looking to the future, organisations extract learning from their activities as a managing change strategy, but what if the opposite was the case? What if organisations in a manner similar to the individual who eats too much cake and says never again repeat the same mistakes? As Santayana (1998) famously warned, those who forget the past are condemned to repeat the past. Martin de Holan et al (2004) differentiate forgetting in terms of accidental and intentional forgetting and entrenched knowledge versus new knowledge. The contribution of history to managing change was highlighted in Chapter 3, and the past also plays a significant role in organisational learning: 'organisations, too, need to understand their past or they too will relive it and grow increasingly out of touch with the changing environment' (Starkey et al 2002, p6). Remembering is an important prerequisite for learning (Van der Bent et al 1999).

Booth and Rowlinson (2006), as part of a wider review of the prospects for management and organisational history, highlight the importance of social memory. They cite Gabriel's (2000) warning about the pervasiveness of organisational nostalgia that mythologises a past which bears little relation to documented history. This may be illustrated through the promotion of corporate museums that selectively remember or forget aspects of an organisation's history. There is believed to be great potential in linking organisational culture with social and collective memory studies. While history implies learning, extracting learning from the past can never be guaranteed. Abrahamson (2000) echoed Santayana that companies that forget their past are condemned to relive their past. Kransdorff (1998) encourages appreciation of the concept of organisational memory in times of change, fearing that if organisational memory is not facilitated, organisations will experience corporate amnesia.

CONCLUDING COMMENTARY

Learning and changing are closely related, with learning informing processes of changing and changing informing processes of learning. However, despite such close relations, the ambiguities surrounding the concepts of learning and changing hamper academic understanding of interrelationships. While the ambiguous language of the learning organisation is one of the reasons for its practical appeal, it becomes difficult to evaluate the rhetorical claims made for the efficacy of such a concept. Critiquing organisational learning and learning organisations is hampered by the different definitions that coexist and the ambiguities of these concepts. The chapter highlighted the existence of organisational forgetting, both as a proactive strategy and happening inadvertently.

CASE STUDY: APPLYING THEORY TO PRACTICE

Manufacturing videotapes: fast-forward to the future

Historical background: Video cassette recorders (VCR) and videotapes had been commercially launched in the 1970s, but it was not until the mid to late 1980s that they became affordable and were to be found in most homes. They allowed people to watch films in the comfort of their own homes and for the first time to record their favourite television programmes. The mid-1980s through to the late 1990s were to be the boom years for VCR and videotape manufacturing. However, in the next decade VCRs and videotape were to be completely eclipsed by digital video disk (DVD), leading to videotape becoming almost obsolete by 2007.

The following case study offers a snapshot of two companies successfully manufacturing videotapes in 1997. Neither company sold direct to the public, but supplied the film distribution companies with the videotapes onto which films were then copied.

Vision-On: It had been Vision-On's most successful year to date and as chief executive of Vision-On, Jo Johnson took great pride in the end-of-year figures. At today's board meeting the directors were determined not to become complacent, yet there were visible signs of satisfaction over what had been a remarkable year. As they went through the key ratios, every ratio had exceeded their earlier projections. Every year for the past five years turnover had increased by at least 50% and their share price was at an all-time record level.

They were only one of two manufacturers of videotapes in the UK and they accounted for 90% of videotapes manufactured in the UK. There was competition in terms of videotapes manufactured overseas, but the bulkiness of the tapes meant that shipping costs were prohibitive. After reviewing the financial information the board reviewed the forecast information, which had been drawn up for the next five years. The management accountants had been asked to work on the cautious side, but even so their figures looked very promising.

Jo turned to Lin Povey as operations director to lead the next part of the board meeting. Lin reported upon the work of the research and development (R&D) team, who were close to patenting a new type of videotape that would eradicate the occasional spooling problems customers had encountered. This problem had been highlighted through extensive surveys of customers that Vision-On undertook. Any defect, however small, was unacceptable and Vision-On believed that the secret of its competitive advantage was based upon its complete commitment to quality management. At their space age production plant there were large posters proclaiming 'Zero deviation is not expected, it is our norm.' The company maintained very high quality standards throughout the production process and any defects were referred to the R&D team so that the learning could be extracted. At any one time the R&D team would be working on at least five special projects to enhance the quality of Vision-On videotapes.

As the meeting ended Jo and Lin joked about cashing in their share options and moving to somewhere warmer. However, both agreed that for the time being they would enjoy the success story that was Vision-On.

Magpie Systems: Magpie Systems was dwarfed by the scale and success of Vision-On. Magpie Systems had been set up by husband and wife team Chris and Catherine Matthews at the beginning of the 1990s at a disused Cornish airbase.

They had used the existing buildings and mainly second-hand equipment to set up a small-scale, cost-effective videotape manufacturing operation. They supplied about 10% of UK-manufactured videotapes and concentrated their operations on independent film distributors.

They were content with the reasonable profits that their company made and they had a reputation for being good employers. The different operations were allocated to different huts at the airbase. Employees were allowed to listen to music in their huts as long as there was a consensus about the choice of music. In each hut, there was a nominal supervisor, but it was understood that as long as work was completed on time and to a good standard, the workers would have considerable autonomy. There were no mission statements or slogans, but a poster of Cornwall with Home Sweet Home written on it was a kind of emblem for Magpie Systems. Chris and Catherine always assured new employees that they did not have big expansion plans and that they were determined to remain based in Cornwall. However, they also impressed upon employees that they were dependent upon their hard work to keep the dream alive.

They had no formalised R&D function, but Chris had benefited from expenses-paid trips to Japan funded by the manufacturers of the VCRs. It was a Friday evening and Chris had just returned from Japan two days earlier. There was a custom that at 3.00 on the last Friday of each month all employees would gather in the mess – this was the hut that they used as their informal social club. The deal was that for three hours they would explore different ways of working and, as Catherine put it, think the unthinkable. In these meetings every employee had an equal voice and the tone of the meeting was non-judgemental with an emphasis upon listening. After the meeting, from 6:00 to 12:00 Chris and Catherine hosted the month-end social with food and drink and a DJ provided courtesy of Saltdean Sunshine Sounds.

Chris opened the meeting screening a short film about Japanese cherry blossom trees. There were mumblings in the audience that Chris might have lost the plot, but everyone went with the flow. At the end of the presentation Chris revealed the DVD that the short film had been recorded onto; it was no bigger than his hand and was greeted with amazement. The DVD was placed in its case and passed around the animated room. Chris was asked many questions and did his best to answer them. The meeting then divided into groups made up of people from each hut. They were tasked with the simple question – what next? After further animated conversation a consensus began to emerge within the room. They would wind down production of videotapes until the end of July. August would be a paid annual holiday and as from the start of September Magpie Systems would resume business manufacturing DVDs.

Case study questions

1 Explain what is happening in Vision-On in terms of organisational defensive routines.

2 Explain what is happening in Magpie Systems in terms of single-loop learning and double-loop learning.

DISCUSSION QUESTIONS

1 What is the appeal of organisational learning for senior managers in organisations?

2 Why do organisations fail to learn?

3 Is the learning organisation a cleverly marketed management fad or something more significant?

4 Who determines what is remembered in organisations?

KEY READINGS

ARGYRIS, C. (1999) *On organizational learning*. Oxford: Blackwell Business.

This book, written over a decade ago, effectively maps many of the debates about organisational learning as configured by Argyris. The book benefits from being polemical in its conceptualisation of organisation learning. Argyris, in seeking to inform the practice of learning and change, is sceptical of critical scholars.

CHILD, J. (2005) *Organization: contemporary principles and practices*. Oxford: Blackwell.

Child devotes a very informative chapter to 'organising for learning'. A strength of the chapter is that Child balances extensive theoretical knowledge of organisational learning with discussion of the operationalisation of the concept inside organisations.

SENGE, P. (2006) *The fifth discipline: the art and practice of the learning organisation*. 2nd ed. London: Random House Business Books.

This book, first published in 1990, has become synonymous with the learning organisation. As this chapter has demonstrated, the views of Senge have attracted bouquets as well as brickbats. However, in encouraging debates about learning organisations, the book made a significant contribution.

PART 4

Developments in
managing change

CHAPTER 15

Power, politics and organisational change

INTRODUCTION

Power and politics have been implicit throughout discussions of managing change featured within this textbook. For example, understanding leading change, resistance to change and communicating change will always be informed by issues of power and politics. Involvement in managerial work inevitably means being involved in power and politics, as the managerial role involves managing 'power', both in terms of exercising it and in being subject to it (Watson 2006). However, despite its centrality to managerial roles, power and politics is frequently not explicitly discussed, either within organisations or within the mainstream management literature. The fear inside organisations is that the disclosure of political activity may not be regarded as valuable corporate or personal publicity (Buchanan and Badham 1999).

Pfeffer (1992b) suggests that we prefer to see the world as a kind of grand morality play, with good guys and bad guys easily identified. In the following quotation (1992b, p49), he explicitly links change and power: 'innovation and change in almost any arena requires the skill to develop power, and the willingness to employ it to get things accomplished'. However, Buchanan and

Badham (2008, pxviii) believe that academics still neglect the shaping role of political behaviour in organisational change, although there has been a recent increase in books seeking to legitimise the managerial use of power (Thompson and McHugh 2009).

This chapter, in focusing upon power, politics and organisational change, draws upon debates from different academic disciplines, such as sociology and political science, to inform understanding about managing change. While definitions of power and politics are contentious, Buchanan and Badham (2008, p11) offer the following helpful working definitions:

Power = the ability to get other people to do what you want them to do.

Politics = power in action, using a range of techniques and tactics.

The study of power has suffered from ambiguous definitions and applications and conflicting philosophical assumptions, which has been made worse by the arguments being conducted in 'highly esoteric idioms' (Johnson and Gill 1993, p134). These concerns still appear applicable today. In the 'Managerial Approaches' section, an overview of the development of theories relating power and politics to management and organisation is presented. This forms the basis for a discussion about power and politics, with specific reference to organisational change. In the 'Critical Perspective', the radical view of Lukes (1974, 2005) about power in general and Hardy (1996) about power and strategic change are featured.

MANAGERIAL APPROACHES

The distinction between the 'Managerial Approaches' and 'Critical Perspective' is far less relevant in this chapter than other chapters, as this chapter seeks to encourage greater engagement with power and politics, both in terms of managerial approaches and critical perspectives.

THEORISING POWER AND POLITICS

Writing about power and politics can be traced back over many decades and within many different academic disciplines. In the following discussion the intention is to introduce – in chronological order – major theories that have influenced management and organisational behaviour. The theories featured are summarised in Box 15.1.

Box 15.1 Major managerial power and politics theories

French and Raven (1959) – Power bases
Crozier (1964) – Power of lower participants
Fox (1974) – Political frames of reference
Etzioni (1975) – Types of power in organisations
Pfeffer (1992b) – Power in organisations

French and Raven (1959) took a resource-based view to understanding power in terms of the power-holder and subordinates; they identified five power bases, which are summarised in Box 15.2.

Box 15.2 Power bases (based upon French and Raven 1959)

Reward power – rewards such as promotion and financial benefits
Coercive power – psychological or material punishment
Referent power – charisma
Legitimate power – emphasis upon roles and job descriptions
Expert power – specialist knowledge and expertise

Box 15.2 identifies the five power bases and clarifies their meanings. In understanding these power bases, French and Raven referred to subordinates' perceptions of a leader, acknowledging that this may be accurate or inaccurate. The power bases are interrelated rather than separate and different power bases may be used in different situations (see Benfari et al 1986 for further development of this approach). The power bases may be differentiated in terms of formal power being coercive power, reward power and legitimate power, and personal power being expert power and referent power.

Crozier (1964) studied maintenance workers in a French tobacco factory. The maintenance workers were perceived as fairly peripheral to production processes in the organisation's bureaucracy. However, they were powerful in the sense that if machinery broke down the production workers were dependent upon the maintenance workers to fix the machines, because while machines were not operating earnings and bonuses would be curtailed. The maintenance workers, in controlling uncertainty, were able to exercise power.

Fox (1974) identified and labelled four different frames of reference on conflict: unitarist, pluralist, interactionist and radical. This framework was to prove subsequently very influential in differentiating perspectives on industrial relations. The unitarist frame of reference assumed a commonality of interests within an organisation, implying harmonious working relations and an absence of conflict. Employees were believed to share common interests, with teamwork often promoted as an example of everyone working together towards a common goal. The pluralist frame of reference depicted organisations as comprising different groups with a range of different interests, inevitably resulting in conflicts. However, these conflicts could be managed through negotiation and compromise. The interactionist frame of reference saw conflict as inevitable in a manner similar to the pluralists, but believed that such conflict was essential for effective performance. The radical frame of reference regarded conflict as an inevitable consequence of capitalist employment relations.

Etzioni (1975) classified organisational relationships in terms of control and the use of power resources. Etzioni's typology comprised three dimensions: power, involvement and relations between power and involvement. It was possible to explain compliance in terms of these three dimensions. Coercive power was concerned with threats or physical sanctions. Remunerative power was concerned with material resources and rewards, and normative power was concerned with symbolic rewards. Three forms of involvement were identified. Alienative involvement was where employees were involved against their wishes. Calculative involvement applied to employees motivated by extrinsic rewards, and moral involvement applied to employees' belief in their organisation's goals. This classification enabled Etzioni to identify different relations between power and involvement. For example, prisons emphasise the use of coercive power resources, businesses emphasise the use of remunerative power resources and political parties emphasise the use of normative power resources. However, these different emphases did not preclude the use of all three.

Pfeffer (1981, 1992a, 1992b) gave considerable impetus to mainstream management literature engaging with power. His concerns about how we accomplish things relate closely to the goal of managing change. In terms of decision-making, Pfeffer (1992b) highlighted that a decision on its own changes nothing, that when a decision is made we do not know if it is good or bad and invariably we spend more time living with the consequences of decisions than the time taken to make the decision. He considered different ways of getting things done in organisations: through hierarchical authority, through developing a strongly shared vision or organisational culture and through power and influence.

Pfeffer (1992b) regarded managing with power as important; at the time he was writing this was not the orthodoxy. His understanding of managing with power may be clarified as follows. Firstly, there is a need to acknowledge the varying interests inside organisations, with the political landscape needing to be diagnosed. Secondly, there is a need to establish the different positions of different individuals. Thirdly, in order to accomplish things there is a need to have more power than those in opposition with a prerequisite being to understand how sources of power can be developed. Fourthly, managing with power entails understanding strategies and tactics, such as timing, using structures, understanding commitment and other forms of interpersonal influence.

The above discussion highlights the increasing acknowledgement of the relevance of theories of power and politics to organisations and management. In the next section the focus is upon relating power and politics to organisational change.

POWER, POLITICS AND ORGANISATIONAL CHANGE

Since the early 1970s the role of power in organisational change initiatives has been increasingly recognised and conceptual thinking has evolved and been enriched by different theoretical assumptions (Bradshaw and Boonstra 2004). Hardy and Clegg (2004, p343) acknowledge that the use of power by management in the context of change appears logical and inevitable: 'if employees do not want to change, then managers must use power – the ability to make them change despite their disinclination – against their resistance'. The presence of change and uncertainty was believed to heighten the intensity of political behaviour (Buchanan and Badham 1999). Buchanan et al (1999), in surveying management experiences and attitudes with regard to organisational development and change, offered empirical insights into managers' perceptions of the political aspects of managing change. Organisational politics were identified as a significant feature of change, with complex and wide-reaching change resulting in more intense politics. Their survey revealed support for politics as beneficial, but equally politics as damaging and distracting.

> This evidence suggests that about one third of managers enjoy the politics game, one third do not, and one third are neutral on the issue. (Buchanan et al 1999, p29)

Hardy and Clegg (2004) acknowledged the inevitable lack of consensus in terms of conceptualisations of power and the interplay between managerial and critical thought and between academics and practitioners. In the face of a lack of consensus, the following discussion is organised around three overviews of power and politics with regard to organisational change, as identified by Buchanan and Badham (2008), Morgan and Sturdy (2000) and Bradshaw and Boonstra (2004). There are inevitably similarities in these overviews, but there are also differences.

Buchanan and Badham (2008) (first edition published in 1999) have given considerable impetus to managerial and academic engagement with the power and politics of organisational change. They identified four underlying beliefs that informed their position. Firstly, political behaviour is more significant than is commonly recognised or admitted and political activity is likely to be heightened during periods of significant organisational change. Secondly, managerialist literature is believed to underplay political behaviour in shaping organisational change in terms of the different commentaries offered. Commentators either deny connections between political behaviour and organisational change or they accept political behaviour, but argue that involvement would be ethically unacceptable. Alternatively, commentators accept the reality of political behaviour, but remain theoretically remote. Thirdly, engagement with political behaviour in the context of organisational change reveals both the positive and negative aspects of such behaviour, rather than a narrow stereotyping of politics as bad. Finally, political behaviour, rather than just being acknowledged, needs to be actively incorporated into management education, training and development.

Buchanan and Badham (2008), in reviewing the power and politics literature with specific reference to organisational change, acknowledge that there is no agreed framework. However, they identify three broad perspectives on power: power as a personal property, power as a relational property and power as an embedded property. The power as personal property perspective regards power as something that you can accumulate and possess. They identify the work of Pfeffer (1992a), cited earlier, as a good illustration of this perspective. The power as a relational property perspective, rather than considering power from the point of view of the person exercising it, looks beyond this and looks for power within different relationships. They identify the work of French and Raven (1959) and Crozier (1964) as good illustrations of this perspective. The power as an embedded property perspective highlights the influence of culture upon power relations.

Power, therefore, is woven into what we take for granted, the order of things, the social and organization structures in which we find ourselves, the rule systems that appear to constitute the 'natural' running of day-to-day procedures. (Buchanan and Badham 2008, p53)

Buchanan and Badham cited Scott-Morgan (1995) as a good illustration of this approach to power. He highlighted how managers establish 'the unwritten rules of the game', which need to be understood in order to better understand organisations and how to progress. The embedded nature of power is discussed further in the 'Critical Perspective' in terms of the writings of Hardy (1996) and Lukes (2005). Journal Research Case 15.1 offers empirical insights into the political behaviour of change agents.

◉ JOURNAL RESEARCH CASE 15.1

Management consultant, head of school, hospital manager and project manager

Paper title: Politics and organizational change: the lived experience
Sector: Management consultancy, education, health and computer manufacturing
Research methods: Interviews (one-and-a-half hours each)
Authors: Buchanan, D. and Badham, R.
Year: 1999
Journal details: *Human Relations*. Vol 52, No 5. pp609–629.

Commentary: Researching the political behaviour of change agents is always going to be methodologically challenging, raising issues around research access and willingness of research subjects to disclose behaviours. The authors report upon a pilot study of senior managers with change implementation responsibilities. Each of the four cases reported in the paper offers interesting insights into the political behaviours of change agents. The authors, in drawing conclusions, suggest that political behaviour was an accepted and pervasive dimension of the role of change agents. The change agents adopted a creative approach to their different contexts. It was possible to view objectionable behaviours as justifiable within specific contexts. The change agents engaged in political behaviour with regard to a combination of circumstances, personal motives and the behaviours of others.

Morgan and Sturdy (2000), in their review of the organisational change literature, identified three approaches: managerialist approaches, political approaches and social approaches. They (2000, p8) defined the political approach as involving '… greater recognition that actors within organisations bring different sets of values and interests into any change context. Political conflict, bargaining and negotiation become the central elements of analysis and the key managerial skill is that of political manipulation.' The work of Fox (1974), cited earlier, is used to explain political approaches to organisational change, which reject the unitary frame of reference in favour of a pluralistic frame of reference, highlighting the influence of competing interest groups. They highlight the emphasis within political approaches of studying ongoing change processes and the internal and external context of change, discussed in Chapter 5. They cite the work of Pettigrew (1985) and Dawson (1994), which favours a political approach to organisational change.

> The political approach to change then promotes more sophisticated 'cultural engineering.' It recognizes the multiplicity of groups involved in the change process and the complexity and contextually bounded nature of change. (Morgan and Sturdy 2000, p17)

Bradshaw and Boonstra (2004, p280) identified four perspectives on power dynamics, which they related to organisational change. In Box 15.3, the essence of these four perspectives is summarised.

Box 15.3 Perspectives on power dynamics (based upon Bradshaw and Boonstra 2004)

manifest–personal power
power explained in terms of person 'A' having more or less power than person 'B'

manifest–structural power
power explained as resting in a position or location

latent–cultural power
power explained as the creation and reproduction of largely latent or unconscious shared meanings

latent–personal power
power explained in terms of how individuals limit themselves and unquestioningly obey

The perspectives on power featured in Box 15.3 may be used in combination. Bradshaw and Boonstra (2004) draw upon notions of polarity, specifically individual power versus collective power and manifest power versus latent power, which were evident in the power and politics literature cited earlier.

The manifest–personal power perspective was informed by early social and psychological research. This perspective views power as the potential ability of an individual to influence a target in a particular system or context. A good example of this perspective was French and Raven (1959), discussed earlier in this chapter. They (2004) acknowledge that the personal power highlighted in this perspective can be stereotyped in the change literature as either dirty tricks or astute strategising. Pettigrew (1975) is cited as another example, illustrating how internal change agents can draw upon at least five interrelated potential power sources.

The manifest–structural power perspective encourages an '... understanding of power that rests in the position or location an interest group, sub-unit, or organisational department holds in the structure of the organisation' (Bradshaw and Boonstra 2004, p284). This perspective shifts the emphasis away from personal traits towards organisational structures. Kanter (1983) was cited as an example of how different power coalitions secure their interests and objectives in organisational change.

The latent–cultural perspective places emphasis upon shared meanings that are largely latent or unconscious. Culture is regarded as reflecting stability and in this way power relations are seen to be natural and unquestionable. Power relations are maintained by those who set agendas and manage meaning. The work of Pettigrew (1977) in terms of the management of meaning through symbolic construction was offered as an example of this perspective.

Manifest–personal power was concerned with how managers, change agents and other individuals use their power in direct, visible and conscious ways. However, latent–personal power offers another means of understanding personal power. Bradshaw and Boonstra (2004) regard this perspective as new and relatively underdeveloped, but potentially fruitful. They regard the perspective as having its roots in psychoanalytic, postmodern and feminist theories. Latent or unconscious power relations become embedded in the psyche of individuals.

> To the extent that an individual is unconsciously complicit and has internalized various mechanisms of control and obedience is the extent to which their freedom to act according to (or even to know) their own values and beliefs is constrained. From this perspective, for example, members of oppressed groups are asked to understand how they collude in maintaining the very systems that oppress them. (Bradshaw and Boonstra 2004, p292)

They offer the works of Knights and Morgan (1991) as an example of postmodern theorising that placed emphasis upon subjectivity and gave impetus to postmodernist accounts of power and change within organisations. Another example of this form of analysis would be the writings of Grey (2003) in his emphasis of the significance of analysing the mundane aspects of our organisational lives.

CRITICAL PERSPECTIVE

In selecting critical perspectives, the dilemma remains that power is a highly contested concept with very few signs of consensus among academic commentators. In the following discussion a pragmatic choice has been made to focus upon two significant critical contributions to the study of power. Lukes' (1974, 2005) development of a radical view on power and Hardy's (1996) highlighting of power informing strategic change have been chosen, particularly because of their impact upon management studies.

POWER: A RADICAL VIEW

In *Power: A radical view*, Lukes offered a compelling explanation of how power over willing subjects was secured. The first edition of the book appeared in 1974, with the second edition appearing in 2005. While the book was aimed at political/social scientists, it offered insights into the exercise of power within organisations that have caught the imagination of management writers. Lukes (2005, p1) sought to answer the question: how can we think about power theoretically and how can we study it empirically? He was particularly interested in the idea that when power was least observable it appeared to be at its most effective. Lukes identified three views of power: one-dimensional, two-dimensional and three-dimensional. In the following discussion, each of these views is explained and illustrated in terms of how each view of power could inform understanding about organisational change in a hypothetical company – International Widgets.

The one-dimensional view of power is sometimes referred to as the pluralist view, although Lukes believed that this label was misleading. Lukes (2005, p19) depicted the one-dimensional view of power as involving '... a focus on behaviour in the making of decisions on issues over which there is an observable conflict of (subjective) interests, seen as express policy preferences, revealed by political participation'. International Widgets entered into negotiations with trade unions and other stakeholders over the closure of its UK factory. The negotiations proved to be difficult as all parties openly attempted to safeguard their interests.

The two-dimensional view of power is explained in terms of a critique of the one-dimensional view of power. In particular, Lukes (2005, p20) cites Bachrach and Baratz's (1970) critique of the one-dimensional view of power as depicting '... a misleadingly sanguine pluralist picture of American politics'. Lukes (2005, pp24/25) depicted the two-dimensional view of power as involving '... a qualified critique of the behavioural focus of the first view... and it allows for consideration of the ways in which decisions are prevented from being taken on potential issues over which there is an observable conflict of (subjective) interests, seen as embodied in express policy preferences and sub-political grievances'. The chief executive of International Widgets explained that the decision to close the UK factory was non-negotiable, but that he was keen to ensure that different stakeholders were fairly compensated.

Lukes explains the three-dimensional view of power again in terms of the limitations of the one-dimensional and two-dimensional views of power.

> ... the three-dimensional view of power involves a thoroughgoing critique of the behavioural focus of the first two views as too individualistic and allows for consideration of the many ways in which potential issues are kept out of politics, whether through the operation of social forces and institutional practices or through individuals' decisions. (Lukes 2005, p28)

Lukes (2005, p40) regarded the three-dimensional view of power as the most radical view, with political systems preventing demands becoming political issues or being made: 'how can one study, let alone explain, what does not happen?' The ethics of the global operations of International Widgets were not part of the discussions. Specifically, the capitalist economic model encouraging the free movement of capital was never discussed.

In Figure 15.1 the three views of power identified by Lukes are usefully summarised. The three views of power made up the body of his book in 1974.

Figure 15.1 Summary of the three views of power

One-dimensional view of power

Focus on (a)   Behaviour
     (a)   Decision-making
     (c)   (Key) issues
     (d)   Observable (overt) conflict
     (e)   (Subjective) interests, seen as policy preferences revealed by political participation

Two-dimensional view of power

(Qualified) critique of behavioural focus
Focus on (a)   Decision-making and nondecision-making
     (b)   Issues and potential issues
     (c)   Observable (overt or convert) conflict
     (d)   (Subjective) interests, seen as policy preferences or grievances

Three-dimensional view of power

Critique of behavioural focus
Focus on (a)   Decision-making and control over political agenda (not necessarily through decisions)
     (b)   Issues and potential issues
     (c)   Observable (overt or convert), and latent conflict
     (d)   Subjective and real interests

Source: Lukes, S. (2005) *Power: a radical view.* 2nd ed. Basingstoke: Palgrave Macmillan published in association with the British Sociological Association, p29.

In the 2005 edition Lukes took the opportunity to add two major new chapters. Over the 30 years that elapsed between the two editions, he acknowledged Foucault's (1980) writing on power: '... Foucault's rhetoric has encouraged many to conceive of power in ways that suggest excitingly subversive implications for how we should think about freedom and rationality' (Lukes 2005, p61). Lukes remained unconvinced by Foucault's rhetoric and troubled by his lack of methodological rigour.

However, Thompson and McHugh (2009, p129), in their review of the contribution of Lukes, highlight a central dilemma in studying power that Lukes himself also raised: '... how do we research things that are hidden, how do we know that power suppresses or hurts people's interests when the outcome is compliance or consent?' They conclude that while his argument has a philosophical persuasiveness, the empirical content and research agenda to support such views remain limited. The final words in this section go to Lukes (2005, p61), who, in reflecting upon power, offered a salutary warning that '... there is no agreement about how to define it, how to conceive it, how to study it and, if it can be measured, how to measure it'.

POWER AND STRATEGIC CHANGE

Hardy (1996) drew upon Lukes (1974) and other radical writers on power to demonstrate how power provided the energy for strategic change. Hardy (1996, S3) was mindful of negative connotations of power and defined power neutrally as '... a force that affects outcomes, while politics is power in action'. Her goal was, through acknowledging the multidimensionality of power, to offer managers mechanisms to move from strategic intent through alignment to realisation. She offered illustrations of how alignment had previously neglected the political implications of organisational change. For example, discussions relating to organisational design and forms, discussed in Chapter 6, appeared neutral yet there were human consequences – winners and losers. In a similar manner, cultural change, discussed in Chapter 13, involved political choices in terms of what was and was not valued. Power was presented as being universally integral to strategic change.

> Hence power is an integral part of strategic change, regardless of whether the organisation is a political cauldron of conflicting interests and power is a way to combat resistance to strategic intentions, or whether it is united by common goals and power is required to facilitate collaborative action. (Hardy 1996, S6)

The way forward was believed to be through a deeper understanding of power, which was informed in particular by Lukes (1974). The model encompassed four dimensions of power: the power of resources, the power of processes, the power of meaning and the power of the system. The power of resources was concerned with traditional conceptualisations linking power to the ability to control scarce resources. In this way power influenced behaviour, which is often referred to as 'carrot and stick' approaches. The power of processes acknowledged power residing in decision-making processes, often referred to as the power of 'non-decision-making'. Non-decision-making protected the status quo, allowing actors to determine outcomes behind the scenes through procedure and political routine.

The power of meaning was the most sophisticated and broadest dimension and highlighted the danger of overlooking how power may prevent conflict from emerging. Hardy (1996, S8) stated that 'Lukes argues that power is often used to shape perceptions, cognitions and preferences so that individuals accept the status quo because they cannot imagine any alternative.' The power of the system referred to the taken-for-granted power that is deeply embedded within an organisational system.

While this was a more sophisticated analysis of power than some of the analyses featured in the 'Managerial Approaches' section, Hardy was not antagonistic towards managers. The whole paper was couched in terms of mobilising power for strategic action:

> When managers attempt strategic change they must use the first three dimensions of power to modify those parts of the existing system that

inhibit the new behaviour necessary to support their initiatives. (Hardy 1996, S9)

The belief was that strategic change was achieved when the power of resources, processes and meaning converged. In subsequent writings Hardy and Clegg (2004) critically reflected upon the relationship between power and change, noting the logic and inevitability of the use of power by management given the high risk of change failure often attributed to employee resistance. They warned (2004, p360) that much of the organisational change literature assists change management failure due to 'its lack of pragmatism about power'. As Bradshaw and Boonstra (2004, p279) suggested, 'transformational change in organisations can be more fully understood and enabled through the simultaneous recognition of the tensions between different perspectives on power'. Their argument was that power merits greater recognition as an integral component of our understanding of managing change, although once again this is not the orthodoxy.

CONCLUDING COMMENTARY

The dynamic nature of power and politics and the dynamic nature of organisational change mean that these concepts are closely related. However, because of definitional ambiguities, competing theories and managers' reluctance to talk openly about the exercise of power and politics, understanding has been hampered. Advances have been made in terms of understanding power and politics with regard to management in general and such developments have informed understanding about power, politics and organisational change. There is no consensus in this field of study and there probably never will be. In the 'Critical Perspective' the radical views of Lukes were introduced, although he probably has as many admirers as detractors. Equally Hardy offered a convincing account of how power was utilised to achieve strategic change. However, debate is ongoing with regard to effectively conceptualising relationships between power and organisational change. Ironically it is likely to be the most powerful professors in the elite universities through utilising the power of resources, the power of processes, the power of meaning and the power of the system that will eventually determine the orthodoxy.

Funding crisis at Musicians in the Community

Musicians in the Community (Mic) had been established in 1972 as a charity to promote the cause of cohesive communities through celebrating music in all its forms. The organisation had increasingly acted as an umbrella organisation for over 100 small music-related charities. Mic offered low-cost consultancy to those organisations that could not afford their own in-house functions, such as HR, marketing and finance. Mic had been established through a large donation from Larry Chaos, the lead singer with the cult 1960s band the Screaming Dogs. Larry had been inspirational as the founder of Mic and had been keen to give something back to people in the communities who bought his music. Larry had died in the mid-1980s, but Mic had benefited from a series of successful funding bids and grown in size.

Mic now had 30 full-time employees, 30 part-time employees and 100 volunteers. The Mic board of trustees was due to meet the following week for their quarterly meeting. However, Beth Sadler, the strident chief executive, had requested an informal Sunday breakfast meeting at her Surrey home. At the meeting Joan Jones, a director at Global Melodies (online music retailer) and one of the trustees, was present, as well as Jennifer October, the musicians' representative on the board, and Daisy Meadows, the employee representative on the board. Daisy and Jennifer had both objected to being summoned to a Sunday morning meeting as they wanted to spend this quality time with their families. Beth had told them both very firmly that non-attendance was not an option and that they were not to inform anyone of their attendance. There were no minutes taken at this meeting, but this is a summary of the key statements.

Beth: 'Thank you for agreeing to give up your Sundays to attend this meeting. I have some very serious news. Our last three funding bids have been unsuccessful, our funds have dwindled and we only have capital reserves to operate for one more month. After that we will be obliged to wind up Mic and all staff, myself included, will be made redundant.'

Daisy: 'Surely there is another option. The finances looked so very strong last year.'

Joan: 'My team of accountants have scrutinised the accounts and I can confirm what Beth has said.'

Jennifer: 'But Larry worked so hard to establish Mic...'

Beth: 'Darling, Larry died of a heroin overdose – he's history.'

Daisy: 'Who knows about this situation?'

Beth: 'Nobody in Mic, but I have been working closely with Global Melodies to try and find a solution; they are the only people who are in the loop. The board of trustees will be informed at our meeting on Wednesday.'

Jennifer: 'Larry hated Global Melodies. He always said that they killed music.'

Joan: 'That type of stereotype is offensive. Apologise now or our legal team will retract the offer.'

Jennifer: 'I am sorry, I...'

Daisy: 'What offer?'

Beth: 'Biscuit anyone?'

Daisy: 'What offer?

Joan: 'I think we better tell them, Beth?'

Beth: 'Joan and myself have been burning the midnight oil and we think we have found a way to take Mic forward.'

Joan: 'We plan to rationalise Mic, but believe that Mic could be reinvented as an online community keeping the Mic logo, ethos etc. We would fund Mic through our charitable trust and develop a new high-profile website.'

Jennifer: 'What is in it for you?'

Joan: 'Very little really, the money involved is chicken feed for a large corporate like ourselves. We would simply require an exclusive link on the website to our download site, but really this is all about philanthropy.'

Jennifer: 'Larry was right, this whole idea sucks!'

Daisy: 'The board will never agree…'

Beth: 'Why do you think you are here? If you vote with us on Wednesday we will have the majority we need for the proposal to be accepted.'

Daisy: 'And if we don't?'

Beth: 'It is bye-bye Mic and bye-bye job, dear. All those great Mic initiatives would end very abruptly, darling, because of your petty actions.'

Joan: 'Do we have your vote?'

Daisy: 'Yes.'

Jennifer: 'Yes, but I am not happy.'

Case study questions

1 Explain what appears to be happening in terms of the exercise of manifest–personal power and manifest–structural power (Bradshaw and Boonstra 2004).

2 Explain what Beth Sadler is doing in terms of Hardy's (1996) four dimensions of power in strategic change.

DISCUSSION QUESTIONS

1 Why are power and politics not discussed more openly inside organisations?

2 How do unitarist and pluralist frames of reference help to explain the managing change literature?

3 What are the academic challenges of explaining organisational change in terms of power and politics?

4 What are the strengths of Hardy's (1996) analysis of strategic change in terms of power?

KEY READINGS

BOONSTRA, J.J. (ed.) (2004) *Dynamics of organizational change and learning*. Chichester: John Wiley & Sons.

This edited collection of readings is infrequently cited yet remains a classic of critical organisational change scholarship. The book is divided into five parts, with a whole part dedicated to power dynamics and organisational change.

BUCHANAN, D. and BADHAM, R. (2008) *Power, politics and organizational change: winning the turf game*. 2nd ed. London: Sage Publications Ltd.

Although intuitively you would imagine a large quantity of literature that relates organisational change to power and politics, serious discussions about the relationships between these concepts are few and far between. Buchanan and Badham are frequently cited by academics studying and researching change. This book benefits from drawing upon relevant social theory while also containing many illustrations of the exercise of power and politics in the workplace.

LUKES, S. (2005) *Power: a radical view*. 2nd ed. Basingstoke: Palgrave Macmillan, published in association with the British Sociological Association.

There is real merit in reading the original reference to when a theory was first articulated. While secondary sources offer shorthand interpretations, they are only interpretations. Lukes offered a contentious account of the dimensions of power in 1974 and, in 2005, his views remained contentious and topical. The book, which inevitably majors upon political science, acts also as a piece of very readable polemical writing.

CHAPTER 16

Ethics and managing change

LEARNING OUTCOMES

After reading this chapter you should be able to:

- differentiate competing theories of business ethics
- appreciate the ethical challenges that managing change raises
- recognise the role of psychological contracts in organisational change
- consider the potential of ethical codes
- reconsider traditional depictions of business ethics
- reflect upon globalisation from an ethical perspective.

INTRODUCTION

Ethics and managing change appear potentially complementary, yet in many ways these fields have developed in parallel. For over 2,000 years the correct ways of behaving, morality and ethical guidance have been the subject of debate among philosophers, religious leaders and others (Rowson 2006). In contrast to the body of knowledge about ethics, recent advances in the study of managing change appear embryonic. Woodall (1996) believed that change management pays little attention to the ethical integrity of managerial behaviour and ethical consequences for employees. However, in the earliest writings about planned approaches to change, ethical concerns were being raised and addressed: 'What right, people will ask, has any man to remake another?' (Lippitt et al 1958, p97). The diverse range of stakeholders in organisations (public, private or third sector) is increasingly acknowledged, which raises questions about reconciling competing interests and, for some, even if competing interests should be reconciled. Campbell and Kitson (2008, p175) highlighted ethical questions that strategic change typically raises:

Could a different strategic solution not be found that had fewer negative impacts? Does the factory have to close?

Do I have to move 300 miles to a new location?

These questions highlight connections between the discussion of power and politics in the previous chapter and this chapter. Managing change decisions will not always be based upon achieving the fairest outcomes. Instead, they will be informed by issues of power and politics. The instability and uncertainty associated with change was believed to create opportunities for abuses of power and the manipulation of information, with individuals and groups vulnerable to exploitation and reluctant to voice opposition to change at such times (Mayon-White 1994). The warning is that organisational change presents unethical managers with an opportunity to act unethically; such issues will be explored in this chapter.

The following working definition of ethics is used for this chapter: 'usually, ethics is understood as reflecting on and recommending concepts of right and wrong behaviour' (Clegg et al 2008, p408). In the 'Managerial Approaches' section, business ethics are introduced, by way of introducing major normative approaches to ethics. The discussion of managing change challenges illustrates the ethical dilemmas that are raised by managing change. Psychological contracts offer a potential informal mechanism for managing employee expectations and ethical codes offer a more formalised mechanism. However, what is ethical remains a contentious philosophical question. The 'Critical Perspective' commences with a critique of the current managerialist configuration of business ethics, and globalisation is featured in terms of the ethical issues it raises. The section concludes with an aspiration to manage change more ethically.

MANAGERIAL APPROACHES

INTRODUCING BUSINESS ETHICS

Any understanding of ethics begins with common-sense views of what is 'right' or 'fair'; the problem is that there are very different views about what these words mean (Ackers 2009). While most people consider their actions to be ethical, there can be considerable variation in their understanding of 'ethical'. This dilemma has been reflected in different approaches to ethics that have developed over the centuries. Four of these approaches, which are often referred to as normative ethics, are: virtue ethics, deontological ethics, ethical learning and growth, and teleological ethics (Fisher and Lovell 2009). Virtue ethics are principle-based in the sense that they refer to the personal characteristics which ensure that individuals make the right choices in ethical situations. The origins of these approaches can be traced back to the Greek philosopher Aristotle, who identified justice as the dominant virtue, whereas Plato identified four virtues: wisdom, courage, self-control and justice.

Deontological ethics can be traced back to the writings of the German philosopher Kant. Kant required actions to be guided by 'universalisable' principles that apply irrespective of the consequences of the actions. The belief was that actions were only morally right if carried out as a duty, not in expectation of a reward. This approach is often understood in terms of the 'Golden Rule', which suggests 'do unto others as you would have done unto yourself' (Fisher and Lovell 2009). The ethical learning and growth approach encouraged processes of learning in the belief that this enabled people to decide for themselves to act ethically. The goal was to become aware of your own ethical potential. Popular management books, such as *The Seven Habits of Highly Effective People* (Covey 1992) and *The Fifth Discipline* (Senge 2006), were believed to encourage such an orientation. Teleological ethics are sometimes referred to as consequentialist in that there is an emphasis upon ethical actions that have the best consequences. The rightness or goodness of actions is not intrinsic to the action; it can only be judged by its consequences (Fisher and Lovell 2009).

It is tempting to choose the 'one best way' in terms of how a manager applies these ethical approaches. However, there are believed to be benefits in using ethical insights from all four approaches (Fisher and Lovell 2009). Watson (2003a), in exploring ethical choices in managerial work, presented the case study of Glenn Ferness, which is featured in Journal Research Case 16.1.

👁 JOURNAL RESEARCH CASE 16.1

Glenn Ferness (senior retail manager)

Paper title: Ethical choice in managerial work: the scope for moral choices in an ethically irrational world
Sector: Retailing
Research methods: Case study research drawing upon ethnography and participant observation, specifically interviews and follow-up conversations with the research subject.
Authors: Watson, T.J.
Year: 2003
Journal details: *Human Relations.* Vol 56, No 2. pp167–185.

Commentary: The focus of this paper was a case study of the ethical approach of Glenn Ferness. Glenn undertook ethically oriented initiatives, compatible with the logic of corporate business success, rather than exclusively doing the right thing for the right reason. Colleagues in her retailing organisation regarded her as being unusually 'ethically aware', although she justified decisions primarily in terms of the business case rather than in ethical terms.

The question is raised: how much scope does the manager in a modern corporation have to act in a way informed by personal rather than corporate moral criteria? (Watson 2003a, p168). In exploring this dilemma, Watson cites Weber's (1947) notion of 'ethical irrationality', suggesting that judgements about right and wrong cannot be established through rational or scientific analysis, because no system of values can make every value consistent with every other value. The implication of this reasoning is significant in that there is not a single set of moral principles to which managers may turn to solve moral dilemmas in their work (Watson 2003a).

While the normative approaches cited earlier drew upon ancient philosophical positions, the theory and practice of business ethics is still evolving. This development is hampered by common business ethics myths (Trevino and Brown 2004). Five of these myths are summarised in Box 16.1.

Box 16.1 Five business ethics myths (based on Trevino and Brown 2004)

Myth one: It's easy to be ethical.
Myth two: Unethical behaviour in business is simply the result of 'bad apples'.
Myth three: Ethics can be managed through formal ethics codes and programmes.
Myth four: Ethical leadership is mostly about leader integrity.
Myth five: People are less ethical than they used to be.

In the following discussion each of the five myths in Box 16.1 is explained. Myth one is that it is easy to be ethical; however, this myth '... disregards the complexity surrounding ethical decision-making, especially in the context of business organisations' (Trevino and Brown 2004, p69). Ethical decisions are regarded as ambiguous with decision-making involving multiple stages, fraught with complications and contextual pressures. Making the right ethical decisions has been debated among philosophers for centuries, suggesting that employees and managers will find ethical decision-making equally challenging.

Myth two is concerned with the idea that unethical behaviour is the result of a few 'bad apples'. A consequence of this myth is that '... the first reaction to ethical problems in organisations is generally to look for a culprit who can be punished and removed' (2004, p72). However, the concern is that such scape-goating downplays the influence of the immediate organisational context upon individuals. Employees are likely to be influenced by their peers in determining what is right or wrong and they are likely to look to managers and leaders for examples of what is acceptable behaviour. Myth three is concerned with managing ethics through formal ethics codes and programmes. Research does support the view that formal ethics and legal compliance may have a positive impact. However, the existence of such codes and programmes does not guarantee effective ethics management. Formal systems in influencing behaviour must be part of a larger, co-ordinated cultural system that supports ethical conduct every day (2004).

Myth four suggests that ethical leadership is mostly about leader integrity. However, they (2004, p77) suggest that ethical leaders '... must demonstrate that they are ethical themselves, they must make their expectations of others' ethical conduct explicit, and they must hold all of their followers accountable for ethical conduct every day'. Myth five suggests that people are less ethical than they used to be. However, they (2004, p77) believe that people are no less ethical than they used to be, but that '... the environment has become quite complex and is rapidly changing, providing all sorts of ethical challenges and opportunities to express greed'. These concerns are very relevant to the managing change theme of this chapter and the focus of the next section.

MANAGING CHANGE ETHICAL CHALLENGES

Ethics gives us a standpoint to decide what is right and wrong and to decide what we ought or ought not to do (Rowson 2006). However, managing change raises particular dilemmas.

> The individual manager has to wrestle with this challenge of continuing change, and is frequently presented with ethical dilemmas as he or she seeks to match the organisation's goals, which may, or may not, be public knowledge, with his or her own conception of what constitutes a fair and acceptable standard of behaviour, and, in turn, to match these with the performance and working methods of individuals and groups within the organisation. (Mayon-White 1994, p196)

In this quotation, the subtleties of managing change ethically begin to surface. Organisational change is dynamic and processual, with the implication that even what is ethical one week may not be ethical the next week. Equally, what is a 'fair and acceptable standard of behaviour' will be highly variable. Salaman (1997) noted that our heads are full of knowledge and full of ideas and images; these ideas, images and values provide shared frameworks, assumptions and moralities, defining and making sense of work and employment.

Establishing an ethical position needs to address such ambiguities. The study of ethics is often made practically relevant through scenarios, dilemmas or case studies requiring students or managers to specify how they would act in such situations. In these situations, ethical choices can be informed by the four normative approaches to ethics discussed in the previous section. Mayon-White's (1994) pioneering paper used examples to illustrate the complex issues raised around managing change ethically, which are summarised in Box 16.2.

Box 16.2 Ethical managing change dilemmas (based upon Mayon-White 1994)

Scenario One – Outsourcing its telephone call centre to Bombay would increase the profits of a private sector company. However, the outsourcing would result in the closure of its UK call centre, which is a major local employer.
Scenario Two – Hospital funding is influenced by how effectively the hospital meets government targets. However, the hospital is failing to meet one of the targets. 'Creative accounting' would enable it to appear to meet the target and secure extra funding for further life-saving operations.
Scenario Three – A manager is known for his coercive style of managing change. The approach has been described as bullying, but the approach minimises resistance and results in the effective implementation of organisational change.

In examining the managing change dilemmas in Box 16.2 it is apparent that ethically managed change can never be completely black and white. These ambiguities may be magnified within emergent approaches to change. Burnes (2009b) argued that emergent approaches to change in emphasising power and politics have been at the expense of Lewin's planned approach to change, which benefited from an ethical basis and stressed democratic participation. In this paper, Burnes reflected back over 25 years dominated by emergent approaches to organisational change and looked forward to the next 25 years of organisational change, which he hoped would be informed by Lewin's ethically based approach to change.

> It has been argued in this article that behavioural change, whether at the individual, group or organisational level, cannot be achieved by imposition, trickery or manipulation. Instead, it requires people to change of their own volition. Therefore, if the new era of ethical behaviour is to become reality, we need an approach to change which is itself ethically based. (Burnes 2009b, p375)

The acknowledgement of psychological contracts between employers and employees offers one means of managing ambiguities that inevitably arise during processes of organisational change.

PSYCHOLOGICAL CONTRACTS AND ORGANISATIONAL CHANGE

Psychological contracts offer an important yet informal mechanism for managing workplace expectations. They have been defined as: 'the invisible or implicit set of expectations that employees have of their organisations (e.g. challenging, stimulating work that allows for career progression) and that their organisations have of them (e.g. loyalty and flexibility), but are not laid down in the formal contract of employment' (Knights and Willmott 2007, p543). Psychological contracts offer a means of considering the ambiguities of employment relations, as well as more tangible employment contracts; workplace relationships are believed to be governed by these less tangible psychological contracts. Morrison (1994) identified three ways in which psychological contracts can be related to change: the dynamic nature of the contract, the effect of change upon the contract, and unspoken expectations about the contract.

Acquisitions (discussed in Chapter 7) illustrate the applicability of psychological contracts to organisational change. Psychological contracts that developed upon joining an organisation, may need to be revised as a consequence of an acquisition: '... individuals will need to form a psychological contract with the new organisation by re-evaluating and accepting their positions in the new firm in light of any changes brought on by the acquisition and subsequent events' (Hubbard 2001, p27). While this is an informal process, if it is not managed the danger is that the benefits of the acquisition will not be realised. The recommendation is that 'if the psychological contract is altered in any way by the acquisition it must be renegotiated. This includes changes brought on either by being acquired or by existing employees being affected by a new acquisition' (Hubbard 2001, p28). The cautionary note is that as the psychological contract is not a conscious agreement, employees tend not to be aware of its existence until it is broken (Hubbard 2001).

The CIPD (2005) report into managing change and psychological contracts reported that the majority of employees were not hostile to change and perceived change as making things better rather than worse. The recommendations for managers, particularly pertinent to discussions in this chapter, included: taking people management issues into account, managing expectations, involving employees, sharing information, consulting with employees and remembering that the line manager's role is often critical. This suggests that there are often opportunities to pre-empt what could potentially become a breach of ethics. The downside of this type of normative guidance is that while it appears reasonable and sensible, by definition there are no guarantees that it will be acted upon, which leads to consideration of more formalised ethical codes.

ETHICAL CODES

Ethical codes are general in tenor, encouraging particular characteristics in employees such as loyalty, honesty, objectivity, probity and integrity and may be differentiated from codes of conduct, which are far more specific (Fisher and Lovell 2009). Eight roles of corporate codes (ethics and conduct) have been identified: damage limitation, guidance, regulation, discipline and appeal, information, proclamation, negotiation and stifling (Fisher and Lovell 2009). In reviewing the disparate managing change literature, ethical codes are not prevalent. This may be a consequence of no single professional body overseeing management of change. The norm within professional bodies is to agree with members' ethical codes as a means of policing the profession (see for example project management, accounting and banking).

The codes of these professions would provide a useful starting point for developing ethical codes with regard to the management of change. Organisational development has encouraged an ethical focus in encouraging commitment to fairness in planned change (Cobb et al 1995). OD may be a better comparator than the other professions as OD has been preoccupied with ethical change agent behaviour and moving towards ethical standards for the OD profession (Woodall 1996). The downside of codes of ethics is that they may treat employees as morally immature, they may not have an impact upon behaviour and they may appear banal and merely common sense (Fisher and Lovell 2009). While acknowledging their intuitive appeal, Fisher and Lovell (2009) identified five possible objections to the development and employment of corporate codes, which are summarised in Box 16.3.

Box 16.3 Possible objections to the development of corporate codes (based on Fisher and Lovell 2009)

1 justification – lack of a universally accepted set of common principles and ethics
2 the inability of rules to govern actions
3 support structures – environment/culture to support codes needs to be in existence
4 the marginality of codes
5 the diminution and ultimate invisibility of individual responsibility

As Box 16.3 highlights, despite the intuitive appeal of corporate codes and their existence in organisations, reservations remain. In encouraging ethical approaches to managing change, it is necessary to look to more radical solutions.

This 'Critical Perspective' develops the argument that business ethics has been configured far too narrowly. Globalisation is featured as an illustration of the ethical dilemmas it raises and finally the development of ethically managed change is encouraged.

AGAINST BUSINESS ETHICS

> Enron, Global Crossing, Tyco, WorldCom, Xerox, ImClone, Andersen and Adelphia are now names on a roll call of accounting fraud, overpaid executives with share options, huge golden parachutes, and employees sacrificed to the bottom line. To put it simply, many people in many places do not trust the market managerial version of the new world order. (Parker 2003, p197)

This quotation, with the benefit of hindsight and the shared experience of the global financial recession, now appears very prophetic. Against such a backdrop of glaring irregularities, the traditional business ethics preoccupation with exploring the moral reasoning about how individual A interacts with individual B appears misguided and petty. Parker and other critical commentators have challenged the current configuration of how business ethics is taught and studied in universities with the aim of asking broader questions about ethical matters and considering alternative forms of organising to the current market managerialism.

Similar concerns were evident when Neimark (1995, p81) asked the provocative question: 'what is it about the structure of our economic system that so often pits profits against people?' In encouraging readers to interrogate their own and society's unexamined assumptions with regard to what is an ethical dilemma and how it can be resolved, Neimark posed four challenges. Firstly, the need to challenge ethics as givens, instead ethics is a product of time and place. Secondly, challenging ethics as limited to interpersonal relations and individual acts, instead ethics needs to be also related to the ideological underpinnings of capitalism. Thirdly, challenging the view that adhering to moral values is sufficient for their realisation. More university ethics courses and corporate training programmes are not the way forward if people do not have access to meaningful work, housing, education and health care. Fourthly, challenging the view that we are solely responsible for how we act in a system. Instead we are answerable for our collective individual acts.

In the current configuration of business ethics, the role of moral philosophy is believed to be overemphasised at the expense of broader social and political debates. Parker (2003) specifically was concerned with how the current configuration of business ethics excludes politics and, through this exclusion, fails to question managerial activity and beliefs in managerialism. His concern was that philosophy is used to underpin and legitimise business ethics, drawing upon philosophers highly selectively, particularly in terms of the omission of many contemporary philosophers. The implication of this line of reasoning is that '… the sorts of questions that business ethics deals with can be greatly enlarged if we share the terrain occupied by philosophers of politics, and that they provide plenty of conceptual tools to make a start with' (Parker 2003, p196).

Ackers (2009) focused upon employment ethics as a subdivision of business ethics and, in particular, the role of HRM in workplace ethics. He regarded HRM as offering an impoverished ethical vision of the employment relationship resting upon three ethical fallacies. Firstly, the golden calf fallacy subordinates human values to business considerations and calculations. The language of HRM '… assumes that business and its economic terminology should shape human aspirations, and not the other way round' (2009, p463). Secondly, the enlightened self-interest fallacy pretends that solely business considerations are sufficient to inform the management of employees without recourse to trade unions or other relevant stakeholders. Thirdly, 'the happy family fallacy assumes that the state and trade unions are unwelcome intrusions into a fundamentally harmonious, unitarist employment relationship' (2009, p464).

ETHICS AND GLOBALISATION

Globalisation '… encompasses a loose, diverse and, at times, contradictory package of ideas' (Collins 2000, p345). Clegg et al (2008) offer a flavour of the different definitions of globalisation, citing Martin (2002), who regarded globalisation as the financialisation of everyday organisational life, and Ritzer (1993), who equated globalisation with Americanisation. They (2008, p581) regard globalisation as '… marked by the integration of deregulating markets and technology and facilitated by telecommunications and ease of transport'. Globalisation is increasingly presented as a contemporary phenomenon, although history offers an informative counterpoint. In the 50 years prior to the First World War, the world economy was regarded as more open and integrated than today (Dicken 2003). And while attention focuses upon contemporary global scandals such as Union Carbide and Bhopal, Fisher and Lovell (2009) remind us about the powerful and global dominating activities in the eighteenth and early nineteenth century of the British East India Company.

Globalisation is frequently presented as a potentially beneficial development, with possibilities for organisations arising out of globalisation including securing greater economies of scale and standardisation, spreading product development and production costs over larger volumes and new opportunities to diversify into different regions or countries (Child 2005). There are close relationships between globalisation debates and managing change debates. Collins (2000, p348) regards globalisation as presenting a mandate for organisational change: 'in the name of globalisation a number of commentators have suggested that far-reaching changes will have to be engineered at home, at work and in our communities, if we are to prosper in the new age, which we are assured, awaits those who are ready to adjust their expectations'. While Collins in his critical review of globalisation was sceptical of the many claims made for globalisation, the interconnectedness of societies and organisations is becoming increasingly apparent, as evidenced by the global financial recession. Clegg et al (2008, p578) suggest that:

> ... Anywhere/anything is potentially or actually linked to anywhere/ anything else in the management of commerce, government, aid, or other globally exchanged goods and services, but especially in movements of international financial flows and foreign currency exchanges that now dwarf the value of international trade in goods.

So while global activities may be traced back over many centuries, there does appear to be new forms of activity requiring new and robust ethical scrutiny. In particular there is a need to develop international perspectives on ethics. Religions, philosophical traditions, cultures and literature all help to establish different ethics and values within different countries, and even within a single country there can be a diversity of ethics and values reflecting historical, economic, religious and cultural backgrounds. For example, Fisher and Lovell's (2009) citation of the work of Chakraborty (1999) illustrates how Vedantic principles (based upon a particular strand of Hinduism) offer a very different perspective on managing change from more traditional Anglo-American perspectives.

Vedantic principles suggest that man-made change goes against natural change, leading to irreparable harm to the environment and relations between people. Constantly changing organisational structures and processes can distract people in terms of their psychological development and the organisational tendency to focus upon the measureable ethically weakens organisations. While no claim is made that these are universally held beliefs in India or that they are empirically proven facts, they illustrate how different belief systems lead to very different evaluations of what is ethical and what is acceptable in terms of managing change. In many developing countries there is a desire to see business ethics reflecting indigenous ethical and religious traditions. However, attempts to produce ethical standards for international business have yet to have a major impact (Fisher and Lovell 2009), raising the important question: does globalisation result in more harm than good? And, as with many of the debates featured in this chapter, the answer is very dependent upon whom you ask.

TOWARDS MANAGING CHANGE ETHICALLY

The aspiration to manage change ethically appears reasonable; however, the dilemma with ethics is that ethics means different things to different people, in particular raising issues of power and politics. The argument developed in this 'Critical Perspective' is that approaches to ethics depicted in the 'Managerial Approaches' section offer a narrow view of ethics that excludes wider social and political issues. Instead, emphasis is placed upon individual responsibilities informed by a selective reading of moral philosophy. The danger is that 'business ethics simply means business as usual' (Parker 2003, p198). Managing change becomes managing the status quo; even the rhetoric of transformational change and revolutionary change masks the preservation of existing social and economic arrangements. The following discussion reflects upon four managing change themes featured in this textbook: power and politics, change communications, change agency and cultural change.

The previous chapter highlighted the contribution of power and politics to understanding managing change. In particular, the radical view of Lukes (2005, p28) explained how '... potential issues are kept out of politics, whether through the operation of social forces and institutional practices or through individuals' decisions'. For example, the closure of a factory is announced, resulting in all employees being made redundant. A managerial approach would review how managers act ethically in their dealings with employees, whereas a critical perspective would question the ethics of closing the factory and making the employees redundant. However, the exercise of power and politics may ensure that critical questions are never raised. The ethics of managing change must be informed by an understanding of power and politics with regard to organisational change.

Change communications, featured in Chapter 11, in focusing upon the effectiveness of communication and potential barriers to such communications, overlooks issues of disclosure and the honesty of communications. Goodman and Truss (2004, p224) drew the following critical conclusion from their case study-based research:

> In general, employees in both organisations felt that they had been informed of changes after, rather than before, the event, that management were out of touch with employee concerns, that others were better informed than they were about the changes, and that they did not understand how the changes would affect them.

Burnes (2004) noted that Lewin, as far back as the 1950s, promoted an ethical and humanist approach to change. This ethical approach informed one of Lewin's main assumptions for OD interventions: 'that the consent and co-operation of all stakeholders in the client organisation should be sought prior to an intervention' (Woodall 1996, p30). This wonderful humanist aspiration was to be lost over time as narrow business interests prevailed (see Burnes' (2009b) earlier concerns about emergent approaches to change). The requirement for consent and co-operation may be contrasted with Kotter and Schlesinger's (1979, p111) frequently cited paper, advocating strategies for change through coercion.

> As with manipulation, using coercion is a risky process because inevitably people strongly resent forced change. But in situations where speed is essential and where the changes will not be popular, regardless of how they are introduced, coercion may be the manager's only option.

This emotive strategy for change inevitably raises ethical concerns. However, these are not exclusively new concerns. Warwick and Kelman (1976, p485) posed the crucial question: is coercion ever ethically justified in social intervention and, if so, under what conditions? People should be free to choose whether they participate in a change programme if they are to gain self-reliance in their problem-solving (Cummings and Worley 2008, p60). In Chapter 13, the focus was upon cultural change and the perceived goal of changing employees' attitudes, values and beliefs. Woodall (1996) identified questionable underlying assumptions of culture management that may be summarised as effective management involves the alignment of values, values can be easily changed, only management can change values and successful organisations have strong cultures.

Woodall's discussion of culture management illustrates the managerialism implicit within many contemporary approaches to managing change. It is very difficult to reconcile such assumptions with earlier discussions about ethical frameworks. In terms of rebalancing culture management, Woodall advocates creating conditions for internal dialogue within organisations about the adoption of new values, which can be related to wider social values. In reflecting upon managing change ethically, the biggest challenge remains the implicit specification of what can and cannot be changed. However, 'believing in the possibility of alternatives is where meaningful debates about both ethics and politics must always begin and also why such debates must take place' (Parker 2003, p199).

CONCLUDING COMMENTARY

Managerial approaches believe that philosophically informed ethical theories offer guidance to individuals on 'being good', which can benefit the individual, their organisation and wider society. Ethically managed change can be enhanced through acknowledging employees' expectations captured within concepts such as the psychological contract, with ethical codes offering a more formalised means of ensuring ethical behaviour, following the lead of OD and other professions. The view of ethics and managing change in the 'Critical Perspective' was far more circumspect, viewing the combination of ethics and managing change as an oxymoron. Business ethics has been configured in such a way that rather than asking awkward questions of managerialism and institutions, the spotlight is upon the actions of individuals and the search for individual bad apples. The implication of this line of reasoning is that in order to move towards ethically managing change, a broader configuration of business ethics is required.

Financial Futures, Oakley's Plastic Mouldings, Greenshires Loans and Savings, and Beautiful Bespoke Jewellery

CASE STUDY: APPLYING
THEORY TO PRACTICE

In the following case study four hypothetical organisational change scenarios are presented, which feature Financial Futures, Oakley's Plastic Mouldings, Greenshires Loans and Savings, and Beautiful Bespoke Jewellery. Please read each of these ethical scenarios.

Scenario One – Financial Futures: Dan Ellington had founded Financial Futures 30 years ago after becoming disillusioned with the clerical job he was doing. Financial Futures provided pensions, savings and investment advice to wealthy clients in the south-east of England. These services were provided through 14 offices, each with its own manager. Dan and the managers would meet every Friday evening without fail for a meal and a chat. Dan was highly charismatic. At the latest Friday gathering Dan offered the managers a once-in-a-lifetime opportunity to invest in the development of Financial Futures into a national rather than exclusively regional operation. Dan believed that the outcome in the long term would be positive, but he was very reluctant to disclose that the regional operation was currently in financial difficulties.

Scenario Two – Oakley's Plastic Mouldings: Oakley's Plastic Mouldings (OPM) had eight factories in the UK, mainly situated in the north of England. They had been highly successful in the past, however in recent years international competition was increasingly gaining ground on them. Although all factories were still profitable, they had decided to close four of their factories and relocate these operations to Malaysia. The dilemma was that the workforce had strong trade union representation and this would inevitably lead to a prolonged dispute, which might jeopardise the whole business. It was decided that if the financial information about each factory was presented in a different way, they could depict the four factories as loss-making and argue that

they needed to be closed in order to safeguard the long-term interests of OPM, which would be in the best interests of the remaining employees.

Scenario Three – Greenshires Loans and Savings: Greenshires Loans and Savings (GLS) operated through a network of 50 branches, with each branch typically employing six staff. The branch managers had invariably been with GLS for many years, initially joining as trainee clerks. When the multinational Associated Loans and Savings (ALS) acquired GLS there had been reassurances that there would be no redundancies in the first three transitional years. This was a generous provision given that unemployment levels were increasing. ALS had decided to maintain the distinct GLS high street brand, but to integrate completely all IT systems. Five branches had undertaken integration on a pilot basis; integration had gone well, but the branch managers had misrepresented their experiences of integration to head office because of fears of further change and in order to safeguard the interests of their staff.

Scenario Four – Beautiful Bespoke Jewellery: Beautiful Bespoke Jewellery (BBJ) was established in 1962 by Bill Smith and had developed an international reputation for making the highest quality bespoke jewellery. The labour costs, particularly the salaries of the jewellery designers, made up a large component of the costs of this highly successful business. Senior management had decided to develop an interactive website, which, through a process of questions, would allow the majority of customers to design their own jewellery. The projections suggested a potential 30% increase in profits arising out of this change initiative, through a 50% decrease in jewellery designers. This initiative had been a closely kept secret. However, in order to develop the website there was a requirement for each jewellery designer to spend a week working with the software designer so that their tacit knowledge could be built into the website.

Case study questions

1 Advise Financial Futures founder Dan Ellington using a virtue ethics normative approach to ethics.

2 Advise Oakley's Plastic Mouldings management using a deontological normative approach to ethics.

3 Advise Greenshires Loans and Savings branch members using an ethical learning and growth normative approach to ethics.

4 Advise Beautiful Bespoke Jewellery senior management using a teleological normative approach to ethics.

DISCUSSION QUESTIONS

1 What are the main impediments to the ethical management of change?

2 Do you believe that universal managing change ethical codes are the way forward?

3 Do psychological contracts have a role to play in contemporary organisations?

4 What ethical challenges does globalisation raise?

KEY READINGS

FISHER, C. and LOVELL, A. (2009) *Business ethics and values: individual, corporate and international perspectives.* 3rd ed. Harlow: FT Prentice Hall.

This popular textbook, first published in 2003, reflects the growing interest in business ethics among both students and academics. Debates featured in the textbook relating to personal values, whistleblowing and globalisation have great relevance to wider society. This textbook is strong on theory, yet succeeds in making complex arguments readily accessible.

JONES, C., PARKER, M. and TEN BOS, R. (2005) *For business ethics.* London: Routledge.

This book is recommended reading for anyone who wants to follow up debates introduced in the 'Critical Perspective' section. The tone of the book is provocative and thought-provoking and articulates a coherent critical challenge to more orthodox accounts of business ethics.

TOFFLER, B.L. and REINGOLD, J. (2003) *Final accounting: ambition, greed and the fall of Arthur Andersen.* New York: Broadway Books.

This book presents an extended case study of the demise of the global accounting and consulting firm Arthur Andersen. Ironically, the firm had a consulting group helping businesses manage their ethics and Toffler ran that practice. However, Toffler quickly became aware that the firm's own ethical culture was lacking. The shift from auditing to management consulting in the 1990s is cited as the reason for the ethical demise of a business that in past had been known for its ethical values.

CHAPTER 17

Change agents and agency

LEARNING OUTCOMES

After reading this chapter you should be able to:

- understand the concepts of change agents and agency
- understand terminology used with regard to change agency
- appreciate the role of tools and techniques in managing change
- recognise managing projects as a managing change methodology
- critically question popular assumptions about change agents and agency
- understand critiques of managing projects approaches to managing change.

INTRODUCTION

The lack of any consensus in either managing change theory or practice has frequently been acknowledged in this textbook. Approaches to organisational change may be categorised in terms of their theoretical contribution at one end of the continuum and their practical application at the other end (Stickland 1998). Change agents and agency traditionally resided at the practical end of such a continuum. This chapter will demonstrate that in recent decades there has been a greater theoretical engagement.

In terms of the origins of the term change agent, 'the term was adopted by the National Training Laboratory staff in 1947 to facilitate discussions among heterogeneous groups of professional helpers' (Lippitt et al 1958, p10). Although the role of the change agent is regarded as one of the most important factors in effecting change (De Caluwe and Vermaak 2003) there is no consensus in terms of terminology or definitions. Change agents play a number of different roles in change processes, with change normally involving a plurality of actors or players (Buchanan and Badham 2008). The term change agency is often favoured over change agent as signposting a group, rather than a single individual, overseeing the change process.

The problematic nature of defining change agency has been acknowledged (Caldwell 2006). Burnes (2009a, p593) defines change agents as '… people responsible for directing, organising and facilitating change in organisations.' Caldwell (2006, p31), citing Lewin (1997), defines the change agent as '... a rational actor who defines, directs and manages feedback during the implementation of change'; this definition is favoured in this chapter.

Managerial approaches to change agents and agency are introduced in terms of further discussion about change agency terminology and theoretical milestones. Approaches to change agency often emphasise managing change tools and techniques, which are explored. Managing change through managing projects is discussed as a form of change agency. In the 'Critical Perspective' change agents and agency and managing change through managing projects are critically questioned.

MANAGERIAL APPROACHES

CHANGE AGENTS AND AGENCY

Caldwell (2006), in the preface to one of the most thorough reviews of agency and change, warned that 'the history of the concept of agency in organizational change theory over the past fifty years makes dismal reading' (see also Hartley et al 1997). The following discussion traces the development of change agency theory and practice with this large caveat in mind.

In reviewing Lewin's (1997) writing from the middle of the last century, Caldwell (2006, p1) highlighted that 'archetypes of agency were identified with models of rational actors and organizational change was conceived as a process that could be effectively planned and managed to achieve instrumental outcomes'. Schon (1963, p77) advocated for champions for radical new inventions: 'it is in the nature of a large organisation to oppose upsetting change and innovation, yet change and innovation there must be'. The quotation intriguingly celebrates an era before change became the espoused organisational norm and the only constant. The paper subsequently talks about product champions who may be related to Schon's interest in inventions and innovation (innovation theory is discussed in Chapter 19).

As well as planned change, the concept of emergent change has been acknowledged in this textbook. Weick (2000, p223) has written about emergent change as follows: 'the hyperbole of transformation has led people to overestimate the liabilities of inertia, the centrality of managerial planning, and the promise of fresh starts, and to underestimate the value of innovative sense making on the front line, the ability of small experiments to travel, and the extent to which change is continuous'. Debates around the planned and/or emergent nature of organisational change have implications for discussions about change agency. Change agency may be regarded as part of a planned approach to managing change. However, the organisational reality of change agency may not be as black and white as either planned or emergent change.

The language of change agents, change agency and change champions can be confusing. The JISCinfoNet (2009) differentiation of the terminology (depicted in Box 17.1) as used by practitioners offers a useful clarification.

Box 17.1 Change agency terminology

Change manager = 'someone with the expertise to lead the change, and can act as a role model for the new reality. May be an experienced project or change manager within the organisation or, possibly, brought in from outside with specific responsibility for managing the change.' (page 20)
Change agent = '… are those people that really make the difference implementing the change at a local level. This will depend on the nature of the change but the role often falls to middle managers because they have the influence and authority to make the change take place.' (page 20)
Change champion = 'These are early adopters, colleagues who want the change implementation to succeed, and believe that the change will be beneficial to the institution. The change champions will be members of staff affected by change. They do not have to have management responsibilities.' (page 22)
Change team = 'The group of staff charged with implementing the change – they must have the confidence of both the management and staff affected by the change.' (page 22)

Source: www.jiscinfonet.ac.uk/infokits/change-management, pages 20–22 (accessed 12 September 2009). Permission granted by JISCinfoNet.

The distinctions featured in Box 17.1 between different roles involved in making change happen are a helpful starting point, yet there is no consensus about this terminology among either practitioners or academics. As a rule of thumb practitioners often make reference to change champions, whereas academics often make reference to change agents and agency. Ulrich (1997) in *Human Resource Champions* presented HR professionals as having the central role of champions in processes of organisational change (discussed further in Chapter 18). This high-profile book gave practitioner impetus to the terminology of change champions (although champions terminology was being used at least as far back as 1963).

Caldwell (2003a, p140), in his review of the literature and empirical research on change agency, offers a fourfold classification of change agents, which is summarised in Box 17.2.

Box 17.2 Fourfold classification of change agents (based upon Caldwell 2003a)

Leadership: change agents as leaders or senior executives
Management: change agents as middle managers or functional specialists
Consultants: change agents as external or internal consultants
Teams: change agents as teams operating at all organisational levels

The classification presented in Box 17.2 begins to counter traditional managerial notions of the chief executive of an organisation acting as the sole heroic change agent. While the chief executive may be the change agent, change agency can also be dispersed throughout organisations and at different levels within organisations. Box 17.2 also highlights opportunities for hybrid forms of change agency, reflecting the unique nature of specific organisational contexts. The notion of dispersed change agency is reflected in recent empirical studies. Doyle's (2001) study, featured in Journal Research Case 17.1, is a good example of such work.

JOURNAL RESEARCH CASE 17.1

Privatised water utility and NHS teaching hospital

Paper title: Dispersing change agency in high velocity change organisations: issues and implications
Sector: Utilities and National Health Service
Research methods: Findings drawn from a detailed questionnaire-based survey, followed up with in-depth qualitative interviewing.
Authors: Doyle, M.
Year: 2001
Journal details: *Leadership and Organization Development Journal.* Vol 22, No 7. pp321–329.

Commentary: This research was explicitly concerned with the dispersal of change agency in two very different organisations, exploring notions that everyone in a changing organisation could be a change agent. These notions are potentially empowering, yet the research is also able to highlight the problems of such dispersal. A policy dilemma emerges from the paper around whether to disperse change agency or to maintain tight management control.

The research featured in Journal Research Case 17.1 offers specific organisational insights into the type of choices and dilemmas that exist around change agency. In their research, Massey and Williams (2006) focused upon the views of change agents in an NHS trust implementing 16 CANDO projects (a tool linked with business improvement programmes). Their research allowed them to make informed suggestions about the practice of change agency, which are summarised in Box 17.3.

Box 17.3 Informing change agency practice in the NHS (based upon Massey and Williams 2006)

1 The team need to be released from daily duties and adequately resourced when first launching an initiative.
2 Change agents need to understand and empathise with the emotional impact and strain that CANDO (or any change programme) can have on individuals.
3 A transitional phase is required in which to engage all change implementers.
4 Training, support, mentoring and shadowing are required where health professionals have not previously been immersed in change management or best practice improvement.
5 Development of change agents informs their understanding of their working environment, offering a more holistic perspective.

Even within public services change agency will take many forms, as the above accounts have demonstrated. Doyle et al (2000) found, in comparing public and private sector responses, that the experience of change in the public sector had been more pressured than in the private sector. In the private sector there are likely to be similarities, but also differences; insider accounts of change agency are informative in such instances given the research access problems mentioned earlier.

Dover (2003) described a major change agent programme (CAP) conducted by Siemens Nixdorf (and later Siemens AG). The key lessons arising from the CAP included incorporating change agents into culture change, blending programme design with post-programme planning and creating realistic post-programme planning. Paton and McCalman (2008), in their guide to the implementation of change management, devote a chapter to what they refer to as the objective outsider as change agent. They offer a persuasive argument for utilising external expertise as part of the change process and draw upon Lippitt (1959). They identified four golden rules that apply to the change agent as objective outsider. These rules are summarised in Box 17.4.

Box 17.4 Change agents: summary of the golden rules (based upon Paton and McCalman 2008)

Rule 1: The relationship between the change agent and the client is a voluntary one and may be severed at any time by either party.
Rule 2: There must be a current or potential problem recognised by senior management about which the change agent has expertise.
Rule 3: The presence of the change agent is temporary, but the change agent should see the project through to completion.
Rule 4: The change agent must be outside the hierarchical power system of the client.

Paton and McCalman (2008) offer a provocative counterpoint to the view that change agency should come from within an organisation, which is informed by their own consultancy practice. It is just one of many choices that change agency raises. The contingency maxim of it appears very relevant here. Caldwell (2006, p64), while acknowledging '... the idea of redefining agency and change is at the core of Pettigrew's mission for contextualism', warns that '... Pettigrew offers little in the way of prescriptive advice on change agency as a form of instrumental intervention' (Caldwell 2006, p62). The scope for research into change agents and agency remains considerable.

MANAGING CHANGE TOOLS AND TECHNIQUES

Managerial approaches to change agency emphasise the use of change tools and techniques, with the use of such tools regarded as a defining characteristic of the change agent. The following discussion draws upon a disparate and largely practitioner-orientated literature in this area. Rigby (2001, p139), in discussing the global consultants Bain and Company survey of management tools, defines a management tool as meaning '… many things, but often involves a set of concepts, processes, exercises, and analytic frameworks'. The norm in discussions is to link management tools and techniques.

Dale and McQuater (1998) offer a differentiation between tools and techniques: '… a "tool" is a simple stand-alone application; whereas a "technique" tends to be a more comprehensively integrated approach to problem solving that might rely on a number of supporting tools'. Peters (1978) emphasised the longevity of the quest for management certainties, citing Frederick Taylor's time and motion studies and his search for highly rational principles of management. Managing change tools and techniques appears to offer change agents certainties in the face of organisational change uncertainties. De Caluwe and Vermaak (2003, p159), in their discussion of the change agent's toolkit, made a distinction between diagnostic models and intervention models. They regarded the accumulation of diagnostic models as an important part of the ongoing professionalisation of change agents and offered examples of organisational-level diagnostic models, which included: the balanced scorecard, portfolio analysis and activity-based costing.

In terms of the better-known intervention models, they identified T-groups, self-steering teams and search groups. The art of change agency appears to be choosing the most appropriate tools for a specific situation. Iles and Sutherland (2001, p19) raise this issue with particular reference to organisational change in the NHS, suggesting that 'no single method, strategy or tool will fit all problems or situations that arise. Managers in the NHS need to be adept at diagnosing organisational situations and skilled at choosing those tools that are best suited to the particular circumstances that confront them'. The challenge for change agents is making informed choices about the most appropriate managing change tools and techniques (see Bain and Company 2009 website for practitioner surveys of management tools and techniques utilisation and satisfaction). In the Organisational Change Field Guide (see Appendix), change-orientated tools are discussed further.

MANAGING CHANGE AS MANAGING PROJECTS

Caldwell (2003a, p137), in his review of change agency, highlighted the role of management consultants in project-managing change, commenting that 'managing change and managing projects are often synonymous'. However, within universities managing projects and managing change tend to be studied in parallel rather than collaboratively, with academics tending to specialise in managing projects and operations management or managing change and organisational development.

There is evidence that managing change authors flirted with managing projects methodologies as a way forward in the early 1990s. Carnall (1991, p57) in *Managing Change* devoted a chapter to the project management of change, writing 'there is good reason to believe that significant changes would benefit from a "project management" approach'. Buchanan and Boddy (1992, p6), by contrast in their pioneering work on change agent competencies, emphasised the interchangeable nature of change agents and project managers: 'it is not possible always to distinguish clearly between these titles, which depend on and vary with the organisational context'.

The literature relating to managing change and managing projects has broadly evolved separately, although with notable exceptions. For some, managing projects may be regarded as a subset of managing change; for example Worren et al (1999, p276) defined the scope of change management as encompassing '... theory and intervention strategies associated with what is known in the academic literature as OD, human resource management (HRM), project management, and strategic change'. Earlier Partington (1996, p16) argued, 'there is a widespread belief within the project management profession that the principles of project management are generic and applicable to all organizations wishing to adopt a project-based management strategy for the management of all kinds of change'.

In terms of the development of project management, the main concern between the late 1940s and the early 1980s was the application of project management to civil engineering and manufacturing. During the 1970s and into the 1980s there was a '... reliance on tools and techniques, and the understanding that projects were used to build or develop, not to change' (Leybourne 2007, p64). As society and organisations have changed project management has responded to this challenge, and Jaafari (2003, p47) suggested that 'without a proper perspective on change as a phenomenon, we cannot understand what possible role project management can play in the complex societies of the 21stCentury...' Leybourne (2007, p69) draws upon his own literature review as well as a review by Kloppenborg and Opfer (2002) to argue that the evolution of the literature highlights '... the movement from a focus on tools and techniques, toward an increasing emphasis on the behavioural elements that impinge on the management of projects'.

The divergence between managing projects and managing change theories appears to relate to rationality. Managing change as projects offers systematic methods and methodologies for managing change that emphasise project lifecycles. Ives (2005, p40) described the traditional approach to project management as involving '... a linear, step-wise approach, where the emphasis is on clearly defining a much-desired outcome via a detailed plan that outlines the milestones that must be accomplished along the way towards achieving the stated outcome'. There is an appealing rationality in what is offered to organisations. Managing change has splintered into many schools of thought and approaches to managing change, as discussed in Chapters 3 and 4. There is neither one best way to study managing change nor one best way to manage change; managing change scholars emphasise the ambiguous and irrational nature of organisational life. Partington (1996, p14), in his review of the organisational change literature, effectively makes this point, noting a large body of literature on the management of organisational change: 'this literature, which includes prescriptive opinion and descriptive accounts as well as research on the subject, has grown just as the perceived usefulness of the "technically rational machine" model of organisation has declined'.

CRITICAL PERSPECTIVE

The quantity and quality of research and theorising with regards to change agency and managing projects has not matched the considerable practitioner interest in these topics. The following 'Critical Perspective' is informed by discussions in many of the earlier chapters of this textbook. In the following 'Critical Perspective' change agents and change agency, as well as managing change as managing projects, are critically questioned.

CRITICALLY QUESTIONING CHANGE AGENTS AND AGENCY

The central problem with traditional conceptions of change agents is the implication that their *raison d'être* is overcoming resistance to change. Doyle (2001), in his review of change agency, wrote: '... any display of reluctance to participate in a change project may identify the individual as a "deviant" or "organisational terrorist" and place their future career prospects and even their job security in jeopardy'. Conceptions of change agents as policing 'organisational terrorists' negate meaningful discourse and dialogue around ongoing processes of changing. The following discussion is organised around four interrelated themes: power and politics, communication breakdowns, dispersal of change agency and the reification of change agents.

There is a tendency in the literature on change agents to focus upon personal skills and competencies (Hartley et al 1997); however, as Buchanan and Badham (1999, p615) highlighted, '... the change agent becomes engaged of necessity in the exercise of power, politics, and interpersonal influence'. Power and politics are very significant to the practice of change agency; however, discussions of power and politics are frequently missing in theories of change agency. Power and politics were the focus of Chapter 15, and those debates are informative in terms of developing understanding about change agency. There are real difficulties in researching change agency, particularly sensitivities around the disclosure of information (Buchanan and Badham 1999). In a fascinating paper Buchanan and Badham offer five accounts of change agents at work with a commentary on their political behaviour. They do acknowledge the limitations of this pilot study, offering the following conclusions from the research. Firstly, the political behaviour of change agents is an accepted and pervasive dimension of the role. Secondly, change agents adopted a considered and creative approach to their situations. Thirdly, some of the behaviours of the change agents may be considered as objectionable, although they can be justified as reasonable in their own contexts. Fourthly, change agents were engaged in political behaviour as a consequence of a combination of organisational circumstances. Fifthly, change agents simultaneously pursued and defended organisational goals as well as personal and career objectives through political behaviour. The overarching conclusion that emerges from the paper is that 'organizational political behavior thus presents positive and negative, "nice and nasty" faces to the observer – and to recipients or victims' (Buchanan and Badham 1999, p609).

The writings of Ford et al (2008) were used in Chapter 12 to explain how change-agent-centric thinking can contribute to the occurrence of resistance to change. One of the issues they raised was how change-agent-centric thinking contributed to communication breakdowns in terms of failing to legitimise change, misrepresenting its chances of success and its failure to call people to action. Ford et al (2008) emphasise the centrality of conversations, discourses and texts in processes of changing (see Oswick et al 2005 for further discussion). The implication of this is that failing to legitimise change undermines change efforts: 'change agents, therefore, must provide discursive justifications that establish the appropriateness and rationality of change adoption, create readiness for change, and increase not only the likelihood of recipient acceptance and participation in the change but also the speed and extent of that acceptance' (Ford et al 2008, p366). Change agents in their preoccupations with overcoming resistance fail to engage in the type of conversations that would allow these discursive justifications to be articulated.

Caldwell (2006, p34) has aired similar concerns: 'ultimately, Lewin's rational systems model of linear change is expert-centred in that the "change agent" or action researcher acts as a feedback mechanism ensuring sequential transitions between states of stability while helping to diffuse or dissipate resistance'. In later discussions about the influence of Edgar Schein on process consultation, Caldwell (2006, p40) poses the question '... does he allow for the possibility of "agency" to emerge from the dialogue between participants or is it circumscribed by the expert intervention techniques and rhetoric of the process consultant?' These scholarly concerns suggest that traditional notions of the expert change agent facilitating change in the face of belligerent employees are in need of revision.

Caldwell (2006, p38) warned that senior management can talk the talk of change agency: 'for example, managers espouse rational theories of strategic action and open dialogue, but they engage in processes of collusion, self-deception and cover-up that subvert rationality'. Again this may be related back to earlier discussions of power, in that change agency may appear to be dispersed without real power to achieve change being devolved. As a response to notions of constant/continuous change, there has been increased interest in dispersing change agency as widely as possible.

However, dispersal needs to be reconciled with each individual maintaining their personal interpretation of change and its meaning to them (Doyle 2001). In a world of multiple meanings, managing a multiplicity of change agents may prove challenging. Doyle (2001) warned that encouraging disparate and unconnected change agent initiatives may seriously undermine the potential coherence and control of change programmes. Doyle (2001, p326) offers the following example from the research project cited earlier: 'in the case of the Water Company, senior managers became alarmed when a spot check revealed 147 separate change initiatives were operating simultaneously'. Caldwell (2006, p160) warns that '... empowering new and sometimes "unaccountable" collective leaders and teams, often with no clear focus or agenda for change can disempower or undermine the fragile interventions of more conventional forms of expert knowledge'.

A further dilemma with dispersed change agency becomes apparent in Buchanan et al's (1999, p26) findings: while change management appeared to be widely distributed in organisations, it was potentially problematic, with 80% agreeing that 'we don't seem to have enough people with the right change management expertise'. The concern here is that although senior managers may favour the dispersal of change agency, employees may not have the breadth of experience/ expertise to act as change agents. Doyle (2001), in drawing upon his research, is able to explore messages that the dispersal and management of change agency might be sending. These messages are summarised in Box 17.5.

Box 17.5 Dispersing change agency messages (based upon Doyle 2001)

1 There is considerable ambiguity about 'empowerment' and 'change agency' terminology.
2 Change leaders cannot make oversimplified assumptions around the motives surrounding the dispersal of change agency.
3 Strategic leaders may lose control over those who manage the change process on their behalf.
4 Problems of greater dispersal of change agency may be partially explained in terms of perception and management style.

These research findings highlight the tensions between top–down management and popular notions of dispersing change agency throughout organisations. Inevitably there must be trade-offs, which can be explained in terms of the earlier discussions of power. The dispersal of change agency discussions can become polarised in terms of either top–down change agency or bottom–up change agency (see Sminia and Van Nistelrooij 2006 for a discussion of the merits of combining a top–down strategic management approach with a bottom–up approach to achieving planned change).

Caldwell (2003a, p134) warned that the '… traditional model of managerial work now looks increasingly outmoded'. Most functional and general managers typically combine change responsibilities with their day job (Buchanan and Badham 2008). It may well be that, rather than reifying change agents as separate, change agency within all managerial work should be acknowledged. This change agency may either be explicitly stated in employment contracts or implicit within psychological contracts. Intriguingly, Peters (1978, p3), in his early writings, argued that '… an effective set of change tools is actually embedded in senior management's daily message sending and receiving activities, and that these tools can be managed in such a way as to energize and redirect massive, lumbering business and government institutions'. This quotation offers a glimpse of the change agency implicit within everyday processes of managing. It is ironic that Peters subsequently fuelled interest in tools, techniques and recipes for managing change. The findings of Buchanan et al (1999) confirmed that the management of continuing change is now more significant than the management of discrete projects.

CRITIQUE OF MANAGING PROJECTS AS MANAGING CHANGE

In the 'Managerial Approaches' section the potential of managing projects as a methodology for managing change was featured. Project management has largely been unremarked upon in critical circles.

> Increasingly, the field of Project Management has promoted itself as a universal and politically-neutral toolkit of techniques appropriate for any activity in any sector, enabling the tight control of discontinuous

work processes, with particular potential for the control of expert labour.
(Hodgson 2002, p804)

In this quotation, Hodgson captures both the managerial appeal of notions
of managing projects and how such an approach works. He regards project
management as benefiting from its professionalisation strategy, particularly
in the USA and the UK. This strategy involved parallel initiatives, which include
formal internal organisation of the occupation, promotion of accredited training
programmes, expansion of credentialism within job markets and the development of
a core 'body of knowledge'.

By way of comparison professionalisation within managing change has been
far less obvious. There has been some internal organisation in terms of OD
departments and OD practitioners, but this has not been the norm. Accrediting
training and credentialism does not exist in any systematic manner. A change
manager is far more likely to hold a generic MBA than a specialist postgraduate
managing change qualification, and the development of a core body of managing
change knowledge does not exist and is never likely to exist. The appeal of
managing change as managing projects may lie within the professional certainties
that project management appears to offer.

> ... Project Management knowledge tends to epitomize and reproduce a
> particularly technicist and instrumental form of modernist rationality. A
> key intention of Project Management models and techniques is to enhance
> the calculability and visibility of those engaged in project work, enabling a
> direct form of control. (Hodgson 2002, p818)

In this Foucauldian analysis, Hodgson demonstrates how power/knowledge is
achieved through calculability and visibility. Instead of the change agent as some
kind of shaman, the project manager's activities are made transparent and open
to inspection by all interested parties – the mystery is apparently removed from
managing change. The appeal of managing change as projects is very apparent in
this form of analysis. Instead of managing change being regarded as ambiguous
and irrational, project-managed organisational change has a very precise
beginning, middle and end. Any organisational change failure may be explained
as failures of the project manager to effectively utilise the project management
body of knowledge. However, although the use of toolkits by change agents
may reassure clients and offer legitimacy, their applicability to the practice of
managing change remains questionable.

> Whereas some professions rely on a well-established and rigorous
> knowledge base, managerial practice is far away from being the mere
> application of a set of well-defined findings or theories. Managers rely
> primarily on tacit, procedural knowledge, derived from direct experience
> and trial-and-error learning. (Worren et al 2002, p1228)

Jarrett (2003, p25) regards tools as originating out of planned change in the 1950s,
with its assumptions '... based on linear, rationalistic thinking, humanistic ideals
and equilibrium conditions'. There have been huge advances in thinking about
managing change since then, particularly in beginning to understand the emergent

nature of organisational change, the irrational nature of human behaviour and the ambiguous nature of change processes. The notion that the project manager's big toolkit can be applied to the vagaries of managing change remains fiercely contested.

CONCLUDING COMMENTARY

The discussion of change agents and agency appears to be integral to any managing change textbook. It is consequently ironic how little coverage change agency receives in traditional managing change textbooks. Change agency may be too close to practice to merit academic engagement, which may explain the disappointing state of research and theory. The practice of change agency, which can be traced back to 1947, has made considerable advances in recent decades, with a language of tools and techniques developing around these practices. Project management has been part of these developments, offering a degree of rationality in the face of managing change ambiguities.

However, critical commentators have begun an ongoing process of questioning the practitioner claims made for change agency. Power and politics, a major theme of this textbook, plays an important role in change agency, which is often overlooked. Change-agent-centric thinking can be problematic in rehashing weary debates about overcoming resistance to change. Empowering notions of dispersing change agency are increasingly being questioned, and it may be time to question the reification of the change agent in favour of acknowledging change agency, which pervades all managerial work.

CASE STUDY: APPLYING THEORY TO PRACTICE

The 23rd Annual Power Tools Manufacturing Conference

The chairman of the Association for Power Tools Manufacturing (APTM) cast a proud eye over the final version of his conference programme. This international conference had run successfully for over two decades and he hoped that this year's conference would be the most successful to date. They had secured the prestigious Greenshires International Conference Centre for the three days and also managed to secure some of the leading names in power tools manufacturing.

The keynote speaker on Monday was the highly respected Maureen Tucker, speaking about 'The white light and white heat of power tools manufacturing'. On Tuesday Doug Yule would present his infamous and amusing 'Case study of the exploding plastic power tool'. On the final day just before the conference dinner, John Cale had agreed to talk about 'The role of change agents in power tools manufacturing'. John had promised that in this keynote address he was planning to offer a controversial way forward for power tools manufacturing, mapping out a charter for change.

The first two days of the conference were very successful, with delegates networking with all of their usual zeal. Attendance at the seminar, plenary and keynote sessions had been very impressive. As the final keynote session drew closer, there was a considerable buzz among the conference delegates. An APTM custom was that leading industry journalists were invited to the final keynote session as a public relations exercise, and among these was Steve Lamacq (editor of *New Manufacturing Tools*). NMT was respected among industry insiders for regularly breaking news about new developments in power tools manufacturing, and Steve had repeatedly criticised old working practices, arguing that the sector needed to come of age. A hush went around the auditorium as John Cale took to the stage. All seats had been taken and people squeezed themselves into aisles and doorways so that they could learn more about his charter for change.

All the lights went down and when the lighting was turned up John Cale was standing next to a 1920s lathe looking at it quizzically. There was a roar of laughter around the auditorium. He announced that we have to let go of the old technology and embrace the white light and white heat of new manufacturing technology (a theme Maureen Tucker had introduced earlier). There was a round of applause as two men wheeled the lathe off stage. He then proclaimed that new technology on its own was not enough and that we needed to work smarter as well as harder. There was a fanfare as his APTM Change Agent's Charter was projected onto a large screen.

The APTM Change Agent's Charter

1. Every manufacturing plant would have a designated change agent.

2. The designated change agent would orchestrate the change process.

3. All change agents would be required to hold a project management qualification.

4. APTM would strictly enforce this qualification requirement.

5. APTM would appraise change agents every 12 months.

6. The change agents would work exclusively with 20 APTM-approved change tools.

7. A taskforce would develop the APTM Change Agency Knowledge Book.

John finished his keynote address with the warning that if 'we do not embrace change agency the future of manufacturing power tools is as doomed as the lathe'. The audience was both shocked and challenged, and despite a loud round of applause the speech had conjured up very mixed feelings. The APTM chairman, who now chaired the Q&A, felt embarrassed that there had been no consultation about this charter prior to the conference.

Len Reed was the first to speak and appeared to be visibly annoyed. He explained that everyone at his Illinois plant was a change agent and that all employees were encouraged to deal with the vagaries of change. Sterling Morrison chuckled that he wasn't sure how Len worked his magic, but that he was in broad agreement. He explained that at his plant he regarded himself as the change agent, but that he worked in consultation with an external consultant and his management teams; as he put it, 'we are just one big happy family'.

Steve Lamacq dramatically stood on his chair, claiming that the charter would take the industry backwards rather than forwards. He demanded evidence that project management would deliver the successful change that John had implied and ripped up his conference programme, stating that an approved list of change tools and a knowledge book was madness. At this point the chairman closed the Q&A, thanking John Cale for his thought-provoking address. The conversation among the delegates was highly animated as they moved into the conference dining room.

Case study questions

1. What support is there in the chapter for the position taken by John Cale?

2. How do debates in the chapter explain the positions taken by Len Reed, Sterling Morrison and Steve Lamacq?

3. How would you advance change agency in the power tools manufacturing sector?

DISCUSSION QUESTIONS

1   Is change agency a prerequisite of managing change?

2   Do we need more or less dispersal of change agency in public service organisations?

3   Why do academics remain suspicious of managing change tools and techniques?

4   Is project management the new change management?

KEY READINGS

CALDWELL, R. (2006) *Agency and change*. **London: Routledge.**

As this chapter has highlighted, academics too frequently sidestep the theory and practice of change agency, which is rather perverse given its centrality to managing change. Caldwell demonstrates that a rigorous theoretical framework can inform practitioner-orientated debates around change agency. Change agency is used as his focus for a thorough discussion of major debates relating to modernism, contextualism, complexity theories and constructionist discourses. The book is a challenging and intellectual read that really does deliver on its subtitle – rethinking change agency.

DE CALUWE, L. and VERMAAK, H. (2003) *Learning to change: a guide for organization change agents*. **London: Sage Publications Ltd.**

It is easy to overlook this fascinating guide for change agents, which may possibly be explained in terms of a historic bias in the managing change literature towards Anglo-American authors. The title suggests a practitioner guide, which the book delivers upon. However, the book is informed by an impressive understanding of the eclectic managing change literature. The book manages to balance theoretical concerns with practical concerns about change agency. The one limitation of this book is its coverage of literature explicitly discussing change agency, which may partially be explained in terms of when it was published.

HODGSON, D.E. and CIMCIL, S. (eds) (2006) *Making projects critical*. **Basingstoke: Palgrave Macmillan.**

This edited collection of readings offers critical perspectives on managing projects. The book was based upon workshops at Bristol Business School with the explicit aim to make projects critical. Concepts rarely discussed with regard to managing projects feature prominently: power, discourse, ontology, rhetoric and uncertainties. The strengths of this book are in highlighting innovative research in very different contexts, such as IT, construction and the Olympics.

CHAPTER 18

HR and managing change

LEARNING OUTCOMES

After reading this chapter you should be able to:

- understand rationales for HR involvement in managing change
- understand HR involvement in managing change
- differentiate theories of HR involvement in managing change
- appreciate the centrality of diversity as a process of changing
- critically question claims made for HR involvement in managing change
- question the extent of advances made in terms of managing diversity.

INTRODUCTION

The centrality of power and politics in managing change was the focus of Chapter 15, which raises questions about who has the power to manage change. In Chapter 17, change agency was discussed generically, and this chapter adopts a narrower focus upon HR involvement in managing change. The awkward question remains, 'can HRM, as a philosophy of competitive advantage concerned with managing innovation and change in the workplace really turn traditional personnel practitioners into change agents?' (Caldwell 2001, p41). Answering this question is central to debates featured in this chapter.

The 'Managerial Approaches' section explores HR involvement in managing change, with specific reference to the work of Storey (1992), Ulrich (1997) and Caldwell (2001). The second part of the 'Managerial Approaches' section focuses upon the advances made in terms of a very specific area of organisational change – managing diversity. In the 'Critical Perspective' the claims made for HR's involvement in managing change and the advances made in HR-enabled diversity changes are questioned.

HR INVOLVEMENT IN MANAGING CHANGE

HR practitioners yearned for years for evidence demonstrating people were an organisation's most important asset and that good HR practice delivered organisational performance (Redman and Wilkinson 2009). In the mid-1990s, a body of research appeared to support such a view, although '... there is a large gap between what HR professionals see as their role and how other managers in the organisation see it' (Redman and Wilkinson 2009, p14). In beginning to clarify HR involvement in managing change, broader HR debates are informative.

Ogilvie and Stork (2003) remind us that change has always been a part of HR; however, the nature of change and HR's role in the design and implementation of change has varied over time. In attempting to review the disparate literature in this area, terminology is problematic. Watson (2006, p404) identified a '... rather messy situation that currently exists whereby the term "human resource management" is used in a confusing variety of ways'. He highlights three ways in which the term HRM is used: as an academic area of study bringing together previously separate topics of personnel management, industrial relations and organisational behaviour; as those aspects of managerial work dealing with employees; and as those areas once referred to as personnel management.

This is not purely a semantic consideration, as implicit within certain models of HRM are beliefs about the level and form of HR involvement in managing change (see Legge 2005 and Storey 2007 for further discussion about the status of HRM). Debates about HR and managing change are closely connected to many other topics covered in this textbook (for example culture, leadership, communications, power and politics). Organisational cultures may encourage or impede HR involvement in organisational change. Also, the involvement of HR in change processes will be influenced by organisational forms as well as strategic choices.

HR involvement in managing change must be understood as part of a bigger challenge that seeks to advance the concept of strategic HRM: 'effective delivery of organisational change requires an alignment between the organisation's corporate and business strategies, its change strategies and its HRM strategy' (Graetz et al 2006, p183). In a similar manner, Armstrong (2009, p437) argued that 'if HR is concerned – as it should be – in playing a major role in the achievement of continuous improvement in organizational capability and individual performance, and in the HR processes that support that improvement, then it will need to be involved in facilitating change'. While these are honourable aspirations, the concern is that HR's involvement in managing change remains at the level of an abstract aspiration.

In the following discussion, three influential frameworks that potentially explain HR involvement in managing change are featured. The frameworks were developed by Storey (1992), Ulrich (1997) and Caldwell (2001). While each framework has unique characteristics, commonalities become evident, and

Caldwell (2001) is able to draw upon chronologically earlier studies in developing his framework. It is worth acknowledging that each writer also uses slightly different terminology. Storey (1992) referred to personnel managers as 'change makers', Ulrich (1997) wrote about HR's visionary role as champions of change, while Caldwell (2001) referred to HR's role as 'transformative' change agents.

In his influential book on the management of human resources, Storey (1992) explained both HR involvement in managing change and the industrial relations implications of such developments. One of the strengths of his case study-based analysis was the scale and scope of the research informing the development of 15 core case studies featured in the book, which included Austin Rover, British Rail, ICI and the NHS. Storey (1992) was able to differentiate interrelationships between change initiatives being imposed unilaterally and negotiated through joint agreements. He also differentiated organisations in terms of those that adopted total change packages and those that adopted discrete change initiatives.

The research highlighted how managing change was the outcome of a series of managerial choices and potentially could be a negotiated process. It is ironic to read the commentary arising out of the case study organisations that informed Storey's analysis: 'a common refrain across the companies was to extol the merits of "eating the elephant a spoonful at a time". As much as anything this was seen as necessary in order to allow middle managers themselves time to handle the changes in bite sized portions' (Storey 1992, p123). There appears to be wisdom in such a view, although it is very difficult to reconcile with contemporary impatience around organisational change.

At the time of writing there was considerable interest in promoting HRM and seeking out case examples of the practice of HRM. However, Storey (1992, p264) was understandably cautious, arguing against '... reification of subtle and incomplete tendencies'. His case study analysis highlighted very different and divergent change initiatives that crossed traditional boundaries. This led Storey (1992, p168) to propose a framework based upon his case study analysis incorporating two dimensions: interventionary/non-interventionary on the horizontal axis and strategic/tactical on the vertical analysis. The four types of personnel practitioner are depicted in Figure 18.1.

The four types of personnel practitioner identified in Figure 18.1 highlighted developments in people management emerging from the case study analysis. The 'advisers' acted as internal consultants. The 'handmaidens' adopted client/contractor relationships with line managers and the 'regulators' '... formulated, promulgated and monitored observance of employment rules' (Storey 1992, p168). The fourth type of personnel management, 'the change maker', is particularly pertinent to debates in this chapter and the closest at that time to the espoused goals of HRM.

The 'change makers' were personnel specialists who made '... a highly proactive, interventionary and strategic contribution' (Storey 1992, p180). In drawing upon his case study analysis, Storey identified two variants of change makers in terms of hard and soft versions of HRM. The hard version identified fully

Figure 18.1 Types of personnel management (Based upon Storey, 1992)

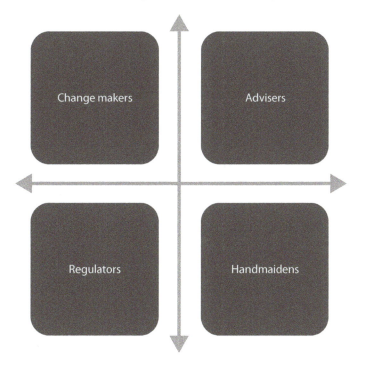

with the business needs of senior management and minimised their personnel persona. The soft version emphasised their role in tapping the creativity and commitment of resourceful humans. Storey (1992, p185) appeared pessimistic about the rhetoric of HR involvement in managing change: 'in sum, even in those cases where "strategic change making" occurs within a mainstream organisation, it cannot be assumed that personnel specialists will be able to claim it as their own'.

By contrast to Storey, Ulrich's (1997) audience in *Human Resource Champions* was primarily HR practitioners and in terms of this goal his work was very influential (Caldwell 2003b). The tone of the book was polemical and prescriptive – for example: 'successful HR change agents replace resistance with resolve, planning with results, and fear of change with excitement about its possibilities' (1997, p152). Ulrich wrote about HR professionals seeking to prescribe a more strategic role for their work. He (1997, p24) was able to identify four key roles that HR professionals must fulfil in order to make their business partnership a reality: strategic human resources, infrastructure, employee contribution and transformation and change. The strategic HR role aligned HR strategies and practices with business strategies. HR professionals through constantly examining and improving HR processes created the infrastructure. HR professionals' involvement in day-to-day problems, concerns and needs of employees enabled the management of employee contributions.

The fourth role for HR professionals was managing transformation and change, which is discussed further because of its relevance to this chapter. Ulrich believed that HR professionals could deliver capacity for change through identifying processes for managing change. The implied metaphor for this work was that of the 'change agent' and that being a change agent was part of the value-added role of HR professionals as business partners: 'HR professionals who are change agents help make change happen; they understand critical processes for change, build commitment to those processes, and ensure that change occurs as intended' (Ulrich 1997, p31).

In his writings, Caldwell made reference to both the work of Storey and Ulrich, among others, while also drawing upon his own research. Caldwell (2001) proposed a new fourfold typology of HR change agency roles, which clarified and expanded earlier discussion about HR change agency roles. The new types identified were champions, adapters, consultants and synergists. Caldwell (2001) undertook a postal questionnaire survey in April 1999. He surveyed personnel and HR managers from a randomly selected sample of 350 companies taken from a listing of 500 major UK companies ranked by 1998 turnover data; the response rate was 28%. Also, face-to-face interviews using a semi-structured agenda were conducted with 12 of the respondents: 'the survey findings appear to indicate the increasing importance of HRM and the change agent role in many large UK companies' (Caldwell 2001, p43).

However, Caldwell warned about variations and complications in the application of change agent typologies for HR professionals. The typology proposed was acknowledged as being deliberately analytical-normative and requiring further empirical research. Caldwell (2001) suggested the classification of HR change agents in terms of four dimensions related to the scale or strategic scope of HR change interventions and the professional identity of the personnel function. In discussing the four change agent roles, Caldwell (2001) offered the following definitions. The change champions were at the very top of their organisations in the roles of directors or chief executives; they led or implemented strategic HR policy changes. The change adapters occupied middle-level HR generalist and personnel specialist roles, building support for change in business units and functions. The change consultants tended to be either external consultants or specialist personnel professionals with expertise or experience in implementing change projects. The change synergists were either '... senior personnel managers or high level external HR consultants capable of strategically co-ordinating, integrating and delivering complex, large scale and multiple change projects across the whole organisation' (Caldwell 2001, p49).

The CIPD's *Reorganising for Success* surveys offer further relevant empirical findings. The CIPD (2003) surveyed more than 800 managers, CEOs, HR directors and managers from private and public sector organisations. A 13% response rate (typical for management surveys) was achieved, with a particularly high response from CEOs in the public sector. The survey methodology allowed the research team to explore if the involvement of HR made a difference to performance:

The findings show that better outcomes are achieved where HR professionals hold formal managerial roles in reorganisation steering groups or management teams. The results are clearest in relation to delivering improvements in employee-related factors, such as morale and retention, and internal effectiveness. Where there is no involvement of HR professionals only a quarter of cases lead to improvement, while the figure rises to around 40% when an HR professional is included on the steering group or management team. (CIPD 2003, pp15/16)

In a follow-up survey into HR's role in change, the CIPD surveyed 594 chief executives, HR directors and directors of other functional areas closely involved in recent reorganisations. Questionnaires were sent out in May 2004 and a 15% response rate was achieved. The six key characteristics of successful reorganisations that were identified were: (1) organisation-wide, holistic change, (2) project management, (3) employee involvement, (4) effective leadership, (5) communication with external stakeholders, and (6) internal and external experience. In the subsequent discussion of the findings, the authors were able to comment specifically upon HR's role in reorganisations:

General or business unit managers normally occupy leadership roles in reorganisations (73% of cases). While normally not performing a leadership function, HR specialists are seen to play a major role by 61% of respondents – HR is clearly involved in an important way. (CIPD 2004, p22)

Graetz et al (2006, p214) note that 'a final, and vital, part of the equation in using HR levers for change is demonstrating what they have delivered in relation to the organisation's performance'. Such an evaluation appears reasonable; however, as Chapter 20 will highlight, evaluating the effectiveness of change initiatives is a complex and multidimensional undertaking, which is likely to be further complicated by attempting to determine the effectiveness of change initiatives and simultaneously evaluate HR's contribution to effective change initiatives.

MANAGING DIVERSITY CHANGES

There has been an increased interest in managing diversity within the management and organisation literature: '... linking equal opportunities initiatives directly with business strategy, the concept of managing diversity is inextricably linked with strategic HRM' (Cassell 2009, p343). Kossek et al (2003, p328) explain how such a strategy may be achieved: 'in order to manage demographic change in economic and labor markets, a common HR change strategy is to increase the diversity of the work force through hiring over time'. These developments potentially offer an applied example of HR's involvement in managing change. The relationship that HR has with senior management is likely to be informed by many factors such as history, culture and organisational politics.

However, it is very unlikely that HR will have autonomy to initiate and manage all the changes it favours: '... whatever change HR advocates and implements, it must either represent the interests of senior management, or "sell" the change by convincing senior managers that change reflects their interests' (Ogilvie and Stork 2003, p265). This is a recurrent theme in this chapter in that while HR may recognise the merits of managing diversity, integrating diversity into business strategies is a separate challenge. Cassell (2009) identified two triggers encouraging managers to focus more upon diversity: changes in demographic trends and the existence of a business case for progressing equal opportunities. Diversity policies are likely to vary considerably. Armstrong (2009) highlighted what could potentially be included in a management of diversity policy: acknowledging difference in workplace cultures and individuals, valuing different qualities that people bring to their jobs, emphasising the elimination of bias in areas such as selection, promotion, performance assessment, pay and learning opportunities, and focusing attention upon individual differences, rather than group differences.

Thomas (2004) presented IBM as an example of managing diversity in which he explained how Lou Gerstner (CEO) in 1995 launched a diversity taskforce initiative that was to become a cornerstone of IBM's HR strategy. Eight taskforces were created that focused upon different groups: 'the goal of the initiative was to uncover and understand differences among the groups and find ways to appeal to a broader set of employees and customers' (Thomas 2004, p98). Gerstner's two central dictates were that IBM needed to get closer to customers, focusing more externally, and secondly focus more upon attracting, retaining, developing and promoting talent. Thomas regarded this successful initiative as benefiting from the four pillars of change: the demonstration of leadership support, the engagement of employees as partners, integrating diversity with management practices and linking diversity goals with business goals.

CRITICAL PERSPECTIVE

The 'Managerial Approaches' section featured developments in terms of HR involvement in managing change and managing diversity. In the following 'Critical Perspective' the focus is not so much upon the legitimacy of such ideals as upon exploring the reality of claims made for HR advances in these areas.

CRITICALLY QUESTIONING HR INVOLVEMENT IN MANAGING CHANGE

The theory and practice of HRM may be regarded as an ongoing conundrum, with the multiple historical roots of HR practice leading to contemporary tensions in HR values, expectations and allegiances (Ogilvie and Stork 2003). HRM has relevance to many different stakeholders and any critical inquiry needs to represent differing perspectives on changing. However, there is a tendency for HRM research to be managerialist and ideologically driven. If HRM is to have academic credibility, all participating actors must be incorporated (Delbridge and Lowe 1997).

Caldwell (2001, p50) acknowledged that 'one of the central problems in analysing HR change agent roles is that they are inseparable from the progressive and proactive agenda of HRM'. The implication is that criticisms of HRM are equally applicable to HR change agent roles. Ogilvie and Stork (2003, p267) acknowledged that HR today is still in a strategic positioning era, which may constrain its involvement in managing change. The dilemma is that HR's involvement in change is closely linked to the strategic positioning of HR; if HR is not meaningfully involved in strategic planning, its involvement in managing change is likely to be operational rather than strategic. As well as this contested theoretical and practical terrain of HRM, exploring connections between HR and organisational change is impeded by the highly ambiguous multiple meanings and definitions that exist for both concepts.

While the research cited in this chapter and earlier chapters furthers understanding, the contextual nature of these findings and the lack of any consensus hamper development of theories specifically about HR involvement in managing change. HR involvement in managing change is likely to be influenced by many contextual variables, as discussed in earlier chapters. Caldwell (2003b, p988), while acknowledging that Ulrich (1997) provided a systematic framework for understanding the emergence of HR roles, notes the prescriptive and didactic nature of his work: 'certainly, Ulrich's model is already widely discussed in the UK and is often trumpeted as the practitioner paradigm towards which the profession should aspire'. However, Caldwell (2003b, p1003), warning that such developments should be viewed with considerable caution, draws the following conclusions about both Storey's (1992) and Ulrich's (1997) contributions: 'yet, as HRM grows in significance, Storey's typology no longer fits a changing organisational context, while Ulrich's prescriptive vision may promise more than HR professionals can ever really deliver'.

Wright's (2008) research highlights another dilemma that arises when researching HR involvement in managing change. Wright (2008), in his interview-based study of Australian HR managers, while focusing upon business partnering and internal consultancy is able to comment upon HR managers occupying change agent roles. For example, Natalie, the learning and development manager in a law firm, characterised her role as follows:

> I am a form of change agent absolutely. I am not the sponsor for change. There is the CEO who is really the sponsor for change. The Executive are champions and sort of directors of the change, and I guess my job is a little bit more implementing change if you like. Even though I help set the scene and sort of tell them what we should be doing, they decide what to do ultimately. (2008, pp1073/4)

The strength of Wright's research is that he is able to offer qualitative insights into HR managers' perceptions of their change agency roles. However, he frequently knowingly refers to the 'imagery' of the HR managers' roles. At the beginning of this chapter HR aspirations to be more closely aligned with business strategies were acknowledged. There is a danger that if you ask HR managers if they perceive themselves as change agents, they will describe themselves as change agents.

This danger may be compounded by role ambiguities relating to HR and problems of defining change agents, discussed in Chapter 17. However, such self-perceptions do not confirm that HR managers/practitioners are the new change agents in organisations as earlier frameworks promised. The good news for practitioners is that '… personnel managers have been past masters at reinventing or reinterpreting their role in their efforts to maintain their credibility and status within a changing world of work' (Caldwell 2003b, p984).

Caldwell and Storey (2007) are well qualified to comment upon subsequent HR developments since the high expectations when Ulrich's (1997) framework was proposed. The tone of their review of the HR function is pessimistic. They acknowledge the daunting nature of integrating HR policies and practices with business strategies. Also, in terms of integrating HR into the line, they (2007, p33) warn that 'in practice, devolution processes may integrate HR to some degree, but equally they can fragment it'. They question the merits of any further search for HR–business strategy integration. In concluding this discussion, HR involvement in change agency does not appear to have fulfilled the high expectations of the previous decade. In Chapter 17, the difficulties of researching change agency were acknowledged, and in a similar manner it is methodologically very difficult to establish the full extent of HR involvement in change agency within a wide range of disparate organisations. It is likely that in certain organisations HR policies have been integrated with business strategies, allowing HR to be fully involved in managing change; however, to date it is impossible to assert that this has become the norm.

THE RHETORIC OF MANAGING DIVERSITY

It can be frustrating attempting to find empirical evidence of successfully managed diversity programmes; case studies often do not contain an evaluative element, and '… sometimes these case study reports focus more on promoting a particular company approach with evangelical zeal, rather than assessing and evaluating the success of a given programme' (Cassell 2009, p350). While there may be talk of managing diversity, it can remain potentially at the level of empty rhetoric rather than real organisational change. In Journal Research Case 18.1, research into diversity management in an American university is featured.

JOURNAL RESEARCH CASE 18.1

Managing diversity in a public sector university in America

Paper title: Increasing diversity as an HRM change strategy
Sector: Large public sector university
Research methods: Examination of a shift in demography towards greater diversity in race and sex composition over an eight-year period. Demographic data collected from the HR information system and a survey of staff (51% response rate).
Authors: Kossek, E.E., Markel, K.S. and McHugh, P.M.
Year: 2003

Journal details: *Journal of Organizational Change Management.* Vol 16, No 3. pp328–352.

Commentary: The caveat with this research is that as it was undertaken in the US, consequently the findings may not transfer to other HR contexts. However, the research is impressive in reporting a longitudinal research-based case study (which is rare in terms of diversity research). Studying demographic changes within a single organisation over time is preferable to a 'snapshot' of a moment in time, and this study is able to highlight one of the dilemmas of managing diversity featured in this chapter. The organisational demography of the case study organisation definitely changed over the eight years. However, the survey findings revealed that work group members did not necessarily agree or hold positive perceptions about the diversity changes made by HR.

Cassell (2009) draws four conclusions from the managing diversity literature. Firstly, there is currently insufficient evidence to assert that organisations that successfully manage diversity are more successful than other organisations. Secondly, there are questions about how transferable US-based 'diversity movement' literature is to other international HR contexts. Thirdly, while diversity is promoted as being in the interests of everyone, hostility towards diversity programmes may exist yet be overlooked or downplayed. For example, Kossek et al (2003, p346), in discussing their findings, suggest 'current employer efforts to increase diversity as an isolated HR strategy may not necessarily lead to increased member agreement that change is favourable'. Fourthly, managing diversity is not such a new phenomenon as the literature often implies. This may be related to the concerns of Konrad et al (2005) that once radical and critical studies of race and gender are being repackaged under the label of diversity studies in order to fit more closely with managerial interests.

CONCLUDING COMMENTARY

The centrality of change agents and agency was the focus of the previous chapter. One group of stakeholders – HR professionals – have claimed to be well placed to take on change agency roles, and this may be seen as part of a larger strategic HRM agenda. The aspiration is certainly understandable, and from the mid-1990s onwards there have been attempts to clarify this involvement. The academic dilemma has been how to differentiate HR's involvement in effective managing change initiatives while acknowledging the significance of organisational change in different contexts. While the rhetoric of HR's strategic involvement in managing change is persuasive, the evidence is less convincing.

One area of managing change where HR is believed to have had an impact is in terms of managing diversity. However, once again a gap is evident between the rhetoric of effectively managed diversity programmes and the reality of persistent workplace inequalities. Diversity initiatives may primarily serve the interests of managers, with the interests of discriminated groups and individuals being a secondary consideration. The goal of encouraging more diverse workplaces is hopefully shared by readers of this textbook. The intention here has not been to challenge this goal, but instead to question the efficacy of HR's involvement in managing change with specific reference to managing diversity. This does not negate the need for work towards more diverse workplaces.

CASE STUDY: APPLYING THEORY TO PRACTICE

Reflecting upon HR change agency roles

At 8:00 on a wet Tuesday night four friends met for their annual reunion at The Arcadian public house. They had all graduated with personnel and development master's degrees a decade earlier at the University of Greenshires. Tonight was the anniversary of their graduation ceremony. In the early years more people had attended, but in later years it had settled down to this grouping of four good friends: Rob Sadler, Lee Ranaldo, Kim Gordon and Thurston Moore.

Inevitably they had each had their share of personal and professional highs and lows over the past decade but all four worked within organisations in a mix of HR, personnel and managerial roles. The conversation began with the everyday trivialities of pub chatter, but quickly moved on to developments in their personal lives: births, marriages, divorces and deaths. Strangely, though, these significant events were merely the context for what was to follow. Although it was never spoken, each of the friends was very keen to benchmark their own progress against the progress of their friends. During the second half of the evening each friend spoke about their current role with specific reference to managing change, in terms of the nature and scope of their work and how they felt about their work. What follows is a summary of each account of progress.

Rob Sadler: Rob explained that he had been in his current role as a personnel officer for the past five years. The job was well paid and he enjoyed many aspects of his work. His biggest frustration was that the job description positioned him as operating reactively for internal clients of the personnel department. He had talked this through with his line manager at appraisals, but his line manager remained adamant that the personnel department was there to serve internal clients. Typical requests to Rob would be for advice on staffing implications of downsizing a particular department or how to remove a difficult employee who was proving resistant to change initiatives. Rob was keen to encourage more participative change management, but this was always defined implicitly and explicitly as outside his role.

Lee Ranaldo: Lee had quickly risen through the ranks to take up the post of Head of Personnel last July. There was a bit of friction between Rob and Lee over Lee's progress as Rob had always had the better grades at university. Lee's secret was that he was far more political than Rob, who tended to be hard-working and sometimes overlooked. Lee regaled the group with stories of his heroic inputs into the monthly senior management board meetings. However, it quickly became apparent to the group that Lee was still 'finding his feet'; while he was now operating at a strategic level, his inputs to senior management meetings tended to be advisory.

Kim Gordon: As Lee basked in the glory of his recent appointment Kim, in a far more understated manner, began to explain her achievements. She had been an HR director with a large, successful electronics manufacturing company for the past five years, achieving more status and greater salary than any of her peers. She never emphasised this as she found the whole process of competition among friends rather crass. However, surprisingly, she explained to her friends that she empathised with some of Rob's frustrations. Two years ago she had nearly resigned from the job. The Japanese parent company utilised very innovative HR practices, which she was convinced could transform UK operations; however, the UK chief executive had remained unconvinced. When he moved into the role of chairman, the incoming chief executive, a very capable Japanese graduate, was far more amenable to her ideas. It was agreed that Kim would become the change manager for a programme of radical changes that would bring UK operations in line with the parent company. Kim reported directly to the chief executive as she began breaking down historical barriers between functional areas of the business. She had to address deep-rooted tensions, but slowly the complex company was beginning to work far more collaboratively. There was a pause in the conversation as everyone comprehended the scale of what Kim was undertaking.

Thurston Moore: Thurston was the last member of the group to check in. Thurston had been by far the least predictable at university and the last ten years had been similarly unpredictable. When literally prodded by Lee, he had ambiguously described himself as a coach; with a little more prodding he explained he was a business solutions coach. Lee felt smug, believing that head of personnel trumped being a business solutions coach. Thurston began to explain the very unusual role that he had found himself occupying in recent years. He had worked for one of the major airline companies, providing internal consultancy and

coaching for the small senior management team. He explained that he did not work nine-to-five hours and the closest relationship he had to a line relationship was his weekly meetings with the chief executive. He enjoyed the mystique of his role and being invited to contribute to all major strategic changes taking place throughout the company. He conceded that he was working exceptionally long hours but was being very well remunerated through a lucrative share ownership scheme. He envisaged two more years in his current role, at which point he would set up as an independent external consultant, hopefully offering his services on an external consultant basis.

Peter flashed the lights of the pub to indicate closing time was imminent and began to clear away the many empty glasses on their table. The group resolved to meet in person in one year's time and in the meantime they would keep in touch by text and email as normal.

Case study questions

1 In terms of the four friends, explain who is likely to be the least and most influential in managing change in their respective companies. (Please assume that the companies are all of a similar size.)

2 Using Storey's (1992) framework, how could the four different change agency roles be analysed?

3 Using Caldwell's (2001) framework, how could the four different change agency roles be analysed?

DISCUSSION QUESTIONS

1 Why do HR managers/practitioners want greater involvement in managing change?

2 Which of the different change agent roles identified by Storey, Ulrich and Caldwell appears most promising as a prescription for future HR activities?

3 Do you believe that HR has become integrated into the strategic management of change?

4 Is the rhetoric of diversity changes a precursor to real change or an impediment to real change?

KEY READINGS

STOREY, J. (1992) *Developments in the management of human resources*. Oxford: Blackwell Business.

While this book is inevitably dated, it is still in print and remains a key piece of literature in this field. Throughout the book Storey highlights how despite the promises of the new HR model being imported from America, the empirical reality of strategic HR advances at that time remained partial and contradictory. The early 1990s witnessed a huge increase in managing change literature, and Storey found himself at the intersection of both HR and managing change debates. While it is easy to be seduced by the rhetoric of these debates, his writings are grounded in thorough research. The book commands academic respect due to his attention to the detail within the research process. In the appendix to the book he acknowledges that he '... recorded 30,000 car miles on study business plus an unmeasured number of miles travelled by train... ' (p280).

STOREY, J. (ed.) (2007) *Human resource management: a critical text*. London: Thomson Learning.

There are ongoing debates about the status and prospects for HRM.

This edited collection of readings is recommended reading for anyone wanting to explore broader HRM debates that underpin the specific managing change debates featured in this chapter. The readings are drawn from leading authorities in the HR field and seek to provoke as well as inform. The chapter by Graeme Salaman on managers' knowledge and the management of change is a particular favourite.

ULRICH, D. (1997) *Human resource champions: the next agenda for adding value and delivering results*. Boston: Harvard Business School Press.

This book was an important milestone in the evolution of strategic HRM and in particular defining a significant role for HR professionals in organisational processes of changing. The book is written in the typical Harvard Business School Press style, managing to appeal and engage managers as well as being cited by academics.

Technological change

INTRODUCTION

Managing change textbooks tend to leave coverage of technological change to separate specialist technology textbooks. However, there are potential dangers in partitioning technological change and organisational change. This partitioning does not mirror the organisational experience of such changes:

> Ever since the first uses of computers in business organisations the development of ICT-based information systems has been inseparable from the dynamics of organisational change. (Mansell et al 2007, p10)

There is a strong case for engaging with technological change as part of a thorough understanding of managing change. In reviewing major debates relating to technological change, the caveat is that the contradictions and competing explanations evident in the organisational change literature are equally evident in the technological change literature. Explanations of technological change informed by the literature from different academic disciplines quickly become apparent. However, as Wilson (1992) noted, writing with specific reference to strategic change, economic theory and management theory are unable to transcend their own paradigmatic boundaries. It is likely that such boundaries will impede the study of technological change in organisations.

The technological change literature comprises a large body of knowledge, which could not be effectively reviewed in the context of a single chapter hence the narrower focus upon relationships between technological change and organisational change. This chapter selectively introduces those technological change debates believed to be particularly pertinent to the managing change focus of this textbook. The 'Managerial Approaches' section clarifies the meaning of technology before offering an overview of different approaches to understanding technological change, with specific attention paid to the contribution of innovation theories. The 'Critical Perspective' offers an overview of the competing perspectives; technological determinism, social determinism and labour process theory, which seek to explain the relationship between technological change and organisational change.

MANAGERIAL APPROACHES

THE MEANING OF TECHNOLOGY

The study of technology requires engagement with what is meant by technology. It is easy to regard technology as a recent phenomenon; however, technology as a human response to the environment has existed throughout human history in various forms (Hatcher 2002). A wide range of technological labels over time have been evident: 'computing machinery, electronic data-processing, computer information processing, information systems, management information systems and information technology' (Orlikowski and Barley 2001, p152). In this way, although the concept of technology is familiar to most people, the meaning of technology reveals subtle differences in how it is understood.

Orlikowski and Scott (2008), acknowledging that technology has been defined and theorised in the management literature in a range of different ways, accept that multiple meanings of technology are also evident in different academic disciplines, such as history, philosophy, psychology and sociology. Technology has a range of meanings, which may be thought of as a spectrum ranging from hardware at one extreme through to social and organisational structures at the other extreme (Scarborough and Corbett 1992). This is a useful starting point for considering competing meanings, avoiding the trap of thinking about technology only in terms of hardware. Another way to understand the meaning of 'technology' is metaphorically. McLoughlin (1999) highlighted how technology has been explained in terms of different metaphors, such as technology as a machine, technology as an organism and technology as an information-processing brain. However, the question remains, what does this slippery term 'technology' refer to?

The term technology is derived from the original Greek *tekhne*, which means art or skill (Grint and Woolgar 1997). In studying technology it is apparent that the definition of 'technology' is closely related to the competing explanations of technology. Grint and Woolgar (1997, p8), in reviewing a range of definitions of technology, cite a definition by Kaplinsky (1984):

> Technology refers to the general material content or process, such as microelectronics; technique refers to the way in which the general technology is developed for a specific purpose often in conjunction with other technologies or work processes.

In the absence of a universal consensus definition of technology, this definition is favoured for this chapter, with both 'technology' and 'technique' relevant to the managing change focus of this textbook.

STUDYING TECHNOLOGICAL CHANGE

Orlikowski and Scott (2008, p3) critically comment upon the management literature on technology in organisations, suggesting that '... for the most part, technology is missing in action'. They find this perplexing given the role that technology plays in organisations and the scale of investment in technology. They substantiate their position through a review of four leading management journals over a decade (from January 1997 to December 2006). In reviewing *The Academy of Management Journal, The Academy of Management Review, Administrative Science Quarterly* and *Organization Science* they found only 4.9% of articles directly addressed the role and influence of technology in organisations. They highlight the paradox that early organisational research recognised the role of technology in organisational affairs (see for example Trist and Bamforth 1951 and Woodward 1958) and that such interest has reduced in recent years.

The following discussion offers a chronological overview of theoretical contributions to understanding technological change during the twentieth century. The caveats about history raised in Chapter 3 remain pertinent here. The intention is to signpost different examples of approaches to understanding technological change, rather than to offer a comprehensive history of technological change. As this is the penultimate chapter of this textbook, contributions from theorists featured in earlier chapters will be acknowledged, rather than repeating their contributions. These theories should not be regarded as an evolution of thinking, as some of these schools of thought remain very influential today. In Box 19.1 different contributions to studying technological change are summarised.

Box 19.1 Understanding technological change (summary of approaches)

- Technology enabling scientific management (Taylor 1911)
- Technology linked to the social system of work (Trist and Bamforth 1951)
- Technology as an independent explanatory variable (Woodward 1958)
- Technology and ideal types of organisation (Burns and Stalker 1961)
- Technology and associated feelings of alienation (Blauner 1964)
- Technology as a strategic choice (Child 1972)
- Technology enabling flexible specialisation (Piore and Sabel 1984)
- Technology enabling process reengineering (Hammer and Champy 1993)
- Technology and adoption processes (Preece 1995)

Taylor (1911), in his espousal of scientific management (discussed in Chapter 3), regarded technology as enabling increased productivity; in this sense he was one of the earliest management writers on technological change. The work of Trist and Bamforth (1951) along with other writers gave impetus to socio-technical systems theory, discussed in Chapter 8, which began to link the technical system of production with the social system of work. Woodward (1958) concluded from research undertaken in south-east Essex that there was a relationship between the type of technology used and organisation structure. She argued that specific forms of organisation structure were suited to particular production systems. Burns and Stalker (1961) again took a contingent view in their analysis of organic structures and mechanistic structures fitting with different production systems, which was discussed in Chapter 6.

Technological change had been promoted positively as a progressive development. However, Blauner (1964) was one of the earliest writers to question this march of progress. He was interested in relationships between alienation, patterns of technology and organisational trends, and through his research identified four forms of alienation: powerlessness, meaninglessness, isolation and self-estrangement. Child (1972), in introducing the concept of strategic choice, made important connections between strategy and technological change. Strategic choice emphasised managerial choice, rather than technology, in shaping work and organisation (McLoughlin and Clark 1994). In this form of analysis, power within processes of organisational change is made explicit, discussed in Chapter 15. Piore and Sabel (1984) applied and extended the idea of 'flexible specialisation', which originated with the regulation school of French social theorists (McLoughlin and Clark 1994). Flexible specialisation has been defined as:

> An approach to employment and work organisation which offers customised products to diversified markets, building trust and co-operative relationships both with employees, who use advanced technologies in a craft way, and other organisations within a business district and its associated community. (Watson 2003b, p68)

Business process reengineering (Hammer and Champy 1993) was presented to organisations as offering a radically different change methodology and by association a radically different future for organisations. Through the power of modern information technology, business processes could be radically redesigned in order to achieve dramatic improvements in their performance.

Preece (1995) was interested in what happens before technology has a physical presence within an organisation. This work may be related to developments in terms of the politics of organisational change, discussed in Chapter 15. Preece (1995) developed a framework supported through empirical work that identified two phases (adoption and introduction). The first four stages constitute the adoption phase and the three remaining stages constitute the introduction phase. It was acknowledged that stages may be iterative, involving going back before further progression ensues.

There is merit in each of the explanations of technological change offered here, and different theorists continue to work to develop more sophisticated explanations while acknowledging early pioneering work. However, as Vurdubakis (2007, p406) warns, social scientists '... have been arguing for decades over what is the most appropriate theoretical framework for integrating the organization's "human" and "technological" dimensions'. What can be asserted is that there is no consensus explanation of technological change, and there never is likely to be. Journal Research Case 19.1 features a research case of implementing new technology.

JOURNAL RESEARCH CASE 19.1

ATC

Paper title: Embellishing the past: middle manager identity and informality in the implementation of new technology
Sector: Air traffic
Research methods: Interviews, observations, attendance at meetings and documentary analysis.
Author: Hallier, J.
Year: 2004
Journal details: *New Technology, Work and Employment.* Vol 19, No 1. pp43–62.

Commentary: ATC was the name used to refer to the case study organisation, which operated in the air traffic sector. The role of ATC was to control the arrivals and departures of aircraft at several small and large airports. There were demands on the organisation to become more commercialised, yet with reduced resources. The technological focus of the case study was the implementation of a new radar and work system in ATC. In particular, the case study highlights problems with the implementation of the new Central Management Function. The research for the case study was undertaken between 1993 and 2001 with the permission of the ATC directors. The case study indicated omissions in the planning of technical change and the neglect of worker concerns during implementation.

THE CONTRIBUTION OF INNOVATION THEORIES

Innovation has been described as the word on everyone's lips (Fagerberg and Verspagen 2009). Consultants persuade companies of its usefulness and politicians are equally keen to stimulate innovation at various levels of government. In the UK, government has encouraged public service organisations to embrace innovation approaches (Mulgan and Albury 2003; Hartley 2005; Audit Commission 2007). The appeal and interrelationships of innovation and the change theme of this textbook are captured in the following quotation:

> Innovation and change are important for organisations. Speaking organisationally, innovation (either of practice or of products) leads to change that allows a company to position itself differently from its competitors. It does things differently (practices) or it offers different things (products/services). (Clegg et al 2008, p374)

In tracing the emergence of the new field of innovation studies, Fagerberg and Verspagen (2009) acknowledge that before 1960 scholarly publications on innovation were few and far between, with one exception: the writings of the Austrian–American social scientist Joseph Schumpeter. Schumpeter (1950) regarded innovation as the main driver of economic development, and this line of reasoning has proved highly influential to innovation scholars ever since. Tidd and Bessant (2009, p15) refer to Schumpeter as the godfather of innovation studies, explaining his simple argument as follows: 'entrepreneurs will seek to use technological innovation – a new product/service or a new process for making it – to get strategic advantage'. The origins of the phrase 'creative destruction', emphasising destroying the old in favour of the new, can be traced back to Schumpeter.

There was a rapid growth in scholarly interest in innovation from the early 1960s, with particularly rapid growth since the 1990s (Fagerberg and Verspagen 2009). One of the early 1960s milestones was the writings of Rogers on the diffusion of innovation:

> In the Diffusion of Innovation, Rogers' (1962) aim was to explain how to inculcate awareness and enthusiasm for technical innovations such that even those most resistant to their adoption might do so. (Mansell et al, 2007, p3)

Different types of innovation are evident such as: products, processes, positions and paradigms (Francis and Bessant 2005). Tidd and Bessant (2009, p16) define innovation as 'a process of turning opportunity into new ideas and of putting these into widely used practice'. They favour a process of innovation that they explain in terms of four key phases of search, select, implement and capture, as depicted in Figure 19.1.

Figure 19.1 A simple model of the innovation process (based upon Tidd and Bessant 2009)

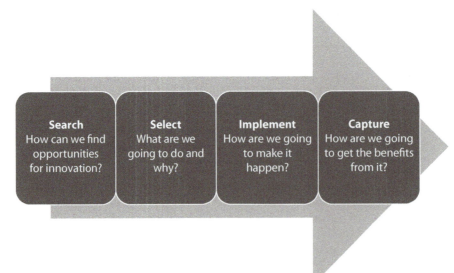

Figure 19.1 depicts the four phases of the innovation process that Tidd and Bessant (2009) highlight. The first phase requires an effective search process to establish how an organisation can survive and thrive. The second phase requires selection of an option that helps an organisation to grow and develop. The implementation phase is concerned with converting ideas into reality. Finally the capture phase is concerned with realising the benefits of an innovation. The model seeks to answer the question: do we have a clear innovation strategy and do we have an innovative organisation?

Innovation studies are strong in explaining the configuration between what the market needs and the available technology; this point of convergence has been labelled the 'technological trajectory' (Dosi 1982). Persistent differences in the sources and directions of technological change have been identified through reviewing studies of technological trajectories (Tidd and Bessant 2009), which are summarised in Box 19.2.

Box 19.2 Summary of differences in sources and directions of technological change (based upon Tidd and Bessant 2009)

- the size of innovating firms
- the type of product made
- the objectives of innovation
- the sources of innovation (for example the supplier of equipment)
- the locus of in-house innovation (for example a research and development laboratory)

The dilemma that emerges from acknowledging differences is that it is dangerous to generalise, yet equally problematic to say that every organisation is different. One effective response has been to identify five major technological trajectories: supplier-dominated, scale-intensive, science-based, information-intensive and specialised suppliers (Tidd and Bessant 2009). The strength of the development of these trajectories is that they are based upon a systematic analysis of more than 2,000 significant innovations in the UK, as well as upon reading historical and case material.

An innovation perspective to technological change encourages an understanding of technology adoption as evolutionary. Innovation is a key 'milestone' in the process, beginning with the invention of a new product, a process or a system and concluding with the diffusion of an artefact within a specified population of 'users' (McLoughlin 1999). In concluding their review of the development of innovation studies, Fagerberg and Verspagen (2009) acknowledge that there is some common ground between innovation studies and management studies. However, the dilemma that they highlight is that innovation studies have developed in terms of the policy implications of economic and social impacts of innovation, which they concede may not attract the same amount of interest from management scholars.

In the following discussion relationships between technological change and organisational change, two areas of study often approached independently, are explored. This is done in the belief that transformations which occur in the nature of work and organising cannot be understood without considering technological changes and the institutional contexts reshaping economic and organisational activity (Orlikowski and Barley 2001). However, the dilemma has been that organisational studies have tended to focus upon the social aspects of organising, and information technology studies have tended to focus upon technical aspects of organising. There are believed to be benefits in cross-fertilisation, and in this 'Critical Perspective' debates featured in earlier sections and further literature are reviewed to address the critical question: how do we adequately account for the changing relationship between technology and forms of organising? The question was originally posed by Jones and Orlikowski (2007) in their overview of ongoing debates in this area. The discussion features three different perspectives identified by Jones and Orlikowski that potentially answer the question: deterministic perspectives, emergent perspectives and labour process perspectives.

DETERMINISTIC PERSPECTIVES

While many theoretical explanations have been offered to explain relationships between technological change and organisational change, deterministic explanations have been the most prominent. Two major forms of deterministic explanation are technological determinism and social determinism, with both offering persuasive explanations of what drives technological change. While there are different varieties of technological determinism, Grint and Woolgar (1997, p7) explained technological determinism as follows:

> This perspective holds that humans (human behaviour and even the course of history) are largely determined by, rather than having influence over, technology. It is a position which has acquired the status of shibboleth.

The work of Woodward (1958) is often cited as an example of technological determinism, although in her subsequent work Woodward (1965) moved away from this position. Knights and Murray (1994) have highlighted the technological determinism within the field of innovation studies in terms of the tendency to depict technologies as developing along trajectories (see for example Nelson and Winter 1982 and Dosi 1982) and within paradigms (see for example Freeman 2007). Pavitt and Steinmueller (2002, p346) warned that the weakness of innovation models is that 'models and theories growing out of economics are weak in coping with the internal organisational dimensions of technological change... ' In essence, in effectively focusing upon the technological side of change, the human side of change is overlooked. Technological determinism has also been highlighted by Knights and Murray (1994) in flexible specialisation analyses of technological change, such as Piore and Sabel (1984).

In seeking to counter the influence of technological determinism it has been argued that people should not be subordinate to machines but instead that machines should be subordinate to people (Rosenbrock 1989). The danger with perceiving technological change as all-pervasive is that theories may be no longer required to have sophistication, describing an inevitable process of diffusion, happening regardless of human intervention. The concern with technological determinism is that human behaviour may be regarded as being largely determined by, rather than having an influence over, technology (Grint and Woolgar 1997). Which raises the question – is technology the force that shapes society, or does society shape technology (Hatcher 2002)?

Social determinism assumes '... that technological changes are themselves socially engineered and/or that work relationships are, in any case, derived from and ultimately determined by, cultural and/or social aspects, rather than technological aspects' (Grint 2005a, p290). The strategic choice (Child 1972) approach introduced in the 'Managerial Approaches' section is a good illustration of social determinism. Strategic choice explanations, in seeking to avoid the technological determinism of contingency approaches, emphasise the social in their explanations of technological change.

The danger with social determinism is that just as technological determinism underplays the role of society in explanations of technological change, social determinism underplays the role of technology in explanations of technological change. The concerns about deterministic perspectives suggest the need for middle ground explanations, which are evident within emergent perspectives.

EMERGENT PERSPECTIVES

Emergent perspectives reflect an intermediate position accommodating both technological and social factors (Jones and Orlikowski 2007). Instead of the either/or approach of technological determinism and social determinism, they regard organisational change as emerging out the complicated interactions between technology, social history and human choices and actions. Grint and Woolgar (1997, p14) clarify this middle ground, although not favouring this position themselves: 'the resulting model portrayed itself as one which avoided extreme determinism of either kind in favour of a conceptual apparatus that included many different elements: technology, people, organisations, genders, interest groups and many others besides'. The studies of technological change undertaken by Trist and Bamforth (1951), which advanced socio-technical systems approaches, illustrate an emergent perspective.

One of the concerns with the emergent perspective relates to what Grint and Woolgar (1997, p7) refer to as 'technicism'. This means that '... technology is assumed to have objective effects which can be measured and predicted and which are largely unaffected by the human actors involved'. While this technicism is far less evident than within technological determinist explanations, there is still believed to be a residue of technicism within this type of explanation. A concern with the emergent perspective is that '... they are not well equipped to account for the dynamic and emergent nature of technological artifacts, as they are modified, corrected, updated, and enhanced during use over time' (Jones and Orlikowski 2007).

LABOUR PROCESS PERSPECTIVES

The labour process perspective offers another explanation of relationships between technological change and organisational change. A good illustration of this perspective was evident within the writings of Braverman (1974). In *Labor and Monopoly Capital*, Braverman (1974) offered a Marxist explanation of how workplace changes increased managerial control and deskilled employees. The contribution of Braverman was in offering an academic challenge to the scientific management of Taylorism, which had (and continues to have) an influence upon the organisation of work. Braverman was able to illustrate his thesis through examples of workplace deskilling of groups such as bank clerks and their experience of the introduction of new technology. His work was influential in explaining the human consequences of capitalist-driven technological change in the workplace. Many criticisms of Braverman's analysis have subsequently been presented; in particular he has been criticised for romanticising notions of skill and craft (Collins 1998). In Box 19.3, arguments featured in this section are summarised through answering the question posed at the beginning of the 'Critical Perspective'.

Box 19.3 Changing relationships between technology and forms of organising

How do we adequately account for the changing relationship between technology and forms of organising?

Organisational change is driven by the intrinsic properties of the technologies adopted (technological determinism).
Organisational change is driven by social forces, rather than technological changes (social determinism).
Organisational change emerges out of interactions between technology, social histories, and contexts and human choices and actions (emergent perspective).
Organisational change is influenced by managerial choices of technologies, which fragment work and deskill and alienate workers (labour process perspective).

In their conclusions, Orlikowski and Scott (2008) encourage the study of technology, work and organisations through a range of different and flexible lenses, urging future research to move beyond separating technology from people, work and organisations. In terms of this further research they suggest that the complex and dynamic relationships of technological influences and organisational processes in specific settings requires greater attention.

CONCLUDING COMMENTARY

Any thorough understanding of managing change must take account of the ongoing technological changes taking place inside organisations in general and the relationships between technological change and organisational change in particular. However, the anticipated large body of knowledge informing understanding about these important developments currently does not exist. The meaning of technology is far more fragmented than would be expected. Many terms such as technical change, information communication technology and new technology result in commentators speaking in different voices and, at times, at cross purposes. In a similar manner the study of technological change reveals a range of competing theories placing different emphases upon different explanatory variables. These hindrances may explain why a review of leading management journals found very little coverage of technological change in organisations in the articles reviewed. The nature of relationships between technological change and organisational change remains open to debate, although these relationships remain as relevant today as they have ever been.

CASE STUDY: APPLYING THEORY TO PRACTICE

Technological change at Perfect Properties

Perfect Properties runs a chain of 300 estate agents' offices in the south of England. Up until some time ago, each office employed on average three full-time staff and two part-time staff. The day-to-day affairs of each office were overseen by the most senior estate agent, referred to as the office manager. The office managers were supported by a centralised head office function. The expectation has always been that each office would make a contribution to the overall profit of Perfect Properties. League tables have been regularly publicised within Perfect Properties, ranking the different contributions from different offices. It used to be informally understood that if an office ever failed to make a contribution to profit, the office manager would 'stand down' from his or her position. Before this year no office manager had ever been required to take this action.

The market for properties has been buoyant for many years, and profits and working life in Perfect Properties has been good. However, over the previous six months there has been a dramatic and unexpected deterioration in the property market. The loss of confidence was precipitated by an international crisis and the property market is now expected to remain stagnant for the next few years. A consequence of this dramatic downturn has been that no fewer than 50 office managers have failed to make a contribution to profit. The overall financial situation is depressing in that Perfect Properties is evidently moving into a loss-making situation and there is no sign of an early recovery in the property market.

The board of Perfect Properties have reviewed four potential strategies, but in the end they have favoured an IT-based solution. The largest costs for Perfect Properties are labour costs, resulting from the large, geographically dispersed office network. Other estate agents in response to the downturn have reduced staff numbers, and Perfect Properties feels it must take a similar course of action. However, the concern is that clients who personally visit offices and talk to staff have often been a potentially lucrative source of business. The solution adopted by the board has been the introduction of a virtual estate agent (VEA) in every office. The VEAs are client-friendly interactive computer terminals. Although Perfect Properties already has a strong Internet presence with its own website, the VEAs are regarded as far more interactive. Initially, the software was designed to respond to the needs of potential purchasers, but in the longer term the VEAs are intended to deal with vendors as well. The VEAs through interactive questionnaires allow users to identify the right area and type of property for them.

This is then linked to the properties that the office and other offices have available, scored against a 0–100 ranking reflecting the level of suitability.

Unfortunately, there was no opportunity to pilot the VEAs, given the unexpected nature of the downturn in the property market. The VEAs were introduced into offices over a very short timeframe. The average staff establishment for each office has meanwhile been reduced from three full-time and two part-time staff to two full-time and one part-time member of staff. Perfect Properties have always employed a proportion of the workforce on short-term contracts, which has enabled this reduction in staff numbers. However, the major staff reduction at the same time as the introduction of major technological change into the offices has not been positively received by employees. The staff disparagingly refer to the VEAs as the 'basic boxes', regarding them as giving an inferior rather than a complementary service. There have even been anecdotal claims that VEAs have been sabotaged by staff members ironically feeding them coffee and sandwiches. However, the VEAs have proved to be very popular with clients. The VEAs appear to appeal to clients in just the way some people prefer to use automated teller machines outside the banks instead of talking to a bank clerk inside a bank branch.

The VEAs are proving to be the salvation of Perfect Properties, attracting many new clients at a very difficult time. Although the initial implementation costs were high, the VEAs have helped to both reduce labour costs and generate more revenue. Over time even the staff in the offices have begun to appreciate how the VEAs help to deal with basic enquiries in an effective manner.

Case study questions

1 What innovation-based rationales for the introduction of the VEAs may be identified?

2 How can the technological changes in Perfect Properties be explained in terms of technological determinism?

3 How can the technological changes in Perfect Properties be explained in terms of social determinism?

4 What could have been done to manage the introduction of the VEAs better?

DISCUSSION QUESTIONS

1 Why do competing explanations of technological change exist?

2 What are the advantages and disadvantages of using an innovation approach to explain managing change?

3 Why are technologically determinist explanations so prevalent?

4 Why has the study of interrelationships between technological change and organisational change proved problematic?

KEY READINGS

GRINT, K. and WOOLGAR, S. (1997) *The machine at work: technology, work and organization*. Cambridge: Polity Press.

The central theme of this provocative book is the relationship between technology and work. The book is particularly strong in terms of coverage of social and cultural contributions to the debate. The book is suited to anyone with grounding in social theory, as some prior knowledge would be useful.

MANSELL, R., AVGEROU, C., QUAH, D. and SILVERSTONE, R. (eds) (2007) *The Oxford handbook of information and communication technologies*. Oxford: Oxford University Press.

This edited handbook offers a thorough overview of major debates relating to information communication technologies. The book benefits from leading authors in the field contributing chapters and adopts a healthy pluralistic approach to advancing theories about information and communication technologies.

TIDD, J. and BESSANT, J. (2009) *Managing innovation: integrating technological, market and organizational change*. 4th ed. Chichester: John Wiley & Sons.

In the search for integration between technological change and organisational change, this textbook offers a solution in terms of managing innovation. This best-selling textbook is highly respected and will appeal to anyone who favours an economics-based approach to change and/or a strategic approach to the management of innovations. The book is a sourcebook of innovation references, as well as being very effectively presented.

PART 5

Conclusions

CHAPTER 20

Evaluating managing change

INTRODUCTION

This textbook began by introducing a series of managing change conundrums, reflecting ongoing debates applicable to both the practice and theory of managing change. One of the major conundrums was concerned with reconciling high expectations invested in managing change with a reported high incidence of organisational change failure. The dilemma that was cited earlier relates to consultants selling managers beautifully presented, forcefully marketed packages promising organisational transformation. Simultaneously academic commentators warn about the advice and recommendations on offer, pointing out inconsistencies, contradictions and simplifications (Salaman and Asch 2003). This has been a major tension within this textbook. Practitioners optimistically focus upon successfully managing change, whereas academics appear preoccupied with pessimistically extracting the learning from failed managing change initiatives. This chapter draws together many of the themes and debates featured in this textbook through a broad overview of managing change in terms of three significant managing change themes: time dimensions, outcomes of managing change and the study of managing change.

The first theme draws upon discussions in this textbook about the role of the past, present and future in explaining why there will always be an element of mystery associated with managing change. Despite more and more models of effective organisational change, studies show that the majority of change programmes tend to fail (Alvesson and Sveningsson 2008). The second theme engages with the outcomes of managing change, specifically in terms of the reported high organisational change failure rates. What is known about organisational change failure rates is addressed in three ways: reviewing organisational change failure literature, reviewing generic explanations of failure rates and identifying potential pitfalls in such evaluations. The third theme is concerned with reflecting upon the study of managing change. This evaluation is specifically concerned with the strengths and weaknesses of studying managing change, opportunities for development and threats to the continued study of managing change.

THE TEMPORAL MYSTERIES OF MANAGING CHANGE

The temporal dimension of organisational change means that attempts to manage change inevitably engage with the uncertainties of an unknown future. The temporal mystery of managing change, both in theoretical and practical terms, is that the past is remembered, the present is perceived and the future is imagined, which is depicted graphically in Figure 20.1.

Figure 20.1 The temporal mysteries of managing change

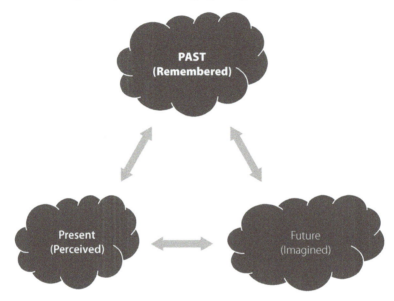

The remembered past, perceived present and the imagined future, depicted in Figure 20.1, are interrelated. This form of display challenges thinking in a linear fashion about moving from the past through the present into the future. Instead, how the past is remembered can inform how the future is imagined and vice versa. Interrelationships between the past, present and future are well documented in society; see for example the writings of Saint Augustine, Albert Einstein, Winston Churchill and George Orwell. However, perversely they are underdeveloped with regard to managing change, although they help to explain difficulties in advancing the theory and practice of managing change.

As Chapter 3 highlighted, the past is remembered. Individuals will have very different recollections of what they remember as the good old days or the bad old days. Equally organisations have histories (featured in Chapter 14) that may be remembered or forgotten as positive or negative. Academics, rather than focus upon a single history, are interested in the different ways history is written (historiography). The historiography of managing change was featured in Chapter 3, revealing how the writings of Kurt Lewin had been misrepresented and how women had been written out of the history of organisational development.

Increasingly, management literature that has been influential in the study of management is being reappraised to illustrate how writers such as F.W. Taylor inaccurately reported their findings to promote scientific management (Wrege and Hodgetts 2000). Organisations through corporate museums present sanitised versions of their histories, with their more shameful episodes often airbrushed away. Kotter (1996), in concluding *Leading Change*, argued that people who embrace the future are happier than those that cling to the past. However, history at the level of individuals, groups/teams, organisations and whole societies endures. Any account of managing change must respect the past and engage with the past, while acknowledging that multiple histories exist.

In Chapter 9 perception was featured and the inevitability of very different perceptions of a common organisational change. How the past is remembered informs how the present is perceived. What we do in the present must be understood in terms of where we have come from historically; the way things are for us in the world is not the only way it can be (Watson 2006). Practitioner-orientated change literature often implies a common perception of organisational change in which all employees pull together to achieve shared goals, as discussed in Chapter 15. This unitarist approach to employee relations is fundamentally flawed. Increasingly, there is an acknowledgement of the very different stakeholders in any organisation and the diversity of individuals that are employed by organisations.

The discussion of power and politics in Chapter 15 highlighted the existence of inequalities with regard to processes of organisational change. Every member of an organisation will have a slightly different perception of their organisation informed by their individual characteristics, culture and history. As well as the present being perceived in very different ways, it is very susceptible to perception distortions. In this textbook, many different perspectives informing understanding about managing change have been featured, as discussed in Chapter 4. These viewpoints can range from Kotter's (1996) enthusiasm for leading change through to Grey's (2003) scepticism about both the feasibility and desirability of managing change. Both the theory and practice of managing change work either implicitly or explicitly with competing perceptions of the present.

The biggest challenge for managing change will always be managing into an imagined future. In seeking to manage into the future, the future by definition remains unknown (March 1981; Dawson 2003). This has proved to be an ongoing challenge for both the theory and practice of managing change. Ludema et al (1997), writing with specific reference to organisational hope, warned that knowledge and hope are regarded as residing at opposite ends of the epistemological continuum, with knowledge belonging to the verifiable past and hope belonging to an imagined future.

This dilemma is equally applicable to the study of managing change – how can social scientists verify enthusiastic claims made for an organisational change that is concerned with an imagined future? The discussions in Chapter 11 about change communications in terms of language and rhetoric highlighted attempts to create a vision of organisational change that galvanises employees in terms of an imagined future. Both the theory and practice of managing change work either implicitly or explicitly with imagined futures.

EVALUATING OUTCOMES OF MANAGING CHANGE

The goal of success is embedded within societies and within individuals. Senior managers want their change initiatives to be successful and perceived by all interested parties as successful. Similarly, most individuals would rather be associated with success rather than failure. The centrality of success is very evident in the practitioner-orientated change literature, which promises successful change if you follow a generic set of steps or recipe, such as Peters and Waterman's (1982) identification of the eight attributes of successful companies.

In terms of learning about managing change, failure may offer better opportunities to learn. Despite the potential learning opportunities of exploring change failures, talking and writing about failure remains an organisational taboo (Thorne 2000; Sennett 2001). However, in the context of studying organisational change ignoring failure is not an option because of the high organisational change failure rates (see Box 20.1). Equally, practitioner preoccupations with being successful and being seen to be successful impede rather than inform understanding about managing change. The 70% organisational change failure rate is cited with depressing frequency, but where did this very specific failure rate originate from?

IN SEARCH OF THE 70% FAILURE RATE

In the 1990s two influential papers – 'Why change programs don't produce change' (Beer et al 1990a) and 'Leading change: why transformation efforts fail' (Kotter 1995) – were published in the practitioner-orientated *Harvard Business Review*. They were to set the tone for an ongoing debate about change failure rates. These papers began a process of questioning the high expectations placed upon managing change, particularly in the 1990s. Neither of these papers offered supporting references or details of any research underpinning the papers; instead, emphasis was placed upon the consultancy experiences of the authors. In both instances the papers promoted books written by the authors (Beer et al 1990b; Kotter 1996), which were also published by Harvard Business School Press. In the case of Beer et al (1990b), case studies that informed their paper were discussed and introduced, whereas Kotter (1996) made passing reference to large companies with which he had worked.

In 1994, Spector and Beer identified a failure rate of upward of 75% specifically for total quality management programmes. However, the 70% organisational change failure first appeared in Beer and Nohria (2000a, p133) in another *Harvard Business Review* paper in which they wrote that 'the brutal fact is that about 70% of all change initiatives fail'. In this paper they argued that based upon their 40 years' experience of studying the nature of corporate change, two archetypes or theories of change exist: Theory E related change to economic value, and Theory O related change to organisational capability (2000a). According to Beer and Nohria, most companies reflected a mix of Theory O and Theory E. They discussed Scott Paper and Champion International as case studies of almost pure forms of these theories and ASDA (UK) as an illustration of how the two theories could be effectively combined in terms of six main dimensions of change. While these case studies were informative, no empirical evidence was cited supporting the famous 70% statistic and the paper contained no supporting references. Either by default or by design, Harvard Business School Press published *Breaking the Code of Change* in 2000 based upon a conference of a similar name. In this edited reader the authors (Beer and Nohria 2000b) drew together many eminent writers and organised their book around Theory E and Theory O, although no new evidence was offered to corroborate the 70% failure rate.

In 2008, Harvard Business Press published *A Sense of Urgency* by Kotter. Headlines featured the high failure rates that Kotter had apparently identified. However, Kotter's exact terminology was far more circumspect.

> From years of study, I estimate today more than 70 per cent of needed change either fails to be launched, even though some people clearly see the need, fails to be completed even though some people exhaust themselves trying, or finishes over budget, late and with initial aspirations unmet. (Kotter 2008, pp12/13)

The 70% failure mantra is again evoked, which may help to sell a book that offers readers tactics to increase the sense of urgency in their respective organisations. While this short discussion has highlighted the role of Harvard Business Press and *Harvard Business Review* in publicising organisational change failure, other commentators have come to similar conclusions. Literature already cited plus further references are summarised in Box 20.1.

Box 20.1 Reporting organisational change failures

'Most change programs don't work because they are guided by a theory of change that is fundamentally flawed.' (Beer et al 1990a, p159)

'25–30 per cent of change efforts succeed'. (Ashkenas 1994)

'Upwards of 75 per cent of TQM interventions fail to live up to the expectations of their champions.' (Spector and Beer 1994, p63)

'... 70% of all change initiatives fail'. (Beer and Nohria 2000a, p133)

'Change management initiatives are largely failures, and the usual explanations for these failures are inadequate.' (Grey 2003, p1)

'... organizational change has an undeniable tendency to produce failure'. (Sorge and van Witteloostuijn 2004, p1212)

'Despite managers and consultants having access to literature on organisational change, a large number of change management programmes still fail.' (Woodward and Hendry 2004, p155)

'Most efforts by executives, managers, and administrators to significantly change the organizations they lead do not work'. (Burke 2008, p11)

Box 20.1 highlights a tendency towards organisational change failure that has been evident for the last two decades. There does appear to be a critical consensus between the likes of Grey and Sorge and van Witteloostuijn as critical commentators and the likes of Beer and Burke with their experiences as business consultants, which highlights the failings of managing change initiatives. This depressing assessment is informative in the context of studying managing change and may not be that different from our everyday life experiences of changing. For example, people stop smoking yet start again and people on diets are invariably unable to maintain their target weights – 'if individuals find change difficult, it is not surprising that organisations do too' (Ulrich 1997, p157).

EXPLAINING ORGANISATIONAL CHANGE FAILURE

In studying this area evaluation pitfalls quickly become apparent, which will be discussed separately. At this stage it is informative to review broad explanations that are often offered for organisational change failures. In Box 20.2 a range of explanations for why organisational change initiatives fail are featured.

Box 20.2 Generic explanations for organisational change failure

Frequency
Frequent organisational changes lead to a greater risk of failure. (Abrahamson 2004a)

Implementation
Only partial and incremental implementation of change is undertaken. (Buchanan and Badham 2008)
Effectively implementing change is problematic. (Boonstra 2004)
The methods are not properly understood or only partly applied. (Buchanan and Badham 2008)
There is an overemphasis upon the content of the change and solving problems. (Gravenhorst and In't Veld 2004)
There is a single issue focus in seeking to realise change. (Gravenhorst and In't Veld 2004)
Our knowledge of planning and implementing change is limited. (Burke 2008)

Top–down/Bottom–up
There is a lack of sufficient support from senior management. (Boonstra 2004).
Top management perspective with a top–down approach. (Gravenhorst and In't Veld 2004)

Cultural challenges
Deep organisational change (cultural change) is difficult. (Burke 2008)
Challenge of changing existing rules, habits, institutional arrangements and values. (Boonstra 2004)

People problems
Problems encountered in change processes (psychological). (Boonstra 2004)
Exercise of pocket veto by members of staff. (De Caluwe and Vermaak 2004)
There is a difficulty in making a case for change when an organisation is doing well. (Burke 2008)

Power and politics
Political issues, particularly in radical strategic change. (Buchanan and Badham 2008)
There is a defence of existing power relations, interests and positions. (Boonstra 2004)

There are inevitably as many explanations of organisational change failure as there are organisational changes; in this sense Box 20.2 should be regarded as selective rather than comprehensive. This textbook has featured many competing perspectives on change and different perspectives will emphasise different explanations for failure. In Box 20.2 generic explanations for organisational change failure have been clustered in order to allow the discussion of themes.

Ironically, Abrahamson (2004) found that the more frequently an organisation changed the greater the risk of failure. Searching for convincing explanations of organisational change failure may overlook the problematic nature of constant change. Poor implementation is a common explanation for failure. This type of explanation tends to protect the status of the change initiative at the expense of those implementing the change (Boonstra 2004). As this textbook has highlighted, change may be implemented from the top–down, the bottom–up or a hybrid of the two. The implication is that preferences in terms of styles of managing change will influence explanations of failure.

Cultural challenges have been offered as another explanation for failure. In Chapter 13, it was acknowledged that while senior managers talk in terms of changing cultures, such projects are long-term and often challenging undertakings. Employees of an organisation are sometimes depicted as the reasons for a failure, with De Caluwe and Vermaak (2004) highlighting the pocket vetoes employees take if they are opposed to a change. Also, understandably people may be unwilling to change when they perceive their organisation to be successful. Finally, there has been a growing acknowledgement of the influence of power and politics upon organisational change, discussed in Chapter 15, and the exercise of power and politics offers another explanation for change failures.

There is merit in these broad explanations of change failure; however, by definition these explanations remain generalisations. This suggests the need to review specific instances of change failure and specific explanations for these failures. Total quality management (TQM) (discussed in the Organisational Change Field Guide (see Appendix)) offers an effective illustration. Spector and Beer (1994) acknowledged a TQM failure rate of upward of 75% in their research into factors supporting or undermining TQM interventions. They focused upon three American organisations involved in financial transaction processing, global banking computing and network services, and commercial nuclear fuels. They argued that successful TQM must follow six steps and that these steps must be undertaken in sequence in order to avoid TQM failure.

Redman and Grieves (1999), in a less prescriptive review of TQM, began by reviewing the literature that explained high TQM failure rates. They (1999, p46) identified five clusters of related explanations for TQM failure: 'a lack of integration between quality management and everyday business practices; difficulties in winning managerial commitment; problems of adapting HR practices to support TQM; the effects of recession and restructuring; and the broad somewhat "catchall" category of poor implementation'. They undertook their case study of TQM at Metco, a UK metal building products manufacturer. They (1999, p57) identified the following key difficulties in TQM implementation specifically at Metco: 'senior manager turnover, an emphasis on short term goals, declining managerial commitment, the impact of redundancy on surviving staff's morale and the failure to manage interpersonal relationships and hence problems with team conflict and communications'. In conclusion they (1999, p58) found that 'in theory TQM offered, or appeared to offer to the company, many things which have yet to materialise or were only briefly realised'.

The above discussion highlights explanations for organisational change failures that can be identified; however, implicit within these explanations is the assumption that if the reasons for failure can be addressed, that change can be successfully managed. This view is not universally supported. For example, King and Anderson (2002, p162) highlighted the general illusion of the manageability of change, suggesting that it is '... composed of three sets of second-order illusory beliefs – the illusion of linearity, the illusion of predictability and the illusion of control'.

The illusion of linearity has been questioned throughout this textbook and is often evident in practitioner-orientated literature. The illusion of linearity was evident in the eight attributes of successful companies (Peters and Waterman 1982) and Kotter's (1995) eight steps. This illusion suggests that change progresses through a series of steps and stages, arriving at a successful outcome. The second illusion is slightly more subtle in suggesting that in following the steps or stages the outcome can be predicted. Again, the predictability of forward-looking organisational change has been questioned throughout this textbook. The final illusion relates to how much control managers have over processes of organisational change. This was most evident in this textbook in terms of discussions about planned change and emergent change, as such approaches make assumptions that managers either do or do not have control over change processes. King and Anderson (2002, p164), despite highlighting these illusions, still believed that managers have a role to play in managing change: 'perhaps the two characteristics most required in managing innovation and change processes are vigilance in detecting the unforeseen as early as possible, and flexibility in reacting to it'.

POTENTIAL PITFALLS OF EVALUATING ORGANISATIONAL CHANGE OUTCOMES

In the final part of this discussion caution is encouraged in terms of placing too much faith in the validity and reliability of the 70% headline failure rate for organisational change. Both practitioners and academics acknowledged a tendency for managing change initiatives to fail; however, these evaluations appear to be more of an art than a science that the failure statistics imply. Any study of managing change outcomes quickly reveals the problematic nature of undertaking such an evaluation in a meaningful way. In Box 20.3, ten potential pitfalls of evaluating organisational change outcomes have been specified.

Box 20.3 The potential pitfalls of evaluating organisational change outcomes

1   the context-specific nature of managing change
2   the latent and espoused rationales of a change initiative
3   the unintended consequences of a change initiative
4   the multidimensional/interdependent nature of a change initiative
5   organisational perceptions of a managing change outcome
6   philosophical basis of managing change evaluations
7   academic perspectives informing evaluations
8   reconciling qualitative and quantitative evaluation findings
9   the dynamic nature of any managing change outcome
10 the sustainability of what has been achieved

Despite the potential pitfalls featured in Box 20.3, there remains a real need to evaluate managing change initiatives to inform the developing body of knowledge about managing change. However, evaluation must be informed by an understanding of potential pitfalls. The following discussion explores each of these potential pitfalls.

In Chapter 5 a contextualist approach to change was introduced and encouraged. The implication is that any evaluation will be unique in terms of the nature of the organisation, the sectoral background and geographical location (1). The managing change literature is biased towards Anglo-American literature, and the danger in generalising the findings from an evaluation of an American organisation to other parts of the world is that national cultures differ considerably. For example, the extensive consultancy experiences of Beer and Kotter working with American businesses are acknowledged; however, such experiences may not be applicable to the experiences of Japanese businesses or Chinese businesses or third sector organisations.

A second potential pitfall relates to the latent and espoused rationales of change initiatives (2). One approach to evaluating a change initiative is to judge it against what it set out to achieve. However, this assumes that the espoused rationale (such as improving customer service) reflects what the management was seeking to achieve, whereas management may have primarily been seeking cost reductions but using improved customer service as a more palatable rationale. Clegg and Walsh (2004) have written about examples of latent functions of managing change, such as utilising the rhetoric of organisational competitiveness and demonstrating to the City that a company is taking an issue seriously.

As well as differentiating between latent and espoused rationales of change, there may be unintended consequences, which benefit an organisation (3). In a similar manner, organisational change initiatives are likely to be multidimensional and interdependent (4). For example, TQM focused upon quality management yet was also concerned with human resource management and cultural change. The focus may be upon a production line, but that production line may be dependent upon an administration department for management information. In this way it becomes difficult and unrealistic to evaluate change initiatives in isolation. Another dilemma in attempting to evaluate managing change initiatives relates to the convergence/ divergence of the different initiatives to which organisations are exposed. Kelemen et al (2000, p154) questioned the belief promoted by Hammer and Champy (1993) that business process reengineering (BPR) and TQM were fundamentally different philosophies of organisation: 'In reality, BPR and TQM practices can draw on similar resources and, in certain settings, be interrelated to the extent that their complex, programmatic effects are difficult, if not impossible, to separate.' This finding complicates our understanding of the rhetorical claims made for TQM. History may reveal that the most important role of TQM was not in terms of quality management, but rather as a precursor to subsequent change initiatives such as BPR.

In this textbook, the concept of organisations comprising many different stakeholders has been favoured, as opposed to a unitarist view that favours a commonality of shared interests. When evaluating a change initiative, competing perceptions of organisational members of the success or failure of change outcomes are likely to exist (5). For example, a diversity management initiative may be hailed as a success by trade unionists, whereas shareholders judge it as a failure because of its cost implications; for every change achieved someone loses something (Harvey 1990). This simple yet important aside acknowledges that there will be winners as well as losers and, consequently, how you evaluate change will be influenced by whether you ask one of the winners or one of the losers.

How change is evaluated is informed by rarely articulated philosophical choices (6). Butler et al (2003, p55) acknowledged that 'all designers of human change programs implicitly or explicitly make use of models which explain why people do what they do'. They conclude their paper that evaluation is a form of knowing informed by the evaluator's epistemology and ontology, discussed in Chapter 4. Epistemology in their paper referred to what evaluators knew about the action thinking programme they were evaluating and ontology referred to their understanding of the reality of the action thinking programme they were evaluating. We adopt different epistemological and ontological positions invariably without acknowledging them; however, they inform the evaluations that we make and by association the outcomes of those evaluations.

In reviewing the literature relating to evaluating organisational change outcomes, academics from very different academic disciplines undertook work informed by very different philosophical positions and academic perspectives (7). For example, an innovation theorist may place emphasis in their evaluation upon the diffusion of an innovation through an organisation, a sector or a country, whereas an organisational behaviour theorist may emphasise resistance to change as part of their evaluation. As well as perceptions, philosophies and academic disciplines underpinning the process of evaluating, there will be preferences for either qualitative or quantitative evaluations or a combination of both (8). Again the perceived legitimacy of qualitative or quantitative data relates to competing epistemological positions. However, preferences also exist inside organisations: '... the traditional criteria for scientific validity do not in themselves guarantee usefulness to practitioners' (Worren et al 2002, p1228). The concern is that managers often focus attention on, and become preoccupied with, the technical side of change, dealing with quantifiable and predictable issues (Bovey and Hede 2001). Handy (1994, p219) highlighted the danger with this line of reasoning in his discussion of the McNamara fallacy:

> The first step is to measure whatever can be easily measured. This is OK as far as it goes. The second step is to disregard that which can't be easily measured or to give it an arbitrary quantitative value. This is artificial and misleading. The third step is to presume that what can't be measured easily really isn't important. This is blindness. The fourth step is to say that what can't be easily measured really doesn't exist. This is suicide.

Handy was concerned that what does not get counted is not valued and money, which is easily counted, becomes the measure of all things. This appears particularly pertinent to evaluating change. For example, in the private sector profit is likely to be an important criterion and in public services reducing costs and providing quality service are likely to be important criteria. In this way the McNamara fallacy highlights the arbitrariness of the earlier 70% failure statistic.

Kotter (1995, p59) conceded that 'the most general lesson to be learned from the more successful cases is that the change process goes through a series of phases that, in total, usually require a considerable length of time'. The outcomes of change will often be dynamic, rather than static (9). For example, an organisational redesign may initially be evaluated as problematic, six months later it may be evaluated as beneficial and five years later as ill-advised. Another related potential pitfall is concerned with the sustainability of a change outcome (10). The greater acknowledgement of the emergent and processual nature of organisational change highlighted change as an ongoing process. This raises questions about sustaining change after the launch phase of a change.

This discussion about the pitfalls of evaluating organisational change outcomes highlights the questionable legitimacy of global statements that 70% of organisational change initiatives fail. While there appears to be a consensus among practitioners and academics about a tendency towards organisational change failure, crude quantification and generalisations about such tendencies impede both the theory and practice of managing change. The evaluation of organisational change outcomes raises questions about the academic study of managing change.

EVALUATING THE STUDY OF MANAGING CHANGE

The literature review that informed the development of this textbook allows conclusions to be drawn about the study of managing change. Many previous evaluations of what is known about managing change have been sceptical (see for example Grey 2003; Clegg and Walsh 2004; Caldwell 2006). Walton and Russell (2004, p145) are indicative of the tone of such evaluations:

> However, there is still little formulaic knowledge about how to create definitive and sustainable change, much less how to measure or evaluate

real change… As some have pointed out, despite over 50 years of being a field, we have little more than rehashed concepts and simplistic ideas.

The frustrations that this quotation communicates are unlikely to be exclusively academic, with practitioners equally aware of high change failure rates discussed in the previous section. Despite such frustrations a vast amount of work has been conducted in the field of organisational change (Clegg and Walsh 2004). In this spirit, the following concluding evaluation identifies strengths, weaknesses, opportunities and threats with reference to the study of managing change, which is graphically depicted in Figure 20.2.

Figure 20.2 Studying managing change – strengths, weaknesses, opportunities and threats

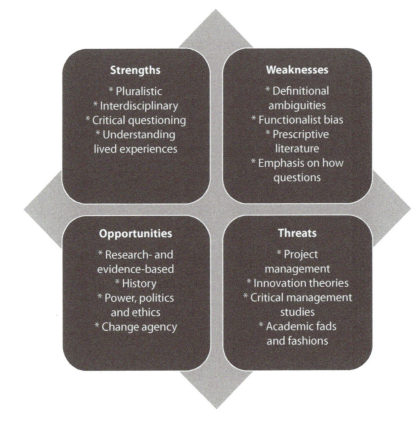

Strengths

* Pluralistic
* Interdisciplinary
* Critical questioning
* Understanding lived experiences

Weaknesses

* Definitional ambiguities
* Functionalist bias
* Prescriptive literature
* Emphasis on how questions

Opportunities

* Research- and evidence-based
* History
* Power, politics and ethics
* Change agency

Threats

* Project management
* Innovation theories
* Critical management studies
* Academic fads and fashions

WHAT ARE THE STRENGTHS OF HOW MANAGING CHANGE IS STUDIED?

Four strengths of how managing change is currently studied are that it is pluralistic, interdisciplinary, critical questioning is evident and there is an increasing understanding about the lived experience of organisational change. *The Academy of Management Review* in a change and pluralism special issue raised the concerns that '… pluralism that is so obvious in society at large is often missing from academic theories' (Eisenhardt 2000, p704). One of the strengths of the study of managing change has been its pluralism, in terms of different academic disciplines, paradigms and perspectives, which were discussed in Chapter 4. Eisenhardt (2000) believed that it was pluralism in ideas, among people and organisations and across industries that drove change.

While practitioner literature invariably emphasises the one best way to manage change, academics are more sceptical about the one best way either to study or manage change. Pettigrew (1990, p269) warned that 'explanations of change are bound to be holistic and multifaceted. Beware of the myth of the singular theory of social or organisational change.' In a similar manner Dawson (2003, p11) warned that '... there can never be a universal theory of organisational change, as change involves a movement to some future state that comprises a context and time that remain unknown'.

The pluralism that informs the study of managing change encourages interdisciplinary studies of managing change. Rather than viewing the study of managing change in terms of a series of academic silos, there is increasing recognition that academic theories work in tandem and that they can inform each other. A good illustration of this has been the recent publication of *Managing Change, Creativity and Innovation* (Andriopoulos and Dawson 2009) in which authors from two very different academic backgrounds advance the field of study through linking rather than separating change, creativity and innovation.

In this textbook popular managing change myths and assumptions have been critically questioned and such critical questioning is evident within academic studies of managing change. Critical questioning allows assumptions, such as resistance as something that managers must overcome, to be challenged. As Chapter 12 demonstrated, changing the terminology from resistance to change to responses to change allows a far more subtle approach to both the theory and practice of managing change.

Collins (1998) adopted the slightly mocking title of 'hero-manager reflections and biographies' to refer to books such as Iacocca with Novak (1986) and Harvey-Jones (1988). These books celebrated the lived experience of senior managers managing change, but invariably remained silent about employees' lived experiences of organisational change. One of the strengths of the study of managing change in recent decades has been an engagement with employees lived experience of organisational change (see for example Dawson 2003 and Buchanan and Badham 2008).

WHAT ARE THE WEAKNESSES OF HOW MANAGING CHANGE IS STUDIED?

Four weaknesses of how managing change is currently studied are that it is plagued with definitional ambiguities, the functionalist paradigm dominates the field of study, prescriptive literature remains influential and study too often focuses upon 'how to manage change' questions at the expense of 'what' and 'why' questions.

Pluralism is a strength of the academic study of managing change; it inevitably blurs the focus of studies. In particular, 'the expansion of the field of organisational change has led to a large amount of concepts, labels and models' (Alvesson and Sveningsson 2008, p13). Evaluating the study of managing change is hampered by the variety of labels used by academics: for example, organisation change management, organisation change, managing change. The functionalist bias in the study of managing change was acknowledged in Chapter 4. The danger with such functionalism is that it contorts the study of managing change so that topics such as ethics are defined as being irrelevant to the mainstream study of managing change.

This textbook has sought to differentiate prescriptive/populist accounts of managing change from more research-orientated academic accounts of managing change. The challenge is that the prescriptive/populist literature far outweighs the academic literature, which means that it remains an influential body of literature. The functionalist/prescriptive influence upon the study of managing change encourages a preoccupation with 'how' questions at the expense of important 'what' and 'why' questions.

WHAT ARE THE OPPORTUNITIES FOR DEVELOPING THE STUDY OF MANAGING CHANGE?

Four opportunities for developing the study of managing change are: greater emphasis upon research-evidence-based approaches, further exploration of the role of history, further study of power, politics and ethics, and greater engagement with change agency.

There remains a huge opportunity for further research into organisational change, which would inform the study of managing change. Action research offers a research design that enables academics to work collaboratively with organisations with regard to furthering understanding about organisational change.

In Chapter 3, the role played by history and historiography in the study of managing change was highlighted. Practitioner interest in organisational memory is being mirrored by growing academic interest in how past changes inform current changes and reappraising what has been written about management in general and managing change in particular. While power, politics and ethics do not normally feature prominently in traditional managing change textbooks, they have an important role to play in informing understanding about managing change. Change agency has received surprisingly little attention in traditional management textbooks; again, the scope for further study is considerable.

WHAT ARE THE THREATS TO THE CONTINUED STUDY OF MANAGING CHANGE?

Four potential threats to the study of managing change are: the field being overtaken by interest in project management and/or innovation theories, critical management studies (CMS) and academic fads and fashions. It can be difficult to differentiate where project management, discussed in Chapter 17, ends and change management begins, and such differentiation is likely to be seen as artificial by practitioners. However, the potential threat is that the study of managing change is eclipsed by project management methods and methodologies.

In a similar manner, innovation theories, discussed in Chapter 19, offer an alternative approach to organisational change. In terms of public sector change, both governments and academics favoured innovation-based frameworks, rather than the established organisational change frameworks. CMS, which was discussed in Chapter 4, has made a large impression upon management studies. However, versions of CMS that favour an anti-performative stance are difficult to reconcile with managing change as a concept or a field of study. Finally, while academics question the fads and fashions of management (Collins 2000), academics appear equally susceptible to fads and fashions. The final threat to the study of managing change is that it simply becomes passé, which would be a pity!

Appendix
The Organisational Change Field Guide

Introducing the Organisational Change Field Guide

In this field guide 20 popular and enduring approaches to organisational change are introduced. The essence and origins of each organisational change are highlighted along with espoused reasons for adoption (Why) and common concerns (Why not). 'Where to look' refers to where particular organisational changes may be most evident and 'What to listen for' refers to typical rhetoric/terminology in use inside organisations. The managerial reference signposts a practitioner-orientated book that offers guidance on the application of a particular approach. The critical reference offers a reference to an academic journal paper critiquing a particular approach.

This guide does not seek to critically evaluate these organisational change initiatives, as they would need to be evaluated within their own specific organisational contexts, but equally the guide does not dismiss these organisational changes as merely fads or fashions. Instead the expectation is that the reader can relate the discussions featured throughout this textbook to specific organisational changes they may encounter as part of their studies or management practice. The organisational changes are discussed separately, although organisations are likely to adopt different initiatives simultaneously. The organisational changes featured in the guide are listed below:

- Action learning
- Appreciative inquiry
- Balanced scorecard
- Benchmarking
- Business process reengineering
- Coaching
- Customer relationship management
- Downsizing
- Employee empowerment
- High-performance work systems
- Investors in People
- Kaizen

- Knowledge management
- Lean Six Sigma
- Learning organisation
- Organisational development
- Outsourcing
- Strategic alliances
- Supply chain management
- Total quality management

1 ACTION LEARNING

ESSENCE AND ORIGINS

Action learning involves a group of typically mature learners studying on courses and/or working in organisations meeting regularly. The time for each set member is equally allocated during the set meeting, offering an opportunity to reflect upon and review actions. Sets are either facilitated by a set facilitator or self-managed. Action learning, particularly when undertaken in association with action research, has been used as a means of facilitating organisational change and extracting learning from organisational change. Reginald Revans developed action learning while advising the UK Coal Board in the 1940s. He subsequently refined and developed action learning in the Health Service in the 1950s and over many decades was a tireless advocate for action learning.

WHY

- Action learning values learning through the questioning of real experiences.
- Action learning encourages the potential development of egalitarian and humanistic values.

WHY NOT

- Action learning is not suitable for everyone.
- The commitment to a set, particularly in terms of time, can be quite intensive.

WHERE TO LOOK

It is evident in more innovative universities. Its application is not associated with particular sectors; however, it has been particularly evident as an approach to management development. It has frequently been used in the National Health Service to develop leaders and managers.

WHAT TO LISTEN FOR

L = P+Q – Learning = programmed knowledge and insightful questioning.

We manage the unknown through questioning.

We find that what our managers learn through action learning sets is highly transferable.

MANAGERIAL REFERENCE

PEDLER, M. (2008) *Action learning for managers.* Aldershot: Gower Publishing Ltd.

CRITICAL REFERENCE

MCLAUGHLIN, H. and THORPE, R. (1993) Action learning – a paradigm in emergence. *British Journal of Management.* Vol 4, No 1. pp19–27.

2   APPRECIATIVE INQUIRY

ESSENCE AND ORIGINS

Appreciative inquiry encourages a search for what is best in people, their organisations and the wider world. Appreciative inquiry emphasises the positive core within organisations and their members. The key phases of appreciative inquiry are known as the 4-D cycle: discovery, dream, design and destiny. The origins of appreciative inquiry can be traced back to David Cooperrider's doctoral dissertation, conferred in 1985. The doctorate introduced appreciative inquiry as a methodology for advancing and understanding innovations in organisations. Cooperrider, working with colleagues, has continued to promote and develop appreciative inquiry.

WHY

- Appreciative inquiry emphasises the positive side of life, which traditionally can be underplayed in organisations.
- Appreciative inquiry offers a tried and tested methodology for facilitating organisational change.

WHY NOT

- The underlying philosophy could be overwhelming for anyone who did not share the appreciative inquiry values.
- Appreciating people as a performance management strategy may be perceived as being manipulative.

WHERE TO LOOK

There are no limits to where appreciative inquiry can be applied. Appreciative inquiry does require senior management support, as well as the broad support of employees. In this sense its adoption is likely to be localised rather than across whole sectors.

WHAT TO LISTEN FOR

Appreciative inquiry gives us a positive foundation of strength to build on in engaging with the future.

The appreciative inquiry philosophy allows us to engage the hearts and minds of our people.

We ask how we might take an appreciative inquiry approach to this?

MANAGERIAL REFERENCE

COOPERRIDER, D.L. and WHITNEY, D. (2005) *Appreciative inquiry: a positive revolution in change.* San Francisco, CA: Berrett Koehler Publishers Inc.

CRITICAL REFERENCE

GRANT, S. and HUMPHRIES, M. (2006) Critical evaluation of appreciative inquiry. *Action Research.* Vol 4, No 4. pp401–418.

3 BALANCED SCORECARD

ESSENCE AND ORIGINS

Balanced scorecards are strategic planning tools that measure performance. In particular they focus upon four perspectives: financial, customer, business processes and learning and growth. However, there is no universal meaning for a balanced scorecard as the application can be highly context-specific. The balanced scorecard can be traced back to the French word *tableau de bord*, meaning dashboard. The work of Robert Kaplan and David Norton in the early 1990s gave major impetus to the application of balanced scorecards.

WHY

- Balanced scorecards help link strategy and operations.
- Balanced scorecards provide a framework for performance measurement.

WHY NOT

- They may be perceived as a tokenistic approach to organisational change.
- They are more of diagnostic tool than an intervention tool.

WHERE TO LOOK

Balanced scorecards are very common and popular among strategists in the public sector, private sector and third sector.

WHAT TO LISTEN FOR

Let's ensure that we achieve at least 75% customer satisfaction.

How do our customers see us?

How will we sustain our ability to change?

MANAGERIAL REFERENCE

KAPLAN, R.S. and NORTON, D.P. (1996) *The balanced scorecard: translating strategy into action*. Boston: Harvard Business School Press.

CRITICAL REFERENCE

COKIN, S.G. (2010) The promise and perils of the balanced scorecard. *Journal of Corporate Accounting and Finance*. Vol 21, Issue 3. pp19–28.

---

4   BENCHMARKING

ESSENCE AND ORIGINS

Benchmarking involves seeking out comparable organisations to compare best practices and processes used by other organisations. This is usually a continuing activity and part of a wider quality management initiative. Benchmarking can be applied to all organisational processes, such as human resource management, accounting and performance management. There are different types of benchmarking, such as strategic, collaborative and internal benchmarking. Benchmarking as a way of working probably originated in Japan. In the West, Rank Xerox in 1979 is regarded as the first organisation to formally adopt benchmarking, with Robert Camp writing up and publicising the Rank Xerox experience.

WHY

- Benchmarking provides a catalyst for organisational cultural change, particularly when confronted with inertia.
- Benchmarking encourages co-operative working with a focus upon continuous improvement.

WHY NOT

- Poor or inadequate implementation of benchmarking could lead to demoralising or meaningless findings.
- There can be difficulties identifying like-with-like comparisons.

WHERE TO LOOK

Benchmarking was originally an exclusively private sector phenomenon. However, in recent years the public and third sectors have embraced the potential of collaborative comparisons.

WHAT TO LISTEN FOR

Let's determine who sets the standard and what the standard is.

Stolen with pride!

Are our best practices really best practices?

MANAGERIAL REFERENCE

STAPENHURST, T. (2009) *The benchmarking book: best practice for quality managers and practitioners*. London: Butterworth-Heinemann.

CRITICAL REFERENCE

BANNISTER, F. (2007) The curse of the benchmark: an assessment of the validity and value of e-government comparisons. *International Review of Administrative Sciences*. Vol 73, No 2. pp171–188.

5 BUSINESS PROCESS REENGINEERING

ESSENCE AND ORIGINS

Business process reengineering, also referred to as BPR, requires the rethinking and redesign of business processes. Dramatic improvements in business performance are believed to be achievable through radical change, both technological and organisational. BPR shifts the organisational emphasis from functions to processes, emphasising entrepreneurialism and the use of information communication technologies. Over time, developments of BPR have included business process: mapping, modelling, improvement and management. The bestselling book *Re-engineering the Corporation* by Michael Hammer and James Champy, published in 1993, initiated BPR.

WHY

- BPR encourages a fundamental rethink of established business processes.
- BPR brings together technological change and organisational change.

WHY NOT

- The methodology is very vague on the human aspects of organisational change.
- Incomplete implementation of BPR can lead to poor results.

WHERE TO LOOK

In the 1990s, BPR in the UK was largely a private sector phenomenon that was subsequently superseded by other organisational change initiatives. However, as private sector interest began to decline there was increased public sector interest in BPR as a transformational change methodology.

WHAT TO LISTEN FOR

Information technology enables us to radically redesign our business processes in order to achieve dramatic improvements in performance.

Those who deliberately obstruct re-engineering efforts need the back of the hand.

Don't automate, obliterate.

MANAGERIAL REFERENCE

JESTON, J. and NELIS, J. (2008) *Business process management: practical guidelines to successful implementations.* London: Butterworth-Heinemann.

CRITICAL REFERENCE

GRINT, K. and CASE, P. (1998) The violent rhetoric of re-engineering: management consultancy on the offensive. *Journal of Management Studies.* Vol 35, No 5. pp557–577.

6 COACHING

ESSENCE AND ORIGINS

Coaching may be regarded as a personal and management development tool. In organisations the focus is upon aligning individual performance with organisational goals. Coaching can be undertaken by both internal coaches and external coaches. Coaching in organisations has been informed by sports coaching and other forms of coaching, which have longer histories. In the past decade coaching in organisations has become a common approach to facilitating learning and development inside organisations.

WHY

- Coaching reflects a belief in the potential within individuals.
- Effective coaching can help individuals align their goals with the goals of their organisation.

WHY NOT

- Counselling or mentoring may be more appropriate approaches.
- Coaching can be resource-intensive in terms of both financial resources and the time undertaking.

WHERE TO LOOK

Coaching is applicable to the goals of public, private and third sector organisations. In organisations where there is a 'coaching culture' it will be more prevalent. As coaching is a resource-intensive form of learning and development, it is often targeted at middle and senior management.

WHAT TO LISTEN FOR

We help individuals clarify their goals in order to align them with the goals of the company.

What did you do in that situation which made the difference?

Let's look to the future, rather than reflect too much upon your past.

MANAGERIAL REFERENCE

ROGERS, J. (2008) *Coaching skills: a handbook*. 2nd ed. Milton Keynes: Open University Press.

CRITICAL REFERENCE

HALL, D.T., OTAZO, K.L and HOLLENBECK, G.P. (1999) Behind closed doors: what really happens in executive coaching. *Organizational Dynamics*. Vol 27, Issue 3. pp39–53.

7 CUSTOMER RELATIONSHIP MANAGEMENT

ESSENCE AND ORIGINS

Customer relationship management (CRM) is a company-wide customer-centric philosophy that is facilitated through the effective application of technology. Collecting data about groups of customers informs understanding about customers and the effectiveness of an organisation's operations. CRM has become increasingly sophisticated as businesses embrace new developments such as the Internet and WAP phones. CRM developed out of database marketing in the 1980s. The main impetus for CRM came in the early 1990s as businesses developed strategies to understand customers' needs and behaviours.

WHY

- Retaining existing customers can be more cost-effective than seeking out new customers.
- The strategy allows businesses to be more responsive to their customers' needs.

WHY NOT

- CRM needs to be effectively implemented and resourced or it could have negative impacts upon customer relations.
- There are resource costs attached to introducing CRM: financial, technological and human resources.

WHERE TO LOOK

CRM has been a private sector development as businesses seek improved returns on investment. However, the technology is enabling public services to redefine relationships with users, particularly through call centre and web-based applications.

WHAT TO LISTEN FOR

Our complaints are down and our customers report improved responsiveness.

Customer loyalty cannot be bought.

We ensure that all our people at all levels accurately collect customer information.

MANAGERIAL REFERENCE

BUTTLE, F. (2008) *Customer relationship management.* 2nd ed. London: Butterworth-Heinemann.

CRITICAL REFERENCE

HARKER, M.J. and EGAN, J. (2006) The past, present and future of relationship marketing. *Journal of Marketing Management.* Vol 22, No 1. pp215–242.

8 DOWNSIZING

ESSENCE AND ORIGINS

Downsizing involves a reduction in employee numbers to increase efficiencies, reduce costs and improve productivity and/or profitability. The origins of the word downsizing can be traced back to the US automobile industry, which used the term to refer to reductions in car size and engine capacity in the 1970s. Since then the term has been adopted as a euphemism for redundancy programmes. While downsizing has been very evident in the private sector it is believed to have originated with 'cutback management' in the public sector in the 1970s and 1980s.

WHY

- Downsizing reduces costs through a reduction in bureaucracy.
- Downsizing increases profitability and/or productivity.

WHY NOT

- The expected cost savings and profitability increases are not always realised.
- Downsizing potentially decreases the morale and increases the resistance to change of existing employees.

WHERE TO LOOK

Downsizing will be more evident in recessionary times. Significant downsizing is anticipated in public services over the next five years.

WHAT TO LISTEN FOR

Cutting staffing needs and working out systemic change can support the streamlined organisation.

Do more with less.

We find stock markets tend to reward our downsizing announcements.

MANAGERIAL REFERENCE

DE MEUSE, K. and MARKS, M.L. (eds) (2003) *Resizing the organization: managing layoffs, divestitures and closings.* San Francisco, CA: Jossey Bass.

CRITICAL REFERENCE

CHADWICK, C., HUNTER, L.W. and WALSTON, S.L. (2004) Effects of downsizing practices on the performance of hospitals. *Strategic Management Journal.* Vol 25. pp405–427.

9   EMPLOYEE EMPOWERMENT

ESSENCE AND ORIGINS

Employee empowerment may be understood as a reaction to the 'one best way' approach encouraged by scientific management. Employee empowerment enables employees to make decisions about their work, in the belief that this autonomy gives them greater responsibility and better equips them to respond to change. Individuals or teams may be empowered dependent upon the organisational context. Empowerment has a long history in spiritual, social and political movements. However, its application to organisations can be traced back to the pioneering writing of Rosabeth Moss Kanter in 1977.

WHY

- Employees are a potentially underutilised resource.
- Empowering employees responds to changes in the knowledge economy.

WHY NOT

- There is a danger of managers only paying lip-service to empowerment.
- There can be difficulties reconciling the strategic direction of the organisation with individual empowerment activities.

WHERE TO LOOK

This approach is highly applicable to the private, public and third sectors. It is often evident within broader quality management initiatives such as total quality management.

WHAT TO LISTEN FOR

We find empowered individuals have a sense of trust, energy and commitment in their work.

Our managers were forgetting that our hired hands also have brains.

Our aim is to nurture an environment in which our employees are productive, empowered and happy.

MANAGERIAL REFERENCE

HOGAN, C.F. (2000) *Facilitating empowerment: a handbook for facilitators, trainers and individuals.* London: Kogan Page Ltd.

CRITICAL REFERENCE

CUNNINGHAM, I. and HYMAN, J. (1999) The poverty of empowerment? A critical case study. *Personnel Review.* Vol 28, Issue 3. pp192–207.

10 HIGH-PERFORMANCE WORK SYSTEMS

ESSENCE AND ORIGINS

High-performance work systems (HPWS) seek to enhance individual performance and organisational performance. Employers provide employees with information, skills and incentives to increase involvement in delivering high performance. Potentially people, work, technology and information are brought together in a single system. Specific work practices are variable but can include employee involvement schemes, job design and reward systems that link pay and performance. Invariably greater emphasis is placed upon the HR function. The terminology can vary considerably, with terms such as 'involvement' and 'commitment' sometimes replacing the term 'performance'. In this sense the origins of these work systems are obscured. There are parallels with the Tavistock Institute's interest in the quality of working life in the 1960s and 1970s. Richard Walton and Edward Lawler both gave impetus to interest in the 1980s.

WHY

- HPWS offers greater integration of different aspects of an organisation.
- HPWS offers potential improvements in terms of improved efficiency and productivity.

WHY NOT

- There is a danger that HPWS is perceived as exploitative.
- HPWS may reflect a managerial aspiration rather than a different work system.

WHERE TO LOOK

High-performance work systems are most suited to situations where products and services are tailored to meeting individual customers' needs, rather than mass market approaches. Advanced manufacturing and the provision of business services are particularly suitable for such approaches.

WHAT TO LISTEN FOR

> We hand-pick key individuals who can bring something special to the company.

> We produce performance through leveraging the effects of motivation and opportunity.

> Our involvement practices create opportunities for engagement.

MANAGERIAL REFERENCE

HOLBECHE, L. (2005) *High performance organisation: creating dynamic stability and sustainable success.* London: Butterworth-Heinemann.

CRITICAL REFERENCE

BOXALL, P. and MACKY, K. (2009) Research and theory on high-performance work systems: progressing the high involvement stream. *Human Resource Management Journal.* Vol 19, Issue 1. pp3–23.

11 INVESTORS IN PEOPLE

ESSENCE AND ORIGINS

Investors in People (IiP) became the leading people management benchmark of business improvement. Investors in People offers an outcome-focused framework that can be applied to a start-up employing two people right up to an employer employing hundreds of thousands of employees. Investors in People responds to different business priorities: managing change, increasing efficiency, maximising profitability, increasing sales, improving productivity and strategic leadership. Investors in People was launched in the UK in 1991 and was born out of the recession.

WHY

- IiP helps organisations to become more effective by harnessing skills of employees to achieve organisational goals.
- As an organisational change methodology, it can be motivating.

WHY NOT

- It can be perceived as a tokenistic rather than an indicator of substantial change.
- There are issues around the rhetoric and reality within organisations of those organisations seeking the award.

WHERE TO LOOK

IiP is evident in the public, private and third sector, with 7 million employees currently having Investors in People recognition in the UK.

WHAT TO LISTEN FOR

Plan, do and review.

We are passionate about business improvement.

Have we involved our people?

MANAGERIAL REFERENCE

INVESTORS IN PEOPLE UK (2006) *Leadership and management handbook: business improvement with Investors in People*. London: The Stationery Office.

CRITICAL REFERENCE

HOQUE, K. (2003) All in all, it's another plaque on the wall: the incidence and impact of the Investors in People standard. *Journal of Management Studies*. Vol 40, Issue 2. pp543–571.

12 KAIZEN

ESSENCE AND ORIGINS

Kaizen involves everyone at every level in the organisation in a philosophy of continuous improvement. The 5S is a high-quality housekeeping management tool emphasising five elements: seiri (sort), seiton (straighten), seiso (scrub), seiketsu (systematise) and shitsuke (standardise). Kaizen events are three-day to five-day breakthrough events, whereas Kaizen blitz are more short-term focused initiatives to improve a process. Kaizen, which means 'improvement' in Japanese, can be traced back to initiatives in Japan in the 1940s and 1950s to improve the quality of products. The concept has since spread worldwide and remains the overarching strategy of Japanese businesses.

WHY

- Kaizen encourages a company-wide culture of improvement.
- Kaizen involves employees in productivity and quality improvements.

WHY NOT

- Poorly implemented Kaizen may prove worse than no Kaizen.
- There are issues around applying Kaizen in very different national cultural contexts.

WHERE TO LOOK

Kaizen is often associated with manufacturing in general and car manufacturing in particular. However, the philosophy of continuous improvement has increasingly caught the imagination of politicians and managers in the public sector.

WHAT TO LISTEN FOR

Be open-minded to continuous improvement.

Let's eliminate muda (waste).

Plan, do, check, act.

MANAGERIAL REFERENCE

ORTIZ, C.A. (2009) *Kaizen and kaizen event implementation.* Harlow: Prentice Hall.

CRITICAL REFERENCE

STYHRE, A. (2001) Kaizen, ethics and care of the operations: management after empowerment. *Journal of Management Studies.* Vol 38, Issue 6. pp795–810.

13 KNOWLEDGE MANAGEMENT

ESSENCE AND ORIGINS

Knowledge management is a response to changes in societies, organisations and individuals, acknowledging developments such as the 'knowledge age', 'knowledge-intensive forms of organisation' and 'knowledge workers'. There is no common definition of knowledge management. Typically definitions refer to practices relating to managing knowledge and its development, sharing, acquisition and creation. Information systems databases are used to manage knowledge in databases, but equally there is interest in managing knowledge developed on the job (tacit knowledge) of employees. Many commentators from different disciplines have informed this field; in terms of management, Peter Drucker was influential in encouraging debate about knowledge workers and their management.

WHY

- Knowledge management encourages employees to be aware of the environment in which they operate.
- Knowledge management captures knowledge that may be particularly important to an organisation.

WHY NOT

- Knowledge management can appear to be a vague aspiration for the uninitiated.
- There is a lack of tried and tested knowledge management methodologies.

WHERE TO LOOK

Knowledge management is more evident in parts of organisations rather than specific sectors. Knowledge management has proved highly applicable to areas such as business administration, information systems and IT developments. In terms of organisation-wide initiatives, pharmaceuticals and the UK National Health Service offer examples of adoption.

WHAT TO LISTEN FOR

We are concerned with know-how and know-why.

Let's ensure that we get the right information to the right people at the right time.

Knowledge is the central concern for this business.

MANAGERIAL REFERENCE

COLLINSON, C. and PARCELL, G. (2004) *Learning to fly: practical knowledge management from leading and learning organizations.* 2nd ed. London: Capstone.

CRITICAL REFERENCE

ALVESSON, M. and KARREMAN, D. (2001) Odd couple: making sense of the curious concept of knowledge management. *Journal of Management Studies.* Vol 38. No 7. pp995–1018.

14 LEAN SIX SIGMA

ESSENCE AND ORIGINS

Lean thinking and Six Sigma can be used separately, but increasingly benefits have been realised through using them in combination. Lean aims to improve flow in the value system while eliminating waste. Six Sigma adds the DMAIC framework and statistical analysis to understand the root causes of problems. The DMAIC framework stands for define, measure, analyse, improve and control. Lean thinking originated in Japan at the car manufacturer Toyota and was publicised in the West in *The Machine that Changed the World* by James P. Womack, Daniel T. Jones and Daniel Roos. Six Sigma was developed by Bill Smith in 1986 at Motorola, drawing upon earlier quality management methodologies developed by the likes of W. Edwards Deming and Joseph M. Juran.

WHY

- Lean Six Sigma delivers rapid transformational improvements.
- Lean Six Sigma improves productivity, reduces waste and lowers costs.

WHY NOT

- Lean Six Sigma is nothing new, just a repackaging of quality management.
- There are questions about the transferability of manufacturing-based solutions to service sector organisations.

WHERE TO LOOK

Early applications were in the private sector, specifically in terms of car manufacturing. Increasingly Lean Six Sigma is regarded as applicable to all sectors, with recent application evident in the UK National Health Service.

WHAT TO LISTEN FOR

We are going to determine the costs of poor quality.

We improve processes by attacking the root causes.

She is currently undertaking her Lean Six Sigma green belt training.

MANAGERIAL REFERENCE

BASU, R. (2008) *Implementing Six Sigma and Lean: a practical guide to tools and techniques.* London: Butterworth-Heinemann.

CRITICAL REFERENCE

NASLUND, D. (2008) Lean, six sigma and lean sigma: fads or real process improvement methods? *Business Process Management Journal.* Vol 14, Issue 3. pp269–287.

15 LEARNING ORGANISATION

ESSENCE AND ORIGINS

The learning organisation is usually associated with Peter Senge's book *The Fifth Discipline*, first published in 1990. Other writers contributed to the concept of learning organisations, with variants including 'the learning company', 'the knowledge-creating company' and 'the living company'. Senge employed the persuasive rhetoric that deep down we are all learners. He identified five component technologies or disciplines of a learning organisation, which were: systems thinking, personal mastery, mental models, building a shared vision and team learning.

WHY

- The learning organisation places emphasis upon individuals, groups and teams as part of the diagnosis of the need for organisational change.
- The learning organisation encourages an organisational culture in which learning is promoted and valued.

WHY NOT

- Learning organisations require a belief in a systemic approach to organisational change.
- The ambiguities of learning organisations make implementation problematic.

WHERE TO LOOK

Applicable to private, public and third sector organisations, although adoption tends to be very localised. It often requires an individual champion or a learning and development department to champion its adoption.

WHAT TO LISTEN FOR

Our workers perform better as they feel more a part of the organisation.

We are interested in the relationships between individual performance and organisational performance.

Our people continually learn to learn together.

MANAGERIAL REFERENCE

SENGE, P.M. (2006) *The fifth discipline: the art and practice of the learning organisation.* New York: Random House Business Books.

CRITICAL REFERENCE

SNELL, R.S. and SALAMAN, G. (2001) Moral foundations of the learning organization. *Human Relations.* Vol 54, Issue 3. pp319–59.

16 ORGANISATIONAL DEVELOPMENT

ESSENCE AND ORIGINS

Organisational development, often referred to as OD, has many components and competing meanings. OD is concerned with organisational improvements and organisational effectiveness. OD is undertaken on a system-wide basis, for example focusing upon a whole factory or a whole organisation. OD involves the application of the behavioural sciences to organisational change, with reinforcement emphasised in particular. OD is concerned with planned change rather than emergent change, and the emphasis upon improving organisational effectiveness is measured. The origins of OD can be traced back to the work of the National Training Laboratories in 1946 in America and, in particular, to the pioneering work of Kurt Lewin. Since then OD as an approach has evolved and been refined, with significant development taking place in the late 1960s and early 1970s.

WHY

- Effective OD offers a systemic and thorough methodology for dealing with the behavioural aspects of organisational change.
- OD has the potential to become part of the organisational culture, rather than merely another fad or fashion.

WHY NOT

- Thorough implementation can be a very resource-intensive means of facilitating organisational change.
- There is a danger that poor implementation of OD may be perceived as ambiguous and have limited impact.

WHERE TO LOOK

While OD has been applied in private, public and third sectors, it is likely to thrive in those organisations that adopt it as their preferred approach to organisational change. For example, in two organisations working in the same sector, one organisation may have an OD department and another may not.

WHAT TO LISTEN FOR

Our OD consultants help staff improve teamwork and group effectiveness as part of the change process.

OD helps organisations solve problems and reach their goals.

An early step in overcoming resistance to change is to understand how individuals experience change.

MANAGERIAL REFERENCE

CUMMINGS, T.G. and WORLEY, C.G (2008) *Organization development and change*. 9th ed. Mason, OH: South-Western Cengage Learning.

CRITICAL REFERENCE

GREINER, L.E. and CUMMINGS, T.G. (2004) Wanted: OD more alive than dead! *Journal of Applied Behavioral Science*. Vol 40, No 4. pp374–391.

17 OUTSOURCING

ESSENCE AND ORIGINS

Outsourcing refers to contracting out a regular business function to a third party. Outsourcing can apply to core value chain activities as well as support activities. Typical areas that have been outsourced include business processes, HR, finance, sales and marketing. However, in recent decades major developments have been in terms of outsourcing IT functions. Outsourcing appears to have been a relatively recent phenomenon of the last two decades. However, forms of outsourcing and activities such as offshoring can be traced back to the writings of the economist Adam Smith. As early as 1954, General Electric Corp was contracting out its information systems.

WHY

- Outsourcing allows fixed costs to be changed into variable costs.
- Outsourcing enables downsizing, allowing an organisation to concentrate upon its core strengths.

WHY NOT

- There may be potentially difficult power relationships with suppliers.
- There may be communication problems.

WHERE TO LOOK

Traditionally perceived as a private sector organisational change initiative, outsourcing is now regularly applied in the private, public and third sectors. Outsourcing is increasingly undertaken on a global basis. Outsourcing is often most evident in terms of its employment consequences.

WHAT TO LISTEN FOR

Outsourcing is transforming industries and the way we work.

Outsourcing is our preferred means of driving change.

Outsourcing is frequently misrepresented and misunderstood; it's all about growing business.

MANAGERIAL REFERENCE

BRAVARD, J. and MORGAN, R. (2006) *Smarter outsourcing: an executive guide to managing successful relationships.* Harlow: FT Prentice Hall.

CRITICAL REFERENCE

DAVIS-BLAKE, A. and BROSCHAK, J.P. (2009) Outsourcing and the changing nature of work. *Annual Review of Sociology.* Vol 35, Issue 1. pp321–340.

18 STRATEGIC ALLIANCES

ESSENCE AND ORIGINS

Strategic alliances are formalised co-operative arrangements between organisations, typically lasting for between two and four years, although they may evolve into mergers or acquisitions. There are different types of strategic alliances, for example joint ventures involve taking an equity stake in a newly formed business, whereas co-operative agreements do not require an equity stake. Alliances in general can be traced back over the centuries, particularly at times of war and in terms of coalition governments. In an organisational sense, history highlights that there have been different forms of co-operation among organisations for many years. Strategic alliances gained prominence in the last two decades, with a high-profile example being the joint venture between Apple Computers and IBM in 1992.

WHY

- Strategic alliances enable organisations to achieve economies of scale and learning.
- Strategic alliances reduce risk, particularly in terms of capital requirements.

WHY NOT

- Strategic alliances can potentially lead to conflicts around organisational goals.
- Potentially, there can be clashes in terms of different organisational cultures.

WHERE TO LOOK

Typically alliances are a private sector phenomenon although equally applicable to public sector and third sector organisations.

WHAT TO LISTEN FOR

We are building a road map which will deliver rich and connected services.

Our strategic alliances are deep, long-term relationships where we invest together in people and resources.

Monitoring of the alliance and contract renegotiations can be reduced where trust exists.

MANAGERIAL REFERENCE

HARVARD BUSINESS REVIEW. (2003) *Harvard Business Review on strategic alliances*. Boston: Harvard Business School Press.

CRITICAL REFERENCE

DAS, T.K. and TENG, B.S. (2000) Instabilities of strategic alliances: an internal tensions perspective. *Organization Science*. Vol 11, No 1. pp77–101.

19 SUPPLY CHAIN MANAGEMENT

ESSENCE AND ORIGINS

Supply chain management places emphasis upon sourcing, procurement, conversion and logistics through an interconnected network of suppliers. The goal of supply chain management is to effectively reduce the inventory of an organisation, which is achieved through three main flows: product flow, information flow and finance flow. Supply chain activities occur at three different organisational levels: strategic, tactical and operational. In the 1960s and 1970s material requirements planning and manufacturing resource planning developed as responses to increasing competition. These developments highlighted the significance of inventories and the potential of technology to enable greater inventory tracking. The first use of the terminology supply chain management was attributed to a paper published in America by R. Keith Oliver and Michael D. Webber.

WHY

- Supply chain management improves activities within the supply chain in terms of greater integration.
- Supply chain management results in improvements in profitability, productivity and competitiveness.

WHY NOT

- Implementation needs to be thorough and effective otherwise there may be inventory problems.

- There are implications for power relations with suppliers of supply chain management.

WHERE TO LOOK

All organisations purchasing supplies will use some form of supply chain management of varying degrees of sophistication. Supply chain management is less visible than other organisational changes, but continues to be significant. Information technology advances will enable more sophisticated forms of supply chain management to develop.

WHAT TO LISTEN FOR

Collaboration has great relevance for all professionals in all industries.

We regard supply chain management as enabling increased sales and margins, rather than as a cost centre.

Plan, source, make, deliver and return.

MANAGERIAL REFERENCE

JACOBY, D. (2009) *Guide to supply chain management: how getting it right boosts corporate performance.* London: Economist Books.

CRITICAL REFERENCE

STOREY, J., EMBERSON, C., GODSELL, J. and HARRISON, A. (2006) Supply chain management: theory, practice and future challenges. *International Journal of Operations and Production Management.* Vol 26, Issue 7. pp754–774.

20 TOTAL QUALITY MANAGEMENT

ESSENCE AND ORIGINS

Total quality management is often referred to by the acronym of TQM. This approach places emphasis upon employees changing their attitudes and behaviour to manage quality holistically through measurement and analysis of quality problems. The origins of TQM can be traced back to Japan's search for quality improvements in the 1940s and 1950s and the guidance offered by Americans such as W. Edwards Deming and Joseph M. Juran. 'Total' refers to quality involving everyone. 'Quality' refers to conformance to requirements and 'management' emphasises that quality must be managed. Deming specified 14 principles, although many quality management initiatives have been labelled as TQM. Three common principles are invariably evident: a customer orientation, a process orientation and a continuous improvement philosophy.

WHY

- TQM encourages greater awareness of the importance of quality management within an organisation.
- TQM can lead to cost savings through enhanced problem-solving and profitability improvements.

WHY NOT

- TQM requires cultural change, which can take a long time to achieve.
- TQM needs to be carefully implemented to be effective.

WHERE TO LOOK

TQM is applicable to public, private and third sector organisations. In the 1980s and the 1990s, high-profile TQM initiatives would have been evident; this is far less likely today. However, in established organisations the legacy of previous TQM initiatives will still be evident.

WHAT TO LISTEN FOR

What are the big problems?

Our processes are completed right, first time every time; defects and waste have been eradicated.

We delight our customers by fully meeting their needs and expectations.

MANAGERIAL REFERENCE

GOETSCH, D.L. and DAVIS, S. (2009) *Quality management for organizational excellence: introduction to total quality management.* London: Pearson Education.

CRITICAL REFERENCE

KNIGHTS, D. and MCCABE, D. (2002) A road less travelled: beyond managerialist, critical and processual approaches to total quality management. *Journal of Organizational Change Management.* Vol 15, Issue 1. pp25–30.

References

ABRAHAMSON, E. (2000) Change without pain. *Harvard Business Review*. Vol 78, No 4. 75–79.

ABRAHAMSON, E. (2004a) Avoiding repetitive change syndrome. *MIT Sloan Management Review*. Vol 45, No 2. 93–95.

ABRAHAMSON, E. (2004b) *Change without pain: how managers can overcome initiative overload, organizational chaos, and employee burnout.* Boston: Harvard Business School Press.

ABRAHAMSON, E. and FAIRCHILD, G. (1999) Management fashion: lifecyles, triggers, and collective learning processes. *Administrative Science Quarterly*. Vol 44, No 4. 708–740.

ACKERS, P. (2009) Employment ethics. In T. REDMAN and A. WILKINSON (ed.) *Contemporary human resource management: text and cases.* Harlow: FT Prentice Hall.

ACKROYD, S. (2002) *The organization of business: applying organizational theory to contemporary change.* Oxford: Oxford University Press.

ACKROYD, S. and THOMPSON, P. (1999) *Organizational misbehaviour.* London: Sage Publications Ltd.

AHN, M.J., ADAMSON, J.S.A. and DORNBUSCH, D. (2004) From leaders to leadership: managing change. *The Journal of Leadership and Organizational Studies.* Vol 10, No 4. 112–123.

ALBRECHT, K. (1983) *Organization development: a total systems approach to positive change in any business organization.* New York: Prentice Hall.

ALVESSON, M. (2002) *Understanding organizational culture.* London: Sage Publications Ltd.

ALVESSON, M. and BILLING, Y.D. (1997) *Understanding gender and organizations.* London: Sage Publications Ltd.

ALVESSON, M. and KARREMAN, D. (2001) Odd couple: making sense of the curious concept of knowledge management. *Journal of Management Studies.* Vol 38, No 7. 995–1018.

ALVESSON, M. and SVENINGSSON, S. (2008) *Changing organizational culture: cultural change work in progress.* London: Routledge.

ALVESSON, M. and WILLMOTT, H. (eds) (1996) *Critical management studies.* London: Sage Publications Ltd.

AMERCIAN MANAGEMENT ASSOCIATION. (1994) *Survey on change management.* New York: American Management Association.

ANDRIOPOULOS, C. and DAWSON, P. (2009) *Managing change, creativity and innovation*. London: Sage Publications Ltd.

ANGWIN, D. (2007) Mergers and acquisitions: a primer. In D. ANGWIN (ed.) *Mergers and acquisitions*. Oxford: Blackwell Publishing.

ANSOFF, H.I. (1965) *Corporate strategy*. New York: McGraw-Hill.

ANTONACOPOULOU, E.P. and GABRIEL, Y. (2001) Emotion, learning and organizational change: towards an integration of psychoanalytic and other perspectives. *Journal of Organizational Change Management*. Vol 14, No 5. 435–451.

ARGYRIS, C. (1973) Personality and organization theory revisited. *Administrative Science Quarterly*. Vol 18. No 2. 141–67.

ARGYRIS, C. (1985) *Strategy, change and defensive routines*. Cambridge, MA: Ballinger.

ARGYRIS, C. (1999) *On organizational learning*. Oxford: Blackwell Business.

ARGYRIS, C. and JACKSON, B. (2001) *Management gurus and management fashions*. London: Routledge.

ARGYRIS, C. and SCHON, D. (1978) *Organizational learning: a theory of action perspective*. Reading, MA: Addison-Wesley.

ARMENAKIS, A.A., HARRIS, S.G. and FIELD, H.S. (1999) Making change permanent: a model for institutionalizing change. In W. PASMORE and R. WOODMAN (eds) *Research in organization change and development*. Volume XII. Greenwich, CT: JAI Press. 97–128.

ARMSTRONG, M. (2009) *Armstrong's handbook of human resource management practice*. 11th ed. London: Kogan Page.

ASCH, S.E. (1952) Effects of group pressure upon the modification and distortion of judgements. In C.E. SWANSON, T.M. NEWCOMBE and E.L. HARTLEY (eds) *Readings in social psychology*. New York: Holt, Rinehart and Winston.

ASH, K., HAMLIN, B. and KEEP, J. (2001) Introduction. In B. HAMLIN, J. KEEP and K. ASH (eds) *Organizational change and development: a reflective guide for managers, trainers and developers*. Harlow: FT Prentice Hall.

ASHKENAS, R. (1994) Beyond the fads: how leaders drive change with results. *Human Resource Planning*. Vol 17, No 2. 25–44.

AUDIT COMMISSION. (2007) *Seeing the light: innovation in local public services*. London: Audit Commission.

BACHRACH, P. and BARATZ, M.S. (1970) *Power and poverty: theory and practice*. New York: Oxford University Press.

BAIN AND COMPANY. (2009) *Management tools and trends 2009*. Available at http://www.bain.com/management_tools/home asp [accessed 7 September 2009].

BALOGUN, J. and HOPE HAILEY, V. (2008) *Exploring strategic change*. 3rd ed. Harlow: FT Prentice Hall.

BALOGUN, J., GLEADLE, P., HOPE HAILEY, V. and WILLMOTT, H. (2005) Managing change across boundaries: boundary shaking practices. *British Journal of Management*. Vol 16, Issue 4. 261–278.

BANNISTER, F. (2007) The curse of the benchmark: an assessment of the validity and value of e-government comparisons. *International Review of Administrative Sciences*. Vol 73, No 2. 171–188.

BARRETT, D.J. (2002) Change communication: using strategic employee communication to facilitate major change. *Corporate Communications: An International Journal*. Vol 7, No 4. 219–231.

BARTLETT, C.A. and GHOSHAL, S. (1989) *Managing across borders: the transnational solution*. London: Century Business.

BARTLETT, C.A. and GHOSHAL, S. (1995) *Transnational management: texts, cases and readings in cross-border management*. Homewood, IL.: R.D. Irwin Inc.

BARTUNEK, J.M. and MOCH, M. (1987) First-order, second-order and third-order change and organization development: a cognitive approach. *Journal of Applied Behavioural Science*. Vol 23, No 4. 483–500.

BASS, B.M. and AVOLIO, B.J. (1994) *Improving organisational effectiveness through transformational leadership*. Thousand Oaks, CA: Sage Publications Inc.

BASU, R. (2008) *Implementing Six Sigma and Lean: a practical guide to tools and techniques*. London: Butterworth-Heinemann.

BATE, P. (1994) *Strategies for cultural change*. Oxford: Butterworth-Heinemann.

BECK, A., BENNETT, P. and WALL, P. (2002) *Communication studies: the essential introduction*. London: Routledge.

BECKHARD, R. and HARRIS, R.T. (1987) The change process: why change? In W.W. BURKE et al (eds) (2009) *Organization change: a comprehensive reader*. San Francisco, CA: Jossey Bass.

BECKHARD, R. and PRITCHARD, W. (1992) *Changing the essence: the art of creating and leading fundamental change in organizations*. San Francisco, CA: Jossey Bass.

BEEKUN, R.I. (1989) Assessing the effectiveness of sociotechnical interventions: antidote or fad? *Human Relations*. Vol 42, No 10. 877–897.

BEER, M. (1980) *Organization change and development: a systems view*. Dallas, TX: Scott Foresman.

BEER, M. and NOHRIA, N. (2000a) Cracking the code of change. *Harvard Business Review*. Vol 78, Issue 3. 133–141.

BEER, M. and NOHRIA, N. (eds) (2000b) *Breaking the code of change*. Boston: Harvard Business School Press.

BEER, M., EISENSTAT, R.A. and SPECTOR, B. (1990a) Why change programs don't produce change. *Harvard Business Review*. Vol 68, Issue 6. 158–166.

BEER, M., EISENSTAT, R.A. and SPECTOR, B. (1990b) *The critical path to corporate renewal*. Boston: Harvard Business School Press.

BELBIN, R.M. (1981) *Management teams*. London: Heinemann Educational Books.

BENFARI, R.C., WILKINSON, H.E. and ORTH, C.D. (1986) The effective use of power. *Business Horizons*. Vol 29, Issue 3. 12–16.

BINNEY, G. and WILLIAMS, C. (1995) *Leaning into the future: changing the way people change organisations*. London: Nicholas Brealey Publishing.

BLAUNER, R. (1964) *Alienation and freedom*. Chicago: Chicago University Press.

BOAL, K.B. and SCHULTZ, P.L. (2007) Storytelling, time, and evolution: the role of strategic leadership in complex adaptive systems. *The Leadership Quarterly*. Vol 18, Issue 4. 411–428.

BOONSTRA, J.J. (2004) Conclusions. In J.J. BOONSTRA (ed.) *Dynamics of organizational change and learning*. Chichester: John Wiley & Sons.

BOOTH, C. and ROWLINSON, M. (2006) Management and organizational history: prospects. *Management and Organizational History*. Vol 1, No 1. 5–30.

BOVEY, W.H. and HEDE, A. (2001) Resistance to organisational change: the role of defence mechanisms. *Journal of Managerial Psychology*. Vol 16, No 7. 534–548.

BOWDITCH, J.L., BUONO, A.F. and STEWART, M.M. (2008) *A primer on organizational behavior*. 8th ed. Chichester: John Wiley and Sons Inc.

BOXALL, P. and MACKY, K. (2009) Research and theory on high-performance work systems: progressing the high involvement stream. *Human Resource Management Journal*. Vol 19, Issue 1. 3–23.

BRADSHAW, P. and BOONSTRA, J. (2004) Power dynamics in organizational change: a multi-perspective approach. In J.J. BOONSTRA (ed.) *Dynamics of organizational change and learning*. Chichester: John Wiley and Sons.

BRAVARD, J. and MORGAN, R. (2006) *Smarter outsourcing: an executive guide to managing successful relationships*. Harlow: FT Prentice Hall.

BRAVERMAN, H. (1974) *Labor and monopoly capital: the degradation of work in the twentieth century*. New York: Monthly Review Press.

BREHM, J.W. (1966) *A theory of psychological resistance*. New York: Academic Press.

BREWIS, J. (2007) Culture. In D. KNIGHTS and H. WILLMOTT (eds) *Introducing organizational behaviour and management*. London: Thomson Learning.

BRIDGES, W. (1986) Managing organizational transitions. *Organizational Dynamics*. Vol 15, No 1. 24–33.

BRIDGES, W. (1995) *Managing transitions: making the most of change*. London: Nicholas Brealey Publishing.

BROOKS, I. (2008) *Organisational behaviour: individuals, groups and the organisation*. 4th ed. Harlow: FT Prentice Hall.

BROWN, A. (1998) *Organisational culture*. 2nd ed. London: FT Pitman Publishing.

BRYMAN, A. and BELL, E. (2007) *Business research methods*. Oxford: Oxford University Press.

BUCHANAN, D. and BADHAM, R. (1999) Politics and organizational change: the lived experience. *Human Relations*. Vol 52, No 5. 609–629.

BUCHANAN, D. and BADHAM, R. (2008) *Power, politics and organizational change: winning the turf game*. 2nd ed. London: Sage Publications Ltd.

BUCHANAN, D. and BODDY, D. (1992) *The expertise of the change agent*. Hemel Hempstead: Prentice Hall (out of print).

BUCHANAN, D., CLAYDON, T. and DOYLE, M. (1999) Organisation development and change: the legacy of the nineties. *Human Resource Management Journal*. Vol 9, No 2. 20–37.

BURKE, R.J. (2006) Why leaders fail: exploring the darkside. *International Journal of Manpower*. Vol 27, No 1. 91–100.

BURKE, W.W. (2006) Where did OD come from? In J.V. GALLOS (ed.) *Organization development: a Jossey Bass reader*. San Francisco, CA: Jossey Bass.

BURKE, W.W. (2008) *Organization change: theory and practice*. 2nd ed. Thousand Oaks, CA: Sage Publications Ltd.

BURKE, W.W., LAKE, D.G. and PAINE, J.W. (eds) (2009) *Organization change: a comprehensive reader*. San Francisco, CA: Jossey Bass.

BURNES, B. (1996) No such thing as… a 'one best way' to manage organizational change. *Management Decision*. Vol 34, No 10. 11–18.

BURNES, B. (2004) Kurt Lewin and the planned approach to change: a re-appraisal. *Journal of Management Studies*. Vol 41, No 6. 977–1002.

BURNES, B. (2006) Preface. In R. CALDWELL *Agency and change*. London: Routledge.

BURNES, B. (2009a) *Managing change: strategic approach to organisational dynamics*. 5th ed. Harlow: FT Prentice Hall.

BURNES, B. (2009b) Ethics and organizational change – time for a return to Lewinian values. *Journal of Change Management*. Vol 9, No 4. 359–381.

BURNES, B., COOPER, C. and WEST, P. (2003) Organisational learning: the new management paradigm? *Management Decision*. Vol 41, No 5. 452–464.

BURNS, J.M. (1978) *Leadership*. New York: Harper and Row.

BURNS, T. and STALKER, G.M. (1961) *The management of innovation.* London: Tavistock Publications.

BURRELL, G. (1992) Back to the future: time and organization. In M. REED and M. HUGHES (eds) *Rethinking organization: new directions in organization theory and analysis.* London: Sage Publications Ltd.

BURRELL, G. and MORGAN, G. (1979) *Sociological paradigms and organisational analysis.* London: Heinemann.

BUTLER, J., SCOTT, F. and EDWARDS, J. (2003) Evaluating organizational change: the role of ontology and epistemology. *TAMARA Journal of Critical Postmodern Organization Science.* Vol 2, No 2. 55–67.

BUTTLE, F. (2008) *Customer relationship management.* 2nd ed. London: Butterworth-Heinemann.

CALAS, M.B. and SMIRCICH, L. (1996) From the 'womans' point of view: feminist approaches to organization studies. In S. CLEGG and C. HARDY (eds) *Handbook on organisations.* London: Sage Publications Ltd.

CALDWELL, R. (2001) Champions, adapters, consultants and synergists: the new change agents in HRM. *Human Resource Management Journal.* Vol 11, No 3. 39–52.

CALDWELL, R. (2003a) Models of change agency: a fourfold classification. *British Journal of Management.* Vol 14. 131–142.

CALDWELL, R. (2003b) The changing roles of personnel managers: old ambiguities, new uncertainties. *Journal of Management Studies.* Vol 40, No 4. 983–1004.

CALDWELL, R. (2003c) Change leaders and change managers: different or complementary? *Leadership and Organization Development Journal.* Vol 24, No 5. 285–293.

CALDWELL, R. (2006) *Agency and change.* London: Routledge.

CALDWELL, R. and STOREY, J. (2007) The HR function: integration or fragmentation? In J. STOREY (ed.) *Human resource management: a critical text.* London: Thomson Learning.

CAMPBELL, R. and KITSON, A. (2008) *The ethical organisation.* Basingstoke: Palgrave Macmillan.

CANGELOSI, V. and DILL, W. (1965) Organizational learning: observations toward a theory. *Administrative Science Quarterly.* Vol 10, No 2. 175–203.

CARNALL, C. (1991) *Managing change.* London: Routledge.

CASSELL, C. (2009) Managing diversity. In T. REDMAN and A. WILKINSON (eds) *Contemporary human resource management: text and cases.* Harlow: FT Prentice Hall.

CHADWICK, C., HUNTER, L.W. and WALSTON, S.L. (2004) Effects of downsizing practices on the performance of hospitals. *Strategic Management Journal*. Vol 25. 405–427.

CHAKRABORTY, S.K (1999) *Values and ethics for organizations: theory and practice*. New Delhi: Oxford University Press.

CHANDLER, A.D. (1962) *Strategy and structure*. Cambridge, MA: MIT Press.

CHARTERED INSTITUTE OF PERSONNEL AND DEVELOPMENT. (2003) *Reorganising for success: CEOs' and HR managers' perceptions*. London: CIPD. Available at: http://www.cipd.co.uk/subjects/corpstrtgy/orgdevelmt/reorg4succ. htm?IsSrchRes=1 [accessed 9 April 2010].

CHARTERED INSTITUTE OF PERSONNEL AND DEVELOPMENT. (2004) *Reorganising for success: a survey of HR's role in change*. London: CIPD. Available at: http://www.cipd.co.uk/subjects/corpstrtgy/orgdevelmt/ reorg4success1004.htm?IsSrchRes=1 [accessed 9 April 2010].

CHARTERED INSTITUTE OF PERSONNEL AND DEVELOPMENT. (2005) *Managing change: the role of the psychological contract*. London: CIPD. Available at: http://www.cipd.co.uk/subjects/empreltns/psycntrct/_mngchngrlpsychcnt. htm?IsSrchRes=1 [Accessed 9 April 2010].

CHILD, J. (1972) Organisation structure, environment and performance: the role of strategic choice. *Sociology*. Vol 6, No 1. 1–22.

CHILD, J. (2005) *Organization: contemporary principles and practices*. Oxford: Blackwell Publishing.

CIULLA, J. (1995) Leadership ethics: mapping the territory. *Business Ethics Quarterly*. Vol 5, No 1. 5–28.

CLAMPITT, P.G., DEKOCH, R.J. and CASHMAN, T. (2000) A strategy for communicating about uncertainty. *Academy of Management Executive*. Vol 14, No 4. 41–57.

CLARK, T. and FINCHAM, R. (eds) (2002) *Critical consulting: new perspectives on the management advice industry*. Oxford: Blackwell Publishers.

CLEGG, C. and WALSH, S. (2004) Change management: time for a change! *European Journal of Work and Organizational Psychology*. Vol 13, No 2. 217–239.

CLEGG, S., KORNBERGER, M. and PITIS, T. (2008) *Managing and organizations: an introduction to theory and practice*. 2nd ed. Los Angeles, CA: Sage Publications Inc.

COBB, A.T., WOOTEN, K.C. and FOLGER, R. (1995) Justice in the making: toward understanding the theory and practice of justice in organizational change and development. In R. WOODMAN and W. PASMORE (eds) *Research in organizational change and development*. Vol 8. Greenwich, CT: JAI Press.

COCH, L. and FRENCH, J.R.P. (jnr) (1948) Overcoming resistance to change. *Human Relations*. Vol 1, No 4. 512–532.

COCKBURN, C. (1991) *In the way of women: men's resistance to sex equality in organizations*. London: Macmillan.

COGHLAN, D. (1994) Managing organizational change through teams and groups. *Leadership and Organization Development Journal*. Vol 15, No 2. 18–23.

COGHLAN, D. and RASHFORD, N.S. (2006) *Organizational change and strategy: an interlevel dynamics approach*. London: Routledge.

COKIN, S.G. (2010) The promise and perils of the balanced scorecard. *Journal of Corporate Accounting and Finance*. Vol 21, Issue 3. 19–28.

COLLINS, D. (1998) *Organizational change: sociological perspectives*. London: Routledge.

COLLINS, D. (2000) *Management fads and buzzwords: critical–practical perspectives*. London: Routledge.

COLLINSON, C. and PARCELL, G. (2004) *Learning to fly: practical knowledge management from leading and learning organizations*. 2nd ed. London: Capstone.

CONGER, J.A. (1990) The dark side of leadership. In G.R. HICKMAN (ed.) *Leading organizations: perspectives for a new era*. Thousand Oaks, CA: Sage Publications Ltd.

CONNER, D.R. (1998) *Managing at the speed of change*. Chichester: John Wiley and Sons.

COOKE, B. (1999) Writing the left out of management theory: the historiography of the management of change. *Organization*. Vol 6, No 1. 81–105.

COOPERRIDER, D.L. and WHITNEY, D. (2005) *Appreciative inquiry: a positive revolution in change*. San Francisco, CA: Berrett Koehler Publishers Inc.

COOPEY, J. (2002) Crucial gaps in the 'learning organization': power, politics and ideology. In K. STARKEY, S. TEMPEST and A. MCKINLAY (eds) *How organizations learn: managing the search for knowledge*. London: Thomson Learning.

COPELAND, T., ROLLER, T. and MURRIN, J. (1993) *Valuation: measuring and managing the value of companies*. New York: John Wiley and Sons.

CORBETT, E.P.J. (1990) *Classical rhetoric for the modern student*. Oxford: Oxford University Press.

CORNELISSEN, J. (2008) *Corporate communication: a guide to theory and practice*. 2nd ed. London: Sage Publications Ltd.

COVEY, S.R. (1992) *The seven habits of highly effective people: powerful lessons in personal change*. London: Simon and Schuster.

CROM, S. and BERTELS, T. (1999) Change leadership: the virtues of deviance. *Leadership and Organization Development Journal*. Vol 20, No 3. 162–167.

CROZIER, M. (1964*) The bureaucratic phenomenon*. Chicago: University of Chicago Press.

CUMMINGS, S. (2002) *Recreating strategy*. London: Sage Publications Ltd.

CUMMINGS, T. and MOLLOY, E. (1977) *Improving productivity and the quality of work life*. New York: Praeger.

CUMMINGS, T.G. and WORLEY, C.G (2008) *Organization development and change*. 9th ed. Mason, OH: South-Western Cengage Learning.

CUNNINGHAM, I. and HYMAN, J. (1999) The poverty of empowerment? A critical case study. *Personnel Review*. Vol 28, Issue 3. 192–207.

DALE, B.G. and MCQUATER, R.E. (1998) *Managing business improvement and quality: implementing key tools and techniques*. Oxford: Blackwell Publishers.

DALY, F., TEAGUE, P. and KITCHEN, P. (2003) Exploring the role of internal communication during organisational change. *Corporate Communications: An International Journal*. Vol 8, No 3. 153–162.

DARWIN, J., JOHNSON, P. and MCAULEY, J. (2002) *Developing strategies for change*. Harlow: FT Prentice Hall.

DARZI, A. (2008) *High quality care for all: NHS next stage review final report*. Department of Health, Norwich: The Stationery Office. Available at: http://www.dh.gov.uk/prod_consum_dh/groups/dh_digitalassets/@dh/@en/documents/digitalasset/dh_085828.pdf [accessed 8 December 2009].

DAS, T.K. and TENG, B.S. (2000) Instabilities of strategic alliances: an internal tensions perspective. *Organization Science*. Vol 11, No 1. 77–101.

DAVIS-BLAKE, A. and BROSCHAK, J.P. (2009) Outsourcing and the changing nature of work. *Annual Review of Sociology*. Vol 35, Issue 1. 321–340.

DAWSON, P. (1994) *Organizational change: a processual approach*. London: Paul Chapman Publishing Ltd.

DAWSON, P. (2003) *Understanding organizational change: the contemporary experience of people at work*. London: Sage Publications Ltd.

DAWSON, S. (1996) *Analysing organisations*. Basingstoke: Macmillan Business.

DE CALUWE, L. and VERMAAK, H. (2003) *Learning to change: a guide for organization change agents*. London: Sage Publications Ltd.

DE CALUWE, L. and VERMAAK, H. (2004) Thinking about change in different colours: multiplicity in change processes. In J.J. BOONSTRA (ed.) *Dynamics of organizational change and learning*. Chichester: John Wiley and Sons Ltd.

DE GEUS, A. (1997) The living company. *Harvard Business Review*. Vol 75, Issue 2. 51–59.

DE MEUSE, K. and MARKS, M.L. (eds) (2003) *Resizing the organization: managing layoffs, divestitures and closings*. San Francisco, CA: Jossey Bass.

DE WIT, B. and MEYER, R. (2004) *Strategy: process, content and context*. London: Thomson Learning.

DEAL, T.E. and KENNEDY, A.A. (1982) *Corporate cultures: the rites and rituals of corporate life*. Reading, MA: Addison-Wesley.

DEAL, T.E. and KENNEDY, A.A. (1999) *The new corporate cultures: revitalizing the workplace after downsizing, mergers and reengineering*. London: Orion Business.

DELBRIDGE, R. and LOWE, J. (1997) Introduction: workplace change and HRM. *The International Journal of Human Resource Management*. Vol 8, No 6. 759–763.

DEMING, W.E. (1986) *Out of the crisis*. Cambridge: Cambridge University Press.

DENT, E.B. and GOLDBERG, S.G. (2000) Challenging 'resistance to change'. *Journal of Applied Behavioral Sciences*. Vol 35, No 1. 25–41.

DENTON, J. (1998) *Organisational learning and effectiveness*. London: Routledge.

DICKEN, P. (2003) *Global shift: reshaping the global economic map of the 21st century*. 4th ed. London: Sage Publications Ltd.

DIGEORGIO, R.M. (2002) Making mergers and acquisitions work: what we know and don't know – Part I. *Journal of Change Management*. Vol 3, No 2. 134–148.

DIGEORGIO, R.M. (2003) Making mergers and acquisitions work: what we know and don't know – Part II. *Journal of Change Management*. Vol 3, No 3. 259–274.

DIMAGGIO, P. and POWELL, W. (1983) The iron cage revisited: institutional isomorphism and collective rationality in organizations. *American Sociological Review*. Vol 48. No 2. 147–60.

DIMAGGIO, P. and POWELL, W.W. (eds) (1991) *The new institutionalism in organisational analysis*. Chicago: University of Chicago Press.

DIXON, N.M. (1994) *The organizational learning cycle: how we can learn collectively*. London: McGraw-Hill.

DOSI, G. (1982) Technical paradigms and technological trajectories – a suggested interpretation of the determinants and directions of technological change. *Research Policy*. Vol 11, No 3. 147–62.

DOVER, P.A. (2003) Change agents at work: lessons from Siemens Nixdorf. *Journal of Change Management*. Vol 3, No 3. 243–257.

DOWNTON, J.V. (1973) *Rebel leadership: commitment and charisma in a revolutionary process*. New York: Free Press.

DOYLE, M. (2001) Dispersing change agency in high velocity change organisations: issues and implications. *Leadership and Organization Development Journal*. Vol 22, No 7. 321–329.

DOYLE, M., CLAYDON, T. and BUCHANAN, D. (2000) Mixed results, lousy process: the management experience of organizational change. *British Journal of Management*. Vol 11, Special Issue. S59–S80.

DRUCKER, P.F. (1954) *The practice of management*. New York: Harper and Row.

DRUCKER, P.F. (1964) *Managing for results*. New York: Harper and Row.

DUNPHY, D. (1996) Organizational change in corporate settings. *Human Relations*. Vol 49, No 5. 541–552.

DUNPHY, D. and STACE, D. (1988) Transformational and coercive strategies for planned organizational change: beyond the O.D. model. *Organization Studies*. Vol 9, No 3. 317–334.

DUNPHY, D. and STACE, D. (1993) The strategic management of corporate change. *Human Relations*. Vol 46, No 8. 905–920.

ECCLES, R.G. and NOHRIA, N. (1992) *Beyond the hype: rediscovering the essence of management*. Boston: Harvard Business School Press.

EISENHARDT, K.M. (2000) Paradox, spirals, ambivalence: the new language of change and pluralism. *Academy of Management Review*. Vol 25, No 4. 703–705.

ELMUTI, D. (1997) Self-managed work teams approach: creative management tool or a fad? *Management Decision*. Vol 35, No 3. 233–239.

ELROD II, P.D. and TIPPETT, D.D. (2002) The 'death valley' of change. *Journal of Organizational Change Management*. Vol 15, No 3. 273–291.

ELVING, W.J.L. (2005) The role of communication in organisational change. *Corporate Communications: An International Journal*. Vol 10, No 2. 129–138.

ETZIONI, A.A. (1975) *Comparative analysis of complex organizations: on power, involvement and their correlates*. Revised ed. New York: Free Press.

EZZAMEL, M., GREEN, C., LILLEY, S. and WILLMOTT, H. (1995) *Changing managers and managing change*. London: Chartered Institute of Management Accountants.

FAGERBERG, J. and VERSPAGEN, B. (2009) Innovation studies – the emerging structure of a new scientific field. *Research Policy*. Vol 38, Issue 2. 218–233.

FAY, B. (1987) The elements of critical social science. In M. HAMMERSLEY (ed.) *Social research: philosophy, politics and practice*. London: The Open University in association with Sage Publications.

FAYOL, H. (1949) *General and industrial management*. London: Pitman.

FIEDLER, F.E. (1964) A contingency model of leadership effectiveness. In L. BERKOWITZ (ed.) *Advances in experimental social psychology*. New York: Academic Press.

FINCHAM, R. and EVANS, M. (1999) The consultants' offensive: re-engineering – from fad to technique. *New Technology, Work and Employment*. Vol 14, No 1. 32–44.

FINCHAM, R. and RHODES, P. (2005) *Principles of organizational behaviour*. Oxford: Oxford University Press.

FINSTAD, N. (1998) The rhetoric of organizational change. *Human Relations.* Vol 51, No 6. 717–740.

FISHER, C. and LOVELL, A. (2009) *Business ethics and values: individual, corporate and international perspectives.* 3rd ed. Harlow: FT Prentice Hall.

FLYNN, F.J. and CHATMAN, J.A. (2001) Strong cultures and innovation: oxymoron or opportunity? In M.L. TUSHMAN and P. ANDERSON (eds) *Managing strategic innovation and change: a collection of readings.* Oxford: Oxford University Press.

FORD, J.D., FORD, L.W. and AMELIO'D, A. (2008) Resistance to change: the rest of the story. *Academy of Management Review.* Vol 33, No 2. 362–377.

FORD, J.D., FORD, L.W. and MCNAMARA, R.T. (2002) Resistance and the background conversations of change. *Journal of Organizational Change Management.* Vol 15, No 2. 105–121.

FOREMAN, J. (2001) Organizational change. In E. WILSON (ed.) *Organizational behaviour reassessed: the impact of gender.* London: Sage Publications Ltd.

FOUCAULT, M. (1980) *Power/knowledge: selected interviews and other writings, 1972–1977.* Brighton: Harvester.

FOURNIER, V. and GREY, C. (2000) At the critical moment: conditions and prospects for critical management studies. *Human Relations.* Vol 53, No 1. 7–32.

FOX, A. (1974) *Beyond contract, work, power and trust relations.* London: Faber and Faber.

FRAHM, J. (2007) Organizational change: approaching the frontier, some faster than others (combined review of five books). *Organization.* Vol 14, No 6. 945–955.

FRANCIS, D. and BESSANT, J. (2005) Targeting innovation and implications for capability development. *Technovation.* Vol 25, No 3. 171–183.

FRANSELLA, F. (1975) *Need to change?* Essential Psychology Series. London: Methuen and Co Ltd.

FREEMAN, C. (2007) The ICT paradigm. In R. MANSELL, C. AVGEROU, D. QUAH and R. SILVERSTONE (eds) *The Oxford handbook of information and communication technologies.* Oxford: Oxford University Press.

FRENCH, E. and DELAHAYE, B. (1996) Individual change transition: moving in circles can be good for you. *Leadership and Organization Development Journal.* Vol 17, No 7. 22–28.

FRENCH, J.R.P. and RAVEN, B.H. (1959) The social bases of power. In D. CARTWRIGHT (ed.) *Studies in social power.* East Lansing, MI: University of Michigan Press.

FRENCH, W.L. and BELL, C.H. (1984) *Organization development: behavioral science interventions for organizational improvement.* Englewood Cliffs, NJ: Prentice Hall.

FRIEDMAN, V., LIPSHITZ, R. and POPPER, M. (2005) The mystification of organizational learning. *Journal of Management Inquiry*. Vol 14, No 1. 19–30.

FULMER, R.M. and KEYS, J.B. (2002) A conversation with Chris Argyris: the father of organizational learning. In K. STARKEY, S. TEMPEST and A. MCKINLAY (eds) *How organizations learn: managing the search for knowledge*. London: Thomson Learning.

GABRIEL, Y. (2000) *Storytelling in organizations*. Oxford: Oxford University Press.

GABRIEL, Y. (2001) The state of critique in organizational theory. *Human Relations*. Vol 54, Issue 1. 23–30.

GALPIN, T.J. (1996) *The human side of change: a practical guide to organization redesign*. San Francisco, CA: Jossey Bass.

GAUGHAN, P.A. (2002) *Mergers, acquisitions and corporate restructurings*. New York: John Wiley and Sons.

GEORGE, J.M. and JONES, G.R. (2001) Towards a process model of individual change in organizations. *Human Relations*. Vol 54. No 4. 419–444.

GERSICK, C. (1988) Time and transition in work teams: toward a new model of group development. *Academy of Management Journal*. Vol 31, No 1. 9–41.

GHAYE, T. (2005) Editorial – reflection as a catalyst for change. *Reflective Practice*. Vol 6, No 2. 177–187.

GILL, R. (2003) Change management – or change leadership? *Journal of Change Management*. Vol 3, No 4. 307–318.

GLADWELL, M. (2006) *Blink: the power of thinking without thinking*. London: Penguin.

GOETSCH, D.L. and DAVIS, S. (2009) *Quality management for organizational excellence: introduction to total quality management*. London: Pearson Education.

GOLEMBIEWSKI, R., PROEHL, C. and SINK, D. (1982) Estimating success of OD applications. *Training and Development Journal*. Vol 36, No 4. 86–95.

GOODMAN, J. and TRUSS, C. (2004) The medium and the message: communicating effectively during a major change initiative. *Journal of Change Management*. Vol 4, No 3. 217–228.

GOODMAN, M.B. (2001) Current trends in corporate communication. *Corporate Communications: An International Journal*. Vol 6, No 3. 117–123.

GRAETZ, F. (2000) Strategic change leadership. *Management Decision*. Vol 38, No 8. 550–562.

GRAETZ, F. and SMITH, A.C.T. (2008) The role of dualities in arbitrating continuity and change in forms of organizing. *International Journal of Management Reviews*. Vol 10, Issue 3. 265–280.

GRAETZ, F., RIMMER, M., LAWRENCE, A. and SMITH, A. (2006) *Managing Organisational Change*. 2nd Australasian ed. Milton, QLD: John Wiley and Sons Australia Ltd.

GRANT, P. and PERREN, L. (2002) Small business and entrepreneurial research: meta-theories, paradigms and prejudices. *International Small Business Journal*. Vol 20, No 2. 185–211.

GRANT, S. and HUMPHRIES, M. (2006) Critical evaluation of appreciative inquiry. *Action Research*. Vol 4, No 4. 401–418.

GRAVENHORST, K.B. and IN 'T VELD, R. (2004) Power and collaboration: methodologies for working together in change. In J.J. BOONSTRA (ed.) *Dynamics of organizational change and learning*. Chichester: John Wiley and Sons.

GREENWOOD, R. and HININGS, C.R. (1988) Organizational design types, tracks and the dynamics of strategic change. *Organization Studies*. Vol 9, Issue 3. 293–316.

GREINER, L.E. (1972) Evolution and revolution as organizations grow. *Harvard Business Review*. Vol 50, Issue 4. 37–46.

GREINER, L.E. and CUMMINGS, T.G. (2004) Wanted: OD more alive than dead! *Journal of Applied Behavioral Science*. Vol 40, No 4. 374–391.

GREY, C. (2000) Review of *Organizational change: sociological perspectives* by David Collins. *Gender, Work and Organization*. Vol 4, No 4. 289–90.

GREY, C. (2003) The fetish of change. *TAMARA Journal of Critical Postmodern Organization Science*. Vol 2, No 2. 1–18.

GREY, C. (2007) Bureaucracy and post-bureaucracy. In D. KNIGHTS and H. WILLMOTT (eds) *Introducing organizational behaviour and management*. London: Thomson Learning.

GRINT, K. (2005a) *The sociology of work*. 3rd ed. Cambridge: Polity Press.

GRINT, K. (2005b) *Leadership: limits and possibilities*. Basingstoke: Palgrave Macmillan.

GRINT, K. and CASE, P. (1998) The violent rhetoric of re-engineering: management consultancy on the offensive. *Journal of Management Studies*. Vol 35, No 5. 557–577.

GRINT, K. and WOOLGAR, S. (1997) *The machine at work: technology, work and organization*. Cambridge: Polity Press.

GUEST, D. (1992) Right enough to be dangerously wrong: an analysis of the *In Search of Excellence Phenomenon*. In G. SALAMAN (ed.) *Human Resource Strategies*. London: Sage Publications Ltd.

HABERMAS, J. (1971) *Toward a rational society*. London: Heinemann.

HALL, D.T., OTAZO, K.L. and HOLLENBECK, G.P. (1999) Behind closed doors: what really happens in executive coaching. *Organizational Dynamics*. Vol 27, Issue 3. 39–53.

HALLIER, J. (2004) Embellishing the past: middle manager identity and informality in the implementation of new technology. *New Technology, Work and Employment*. Vol 19, No 1. 43–62

HAMBRICK, D.C. and CANNELLA, A.A. (jnr) (1989) Strategy implementation as substance and selling. *Academy of Management Executive*. Vol 3, No 4. 278–285.

HAMMER, M. and CHAMPY, J. (1993) *Reengineering the corporation: a manifesto for business revolution*. London: Nicholas Brealey.

HANCOCK, P. and TYLER, M. (2009) Emotion at work. In T. REDMAN and A. WILKINSON (eds) *Contemporary human resource management: text and cases*. Harlow: FT Prentice Hall.

HANDY, C.B. (1978) *The gods of management*. Harmondsworth: Penguin.

HANDY, C. (1994) *The empty raincoat: making sense of the future*. London: Random House UK Ltd.

HANNAN, M.T. and FREEMAN, F. (1977) The population ecology of organizations. *American Journal of Sociology*. Vol 82, No 5. 929–964.

HARDY, C. (1996) Understanding power: bringing about strategic change. *British Journal of Management*. Vol 7 (special issue). S3–S16.

HARDY, C. and CLEGG, S. (2004) Power and change: a critical reflection. In J.J. BOONSTRA (ed.) *Dynamics of organizational change and learning*. Chichester: John Wiley and Sons.

HARKER, M.J. and EGAN, J. (2006) The past, present and future of relationship marketing. *Journal of Marketing Management*. Vol 22, No 1. 215–242.

HARRIS, L. (2002) The learning organisation – myth or reality? Examples from the UK retail banking industry. *The Learning Organization*. Vol 9, No 2. 78–88.

HARRISON, R. (1972) Understanding your organization's character. *Harvard Business Review*. Vol 50, No 3. 119–128.

HARRISON, R. (1995) *The collected papers of Roger Harrison*. London and New York: McGraw-Hill.

HARTLEY, J. (2005) Innovation in governance and public services: past and present. *Public Money and Management*. Vol 25, No 1. 27–34.

HARTLEY, J. and BENINGTON, J. (2006) Copy and paste, or graft and transplant? Knowledge sharing through inter-organizational networks. *Public Money and Management*. Vol 26, No 2. 101–108.

HARTLEY, J., BENNINGTON, J. and BINNS, P. (1997) Researching the role of internal-change agents in the management of organizational change. *British Journal of Management*. Vol 8. 61–73.

HARVARD BUSINESS REVIEW. (2003) *Harvard Business Review on strategic alliances*. Boston: Harvard Business School Press.

HARVEY, T.R. (1990) *Checklist for change: a pragmatic approach to creating and controlling change*. Boston: Allyn and Bacon.

HARVEY JONES, J. (1988) *Making it happen*. Glasgow: Collins.

HATCHER, T. (2002) *Ethics and HRD*. Cambridge, MA: Perseus Publishing.

HENDRY, C. (1996) Understanding and creating whole organizational change through learning theory. *Human Relations*. Vol 48, No 5. 621–41.

HERSHEY, P. and BLANCHARD, K.H. (1969) Life-cycle theory of leadership. *Training and Development Journal*. Vol 23, No 5. 26–34.

HERZBERG, F., MAUSNER, B. and SNYDERMAN, B. (1959) *The motivation to work*. New York: Wiley.

HOCHSCHILD, A.R. (2003) *The managed heart: commercialization of human feeling*. 20th Anniversary ed. Berkeley: University of California Press.

HODGKINSON, G.P. and WRIGHT, G. (2002) Confronting strategic inertia in a top management team: learning from failure. *Organization Studies*. Vol 23, No 6. 949–977.

HODGSON, D. (2002) Disciplining the professional: the case of project management. *Journal of Management Studies*. Vol 39, No 6. 803–821.

HODGSON, D.E. and CIMCIL, S. (eds) (2006) *Making projects critical*. Basingstoke: Palgrave Macmillan.

HOFSTEDE, G. (1984) *Culture's consequences: international differences in work related values*. Beverley Hills, CA: Sage Publications Inc.

HOFSTEDE, G. (1991) *Cultures and organizations, software of the mind*. Maidenhead: McGraw-Hill.

HOGAN, C.F. (2000) *Facilitating empowerment: a handbook for facilitators, trainers and individuals*. London: Kogan Page Ltd.

HOLBECHE, L. (2005) *High performance organisation: creating dynamic stability and sustainable success*. London: Butterworth-Heinemann.

HOLMES, T.H. and RAHE, R.H. (1967) The social readjustment rating scale. *Journal of Psychosomatic Research*. Vol 11, No 2. 213–218.

HOPE HAILEY, V. and BALOGUN, J. (2002) Devising context-sensitive approaches to change: the example of GlaxoWellcome. *Long Range Planning*. Vol 35, Issue 2. 153–178.

HOQUE, K. (2003) All in all, it's another plaque on the wall: the incidence and impact of the Investors in People standard. *Journal of Management Studies*. Vol 40, Issue 2. 543–571.

HUBBARD, N. (2001) *Acquisition: strategy and implementation*. Revised edition. Basingstoke: Palgrave Macmillan.

HUCZYNSKI, A.A. (2006) *Management gurus*. 2nd ed. London: Routledge.

HUGHES, M. (2009) Reengineering works: don't report, exhort. *Management and Organizational History*. Vol 4, No 1. 105–122.

IACOCCA, L. and NOVAK, W. (1986) *Iacocca*. London: Bantam Books.

IHATOR, A.S. (2004) Corporate communication: reflections on twentieth century change. *Corporate Communications: An International Journal*. Vol 9, No 3. 243–253.

ILES, V. and SUTHERLAND, K. (2001) *Managing change in the NHS: organisational change*. NHS Service Delivery and Organisation R&D Programme. Available at: http://www.sdo.nihr.ac.uk/files/adhoc/change-management-review.pdf [accessed 9 April 2010].

INVESTORS IN PEOPLE UK (2006) *Leadership and management handbook: business improvement with Investors in People*. London: The Stationery Office.

ITZIN, C. and NEWMAN, J. (eds) (1995) *Gender, culture and organizational change: putting theory into practice*. London: Routledge.

IVES, M. (2005) Identifying the contextual elements of project management within organizations and their impact on project success. *Project Management Journal*. Vol 36, No 1. 51–50.

JAAFARI, A. (2003) Project management in the age of complexity and change. *Project Management Journal*. Vol 34, No 4. 47–57.

JACKSON, B. (2001) *Management gurus and management fashions*. London: Routledge.

JACOBY, D. (2009) *Guide to supply chain management: how getting it right boosts corporate performance*. London: Economist Books.

JANIS, I.L. (1972) *Victims of groupthink: a psychological study of foreign policy decisions and fiascos*. Boston: Houghton Mifflin.

JARRETT, M. (2003) The seven myths of change management. *Business Strategy Review*. Vol 14, Issue 4. 22–29.

JESTON, J. and NELIS, J. (2008) *Business process management: practical guidelines to successful implementations*. London: Butterworth-Heinemann.

JICK, T.D. (1990) The recipients of change. In W.W. BURKE et al (eds) *Organization change: a comprehensive reader*. San Francisco, CA: Jossey Bass.

JISCinfoNET *Change Management infoKit*. Available at: www.jiscinfonet.ac.uk/infokits/change-management [accessed 12 September 2009].

JOHNSON, G. (1992) Managing strategic change – strategy, culture and action. *Long Range Planning*. Vol 25, No 1. 28–36.

JOHNSON, G., SCHOLES, K. and WHITTINGTON, R. (2008) *Exploring corporate strategy*. 8th ed. Harlow: FT Prentice Hall.

JOHNSON, P. and GILL, J. (1993) *Management control and organizational behaviour*. London: Paul Chapman Publishing Ltd.

JONES, C., PARKER, M. and TEN BOS, R. (2005) *For business ethics*. London: Routledge.

JONES, E., WATSON, B., GARDNER, J. and GALLOIS, C. (2004) Organizational communication: challenges for the new century. *Journal of Communications*. Vol 54, No 4. 722–50.

JONES, G. (2010) *Organizational theory, design and change*. 6th ed. Boston: Pearson.

JONES, M. and ORLIKOWSKI, W.J. (2007) Information technology and the dynamics of organizational change. In R. MANSELL, C. AVGEROU, D. QUAH and R. SILVERSTONE (eds) *The Oxford handbook of information and communication technologies*. Oxford: Oxford University Press.

JONES, R.A., JIMMIESON, N.L. and GRIFFITHS, A. (2005) The impact of organizational culture and reshaping capabilities on change implementation success: the mediating role of readiness for change. *Journal of Management Studies*. Vol 42, No 2. 361–386.

JORGENSEN, H.H., OWEN, L. and NEUS, A. (2009) Stop improvising change management! *Strategy and Leadership*. Vol 37, No 2. 38–44.

JOYCE, P. (1998). Management and innovation in the public service. *Strategic Change*. Vol 7, No 1. 19–31.

KANTER, R.M. (1983) *The change masters*. New York: Simon and Schuster.

KANTER, R.M., STEIN, B.A. and JICK, T.D. (1992) *The challenge of organizational change*. New York: The Free Press.

KAPLAN, A. (1964) *The conduct of inquiry*. San Francisco, CA: Chandler Publishing.

KAPLAN, R.S. and NORTON, D.P. (1996) *The balanced scorecard: translating strategy into action*. Boston: Harvard Business School Press.

KAPLINSKY, R. (1984) *Automation: the technology and society*. Harlow: Longman.

KELEMEN, M., FORRESTER, P. and HASSARD, J. (2000) BPR and TQM: divergence or convergence? In D. KNIGHTS and H. WILLMOTT (eds) *The reengineering revolution: critical studies of corporate change*. London: Sage Publications Ltd.

KELLERMAN, B. (2004) *Bad leadership*. Boston: Harvard Business School Press.

KETS DE VRIES, M.F. (1989) *Prisoners of leadership*. New York: John Wiley and Sons.

KETS DE VRIES, M.F.R. (2006) *The leader on the couch: a clinical approach to changing people and organisations*. Chichester: John Wiley and Sons Ltd.

KING, N. and ANDERSON, N. (2002) *Managing innovation and change: a critical guide for organizations*. London: Thomson Learning.

KIRTON, M.J. (2003) *Adaption-innovation: in the context of diversity*. London: Routledge.

KLOPPENBORG, T.J. and OPFER, W.A. (2002) The current state of project management research: trends, interpretations, and predictions. *Project Management Journal*. Vol 33, No 2. 5–18.

KNIGHTS, D. and COLLINSON, D. (1987) Disciplining the shopfloor: a comparison of the disciplinary effects of managerial psychology and financial accounting. *Accounting, Organizations and Society*. Vol 12, No 5. 457–477.

KNIGHTS, D. and MCCABE, D. (2002) A road less travelled: beyond managerialist, critical and processual approaches to total quality management. *Journal of Organizational Change Management*. Vol 15, Issue 1. 25–30.

KNIGHTS, D. and MCCABE, D. (2003) *Organization and innovation: guru schemes and American dreams*. Maidenhead: Open University Press.

KNIGHTS, D. and MORGAN, G. (1991) Corporate strategy, organizations and subjectivity. *Organization Studies*. Vol 12, No 2. 251–74.

KNIGHTS, D. and MURRAY, F. (1994) *Managers divided: organisational politics and information technology management*. Chichester: John Wiley and Sons.

KNIGHTS, D. and WILLMOTT, H. (2007) Management and leadership. In D. KNIGHTS and H. WILLMOTT (eds) *Introducing organizational behaviour and management*. London: Thomson Learning.

KNIGHTS, D. and WILLMOTT, H. (eds) (2007b) *Introducing organizational behaviour and management*. London: Thomson Learning.

KOLB, D. (1984) *Experiential learning: experience as the source of learning and development*. Englewood Cliffs, NJ: Prentice Hall.

KONRAD, A.M., PRASAD, P. and PRINGLE, J. (eds) (2005) *Handbook of workplace diversity*. London: Sage Publications Ltd.

KOSSEK, E.E., MARKEL, K.S. and MCHUGH, P.M. (2003) Increasing diversity as an HRM change strategy. *Journal of Organizational Change Management*. Vol 16, No 3. 328–352.

KOTTER, J. (1990) *A force for change: how leadership differs from management*. New York: Free Press.

KOTTER, J.P. (1995) Leading change: why transformation efforts fail. *Harvard Business Review*. Vol 73, Issue 2. 59–67.

KOTTER, J.P. (1996) *Leading change*. Boston: Harvard Business School Press.

KOTTER, J.P. (2008) *A sense of urgency*. Boston: Harvard Business School Press.

KOTTER, J.P. and HESKETT, J.L. (1992) *Corporate culture and performance*. New York: The Free Press.

KOTTER, J.P. and SCHLESINGER, L.A. (1979) Choosing strategies for change. *Harvard Business Review*. Vol 57, No 2. 106–114.

KRANSDORFF, A. (1998) *Corporate amnesia: keeping know-how in the company.* London: Butterworth-Heinemann.

KUBLER-ROSS, E. (1969) *On death and dying.* New York: Touchstone.

LAJOUX, A.R. (1998) *The art of M&A integration.* New York: McGraw-Hill.

LAVE, J. and WENGER, E. (1991) *Situated learning: legitimate peripheral participation.* Cambridge: Cambridge University Press.

LAWRENCE, P.R. and LORCSH, J.W. (1967) *Organisation and environment.* Cambridge, MA: Harvard University Press.

LEANA, C.R. and BARRY, B. (2000) Stability and change as simultaneous experiences in organisational life. *Academy of Management Review.* Vol 25, No 4. 753–759.

LEAVITT, H.J. (1964) Applied organizational change in industry: structural, technical and human approaches. In W.W. COOPER, H.J. LEAVITT and M.W. SHELLY (eds) *New perspectives in organization research.* New York: Wiley.

LEGGE, K. (2005) *Human resource management: rhetorics and realities.* Anniversary edition. Basingstoke: Palgrave Macmillan.

LEWIN, K. (1947) Frontiers in group dynamics. In D. CARTWRIGHT (ed.) *Field theory in social science.* London: Social Science Paperbacks.

LEWIN, K. (1951) *Field theory in social science.* New York: Harper and Row.

LEWIN, K. (1997) *Resolving social conflicts and field theory in social science.* (Reissue of two previous anthologies).Washington, DC: American Psychological Association.

LEWIS, L.K. (2000) Communicating change: four cases of quality programs. *The Journal of Business Communication.* Vol 37, No 2. 128–155.

LEWIS, L.K. and SEIBOLD, D.R. (1998) Reconceptualizing organizational change implementation as a communication problem: a review of literature and research agenda. In M.E. ROLOFF (ed.) *Communication yearbook.* Vol 21. Thousand Oaks, CA: Sage Publications Ltd.

LEWIS, L.K., SCHMISSEUR, A.M., STEPHENS, K.K. and WEIR, K.E. (2006). Advice on communicating during organizational change: The content of popular press books. *Journal of Business Communication.* Vol 43, No 2. 113–137.

LEYBOURNE, S.A. (2006) Managing change by abandoning planning and embracing improvisation. *Journal of General Management.* Vol 31, No 3. 11–29.

LEYBOURNE, S.A. (2007) The changing bias of project management research: a consideration of the literatures and an application of extant theory. *Project Management Journal.* Vol 38, No 1. 61–73.

LIKERT, R. (1967) *The human organization: its management and values.* New York: McGraw-Hill.

LINDBOLM, C.E. (1959) The science of muddling through. *Public Administration Review*. Vol 19, No 2. 79–88.

LINES, R. (2004) Influence of participation in strategic change: resistance, organizational commitment and change goal achievement. *Journal of Change Management*. Vol 4, No 3. 193–215.

LIPPITT, R. (1959) Dimensions of the consultant's job. *Journal of Social Issues*. Vol 15, No 2. 5–11.

LIPPITT, R., WATSON, J. and WESTLEY, B. (1958) *The dynamics of planned change*. New York: Harcourt, Brace and Company.

LLEWELLYN, S. and TAPPIN, E. (2003) Strategy in the public sector: management in the wilderness. *Journal of Management Studies*. Vol 40, No 4. 955–982.

LOH, M. (1997) *Re-engineering at work.* Aldershot: Gower Publishing Ltd.

LOVALLO, D. and KAHNEMAN, D. (2003) Delusions of success: how optimism undermines executives' decisions. *Harvard Business Review*. Vol 81, Issue 7. 56–63.

LUDEMA, J.D., WILMOT, T.B. and SRIVASTVA, S. (1997) Organizational hope: reaffirming the constructive task of social and organizational inquiry. *Human Relations*. Vol 50, No 8. 1015–1052.

LUKES, S. (1974) *Power: a radical view*. London: Macmillan.

LUKES, S. (2005) *Power: a radical view*. 2nd edition. Basingstoke: Palgrave Macmillan published in association with the British Sociological Association.

MACY, B., BLIESE, P. and NORTON, J. (1994) Organisational change and work innovation: a meta-analysis of 131 North American field experiments 1962-1990. In R. WOODMAN and W. PASMORE (eds) *Research in organisation change and development*. Vol 7. Greenwich, CT: JAI Press.

MANNING, P.K. (1992) *Organizational communication*. New York: Aldine De Gruyter.

MANSELL, R., AVGEROU, C., QUAH, D. and SILVERSTONE, R. (eds) (2007) *The Oxford handbook of information and communication technologies*. Oxford: Oxford University Press.

MANSELL, R., AVGEROU, C., QUAH, D. and SILVERSTONE, R. (2007) The challenges of ICTS. In R. MANSELL, C. AVGEROU, D. QUAH and R. SILVERSTONE (eds) *The Oxford handbook of information and communication technologies*. Oxford: Oxford University Press.

MARCH, J.G. (1981) Footnotes to organizational change. *Administrative Science Quarterly*. Vol 26, Issue 4. 563–577.

MARRIS, P. (1974) *Loss and change*. London: Routledge and Kegan Paul.

MARSHAK, R.J. (2006) *Covert processes at work: managing the five hidden dimensions of organizational change*. San Francisco, CA: Berrett Koehler Publishers, Inc.

MARTIN, R. (2002) *Financialization of daily life*. Philadelphia, PA: Temple University Press.

MARTIN DE HOLAN, P., PHILLIPS, N. and LAWRENCE, T.B. (2004) Managing organizational forgetting. *MIT Sloan Management Review*. Vol 45, No 2. 45–51.

MASSEY, L. and WILLIAMS, S. (2006) Implementing change: the perspective of NHS change agents. *Leadership and Organization Development Journal*. Vol 27, No 8. 667–681.

MATHENY, J.A. (1998) Organizational therapy: relating a psychotherapeutic model of planned personal change to planned organizational change. *Journal of Managerial Psychology*. Vol 13, No 5/6. 394–405.

MAYO, E. (1933) *The human problems of an industrial civilization*. New York: Macmillan.

MAYON-WHITE, W.M. (1994) The ethics of change management: manipulation or participation? *Business Ethics*. Vol 3, No 4. 196–200.

MCADAM, R. and MITCHELL, N. (1998) Development of a business process re-engineering model applicable to the public sector. *Total Quality Management*. Vol 9, No 4. 160–164.

MCCABE, D. (1999) Total quality management: anti-union Trojan horse or management albatross? *Work, Employment and Society*. Vol 13, No 4. 665–691.

MCGREGOR, D. (1960) *The human side of enterprise*. New York: McGraw-Hill.

MCLAUGHLIN, H. and THORPE, R. (1993) Action learning – a paradigm in emergence. *British Journal of Management*. Vol 4, No 1. 19–27.

MCLOUGHLIN, I. (1999) *Creative technological change: the shaping of technology and organisations*. London: Routledge.

MCLOUGHLIN, I. and CLARK, J. (1994) *Technological change at work*. Buckingham: Open University Press.

MERRON, K. (1993) Let's bury the term 'resistance'. *Organizational Development Journal*. Vol 11, No 4. 77–86.

MILES, R.E. and SNOW, C.C. (1984) Fit, failure and the hall of fame. *California Management Review*. Vol 26, No 3. 10–28.

MILLER, D. (1990) *The Icarus paradox*. New York: Harper Collins.

MILLER, D. and FRIESEN, P.H. (1984) *Organizations: a quantum view*. Englewood Cliffs, NJ: Prentice Hall.

MINTZBERG, H. (1983) *Structure in fives: designing effective organizations*. Englewood Cliffs, NJ: Prentice Hall.

MINTZBERG, H. (1987) The strategy concept 1: five Ps for strategy. *California Management Review*. Vol 30, No 1. 11–24.

MINTZBERG, H., AHLSTRAND, B. and LAMPEL, J. (2009) *Strategy safari: the complete guide through the wilds of strategic management*. 2nd ed. London: FT Prentice Hall.

MOHR, L.B. (1999) One hundred theories of organizational change: the good, the bad and the ugly. In H.G. FREDERICKSON and J.M. JOHNSTON (eds) *Public management reform and innovation: research, theory and application*. Tuscaloosa, AL.: The University of Alabama Press.

MORGAN, G. (1989) *Creative organization theory: a resource book*. Newbury Park, CA: Sage Publications Inc.

MORGAN, G. and STURDY, A. (2000) *Beyond organizational change: structure, discourse and power in UK financial services*. London: Macmillan.

MORRISON, D. (1994) Psychological contracts and change. *Human Resource Management*. Vol 33, No 3. 353–372.

MORRISON, E.W. and MILLIKEN, F.J. (2000) Organizational silence: a barrier to change and development in a pluralistic world. *Academy of Management Review*. Vol 25, No 4. 706–725.

MULGAN, G. and ALBURY, D. (2003) *Innovations in the public sector*. London: Cabinet Office.

NADLER, D.A. and GERSTEIN, M.S. (1992) Designing high-performance work systems: organizing people, work, technology, and information. In J.V. GALLOS (ed.) *Organization development: a Jossey Bass reader*. San Francisco, CA: Jossey Bass.

NADLER, D.A. and TUSHMAN, M.L. (1990) Beyond the charismatic leader: leadership and organizational change. In M.L. TUSHMAN and P. ANDERSON (eds) *Managing strategic innovation and change: a collection of readings*. New York: Oxford University Press.

NADLER, D.A. and TUSHMAN, M.L. (1997) *Competing by design: the power of organizational architecture*. Oxford: Oxford University Press.

NASLUND, D. (2008) Lean, six sigma and lean sigma: fads or real process improvement methods? *Business Process Management Journal*. Vol 14, Issue 3. 269–287.

NEIMARK, M.K. (1995) The selling of ethics: the ethics of business meets the business of ethics. *Accounting, Auditing and Accountability Journal*. Vol 8, No 3. 81–96.

NELSON, R. and WINTER, S. (1982) *An evolutionary theory of economic change*. Boston: Harvard University Press.

NONAKA, I. (1991) The knowledge-creating company. *Harvard Business Review*. Vol 69. November/December. 96–104.

NORTHOUSE, P.G. (2010) *Leadership: theory and practice*. 5th ed. Thousand Oaks, CA: Sage Publications Inc.

OGBONNA, E. and WILKINSON, B. (2003) The false promise of organizational culture change: a case study of middle managers in grocery retailing. *Journal of Management Studies*. Vol 40, No 5. 1151–1178.

OGILVIE, J.R. and STORK, D. (2003) Starting the HR and change conversation with history. *Journal of Organizational Change Management*. Vol 16, No 3. 254–271.

ORLIKOWSKI, W.J. and BARLEY, S.R. (2001) Technology and institutions: what can research on information technology and research on organizations learn from each other? *MIS Quarterly*. Vol 25, No 2. 145–165

ORLIKOWSKI, W.J. and SCOTT, S.V. (2008) *Sociomateriality: challenging the separation of technology, work and organization*. London School of Economics and Political Science, Department of Management, Working Paper Series, Paper No 174.

ORTENBLAD, A. (2007) Senge's many faces: problem or opportunity? *The Learning Organization*. Vol 14, No 2. 108–122.

ORTIZ, C.A. (2009) *Kaizen and kaizen event implementation*. Harlow: Prentice Hall.

OSWICK, C., GRANT, D., MICHELSON, G. and WAILES, N. (2005) Looking forwards: discursive directions in organizational change. *Journal of Organizational Change Management*. Vol 18, No 4. 383–390.

PAGE, T. (1998) *The diary of a change agent*. Aldershot: Gower.

PALMER, I. and DUNFORD, R. (2002) Out with the old and in with the new? The relationship between traditional and new organizational practices. *International Journal of Organizational Analysis*. Vol 10, Issue 3. 209–225.

PALMER, I. and DUNFORD, R. (2008) Organizational change and the importance of embedded assumptions. *British Journal of Management*. Vol 19, Special Issue. S20–S32.

PALMER, I., DUNFORD, R. and AKIN, G. (2009) *Managing organizational change: a multiple perspectives approach*. 2nd ed. Boston: McGraw-Hill International Editions.

PARKER, M. (2003) Introduction: ethics, politics and organizing. *Organization*. Vol 10, No 2. 187–203.

PARTINGTON, D. (1996) The project management of organizational change. *International Journal of Project Management*. Vol 14, No 1. 13–21.

PATON, R. and DEMPSTER, L. (2002) Managing change from a gender perspective. *European Management Journal*. Vol 20, No 5. 539–548.

PATON, R.A. and MCCALMAN, J. (2008) *Change management: a guide to effective implementation*. 3rd ed. London: Sage Publications Ltd.

PAVITT, K. and STEINMUELLER, W.E. (2002) Technology in corporate strategy: change, continuity and the information revolution. In A. PETTIGREW, H. THOMAS and R. WHITTINGTON (eds) *Handbook of strategy and management*. London: Sage Publications Ltd.

PEARCE, J.A. and RAVLIN, E.C. (1987) The design and activation of self-regulating work groups. *Human Relations*. Vol 40, No 11. 751–782.

PEDLER, M. (2008) *Action learning for managers*. Aldershot: Gower Publishing Ltd.

PEDLER, M., BURGOYNE, J. and BOYDELL, T. (1991 and 1997) *The learning company: a strategy for sustainable development*. 1st and 2nd eds. London: McGraw-Hill.

PERREN, L. and MEGGINSON, D. (1996) Resistance to change as a positive force: its dynamics and issues for management development. *Career Development International*. Vol 1, No 4. 24–28.

PETERS, T.J. (1978) Symbols, patterns, and settings: an optimistic case for getting things done. *Organizational Dynamics*. Vol 7, Issue 2. 3–23.

PETERS, T. (1988) *Thriving on chaos*. London: Macmillan Limited.

PETERS, T.J. and WATERMAN, R.H. (1982) *In search of excellence: lessons from America's best run companies*. New York: Harper and Row.

PETTIGREW, A.M. (1973) *The politics of organizational decision making*. London: Tavistock Publications.

PETTIGREW, A. (1975) Towards a political theory of organizational intervention. *Human Relations*. Vol 28, No 3. 191–208.

PETTIGREW, A.M. (1977) Strategy formulation as a political process. *International Studies of Management and Organization*. Vol 7, No 2. 78–87.

PETTIGREW, A.M. (1979) On studying organizational cultures. *Administrative Science Quarterly*. Vol 24, No 4. 570–581.

PETTIGREW, A.M. (1985) *The awakening giant: continuity and change in ICI*. Oxford: Blackwell Publishing.

PETTIGREW, A.M. (1990) Longitudinal field research on change theory and practice. *Organization Science*. Vol 1, No 3. 267–292.

PETTIGREW, A.M. (1992) On studying managerial elites. *Strategic Management Journal*. Vol 6, No 16. 163–182.

PETTIGREW, A.M. (2002) Andrew Pettigrew on executives and strategy: An interview by Kenneth Starkey. *European Journal of Management*. Vol 20, No 1. 20–34.

PETTIGREW, A.M. (2003) Strategy as process, power and change. In S. CUMMINGS and D. WILSON (eds) *Images of strategy*. Oxford: Blackwell Publishing.

PETTIGREW, A.M. and FENTON, E.M. (eds) (2000) *Innovating new forms of organizing*. London: Sage Publications Ltd.

PETTIGREW, A.M. and WHIPP, R. (1993) *Managing change for competitive success*. Chichester: Wiley Blackwell.

PETTIGREW, A., FERLIE, E. and MCKEE, L. (1992) *Shaping strategic change: making change in large organizations*. London: Sage Publications Ltd.

PETTIGREW, A., MASSINI, S. and NUMAGAMI (2000) Innovative forms of organising in Europe and Japan. *European Management Journal*. Vol 18, No 3. 259–273.

PETTIGREW, A., THOMAS, H. and WHITTINGTON, R. (2002) Strategic management: the strengths and limitations of a field. In A. PETTIGREW, H. THOMAS and R. WHITTINGTON (eds) *Handbook of strategy and management*. London: Sage Publications Ltd.

PFEFFER, J. (1981) *Power in organizations*. Boston: Pitman.

PFEFFER, J. (1992a) *Managing with power: politics and influence in organizations*. Boston: Harvard Business School Press.

PFEFFER, J. (1992b) Understanding power in organizations. *California Management Review*. Vol 34, Issue 2. 29–50.

PIDERIT, S.K. (2000) Rethinking resistance and recognizing ambivalence: a multidimensional view of attitudes toward an organizational change. *Academy of Management Review*. Vol 25, No 4. 783–794.

PIORE, M.J. and SABEL, C.F. (1984) *The second industrial divide: possibilities for prosperity*. New York: Basic Books.

POOLE, M. and MANSFIELD, R. (1992) Managers' attitudes to human resource management: rhetoric and reality. In P. BLYTON and P. TURNBULL (eds) *Reassessing human resource management*. London: Sage Publications Ltd.

PREECE, D. (1995) *Organisations and technical change: strategy, objectives and involvement*. London: Routledge.

PRICE, D. (2009) The context of change. In D. PRICE (ed.) *The principles and practice of change*. Basingstoke: Palgrave Macmillan in association with the Open University.

PRICE, D. (ed.) (2009) *The principles and practice of change*. Basingstoke: Palgrave Macmillan in association with the Open University.

PROBST, G. and BUCHEL, B. (1997) *Organizational learning*. London: Prentice Hall.

PUGH, D.S. and HICKSON, D.J. (2007) *Writers on organizations*. London: Penguin Books. London.

QUINN, J.B. (1980) *Strategies for change: logical incrementalism*. Homewood, IL: R.D. Irwin, Inc.

QUIRKE, B. (1995) *Communicating change*. London: McGraw-Hill Book Company.

QUIRKE, B. (2008) *Making the connections: using internal communication to turn strategy into action*. 2nd ed. Aldershot: Gower Publishing Limited.

RAFFERTY, A.E. and GRIFFIN, M.A. (2006) Perceptions of organizational change: a stress and coping perspective. *Journal of Applied Psychology*. Vol 91, No 5. 1154–1162.

RANDALL, J. (2004) *Managing change/changing managers*. London: Routledge.

RASHFORD, N.S. and COGHLAN, D. (1989) Phases and levels of organisational change. *Journal of Managerial Psychology*. Vol 4, Issue 3. 17–22.

REDMAN, T. and GRIEVES, J. (1999) Managing strategic change through TQM: learning from failure. *New Technology, Work and Employment*. Vol 14, No 1. 45–61.

REDMAN, T. and WILKINSON, A. (2009) Human resource management: a contemporary perspective. In T. REDMAN and A. WILKINSON (eds) *Contemporary human resource management: text and cases*. Harlow: FT Prentice Hall.

REED, P.J. (2001) *Extraordinary leadership: creating strategies for change*. London: Kogan Page.

REES, C. and EDWARDS, T. (2003) *HR's contribution to international mergers and acquisitions*. London: Chartered Institute of Personnel and Development.

REVANS, R.W. (1982) *The origins and growth of action learning*. Bromley: Chartwell-Bratt.

REYNOLDS, J., CALEY, L. and MASON, R. (2002) *How do people learn?* London: Chartered Institute of Personnel and Development.

REYNOLDS, R. (1994) *Groupwork in education and training: ideas in practice*. The Educational and Training Series. London: Kogan Page Limited.

RIEL, C.B.M van and FOMBRUN, C.J. (2007) *Essentials of corporate communication*. London: Routledge.

RIGBY, D. (2001) Management tools and techniques: a survey. *California Management Review*. Vol 43, No 2. 139–160.

RITZER, G. (1993) *The McDonaldization of society*. Newbury Park, CA: Pine Forge.

ROBBINS, H. and FINLEY, M. (1998) *Why teams don't work*. London: Orion Business.

ROBBINS, S.P. and JUDGE, T.A. (2009) *Organizational behavior*. 13th ed. New Jersey: Pearson Prentice Hall.

ROBERTSON, P.J. and SENEVIRATNE, S.J. (1995) Outcomes of planned organisational change in the public sector: a meta analytic comparison to the private sector. *Public Administration Review*. Vol 55, No 6. 547–558.

ROGERS, E. (1962) *Diffusion of innovations*. New York: The Free Press.

ROGERS, J. (2008) *Coaching skills: a handbook*. 2nd ed. Milton Keynes: Open University Press.

ROGERS, L. (2010) Labour hid the ugly truth about the National Health Service. Available at: http://www.timesonline.co.uk/tol/news/uk/health/article7052606.ece (accessed 14 April 2010).

ROMANELLI, E. and TUSHMAN, M.L. (1994) Organizational transformation as punctuated equilibrium: an empirical test. *Academy of Management Journal*. Vol 37, No 5. 1141–1166.

ROSE, N. (1989) *Governing the soul: the shaping of private self*. London: Routledge.

ROSENBROCK, H.H. (1989) *Designing human-centred technology*. London: Springer Verlag.

ROWSON, R. (2006) *Working ethics: how to be fair in a culturally complex world*. London: Jessica Kingsley Publishers.

RUBERY, J., EARNSHAW, J., MARCHINGTON, M., COOKE, F.L. and VINCENT, S. (2002) Changing organizational forms and the employment relationship. In G. SALAMAN, J. STOREY and J. BILLSBERRY (eds) *Strategic human resource management theory and practice*. London: OU Business School in association with Sage Publications.

SALAMAN, G. (1997) Culturing production. In P. DU GAY (ed.) *Production of culture/cultures of production*. London: Sage Publications in association with the Open University.

SALAMAN, G. (2007) Managers' knowledge and the management of change. In J. STOREY (ed.) *Human resource management: a critical text*. 3rd ed. London: Thomson Learning.

SALAMAN, G. and ASCH, D. (2003) *Strategy and capability: sustaining organizational change*. Oxford: Blackwell Publishing.

SANTAYANA, G. (1998) *The life of reason*. London: Prometheus Books.

SATHE, V. (1985) *Culture and related corporate realities*. Homewood, IL: Irwin.

SAUQUET, A. (2004) Learning in organizations: schools of thought and current challenges. In J.J. BOONSTRA (ed.) *Dynamics of organizational change and learning*. Chichester: John Wiley and Sons.

SCARBROUGH, H. and CORBETT, J.M. (1992) *Technology and organization: power, meaning and design*. London: Routledge.

SCHEIN, E.H. (1980) *Organizational psychology*. Englewood Cliffs, NJ: Prentice Hall.

SCHEIN, E.H. (1990) Organizational culture. *American Psychologist*. Vol 45, Part 2. 109–119.

SCHEIN, E.H. (2004) *Organizational culture and leadership*. San Francisco, CA: Jossey Bass.

SCHEIN, E.H. (2006) So how can you assess your corporate culture? In J.V. GALLOS (ed.) *Organization development: a Jossey Bass reader*. San Francisco, CA: Jossey Bass.

SCHNEIDER, D.M. and GOLDWASSER, G. (1998) Be a model leader of change. *Management Review*. Vol 87, No 3. 41–45.

SCHON, D.A. (1963) Champions for radical new inventions. *Harvard Business Review*. Vol 41, No 2. 77–86.

SCHUMPETER, J. (1950) *Capitalism, socialism and democracy*. New York: Harper and Row.

SCOTT-MORGAN, P. (1995) *The unwritten rules of the game*. New York: McGraw-Hill.

SENGE, P. (1990 & 2006) *The fifth discipline: the art and practice of the learning organisation*. London: Random House Business Books.

SENNETT, R. (2001) Failure. In G. SALAMAN (ed.) *Understanding business organisations*. London: Routledge in association with the Open University.

SINCLAIR, A. (1992) The tyranny of a team ideology. *Organization Studies*. Vol 13, No 4. 611–626.

SKINNER, B.F. (1948) *Walden two*. New York: Macmillan.

SKINNER, B.F (1974) *About behaviourism*. London: Jonathan Cape.

SMINIA, H. and VAN NISTELROOIJ, A. (2006) Strategic management and organization development: planned change in a public sector organization. *Journal of Change Management*. Vol 6, No 1. 99–113.

SNELL, R.S. and SALAMAN, G. (2001) Moral foundations of the learning organization. *Human Relations*. Vol 54, Issue 3. 319–59.

SORGE, A. and VAN WITTELOOSTUIJN, A. (2004) The (Non) sense of organizational change: an essay about universal management hypes, sick consultancy metaphors and healthy organization theories. *Organization Studies*. Vol 25, No 7. 1205–1231.

SPECTOR, B. and BEER, M. (1994) Beyond TQM programmes. *Journal of Organizational Change Management*. Vol 7, No 2. 63–70

SPICER, A., ALVESSON, M. and KARREMAN, D. (2009) Critical performativity: the unfinished business of critical management studies. *Human Relations*. Vol 62, No 4. 537–560.

STACEY, R.D. (2007) *Strategic management and organisational dynamics: the challenge of complexity*. London: FT Prentice Hall.

STAPENHURST, T. (2009) *The benchmarking book: best practice for quality managers and practitioners*. London: Butterworth-Heinemann.

STARKEY, K., TEMPEST, S. and MCKINLAY, A. (2002) Introduction. In K. STARKEY, S. TEMPEST and A. MCKINLAY (eds) *How organizations learn: managing the search for knowledge*. London: Thomson Learning.

STEINER, C. (2001) A role for individuality and mystery in 'managing' change. *Journal of Organizational Change Management*. Vol 14, No 2. 150–167.

STICKLAND, F. (1998) *The dynamics of change*. London: Routledge.

STOREY, J. (1992) *Developments in the management of human resources*. Oxford: Blackwell Business.

STOREY, J. (2005) New organizational forms and their links with HR. In G. SALAMAN, J. STOREY and J. BILLSBERRY (eds) *Strategic human resource management theory and practice*. London: OU Business School in association with Sage Publications.

STOREY, J. (ed.) (2007) *Human resource management: a critical text*. London: Thomson Learning.

STOREY, J., EMBERSON, C., GODSELL, J. and HARRISON, A. (2006) Supply chain management: theory, practice and future challenges. *International Journal of Operations and Production Management*. Vol 26, Issue 7. 754–774.

STURDY, A. (2004) The adoption of management ideas and practices: theoretical perspectives and possibilities. *Management Learning*. Vol 35, No 2. 155–179.

STURDY, A. and GREY, C. (2003) Beneath and beyond organizational change management: exploring alternatives. *Organization*. Vol 10, No 4. 651–662.

STYHRE, A. (2001) Kaizen, ethics and care of the operations: management after empowerment. *Journal of Management Studies*. Vol 38, Issue 6. 795–810.

TAYLOR, F.W. (1911) *The principles of scientific management*. New York: Harper and Row.

THOMAS, D.A. (2004) Diversity as strategy. *Harvard Business Review*. Vol 82, Issue 9. 98–108.

THOMPSON, P. and MCHUGH, D. (2009) *Work organisations: a critical approach*. 4th ed. Basingstoke: Palgrave Macmillan.

THOMPSON, P. and O'CONNELL DAVIDSON, J. (1995) The continuity of discontinuity: managerial rhetoric in turbulent times. *Personnel Review*. Vol 24, No 4. 17–33.

THORNE, M.L. (2000) Interpreting corporate transformation through failure. *Management Decision*. Vol 38, No 5. 305–314.

TICHY, N.M. (1983) *Managing strategic change: technical, political and cultural dynamics*. New York: John Wiley and Sons.

TIDD, J. and BESSANT, J. (2009) *Managing innovation: integrating technological, market and organizational change.* 4th ed. Chichester: John Wiley and Sons.

TIMMERMAN, C.E. (2003) Media selection during the implementation of planned organizational change. *Management Communication Quarterly.* Vol 16, No 3. 301–340.

TOFFLER, B.L. and REINGOLD, J. (2003) *Final accounting: ambition, greed and the fall of Arthur Andersen.* New York: Broadway Books.

TOURISH, D. and PINNINGTON, A. (2002) Transformational leadership, corporate cultism and the spirituality paradigm: an unholy trinity in the workplace? *Human Relations.* Vol 55, No 2. 147–172.

TREVINO, L.K. and BROWN, M.E. (2004) Managing to be ethical: debunking five business ethics myths. *Academy of Management Executive.* Vol 18, No 2. 69–81.

TRIST, E.L. and BAMFORTH, K.W. (1951) Some social and psychological consequences of the longwall method of coal-getting. *Human Relations.* Vol 4, No 1. 3–38.

TROMPENAARS, F. and WOOLLIAMS, P. (2003) A new framework for managing change across cultures. *Journal of Change Management.* Vol 3, No 4. 361–375.

TSOUKAS, H. (2005). Afterword: why language matters in the analysis of organizational change. *Journal of Organizational Change Management.* Vol 18, No 1. 96–104.

TSOUKAS, H. and CHIA, R. (2002) On organizational becoming: rethinking organizational change. *Organization Science.* Vol 13, No 5. 567–582.

TUCKMAN, B.W. (1965) Development sequence in small groups. *Psychological Bulletin.* No 63. 384–399.

TUCKMAN, B.W. and JENSEN, M.C. (1977) Stages of small-group development revisited. *Group and Organizational Studies.* Vol 2, No 4. 419–427.

ULRICH, D. (1997) *Human resource champions: the next agenda for adding value and delivering results.* Boston: Harvard Business School Press.

URWICK, L. (1947) *The elements of administration.* 2nd ed. London: Pitman.

VAN DE VEN, A.H. and POOLE, M.S. (1995) Explaining development and change in organizations. *Academy of Management Review.* Vol 20, No 3. 510–540.

VAN DE VEN, A.H. and POOLE, M.S. (2005) Alternative approaches for studying organizational change. *Organization Studies.* Vol 26, No 9. 1377–1404.

VAN DER BENT, J., PAAUWE, J. and WILLIAMS, R. (1999) Organizational learning: an exploration of organizational memory and its role in organizational change processes. *Journal of Organizational Change Management.* Vol 12, No 5. 377–404.

VINCE, R. (2002a) Organizing reflection. *Management Learning*. Vol 33, No 1. 63–78.

VINCE, R. (2002b) The politics of imagined stability: a psychodynamic understanding of change at Hyder plc. *Human Relations*. Vol 55, No 10. 1189–1208.

VURDUBAKIS, T. (2007) Technology. In D. KNIGHTS and H. WILLMOTT (eds) *Introducing organizational behaviour and management*. London: Thomson Learning.

WALSTON, S.L. and CHADWICK, C. (2003) Perceptions and misperceptions of major organizational changes in hospitals: do change efforts fail because of inconsistent organizational perceptions of restructuring and reengineering? *International Journal of Public Administration*. Vol 26, No 14. 1581–1605.

WALTON, E. and RUSSELL, M. (2004) Organizational change: strategies and interventions. In J.J. BOONSTRA (ed.) *Dynamics of organizational change and learning*. Chichester: John Wiley and Sons Ltd.

WARWICK, D.P. and KELMAN, H.C. (1976) Ethical issues in social intervention. In W.G. BENNIS, K.D. BENNE, R. CHIN and K.E. COREY (eds) *The planning of change*. 3rd ed. New York: Holt, Rinehart and Winston.

WATSON, G. (1967) Resistance to change. In W.W. BURKE, D.G. LAKE and J.W. PAINE (eds) *Organizational change: a comprehensive reader*. San Francisco, CA: Jossey Bass.

WATSON, T.J. (1995) In search of HRM: beyond the rhetoric and reality distinction or the case of the dog that didn't bark. *Personnel Review*. Vol 24, No 4. 6–16.

WATSON, T.J. (2003a) Ethical choice in managerial work: the scope for moral choices in an ethically irrational world. *Human Relations*. Vol 56, No 2. 167–185.

WATSON, T.J. (2003b) *Sociology, work and industry*. London: Routledge.

WATSON, T.J. (2006) *Organising and managing work*. 2nd ed. Harlow: FT Prentice Hall.

WEBER, M. (1947) *The theory of social and economic organization (trans)*. Glencoe, IL: The Free Press.

WEICK, K. (1979) *The social psychology of organizing*. Reading, MA: Addison-Wesley.

WEICK, K.E. (1998) Improvisation as a mindset for organizational analysis. *Organization Science*. Vol 9, No 5. 543–555.

WEICK, K.E. (2000) Emergent change as a universal in organizations. In M. BEER and N. NOHRIA (eds): *Breaking the code of change*. Boston: Harvard Business School Press.

WEISS, J.W. (2001) *Organizational behavior and change: managing diversity, cross-cultural dynamics and ethics*. Cincinnati, OH: South Western Thomson Learning.

WEST, M.A., HIRST, G., RICHTER, A. and SHIPTON, H. (2004) Twelve steps to heaven: successfully managing change through developing innovative teams. *European Journal of Work and Organizational Psychology*. Vol 13, No 2. 269–299.

WHIPP, R. (1996) Creative deconstruction: strategy and organization. In S.R. CLEGG, C. HARDY and W.R. NORD (eds) *The SAGE Handbook of organization studies*. London: Sage Publications Ltd.

WHITTINGTON, R. (2001) *What is strategy and does it matter?* London: Routledge.

WILLCOCKS, L. and MASON, D. (1987) *Computerising work: people, systems design and workplace relations*. London: Paradigm.

WILLMOTT, H. (1993) Strength is ignorance; slavery is freedom: managing culture in modern organizations. *Journal of Management Studies*. Vol 30, No 4. 515–552.

WILSON, D. (1992) *A strategy for change*. London: Routledge.

WILSON, E. (ed.) (2001) *Organizational behaviour reassessed: the impact of gender*. London: Sage Publications Ltd.

WILSON, E. (2001) Organizational culture. In E.M. WILSON (ed.) *Organizational behaviour reassessed: the impact of gender*. London: Sage Publications.

WILSON, F.M. (2010) *Organizational behaviour and work: a critical introduction*. 3rd ed. Oxford: Oxford University Press.

WITZEL, M. (2003) *Fifty key figures in management*. Routledge Key Guides. London: Routledge.

WOMACK, J., JONES, D. and ROOS, D. (1990) *The machine that changed the world*. London: Macmillan.

WOODALL, J. (1996) Managing culture change: can it ever be ethical? *Personnel Review*. Vol 25, No 6. 26–40.

WOODMAN, R.W. (2008) Discourse, metaphor and organizational change: the wine is new, but the bottle is old. *British Journal of Management*. Vol 19. S33–S37.

WOODWARD, J. (1958) *Management and technology*. London: HMSO.

WOODWARD, J. (1965) *Industrial organization: theory and practice*. London: Oxford University Press.

WOODWARD, S. and HENDRY, C. (2004) Leading and coping with change. *Journal of Change Management*. Vol 4, No 2. 155–183.

WORREN, N., MOORE, A. and ELLIOTT, R. (2002) When theories become tools: toward a framework for pragmatic validity. *Human Relations*. Vol 55, No 10. 1227–1250.

WORREN, N.A.M., RUDDLE, K. and MOORE, K. (1999) From organizational development to change management: the emergence of a new profession. *The Journal of Applied Behavioral Science*. Vol 35, No 3. 273–286.

WREGE, C.D. and HODGETTS, R.M. (2000) Frederick W. Taylor's 1899 pig iron observations: examining fact, fiction, and lessons for the new millennium. *Academy of Management Journal*. Vol 43, No 6. 1283–1291.

WREN, D.A. (1987) Management history: issues and ideas for teaching and research. *Journal of Management*. Vol 13, No 2. 339–350.

WRIGHT, C. (2008) Reinventing human resource management: business partners, internal consultants and the limits of professionalization. *Human Relations*. Vol 6, No 8. 1063–1086.

Subject Index

Name Index

Note: This index lists individuals quoted or mentioned in the text, either as authors or in other contexts, and organisations mentioned as employers and in similar contexts. It does not include authors given purely as reference sources, either within the text or in the Discussion Questions or Key Readings sections, or the names of co-authors not given in the text.

Waterman, R.H., 6, 48, 180, 181
Watson, G., 164
Watson, T.J., 47, 50, 52–53, 109, 158, 186, 226, 253, 268
Webber, M.D., 318
Weber, M., 29, 79
Weick, K.E., 8, 96–97, 239
Weiss, J.W., 155, 182
Westpac Bank, 94
Whipp, R., 141
Wilkinson, A., 185, 253
Williams, R., 241
Willmott, H., 49, 51, 145, 187, 229

Wilson, D., 7, 43, 93, 97, 185, 200, 265
Wilson, E., 35, 188
Winter, S., 96
Witzel, M., 27, 29, 32, 79
Woodall, J., 224, 234–235
Woodman, R.W., 159
Woodward, J., 268, 272
Woodward, S., 123, 138, 141
Woolgar, S., 267, 272–273
Worley, C.G., 93, 139, 166
Worren, N., 244, 248, 290
Wright, C., 259

9 781843 982418